This book is due for return not later than the last date stamped below, unless recalled sooner.

Implementing EU Pollution Control

This book examines the role of law in European Union
integration processes through a detailed analysis of the
implementation of the EU Directive on Integrated Pollution
Prevention and Control at European level and in the UK and
Germany. It questions traditional conceptions which perceive
law as the 'formal law in the books', as instrumental and as
relatively autonomous in relation to its social contexts. The book
also discusses in depth how the key legal obligation of the
Directive, to employ 'the best available techniques', is actually
implemented.

This research locates the analysis of the implementation of
the IPPC Directive in the wider context of current political
science and sociology of law debates about the role of law in
EU integration processes, the nature of EU law, new modes
of governance and the significance of 'law in action' for
understanding legal process.

BETTINA LANGE is a Lecturer in Law and Regulation at the Centre
for Socio-Legal Studies, University of Oxford.

Books in the series

EU Enlargement and the Constitutions of Central and Eastern Europe
Anneli Albi

Social Rights and Market Freedom in the European Economic Constitution:
A Labour Law Perspective
Stefano Giubboni

The Constitution for Europe: A Legal Analysis
Jean-Claude Piris

The European Convention on Human Rights
Steven Greer

European Broadcasting Law and Policy
Lorna Woods and Jackie Harrison

Transforming Citizenship? The European Union, Electoral Rights and the Restructuring
of European Political Space
Jo Shaw

Implementing EU Pollution Control: Law and Integration
Bettina Lange

Implementing EU Pollution Control

Law and Integration

Bettina Lange

CAMBRIDGE
UNIVERSITY PRESS

CAMBRIDGE UNIVERSITY PRESS
Cambridge, New York, Melbourne, Madrid, Cape Town, Singapore,
São Paulo, Delhi

Cambridge University Press
The Edinburgh Building, Cambridge CB2 8RU, UK

Published in the United States of America by Cambridge University Press,
New York

www.cambridge.org
Information on this title: www.cambridge.org/9780521883986

First published 2008

Printed in the United Kingdom at the University Press, Cambridge

A catalogue record for this publication is available from the British Library

ISBN 978-0-521-88398-6 hardback

To Susan

Contents

Series editors' preface

Implementing EU Pollution Control is an important book contributing to the sociology of (EU) law. It combines a radical reconceptualisation of the relationship of law and integration in the context of EU integration studies, drawing upon the sociological and critical theories, with an extended case study looking at the 'law in action' in the environmental field. Eschewing 'grand theories' of European integration or of the role of law in European integration, it takes as its central question the role of law in European integration. However, it proceeds not by treating law as a static unchanging concept (the 'law in the books') but by focusing on the micro specifics of 'law in action', specifically the implementation of EU pollution control in the hands of national officials in Germany and the UK. The claim is not so much that law 'integrates' (or indeed that it does not), but rather that the issue of the role of law in the context of the social, economic and political processes occurring in relation to the EU is above all an empirical one, and not resolvable either by application of legal reasoning techniques or by grand theorising.

The book is therefore an important step forward in analysis, combining both a rigorous theoretical framework with detailed and careful empirical work, based on extensive interviews with pollution control officials in the UK and Germany. It challenges traditional theories regarding the relationship between law and integration, which treat law as a static independent variable and fail to account for the broader image of law which has emerged through socio-legal studies and critical legal studies over a number of decades. It uses instead a law in action analysis, which is novel in the field of EU legal studies, where there has thus far been very little work which has brought the insights and methods of socio-legal studies to bear upon the empirical detail of the implementation of EU law. What is important about the empirical work is that it reveals EU law in action to be a work in progress, not a static state of affairs. For example, the implementation of aspects of the EU Directive on Integrated Pollution Prevention and Control (IPPC) involves constant debate and contestation between the interested parties including both national officials and other social actors around best practices and the determination of the all important 'best available techniques' for limiting pollution from installations. Specifically, however, the analysis draws upon Foucauldian notions of power in relation to discourse and language in order to identify the specific ways in which norms are formed and transformed in the context of implementation.

We are delighted to be publishing *Implementing EU Pollution Control* in the *Cambridge Series on European Law and Policy* not only as a contribution to EU legal studies, but also as a contribution to understanding law in relation to EU integration more generally, and, indeed, as an important contribution to socio-legal studies.

Laurence Gormley
Jo Shaw

Acknowledgements

The research for this book has been funded through grants from the German Academic Exchange Service, Aberystwyth University Research Fund and the UK Socio-Legal Studies Association. Writing up of the research was facilitated through a Jean-Monnet Fellowship at the European University Institute, Florence, Italy and through research leave granted by Keele University. I am grateful to these organisations for their financial support.

I would also like to acknowledge helpful feedback and comments from participants at the annual UK Socio-Legal Studies Association conferences at which sections of this book were presented as papers, from colleagues at Keele during law school staff seminars and participants in the Hart Legal Workshops 2006 and 2007 at the Institute of Advanced Legal Studies, University of London.

I would like to thank Nicholas Walker for reading the entire manuscript and providing detailed suggestions for improving my English language writing. Mary Ewert, Katrin Wiegand and Gillian Potter-Merrigan provided excellent professional transcription services for the interviews with UK and German licensing officers.

Special thanks go to the UK and German permitting officers, as well as the BREF writers who participated in the study and who gave generously of their time while being busy at work. For confidentiality reasons they have to remain anonymous. The views expressed in this book are my own and do not necessarily reflect the perspectives of the individuals and organisations who participated in the research on the implementation of the IPPC Directive.

Bettina Lange
Keele, April 2007

Update on the IPPC Directive

Since delivery of the typescript of this book to Cambridge University Press in April 2007 there have been further developments in relation to the IPPC Directive. The EU Commission's Communication from 2003 'On the Road to Sustainable Production: Progress in Implementing Council Directive 96/61/EC concerning integrated pollution prevention and control' started a consultation process on the further development of the IPPC Directive (referred to in chapter 1). By the end of 2005 the Commission had also commissioned various consultants' projects for more detailed information input into the reform process. The EU Commission is currently examining the results of this consultation. This will be concluded at the end of 2007 and a revision of the IPPC Directive may be proposed.

The review is not intended to change the underlying principles of the IPPC Directive. Some smaller technical amendments have been discussed such as the clarification of terms currently used in the text of the Directive as well as questions of scope, such as whether particular waste treatment plants should also be covered by the IPPC Directive. There is also a proposal to tighten up the exchange of information about the best available techniques among member states and industry which is organised by the Commission under Art. 16 (2) of the IPPC Directive. Member states may be required to submit to the Commission information on pollution abatement techniques used in plants within two months of the request. But the reform of the IPPC Directive also addresses wider associated issues, such as the impact of its implementation on the competitiveness of industry in the EU. A new consultants' study has been commissioned which will examine whether implementation of the IPPC Directive distorts competition between those plants in an industrial sector which are covered by the Directive and those that are not because their activities fall below the threshold specified in Annex I to the Directive. The study will also consider impacts of the IPPC Directive on the competitiveness of small- and medium-sized businesses and whether different national approaches to its implementation distort competition between member states. The review is also exploring how operators of industrial facilities can be encouraged – for instance through economic incentives – to go beyond regulatory compliance with the minimum requirements of the best available techniques standard and to strive for continuous improvement in their pollution control procedures.

Finally, the current review process is also considering various options for streamlining and clarifying interactions between the IPPC Directive and other EU industrial emissions control legislation. Legal obligations imposed by the IPPC Directive overlap with other EU emissions control legislation, such as the Large Combustion Plant Directive 2001/80/EC, the Waste Incineration Directive 2000/76/EC, the Solvent Emissions Directive 1999/13/EC, the Landfill Directive 1999/31/EC and the Seveso II Directive 1996/82. Moreover, nitrogen oxides and sulphur dioxide emissions are controlled both under the IPPC Directive and possible EU and national, such as the Dutch and Slovakian trading schemes for these emissions. Streamlining, which also promotes the wider EU programme of 'simplifying legislation', addresses whether authorisation requirements imposed upon operators are compatible under these various legal regimes. Streamlining could take a number of forms, such as the implementation of related EU emissions control legislation through the BAT standard in IPPC permits. Another option involves the integration of various pieces of EU emissions control legislation into the IPPC Directive, and hence to create a new single Framework Directive on industrial emissions with a broad scope.

The current IPPC reform process has implications for the research findings discussed in this book. The closer integration of the IPPC Directive with other EU industrial emissions control legislation will render the best available techniques (BAT) technology standard probably even more central to EU emissions control. Further empirical analysis will be needed in order to understand how streamlining may affect the way BAT standards are determined in practice. The book argues that BAT standards sometimes simply remain open. It remains to be seen whether a more direct and explicit link between the legal obligations of the IPPC Directive and those of other EU emissions control legislation will help to bring about closure in definitions of the BAT standard. The current reform of the IPPC Directive also further highlights key themes discussed in this book. The reform process seeks to enhance the effectiveness of the IPPC Directive. The book is sceptical about the potential of law to regulate in an instrumental fashion and hence it will be interesting to see whether a revised IPPC Directive will really deliver the intended specific regulatory outcomes. Moreover the IPPC Directive reform process sheds further light on issues that are central to this book's account of the Directive. The Commission will compile further, more recent information about potential variation in the ways in which member states implement the IPPC Directive. The book suggests that there are some differences in the way in which the UK and Germany implement the Directive. Finally reform of the IPPC Directive through provisions which will encourage operators to go beyond regulatory compliance with a minimum BAT standard further strengthens a key characteristic of BAT also discussed in this book, i.e. that BAT is a dynamic, not a static fixed technology standard and hence can be plant specific.

Bettina Lange
Oxford, October 2007

Abbreviations

ALARA	As Low as Reasonably Achievable, an alternative technology standard to 'the best available techniques'
BAT	Best Available Techniques
BATNEEC	Best Available Techniques Not Entailing Excessive Cost, as referred to in section 7 of EPA 1990
BimSchG	*Bundesimmissionsschutzgesetz*, German federal air immissions control law
4. BimSchV	*Vierte Bundesimmissionsschutzverordnung*, fourth German federal air immissions control regulation. This lists the plants which require a licence under the *Bundesimmissionsschutzgesetz* and includes the plants listed in Annex I of the IPPC Directive
BMU	Bundesministerium für Umwelt, Naturschutz und Reaktorsicherheit, German federal environmental ministry
BREF	Best Available Techniques Reference Document
CDQ	Coke Dry Quenching, a technique for cooling coke through dry inert gases
CEFIC	European Chemical Industry Council, a trade association which represents the interests of the chemical industry in the EU
CSQ	Coke Stabilisation Quenching, a technique for cooling coke through wet quenching, i.e. spraying of the hot coke with water
DEFRA	Department for the Environment, Food and Rural Affairs
DG	Directorate General of the EU Commission

EA	Environment Agency for England and Wales
ECSC	European Coal and Steel Community
EEB	European Environmental Bureau
EEC	European Economic Community
EIPPC Bureau	European IPPC Bureau, Seville, Spain
ELV	Emission Limit Value
EMAS	Eco-Management and Audit Scheme
EPA	Environmental Protection Act 1990
EPOPRA	Environmental Protection Operator and Pollution Risk Appraisal
EU	European Union
EURATOM	European Atomic Energy Community
EUROFER	European Confederation of Iron and Steel Industries, trade association which represents the interests of the EU iron and steel industry
IEF	Information Exchange Forum
IEG	IPPC Experts Group
IPC	Integrated Pollution Control under Part I of the UK Environmental Protection Act 1990
IPPC	Integrated Pollution Prevention and Control under the EU IPPC Directive
IPTS	Institute for Prospective Technological Studies, Seville, Spain. It hosts the EIPPC Bureau and is one of the seven scientific institutes of the European Commission's Joint Research Centre
KrW-/AbfG	*Kreislaufwirtschafts- und Abfallgesetz*, German federal waste management Act
LUA	*Landesumweltamt* (*Land* environmental protection agency)
NFU	National Farmers Union, UK
NGO	Non-Governmental Organisation
OMC	Open Method of Coordination, a new governance tool employed by the EU in order to coordinate activities between Member States in areas deemed politically sensitive and/or where the EU has limited legal competencies
OSPAR	1992 OSPAR Convention on the protection of the marine environment of the North-east Atlantic
PM	Particulate matter, i.e. dust

PPC Regs	Pollution Prevention and Control (England and Wales) Regulations 2000, SI 2000 No. 1973
SEA	Single European Act
SEPA	Scottish Environment Protection Agency
SPG	Strategic Permitting Group, group set up by the UK Environment Agency for the centralised licensing of IPPC plants
TA	*Technische Anleitung*, technical instruction, tertiary rules defining the BAT standard in Germany
TWG	Technical Working Group
UBA	Umweltbundesamt, German Federal Environmental Authority
UNICE	Union of Industrial and Employers' Confederations of Europe, now called 'Business Europe, Confederation of European Business'. It represents EU industry and employers' interests
VDI	Verein Deutscher Ingenieure, Association of German Engineers
WHG	*Wasserhaushaltsgesetz*, German federal water law

1   Introduction

What is law in European Union integration?

This book discusses relationships between law and integration. It focuses on legal integration in the European Union. By integration I mean:[1]

the process whereby political actors in several distinct national settings are persuaded to shift their loyalties, expectations and political activities toward a new centre, whose institutions possess or demand jurisdiction over the pre-existing national states.

(Haas, 1958: 16)

This definition recognises the interplay between various dimensions of integration. The shifting of loyalties, expectations and political activities towards a new EU centre also reveals a social aspect to EU integration. Political dynamics are analysed through reference to the building of new EU institutions (Wiener and Diez, 2004: 1). In discussing law and integration relationships this book focuses on the question: what is law in European Union (EU) integration? The book's emphasis is thus on analytical rather than normative issues. It departs from a current emphasis on normative concerns in EU integration studies, framed by lawyers as issues of control, accountability, transparency and legitimacy in the exercise of power in the EU (Armstrong and Shaw, 1998: 148; Wincott, 1995). While the empirical data discussed in this book shed light on these normative concerns, the book's main goal is to advance an understanding of the nature of law in EU integration processes. The book questions conceptualisations of law as formal, instrumental and relatively autonomous from its social contexts. It analyses law and society relationships in the context of EU integration without developing normative claims about how law and society should interact.[2]

The question 'what is law in EU integration?' raises two issues. First, how can we conceptualise law in EU integration processes? What idea of 'law' are we invoking when we say that 'law' is implicated in EU integration? Second, what is the role of law in comparison to other aspects, such as economic, political, technical and social drivers of EU integration processes? Is there a clearly separate legal dimension to EU integration which can be distinguished from political, economic, technical and social dynamics? Answers to the first question will have implications for the second question about links between legal and other dimensions of EU integration.

So why do these questions matter? It is clear that law is central to EU integration. For some analysts legal integration is even the first important form of Europeanisation (Stone Sweet, 2004: 240). Both primary legislation, such as the Treaties establishing the European Union, as well as secondary legislation are crucial to integration. Secondary legislation is particularly central to the EU's capacity to govern, since EU institutional actors only have limited use of other tools of government, such as taxation, redistribution and direct law enforcement. It seems that law is even becoming more important in EU integration, due to the rise in judicial governance by the European Court of Justice and the Court of First Instance (ibid.: 7). Demand for rule clarification, monitoring and enforcement by the European Courts is increasing, also due to the constitutionalisation of the Treaties (ibid.: 238). Juridification and especially judicialisation are often perceived as crowding out the social, political and economic dynamics of EU integration. This book questions this perspective by examining the inclusion of technical, political and economic dynamics in the construction of 'law'. By examining these 'contexts in law', the book seeks to contribute to 'EU law in context' debates. It starts from the idea that law is central to processes of integration in the EU. But it is by no means clear what conception of law can best explain the outcomes of integration. There is as yet no EU state. Hence, traditional, modern conceptions of state law developed in association with the rise of the nation state in Western Europe in the eighteenth and nineteenth century have limited application. Moreover, social actors involved in EU integration processes do not necessarily have a clear, settled view of the nature of EU law. There was lively and controversial debate among German and UK permitting officers who issue licences for plants regulated under the EU Directive on Integrated Pollution Prevention and Control (IPPC), which is at the heart of the book's empirical analysis. There was also debate among engineers in EU technical working groups, civil servants in national environmental administrations, as well as operators, about the nature and key characteristics of the technology standard imposed by the IPPC Directive. Finally, asking 'what is law in EU integration?' matters because how we conceive law shapes how we think about its role in EU integration. Hence, analysing the nature of EU law, including rendering assumptions about law explicit, can contribute to the development of EU integration theories. But how does the book seek to analyse the nature of law in EU integration?

Law and integration relationships through the prism of the EU Directive on Integrated Pollution Prevention and Control

Key features of the IPPC Directive

This book addresses the question 'what is law in EU integration?' through an analysis of the implementation of the EU Directive on Integrated Pollution Prevention and Control (96/61/EC). The IPPC Directive establishes a pollution control regime that seeks to prevent and minimise emissions in relation to air, water and land from new and existing[3] mainly large industrial[4] operators. The Directive also regulates further environmental impacts through requirements on energy efficiency, waste minimisation, noise, accident prevention and site restoration after installation closure.[5] Control of all of these releases is achieved in an integrated manner through one single IPPC permitting procedure.[6] IPPC permit conditions further specify operators' obligations. They are set with reference to a technology standard. According to Art. 3 of the IPPC Directive member state regulatory authorities shall ensure that operators employ the 'best available techniques' (BAT) in order to prevent emissions to all three environmental media, air, water and land. Art. 2 (11) of the Directive provides only a rudimentary definition of 'the best available techniques':

BAT shall mean the most effective and advanced stage in the development of activities and their methods of operation which indicate the practical suitability of particular techniques for providing in principle the basis for emission limit values designed to prevent and, where that is not practicable, generally to reduce emissions and the impact on the environment as a whole.

So, how are 'the best available techniques' defined in practice? The BAT standard is further specified at the EU, member state and local permitting level. At the EU level Art. 16 (2) of the IPPC Directive requires the Commission to organise an 'exchange of information' on what constitute 'the best available techniques':

The Commission shall organize an exchange of information between member states and the industries concerned on best available techniques, associated monitoring, and developments in them. Every three years the Commission shall publish the results of the exchanges of information.[7]

The IPPC Directive does not specify how this information exchange is to be organised. The EU Commission has therefore developed its own procedure (Emmott et al. 2000). It has set up Technical Working Groups (TWGs), one for each of the industrial sectors covered by the IPPC Directive.[8] These TWGs comprise representatives from member states' environmental administrations, often from permitting authorities, such as chemists and engineers with experience in licensing industrial installations. TWGs also include industry representatives, such as staff from the Confederation of European Business (UNICE),[9] or sector-specific EU-wide trade associations,[10] and sometimes representatives drawn directly from large industrial operators. According to Art. 16 (2) IPPC Directive member states and industry representatives participate in the information exchange. But upon its own initiative the Commission also invites environmental NGOs to participate in TWGs. The Commission has also set up and chairs the Information Exchange Forum (IEF). In terms of composition this forum nearly mirrors the TWGs. It comprises member states' representatives from the higher levels of their environmental administrations, such as national environmental ministries, as well as industry and environmental NGO members. While the TWGs are to focus on specific technical issues, the IEF is meant to deal with wider EU policy decisions in the determination of 'the best available techniques'. The results of this information exchange are published by the Commission[11] as BAT reference documents (BREFs).[12] There is one 'vertical' BREF for each industrial sector covered by the IPPC Directive, such as the production of non-ferrous metals, inorganic chemicals, cement and lime as well as iron and steel, to name a few of the sectors covered by the IPPC Directive.[13] All vertical BREFs are structured in six chapters which report the same type of information for the different sectors.[14] While the first chapter contains 'General Information' about the industry, including its size, economic constraints, markets and production sites, the second chapter reviews 'Applied Processes and Techniques' in the industry. The third chapter reports the emissions as well as raw material, energy and water consumption which are associated with the production and pollution control techniques under review in the BREF. The fourth chapter then narrows down the range of techniques which have been considered in the third chapter to just those techniques which will be considered in the determination of BAT.[15] The fifth and main BREF chapter presents the BAT conclusion. This consists of a recommendation of one or several techniques which are considered to constitute 'the best available techniques' for the sector. This chapter also provides information about the emissions which are associated with the use of these techniques.[16] A final sixth chapter identifies 'emerging techniques'.[17] According to Art. 2 (11), last sentence and Annex IV No. 12 of the IPPC Directive local member state permitters have to take into account these BREFs when determining BAT for specific plants, but are not bound by them.

Amendments of the IPPC Directive

The IPPC Directive was passed on 24 September 1996. It was published on the 10 October in the Official Journal of the EU and came into force on the 30 October 1996.[18] It has been amended twice. In order to consolidate and clarify the Directive text the EU Commission has now put forward a proposal for the codification of the Directive. This integrates the two amendments into the text of the IPPC Directive.[19] The Public Participation Directive 2003/35/EC required member states to ensure that members of the public are given 'early and effective opportunities' to participate in IPPC permitting.[20] It also added Annex V to the IPPC Directive which lists a range of criteria governing public participation. The public must now also be consulted in relation to *draft permits*. This enhances citizens' opportunities for input into the permitting process. Before this amendment the public only had a right to comment on *permit applications*. The possibility for citizens to comment on draft permits opens up what is often a closed process of permit negotiation between regulators and operators. Moreover, para. 2 of Annex V strengthens and extends citizens' rights of access to a range of information used in IPPC permitting. It also supports rights of access to justice, thus enabling challenges before the courts to decisions made under the IPPC Directive.[21] The second amendment of the IPPC Directive occurred through Directive 2003/87/EC on emissions trading. This Directive establishes that for installations regulated both under the IPPC and the EU Emissions Trading Directive no emission limit values will be imposed for greenhouse gases traded under Directive 2003/87/EC.[22]

Moreover, member states will not be required to impose energy efficiency requirements for installations within the jurisdiction of both the IPPC and the EU Emissions Trading Directive. This potentially weakens the IPPC Directive's contribution to combating climate change (ENDS Report No. 319, August 2001: 17).

Last but not least, as required by Art. 16 (3) of the IPPC Directive, the EU Commission is now reviewing the Directive. It has started a consultation process with member states, industry and other interested groups to discuss revisions. The Commission is considering a more harmonised approach to setting emission limit values in IPPC permits, also through more detailed requirements in the Directive text.[23] The review also addresses how to clarify interactions between the IPPC Directive and possible EU or national emissions trading schemes for nitrogen oxides and sulphur dioxide emissions from large industrial operators. The Commission review includes a search for tools which could stimulate plant operators to go beyond 'mere compliance' with the Directive and to further improve the environmental performance of their installations. A final report of this ongoing review process is expected in 2007. Having outlined key features of the IPPC Directive, including its amendments, I now turn to a discussion of its implementation in the UK and Germany.

Implementation of the IPPC Directive in the UK and Germany

The practical implementation of the IPPC Directive is not without problems. The Commission has started infringement proceedings under Art. 226 EC Treaty against a number of member states.[24] The EU Commission brought a successful case against the UK for failure to implement the IPPC Directive in time – by 30 October 1999 – in Northern Ireland and in Great Britain in relation to off-shore installations (ENDS Report No. 326, March 2002). But an EU Commission report on progress with implementing the Directive across the EU – four years after the expiry of the 30 October 1999 deadline – noted that so far only the UK had incorporated correctly all aspects of the Directive (COM (2003) 354).[25] The EU Commission is now seeking to speed up implementation of the Directive. It has issued guidance to member states advising on the interpretation of certain key provisions of the Directive, such as the capacity thresholds in Annex I to the Directive which specify what production capacity a plant has to have in order to be regulated by the Directive. The Commission has also set indicators measuring the number of permits issued for existing installations, in order to monitor progress of member states in meeting the deadline of 30 October 2007 by which existing installations must also comply with the requirements of the IPPC Directive (First Report on the implementation of the IPPC Directive, 3 November 2005, COM (2005) 540 final, p. 8). But how have Germany and the UK actually implemented the IPPC Directive so far?

Implementation of the IPPC Directive in Germany

Key actors

Key policy decisions about the implementation of the IPPC Directive in Germany were taken by the federal environmental ministry.[26] It provided the draft for the Artikelgesetz which implements the IPPC Directive into German national law, by amending the main federal air immissions control statute, the *Bundesimmissionsschutzgesetz* (BimSchG), the main federal water pollution control statute, the *Wasserhaushaltgesetz* (WHG) and the major federal waste management statute, the *Kreislaufwirtschafts- und Abfallgesetz* (KrW-/AbfG). In accordance with para. 48 BimSchG the German federal environmental ministry also presented to the upper chamber of the German Parliament, the Bundesrat,[27] a revised version of the technical instructions for air, the TA *Luft*. These flesh out the meaning of the BAT technology standard in German environmental law, especially for installations with significant emissions into the air. For discharges into water there is secondary legislation, the *Verordnung über Anforderungen an das Einleiten von Abwasser in Gewässer*[28] which specifies in forty-five appendices 'the best available techniques' for specific areas of industry. There are also technical instructions (TA) which develop BAT standards for waste management facilities dealing with hazardous wastes (TA *Abfall*). There are also separate technical instructions listing BAT measures for installations which reuse, treat or dispose of household wastes (TA *Siedlungsabfall*). Furthermore, there are technical instructions which deal with noise emissions (TA *Lärm*).

In contrast to the UK there is no single unified regulator in Germany responsible for permitting IPPC installations. Different sections of the various environmental administrations in the relevant *Bundesland* issue permit conditions relating either to emissions to air, water or land. Hence, Germany has taken advantage of Art. 7 of the IPPC Directive which states that an 'integrated approach to permitting' only requires coordination of the conditions and procedure for the granting of IPPC permits, where more than one competent authority is involved. Para. 13 of the BimSchG provides a so-called limited 'concentration effect',[29] according to which a range of other relevant permits for the construction and operation of an IPPC installation, such as planning permission,[30] are included in the IPPC permit issued under para. 4 BimSchG. German IPPC permits include conditions in relation to releases to air and land. But discharge consents for emissions to surface waters under the WHG and to sewers are issued separately and thus are not included in this limited concentration effect under para. 13 BimSchG. Under para. 10 (5), second sentence, the German IPPC licensing authority has to ensure, however, a 'full coordination' of the media-specific licensing procedures and the conditions affecting different environmental media in an IPPC licence.[31] But this does not grant a right to the IPPC licensing authority to override or impose its view of what amounts to appropriate coordination of licence conditions in the case of differing views held by the licensing authority and the water authority (Kloepfer, 2004: 1278). Hence, Germany's implementation of the IPPC Directive is an example of an approach to permitting which is not fully integrated.

Who exactly becomes involved in permitting German IPPC installations varies according to the particular Bundesland[32] in which the plant is situated.[33] The administrative structures, including the environmental administration, varies between the different Bundesländer. The Bundesland in which the empirical research was carried out has a three-tier administrative structure. The first tier of the environmental administration consists of the Landesumweltministerium, the Land environmental ministry, which is part of the Land government.[34] Especially in the case of large, politically significant operators, the Land environmental ministry can become indirectly involved in the IPPC permitting process.[35] District governments[36] are the second administrative tier in most of the German Länder.[37] In the Land in which the research was carried out the district government is responsible for licensing IPPC installations. City authorities[38] and communes[39] constitute the third and lowest level of the administration. They can be consultees in IPPC licensing procedures.

Key procedures

In contrast to the UK, Germany has not issued national 'best available techniques' guidance documents to permitting authorities. Instead, fairly media specific regulations, which are binding upon permitters, have been revised, also in order to incorporate the IPPC Directive into national law. Key among these are the revised technical instructions on air emissions, the so-called TA *Luft* of 24 July 2002. There are also technical instructions on noise, waste water, land, waste and household waste.[40]

Permitting of new IPPC installations is carried out in Germany under para. 4 of the BimSchG. Regulations issued under the BimSchG,[41] the so-called 4. BimSchV, list all the installations which are covered by the German IPPC regime.[42] Existing plants are brought under IPPC control through amendments of their existing BimSchG permits under para. 17 BimSchG.[43] According to para. 6 (1) BimSchG, once operators demonstrate in their permit application that they can fulfil the requirements of para. 5 BimSchG – which replicates the 'basic obligations of the operator' from Art. 3 of the IPPC Directive – the German regulatory authority *has to grant* the IPPC permit. Hence, once the operator complies with the requirements of Art. 5 BimSchG he has a *right* to the IPPC permit. This also strengthens the operator's bargaining position in permit negotiations with the regulatory authority. In contrast to this – and potentially closer to the text of the IPPC Directive – the UK regulator exercises discretion under Reg. 10 (2) of the PPC Regs. (England and Wales) 2000 when deciding whether to grant or refuse the operator's application for an IPPC permit. This is the case even if the operator has fulfilled all the duties arising from Art. 3 of the IPPC Directive.

The BAT technology standard from the IPPC Directive is implemented in German national law through para. 5(2) BimSchG. It requires IPPC installations to prevent detrimental impacts on the environment in particular through employing 'the best available techniques' ('Stand der Technik').[44] The term 'Stand der Technik' referred also to the technology standard required under the BimSchG before the implementation of the IPPC Directive. Hence, use of the same term – 'Stand der Technik' – for the new and slightly different IPPC BAT technology standard builds a degree of continuity between the previous and the new German IPPC pollution control regime. Some commentators perceive the IPPC BAT standard as less onerous than the previous German technology standard, because the former is considered to provide more scope for cost considerations in the definition of the 'best available techniques' (Winter, 1999: 77; Kloepfer, 1998: 144, 929). Having outlined key elements of the incorporation of the IPPC Directive in Germany, I will now turn to its implementation in the UK.

Implementing the IPPC Directive in the UK

Key actors

Key policy decisions about the implementation of the IPPC Directive in the UK were taken by the Department for the Environment, Food and Rural Affairs (DEFRA) in consultation with the Environment Agency (EA). The Department drafted the two key legal instruments which implement the IPPC Directive in the UK. First, the Pollution Prevention and Control Act 1999[45] provides a basic framework for the implementation of the IPPC Directive in the UK. It is fleshed out through the more detailed provisions of the Pollution Prevention Control (England and Wales) Regulations 2000 (PPC Regs.) made under section 2 of the PPC Act 1999.[46] In the UK the Environment Agency for England and Wales (EA) and the Scottish Environment Protection Agency (SEPA) administer the IPPC system for about 85 per cent of installations regulated through the IPPC Directive, known as Part A (1) installations (Bell and McGillivray, 2006: 774). UK local authorities administer IPPC pollution control for a small number of less polluting IPPC installations, also known as Part A (2) installations.[47]

Initially EA area offices issued licenses for IPPC installations. This, however, was additional work for area officers who otherwise supervise sites and enforce legal regulation. Hence, in order to speed up implementation of the IPPC Directive the EA set up four strategic permitting groups (SPGs) which focus exclusively on the permitting of IPPC sites.[48] New staff have been recruited to these SPGs and area officers have been seconded to them. Moreover, the EA involves environmental consultancies in IPPC permitting work. Consultants prepare draft permits which are checked and finally issued by the EA. The data for the empirical part of the research were collected from one of the four SPGs in England. Having outlined key actors involved in the implementation of the IPPC Directive in the UK I now want to consider the key procedures through which the Directive is applied in the UK.

Key procedures

The IPPC Directive was based upon a UK proposal. In fact it has been considered as an example of the 'British' approach to pollution control, by being 'flexible' and 'pragmatic' and allowing for the adaptation of pollution control standards to specific circumstances in accordance with the concept of BAT (Bell and McGillivray, 2006: 791). Hence, it is not surprising that UK implementation replicates key structures of the

Directive itself. Reg. 11(2) of the PPC Regs. requires operators to take all measures to prevent pollution of the environment as a whole, in particular through the application of BAT. In order to flesh out the IPPC BAT technology standard, the Environment Agency has issued UK national guidance documents for the different sectors regulated by the IPPC Directive. These follow the format of the EU BREF documents.[49] Like the EU BREFs these 'Sector Guidance Notes' are not binding upon UK permitting officers, but are usually taken into account when BAT is determined in specific IPPC permits. The UK Sector Guidance Notes describe various BAT techniques and specify emission limit values for BAT technologies. But it is a hallmark of the UK approach that a focus on compliance with emission limit values should not replace the application of flexible BAT to an installation as 'the real standard' (Bell and McGillivray, 2006: 780).[50] This is in contrast to the German approach which focuses on compliance with emission limit values – specified in the various technical instructions – in order to implement the BAT standard.

Why the IPPC Directive?

The IPPC Directive is the empirical research focus here for several reasons. First, an analysis of the Directive is timely. It is a recent key instrument of EU pollution control law which is still being implemented in various EU member states, including new ones. Second, the Directive is of wider significance because it constitutes the core of EU pollution control law. It links up with other key EU environmental legislation, such as the Large Combustion Plant Directive,[51] the Waste Incineration Directive, the Solvents Directive,[52] the Seveso Directive on the Control of Major Accident Hazards, the National Emissions Ceiling Directive and the Landfill Directive. These other Directives set limits for the emission of certain substances, such as for oxides of sulphur and nitrogen oxides in the case of the Large Combustion Plant Directive, and specific standards for the operation of waste incineration plants and landfills, regulated also under IPPC, in the case of the Waste Incineration[53] and Landfill Directives.[54] Hence, pollution control standards set out in other key pieces of EU environmental legislation are effectively implemented through conditions in IPPC permits.[55] The EU Commission wants to further strengthen and clarify links between the IPPC Directive and other EU pollution control regimes, also through a proposal for a single EU Framework Directive which would bring together in one legislative text the IPPC Directive, as well as the Large

Combustion Plant and Waste Incineration Directives (ENDS Report, No. 363, April 2005: 58; ENDS Report No. 370, November 2005, p. 44).[56]

Second, the IPPC Directive is also of wider significance because its key regulatory tool, a technology standard, is employed in various other national, EU and international pollution control regimes. Hence, understanding the practical operation of the BAT technology standard in the context of the IPPC Directive may also generate insights into technology standards used in other pollution control regimes. Technology standards had been harnessed in both German and UK environmental regulation long before the introduction of the IPPC Directive. The first version of the German federal air pollution control statute, the *Bundesimmissionsschutzgesetz* of 1974 required operators of industrial installations to employ the 'Stand der Technik' or state of the art technology, in order to reduce emissions into the air. Similarly, section 7 (2) (a) of the UK Environmental Protection Act 1990 already required operators of installations to employ 'the best available techniques not entailing excessive costs'. In fact in most OECD countries technology standards are a cornerstone of environmental regulation (Rajotte, 2000).[57]

Technology standards, however, have not just been employed in national environmental regulation. They are also a key element of international environmental law. The 1992 OSPAR Convention seeks to protect the marine environment of the North-east Atlantic.[58] Art. 2 para. 2 (b) (i) requires the Contracting Parties to the Convention to apply 'the best available techniques' for the control of marine pollution.[59] Finally, technology standards also feature in other EU environmental legislation, not just the IPPC Directive. Directive 84/360/EEC[60] combats air pollution from industrial plants. Art. 4 of this Directive requires member states' competent authorities to ensure that 'all appropriate preventative measures against air pollution have been taken, including the application of the best available technology, provided that the application of such measures does not entail excessive costs'.

Third, and most importantly, the IPPC Directive is of wider significance and was therefore chosen as the focus for this empirical research because it allows us to address key questions about the nature of EU law. The BAT technology standard brings into focus the interrelationships between legal, economic, political and technical dynamics in the process of EU integration. Wider economic factors, such as developments in markets in pollution abatement technology and profitability of regulated plants, can influence what gets installed as BAT production and pollution reduction techniques across the EU. More specifically, according to Art. 2 (11) (second indent) IPPC Directive, economic factors, such as the 'costs and advantages' of techniques, should be taken into account when the legal obligation to install the 'best available techniques' is determined for a specific site. But political factors, such as national environmental policy preferences as well as regulated industries' interests, can also influence what gets to be considered as 'the best available techniques' under the IPPC Directive. Hence, analysis of the BAT technology standard sheds light on the question whether there is a distinct 'legal' dimension to the process of EU integration. But how does the research address these questions about the nature of law in EU integration?

A brief note on research methods

This book analyses the nature of EU law through three qualitative empirical[61] case studies which examine key sites of discourse about what constitute 'the best available techniques'. I am interested in the narratives which participants in BAT determinations construct concerning law and integration. Hence, the research pays close attention to the discourses which are mobilised when social actors debate what should be considered as 'the best available techniques'. These discourses matter, because they are not mere representations of the social world. They constitute social action.[62] The analysis traces how actors strategically use discourses in debates about what should be considered as 'the best available techniques'. But it also addresses how discourses regulate what arguments can be mobilised about 'the best available techniques' and therefore how discourses constitute 'actors'. Hence, the analysis draws on Foucault's ideas about discourse and inductively develops propositions grounded in the empirical data.

The first case study examines how determinations of what are 'the best available techniques' are achieved during the process of debating and drafting the EU BAT Reference (BREF) guidance documents. How do members of EU technical working groups define and construct normativity when selecting 'the best available techniques'? Why are some techniques singled out as 'the best available techniques'?[63] The second and third case studies provide data about how 'the best available techniques' are determined in a UK and German regulatory authority by permitting officers and operators when IPPC permits are written for specific installations. Two countries are the minimum number necessary in order to discuss potential integration effects generated by the IPPC Directive, such as harmonised definitions of 'the best available techniques'. The UK and Germany were chosen for several reasons. First, there are about 35,542 existing installations in the EU which fall within the IPPC regime.[64] Most of these are situated in four member states, Germany, France, Spain and the UK. In fact the largest number of existing IPPC installations – circa 8068 – are located in Germany. The fourth largest number of existing IPPC installations – circa 4299 – are found in the UK. Hence, given that about a third of IPPC installations in the EU are licensed by German or UK regulatory authorities, empirical data in relation to IPPC implementation in these two countries are likely to be significant,

Second, Germany and the UK were chosen for the case studies because they have had sufficiently distinct national approaches to pollution control before the implementation of the IPPC Directive. UK pollution control has traditionally relied on environmental quality standards.[65] Moreover, environmental law in the UK often provides significant discretion for permitting officers in the setting of environmental standards. In contrast to this, German pollution control regimes rely considerably on binding emission limit values.[66] In addition, German permitting officers' discretion is curtailed by a more legalistic approach towards permitting which draws on a dense network of detailed secondary and tertiary rules. German and UK pollution control regimes also differed before the implementation of the IPPC Directive because the UK had already established an integrated pollution control regime (IPC) under Part 1 of EPA 1990 which was in fact the basis for the UK proposal for the EC IPPC Directive. A hallmark of this regime and the IPPC Directive is a holistic approach towards permitting whereby emissions from installations to all three interconnected environmental media, air, water and land are regulated in an integrated way. For instance, when limits are set for an installation's emissions of pollutants into water, a simple transfer of pollutants into another environmental medium such as land should be avoided. Such pollution transfers can occur when a filter sludge is generated in a waste water treatment plant. While this removes pollutants from the plant's effluent stream, it may contribute to the pollution of land when the sludge is disposed of in a landfill site.

In contrast to this aspiration for an integrated approach, separate parts of the German environmental bureaucracy have set standards for emissions into air, water and land which are also regulated by separate legal provisions.[67] Hence, the UK and Germany have possessed sufficiently different systems of pollution control in order to address the question whether the IPPC Directive – and in particular what type of 'law' generated during its practical implementation – has contributed to an EU integration effect. The purpose of the two case studies is to analyse what contribution 'law' as well as technical, political and economic dynamics make to the determination of 'the best available techniques' and whether there is some indication that harmonised definitions of 'the best available techniques' are emerging. The UK and German case studies therefore do not seek to identify, compare and contrast key characteristics and styles of implementing the IPPC Directive in Germany and England for their own sake. So what then are the key argument and contribution of the book?

Argument and contribution of the book

The empirical research seeks to question theoretical assumptions about the nature of law in EU integration by examining what law is generated in practice during the implementation of the IPPC Directive. Hence, the book pursues a different perspective on the relationship between law and EU integration than is commonly assumed. Often a specific, predetermined concept of law, which perceives law as the 'formal law in the books', as relatively autonomous from its social contexts and as capable of being wielded in an instrumental manner, underpins explanatory accounts of EU integration. Law is the independent variable and integration outcomes are the dependent variable. This book reverses this relationship and treats integration outcomes as the independent variable and law as the dependent variable. The question then is how law has to be conceptualised in order to account for EU integration outcomes. What types of law feature in EU integration processes? The book suggests that this is an empirical question which needs to be answered with reference to an analysis of what law is actually generated in real life EU integration processes. Hence, the book focuses on 'EU law in action'. It emphasises the importance of implementation practices as a source of law and thus the limited applicability of 'formal' definitions of law as the 'law in the books'. It also argues that there are limits to the instrumental use of 'law' which arise from close connections between law and its social contexts. This analysis seeks to contribute to various literatures.

First of all this book adds to the existing literature on the IPPC Directive. There are currently three types of contributions to debates about the IPPC Directive. First, some accounts focus on doctrinal analysis of the text of the IPPC Directive as well as UK and German implementing measures (Kloepfer, 2004; Farthing et al., 2003; Zoettl, 2000; Doppelhammer, 2000; Backes and Betlem, 1999; Long, 1999; Emmott and Haigh, 1996; Schnutenhaus, 1995). They discuss possible different interpretations of the text of the Directive and thus point to unresolved questions about key concepts, such as the meaning of BAT, the relevance of economic and local environmental considerations in the determination of pollution control standards, and in particular the notion of integrated pollution control. Some contributions also examine the interrelationship between the IPPC Directive and other EU environmental legislation on water and air protection (Pallemaerts, 1996). Some legal analyses of the Directive also discuss its implementation in different EU member states (see, for example, Backes and Gerrit, 1999; Emmott, 1997).

Second, the EU Commission as well as national environmental agencies have commissioned a number of applied policy studies of the IPPC Directive. They focus on the practical implementation of the Directive by member state regulatory authorities and regulated installations.[68] Their main purpose is to gather information about what hinders and promotes 'successful and effective implementation' of the IPPC Directive. Some studies focus on economic obstacles to the implementation of the IPPC Directive. For instance, one study addresses operators' arguments that implementation of BAT can adversely affect their competitiveness. It concludes that environmentally high performing plants which have already adopted BAT are also economically successful in the long run (Hitchens et al., 2001).[69] Another study examines data on the costs of implementing BAT, focusing on the ceramics industry in Flanders, Belgium. It recommends drawing on cost data from a number of sources, not just technology suppliers, in order to determine more accurately the economic feasibility of BAT.[70]

Other studies examine whether the IPPC Directive simply ensures environmental protection, or can also stimulate innovation in clean production and pollution reduction techniques. In the UK a DTI-led study in which DEFRA and the EA participated examines practical case examples. It suggets that IPPC is effective in encouraging the diffusion of existing innovative technologies among operators, but does not really stimulate the development of new clean production and pollution reduction technologies (ENDS Report, No. 363, April 2005: 4–5). The IPPC Directive's role in stimulating technological innovation will also be further examined in the context of the EU Commission's official review of the IPPC Directive. Moreover, the question whether an integrated system of pollution control and permitting is emerging across the EU has been examined, sometimes from a comparative perspective (Bohne, 2006, 1998). The EU Commission is seeking to enhance the effectiveness of the IPPC Directive by improving understanding of its interaction with other pollution control regimes. The Commission is therefore proposing to conduct research into the relationships between licensing under the IPPC Directive and emissions trading in sulphur dioxide and nitrogen oxides.[71] Finally, the Commission is conducting a comprehensive EU wide audit which examines how far various member states have successfully implemented the Directive at installation level (Entec, Draft Final Report, 2006, ENDS Report No. 363, April 2005: 58; Commission Communication on the Implementation of the IPPC Directive, 2003).[72]

Third, some contributions to the existing literature on the IPPC Directive place the Directive in the wider context of debates about new forms of EU governance and regulation, including those which are science-based (Chalmers, 2000; Scott, 2000; Pallemaerts, 1996). The IPPC Directive is considered as an example of a shift from uniform to more flexible forms of EU governance. It leaves considerable flexibility to member states on what emission limit levels to set in permits for installations (for an argument that it does not provide for enough flexibility, see Faure and Lefevere, 1996). It is prescriptive mainly in relation to the procedure and criteria for setting emission limits. This also leaves open what the appropriate balance is between governance by scientific rationality and wider social concerns harnessed through public participation in standard setting under the IPPC Directive (Chalmers, 2000: 581).

The empirical data discussed in this book will be of interest to policy makers seeking to understand the practical implementation of the IPPC Directive because the data illustrate a range of obstacles to the 'successful' implementation of the IPPC Directive in member states. They suggest that national environmental administrations seek to adapt the implementation of the IPPC Directive to their pre-existing national systems of industrial pollution control and entrenched practices of determining technology standards. The Directive provides a significant challenge to existing procedures for permitting sites both in the UK and Germany. Holistic, integrated permitting which takes into account emissions to all three interconnected media – air, water and land – is different from traditional, compartmentalised, media-specific permitting in German environmental bureaucracies. The strengthened public participation provisions in the IPPC Directive[73] are a significant departure from previous public consultation provisions in the UK. The regulatory authority now also has to consult the public on the draft licences agreed with operators. Prior to these strengthened public participation provisions, regulatory authorities only consulted citizens on the IPPC licence *application*.[74] Hence, the book discusses issues of interest to environmental policy makers and lawyers.

It also questions assumptions which underpin certain contributions to the existing literature on the IPPC Directive. For instance, the EU Commission IPPC audit study assumes that there is a clear definition of the key legal obligations imposed by the Directive and hence that there can be specific answers to the question whether member states 'comply in practice' with the Directive. But this book explores whether we know what 'law' in EU integration really is. It asks whether, in the light of evidence of the active construction of 'EU law in action', it makes sense to hold on to the idea that we can theoretically and abstractly determine through doctrinal analysis the contents and meaning of EU legal obligations which can then be compared and contrasted with the 'reality of the living law'. Once we problematise what 'law' is, it becomes more difficult to know what actually constitutes compliance with the legal provisions of the IPPC Directive.[75]

The book is also relevant for EU lawyers and policy makers interested in wider debates about new forms of EU governance. The IPPC Directive is an example of a hybrid form of law, combining 'soft' and 'hard' law provisions. Such 'hybrid' forms of law are considered as a hallmark of new forms of EU governance (Trubek, Cottrell and Nance, 2005). The text of the IPPC Framework Directive itself constitutes 'hard' law, generated through the 'classic community method', involving co-decision between the Council of Ministers and the European Parliament. Moreover, emission limits set in other EU 'hard' law Directives are taken into account as minimum standards when local permitters determine BAT for a specific installation. But elements of the BAT technology standard are akin to 'soft' law. The Directive only prescribes the procedure for defining it, not the actual BAT standard. Guidance about 'the best available techniques' is determined at the EU level through a committee procedure which involves technical and political deliberation. This is a departure from standard setting through the 'classic community method' and thus another feature of new forms of EU governance.

Finally, and most importantly, the book seeks to add a new perspective to existing literatures by linking an analysis of the implementation of the IPPC Directive to wider questions about the nature of law in EU processes of integration. It examines what technology standards are actually generated during the implementation of the IPPC Directive and analyses these as examples of 'EU law in action'. Hence, the book seeks to establish new links between debates about 'law in action' in the sociology of law literature and debates about the role of law in EU integration and thus theories of EU integration. The book moves beyond an analysis of 'law in action' simply in a national context to an analysis of 'EU law in action' in a transnational legal order. It also examines 'law in action' not just in terms of social actors' behavioural tactics and strategies in relation to law, but also in terms of the discourses they mobilise. Whilst realist and sociological jurisprudence left a strong modernist legacy for 'law in action' research, this book takes on board the 'linguistic turn' in socio-legal research. Its empirical analysis pays close attention to social actors' oral discourse and written accounts constructed during the implementation of the EU IPPC Directive. Through attention to the 'law in action' the book seeks to develop a sociological analysis of EU law. It aims to contribute to a critical sociology of integrating law which questions the inevitability and naturalness of 'law' in governing social relations and achieving integration.

Outline of the book

Chapter 2 begins with a discussion of what I call 'traditional' perspectives on the role of law in EU integration. It traces how perceptions of law as the formal law 'in the books', as relatively autonomous from its social contexts and as capable of being wielded in an instrumental manner, have informed certain accounts of the role of law in EU integration. Chapter 3 then discusses literature which adds a critical perspective by questioning these traditional conceptions of law in EU integration, for instance, by recognising 'soft law' and new forms of normativity employed in innovative forms of EU governance. Chapter 3 argues that these critical perspectives can be developed further, in particular through reference to debates in the sociology of law literature about the 'law in action'. Chapter 4 therefore provides an introduction to key themes in 'law in action' research. It highlights relationships between a 'social' and a 'legal' sphere as a key aspect of

'EU law in action'[76] concepts. Chapters 5, 6, 7 and 8 then discuss data from the empirical case studies in order to develop an 'EU law in action' analysis. Chapter 5 examines how the BAT technology standard is further defined in the EU Technical Working Groups, the first level of the implementation of the EU Directive. Chapter 6 discusses a key characteristic of the BAT technology standard, generated also through German and UK local permitting practices. Attempts to define what constitute 'the best available techniques' lead to variation in open and closed BAT norms.[77] Chapter 6 argues that discourses play a central role in this process. Chapter 7 then focuses on an analysis of an economic discourse in BAT determinations. It highlights how closely the discussion of cost considerations in BAT determinations can be linked to political and technical discourses about what constitutes 'BAT'. Chapter 8 then further examines the idea that it becomes difficult to separate 'law' from its 'contexts' in the determination of what constitute 'the best available techniques'. It tackles the question whether a distinct category of 'law' can be said to generate EU integration results through a comparison of a coke oven licensing procedure in the UK and Germany. The comparison of the two licensing procedures shows that similar BAT techniques were chosen for the cooling of coke oven gas. Hence, there is an integration effect. But can it be argued that this was produced by IPPC Directive 'law'? The concluding chapter 9 then draws together the main findings of the research.

Notes

1. Also a horizontal and vertical dimension to legal integration must be recognised. On a horizontal level legal integration consists in the Council's attempts to harmonise formal legal standards in different member states through EC legislation. In particular where EC legislation draws on member states' policy initiatives transnational exchanges between member state societies are one aspect of legal integration (Stone, referred to in Wiener and Diez, 2004: 16). But legal integration also has a vertical dimension by virtue of EC law affecting the national legal orders of the different member states (Slaughter and Mattli, referred to in Armstrong (1998: 159).
2. Some critical legal studies approaches develop alternative visions of legal doctrine, such as 'deviationist' or 'enlarged' doctrine (Unger, 1983: 585).
3. The Directive applies to new installations, i.e. those which commence operations on or after 31 October 1999. Existing installations, i.e. those which operated before 31 October 1999 will have to achieve full compliance with the Directive by the 30 October 2007.

4. Installations subject to the obligations of the Directive are listed in Annex I. They cover activities from the energy industry, the production and processing of metals, the mineral industry, the chemical industry, waste management activities, pulp and paper production, textile pre-treatment and dying, tanning, slaughterhouses as well as intensive pig and poultry rearing. Furthermore, surface treatments, carbon and electrographite production as well as food production are also covered.

5. In the EU of fifteen member states about 45,000 large industrial installations come within the IPPC regime: Report from the Commission to the Council and the European Parliament, Brussels, 8 November 2005, COM (2005) 540 final, p. 2.

6. In Germany licences for discharges to water are still issued separately.

7. In the proposal for a consolidated version of the IPPC Directive this is now Art. 17.

8. For instance, there is a TWG for the iron and steel sector, for the non-ferrous metal sector, for the paper and pulp industry, for large combustion plants, for food and drinks manufacture etc.

9. This organisation has now changed its name to 'Business Europe'. For more information see www.businesseurope.eu/Content/Default.asp?

10. Such as the European Council of the Paint, Printing Ink and Artists' Colours Industry (CEPE).

11. While DG Environment leads the BREF drafting process, particularly by chairing the IEF, the BREFs are published by the EU Commission as a collective body. This means that all the different Commission Directorates have to agree to publish the draft BREFs. At times there were disagreements between DG Enterprise and Industry, on the one hand, and DG Environment, on the other, about the contents of a draft BREF.

12. By 7 December 2006 the first round of thirty-one BREFs had been completed. BREFS are periodically reviewed and their technical information updated. This process has been started for the BREF for the iron and steel sector, the cement and lime sector, non-ferrous metals and the manufacture of glass.

13. Some BREFs are written not for specific industrial sectors, but on issues which cut across different sectors. These 'horizontal' BREFs deal with topics, such as cross-media and economic issues in the definition of BAT, cooling techniques and monitoring of emissions from installations.

14. It takes about three years for a BREF document to be drafted at the EU level: ENDS Report No. 372, January 2006, p. 48.

15. In the early stages of BREF writing these were called 'BAT candidates'.

16. Frank Farrell, 'How Economic Issues were Dealt with in the Non-Ferrous Metals BREF', p. 2 and see the official 'IPPC BREF Outline and Guide' on http://www.eippcb.jrc.es/pages/Boutline.htm.

17. For further information see 'IPPC BREF outline and guide', ibid.

18. Art. 21 para. 1 of the IPPC Directive requires that member states have to incorporate the IPPC Directive within 3 years into their national law. Hence,

member states had time until 30 October 1999 to implement the Directive into their national laws.

19. See Proposal for a Directive of the European Parliament and of the Council, concerning integrated pollution prevention and control, Brussels, 25.09.2006, COM (2006) 543 final.

20. See Art. 15 of the proposal for a consolidated version of the IPPC Directive.

21. As laid down in Art. 16 of the proposal for a consolidated version of the IPPC Directive.

22. According to Art. 9 (3) of the proposed consolidated version of the IPPC Directive which clarifies the link between the two Directives.

23. For instance, member states currently use different parameters for setting emission limit values ELVs. Some set ELVs as the mass of pollutant per discharge flow, i.e. 20 mg of cadmium per 1 litre of the factory's effluent discharged into the river. Others set ELVs as mass of pollutant per mass of product produced, i.e. an ELV of 20 mg of cadmium per each 1 kg of galvanised steel produced (ENDS Report, No. 370, November 2005: 44).

24. Infringement proceedings under Art. 226 EC Treaty have also been taken against Spain, Belgium, Denmark, France, Greece, the Netherlands, Luxembourg and Austria. The Commission had also considered infringement proceedings against Germany for late implementation which were, however, terminated, once it became clear that Germany had made substantial progress towards implementation in compliance with the legal deadlines.

25. There has been slow implementation of the IPPC Directive, especially in Spain, Portugal and Italy, as well as considerable variation between member states in implementing the IPPC Directive (see EU Commission, First Report on the implementation of the IPPC Directive, 3 November 2005, COM (2005) 540 final, pp. 3, 8) at http://ec.europa.eu/environment/ippc/ippc_report.htm). In order to facilitate implementation of the Directive the Commission has also launched an 'IPPC Implementation Action Plan'. For further information see http://ec.europa.eu/environment/ippc/ippc_ implementation.htm.

26. The Bundesministerium für Umwelt, Naturschutz und Reaktorsicherheit (BMU).

27. The Bundesrat represents the interests of the Länder in the German federal structure.

28. Die Abwasserverordnung.

29. In German Konzentrationswirkung.

30. This is different from the UK. For most IPPC installations planning consent can be obtained independently from the planning authority either before or after obtaining a PPC permit (Farthing, Marshall et al., 2003: 32).

31. This duty to strive for 'full coordination' was introduced into the BimSchG in order to comply with Art. 7 of the IPPC Directive.

32. As a federal state Germany consists of a number of different states, called Länder or Bundesländer.

33. According to Art. 84 of the German constitution (the Basic Law – *Grundgesetz*) the *Länder* implement and enforce federal environmental statutes, such as the *Bundesimmissionsschutzgesetz* as well as their own *Land* environmental statutes. The *Länder* also implement federal environmental regulations passed under federal environmental statutes according to Art. 84 para. 2 GG, such as the TA *Luft* and other technical instructions which flesh out the BAT technology standard under the IPPC Directive.

34. This is also called the *oberste Umweltschutzbehörde*, the highest environmental authority.

35. See also the discussion in chapter 7. Part of this first tier of *Land* environmental administration are also the upper *Land* authorities (*obere Landesbehörde*). A number of *Länder* have an upper *Land* authority which deals with environmental issues, such as the Hessisches Landesamt für Umwelt und Geologie. For more information see http://www.hlug.de/.

36. *Regierungspräsidenten* or *Bezirksregierungen*.

37. Exceptions here are the city states, such as Bremen, Hamburg and Berlin. Among the large *Länder* (*Flächenstaaten*) the exceptions are Saarland, Schleswig-Holstein, Brandenburg and Mecklenburg-Vorpommern.

38. *Kreisfreie Städte*.

39. *Kreise*.

40. TA *Lärm*, TA *Abwasser*, TA *Boden*, TA *Abfall* and TA *Siedlungsabfall*.

41. The regulations were issued under para. 4 (1), third sentence, of the BimSchG in connection with para. 19 (1) BimSchG.

42. There are differences, however, between the list of installations covered in Annex I of the IPPC Directive and those listed in the 4th BimSchV. The 4th BimSchV was drawn up in particular with reference to the air pollution potential of plants while the list in Annex I to the IPPC Directive was compiled also with reference to the water and land contamination potential of installations. Furthermore the German list includes plants which were considered in need of IPPC regulation due to their explosion and fire-hazard potential (Kloepfer, 1998: 927).

43. In so-called *Sanierungsverfahren*.

44. § 3 (6) of the BImSchG of 26 September 2002 defines as 'Stand der Technik' the 'state of development which innovative techniques, measures or modes of operating a plant have achieved. These must be practically suited to limit emissions into air, water and soil, to guarantee the safety of a plant and an environmentally acceptable waste disposal or otherwise to contribute to the prevention and minimisation of impacts onto the environment and thus to ensure a generally high level of the protection of the environment as a whole. In order to determine the "Stand der Technik" in particular the criteria of the Annex have to be considered.' In German: 'Stand der Technik im Sinne dieses Gesetzes ist der Entwicklungsstand fortschrittlicher Verfahren, Einrichtungen oder Betriebsweisen, der die praktische Eignung einer Maßnahme zur Begrenzung von Emissionen in Luft, Wasser and Boden, zur Gewährleistung der Anlagensicherheit, zur Gewährleistung

einer umweltverträglichen Abfallentsorgung oder sonst zur Vermeidung oder Verminderung von Auswirkungen auf die Umwelt zur Erreichung eines allgemein hohen Schutzniveaus für die Umwelt insgesamt gesichert erscheinen lässt. Bei der Bestimmung des Standes der Technik sind insbesondere die im Anhang aufgeführten Kriterien zu berücksichtigen.' Apart from the more specific reference to plant safety and environmentally acceptable waste disposal from an IPPC plant, § 3 (6) BimSchG reproduces the definition of the 'best available techniques' from Art. 2 (11) of the IPPC Directive in the text of the German legislation. The annex to the German legislation is a replication of the Annex I criteria for the definition of BAT in the IPPC Directive.

45. SI 2000/1973.
46. Similar PPC regulations have been issued for Scotland and Northern Ireland as well as for off-shore installations (SI 2001/1091).
47. In the UK about 6,500 installations are covered under the IPPC regime. UK Article 16 (3) Report to the EU Commission, 31 December 2002 (DEFRA, 2003).
48. About 150–200 staff work in these four central strategic permitting groups.
49. Where no EU BREF documents had been drafted by the time a particular sector became due to be licensed in the UK, the Environment Agency took into account the previous UK sector guidance notes which had been written for the IPC pollution control regime under Part I of EPA 1990.
50. This point was further developed in *Thornby Farms v. Daventry District Council* [2002] Env LR 28 in relation to the previous BATNEEC standard ('best available techniques not entailing excessive cost', as referred to in section 7 of EPA 1990).
51. Directive 2001/80/EC on the limitation of emissions of certain pollutants into the air from large combustion plants, OJ L 309, 27.11.2001, p. 1.
52. Council Directive 1999/13/EC of 11 March 1999 on the limitation of emissions of volatile organic compounds due to the use of organic solvents in certain activities and installations, OJ L 85, 29.3.1999, p. 1.
53. Directive 2000/76/EC OJ L 332, 28.12.2000, p. 91.
54. One of the issues here is that regulatory authorities may simply transfer emission standards from the waste incineration and the landfill Directive into IPPC permits for these installations, while the BAT concept under the IPPC Directive may actually require tighter standards because the quality of the local environmental media into which pollutants are discharged also has to be considered under BAT (ENDS Report No. 377, June 2006, p. 43).
55. How far the IPPC Directive and other pieces of EU environmental legislation are integrated in practice varies between member states. The UK, for instance, is seeking to achieve greater integration and efficiency through the introduction of a single permitting programme in England and Wales for installations covered both under EU waste legislation and the IPPC Directive. This new regime is due to come into operation in spring 2008 (ENDS Report No. 380, September 2006, pp. 38–39).

56. Some member states have tried to develop further links between the IPPC Directive and other elements of pollution control regimes. The UK, for instance, has commissioned research into the link between the EU environmental management standard, EMAS (eco-management and auditing scheme under EU Regulation 761/01), and IPPC controls. The suggestion was that reporting and monitoring requirements in IPPC permits may be fulfilled through reporting and monitoring work which an EMAS certified company may already undertake (ENDS Report, No. 323, December 2001:12).

57. Also section 109 (3) (c) of the Environmental Protection Act 1990 requires a person who is keeping genetically modified organisms to use 'the best available techniques not entailing excessive cost' for keeping the organisms under his control and for preventing any damage to the environment which could arise from the keeping of the genetically modified organisms.

58. The are currently fifteen signatories to the 1992 OSPAR Convention, including Belgium, Denmark, Finland, France, Germany, Iceland, the Netherlands, Norway, Portugal, Spain, Sweden, the UK, Luxembourg, Switzerland and the Commission of the European Communities.

59. The development of guidance documents on what constitute 'the best available techniques' by OSPARCOM (the OSPAR Commission) feeds into the definition of BAT under the IPPC Directive. For instance, guidance under OSPARCOM on 'the best available techniques' for ammonia production contributed to the work on the draft IPPC BREF on ammonia production. OSPARCOM recommends that mercury cells in ammonia production will be phased out by 2010. But in practice the replacement of mercury cells in many European countries has been patchy over the last 15–20 years (ENDS Report No. 309, October 2000, p. 52). OSPARCOM has also published BAT guidance documents on 'best available techniques for the Primary Production of Non-Ferrous Metals' and 'best available techniques for the vinyl chloride industry'.

60. OJ 1984 L 188, p. 20.

61. The data were collected through semi-structured interviews with members of EU technical working groups and permitting staff in national environmental regulatory authorities who deliberate and decide on what should be considered as 'the best available techniques' for installations. Qualitative data were also collected from various files compiled by organisations involved in the assessment of 'the best available techniques'. These were background files kept by the European EIPPC Bureau which coordinates the writing of EU guidance documents as well as files from a German and a UK regulatory authority on the process of licensing IPPC installations.

62. I therefore refer to economic, political and technical discourses which are mobilised in the determination of BAT, not just economic, political and technical constructions of the process of choosing 'the best available techniques'.

63. This case study draws on a two months' stay in the Commission's EIPPC Bureau which was set up to coordinate the work of Technical Working

Groups (TWGs) for the various sectors covered by the IPPC Directive. Qualitative empirical data were collected through semi-structured interviews with staff writing the BREFs and through analysis of background files for the BREF on the iron and steel sector, the non-ferrous metals sector and large combustion plants.

64. Entec report, 2006: ii. This figure is based on available data from twenty-two out of the twenty-five EU member states.

65. In the case of pollution control through environmental quality standards the absorptive capacities of the receiving environmental medium, such as air, water or land, are taken into account. For instance, an environmental quality standard may stipulate that there should be no more than 2 mg of SO2 per cubic metre in the medium of air. The natural ability of air to disperse pollutants will also contribute to the achievement of this environmental quality standard.

66. Emission limit values set fixed standards independent of any absorptive or dispersing capacities of environmental media. They control pollutants directly at the source of emissions from installations for instance. An emission limit standard would stipulate, for example, a limit of 5 mg of cadmium per litre of water discharged by a factory pipe into a river.

67. Moreover, the UK, for instance, has relied more than Germany on environmental quality standards than emission limit values.

68. See, for instance, Report from the Commission to the Council and the European Parliament on the Implementation of Directive 96/61/EC concerning integrated pollution prevention and control, Brussels, 8 November 2005, COM (2005) 540 final.

69. The report was based on a comparison of the economic performance of plants which have already adopted most elements of BAT as described in their sector BREFs and plants which have not yet adopted BAT. The case studies on which this study relied involved the cement, non-ferrous metals as well as pulp and paper sector. The EU Commission subsequently commissioned another study on 'Different Approaches to Implement the IPPC Directive and the Impact on Competitiveness' as a further input into its review of the IPPC Directive.

70. While technology suppliers' data were found to be realistic about the investment costs of the techniques, they overestimated the costs of operating BAT techniques, once installed. Moreover, the study found that pollution reduction techniques' efficiencies were lower than suggested by equipment suppliers.

71. In particular the UK and the Netherlands want to see IPPC BAT conditions on SO2 and NOX replaced with emission trading in these acid gases (ENDS Report, No. 358, November 2004: 60).

72. This study involves the close examination of permits issued by member state regulatory authorities in order to determine whether actual permitting practice and BAT conditions comply with the requirements of the IPPC Directive. It is planned that about thirty EU installations from the

iron and steel, pulp and paper, cement, non-ferrous metals and chemicals sectors will participate.

73. Introduced through the amendment of the IPPC Directive by the Public Participation Directive.

74. The IPPC Directive now also requires regulatory authorities to provide a publicly accessible account of the reasoning behind their permitting decisions. While this already occurs in German licensing practices this is a new requirement for UK regulatory authorities.

75. That it is by no means clear what constitutes compliance with the provisions of the IPPC Directive is also illustrated by the dispute between the EU Commission and some member states, such as the UK, on whether full compliance with the provisions of the IPPC Directive and the BAT standard in particular has to be achieved by 30 October 2007 or whether compliance with the Directive is also achieved through the imposition merely of improvement conditions which allow for the completion of BAT actions at a date later than 30 October 2007.

76. I use the term EU law to refer to the IPPC Directive and other formal EU legislation. I also include in the term 'EU law in action' national implementing measures and activities, such as the permitting of specific installations under the Directive.

77. I use the term BAT norm also for BAT determinations in the BREFs, although they only constitute guidance to permitters in local permitting authorities and hence are not legally binding. Hence, the term 'BAT norm' refers also to standards which have the potential to become formally legally binding. BAT techniques listed in BREFs already contain an element of normativity in that they constitute an already narrower selection of all possible techniques which could be considered as BAT. They are therefore persuasive, though not formally legally binding, in debates about what constitutes BAT.

2   Traditional perspectives on the role of law in EU integration

Introduction

This chapter discusses a number of contributions which form what I call 'traditional perspectives' on law and European integration. The literature in this area is rich and multifaceted. The label 'traditional perspectives' does not fully capture all its subtleties and variety. Hence, my construction of 'traditional perspectives' in this chapter is a heuristic device. By drawing out key ideas which inform these traditional perspectives on law in EU integration, I seek to clarify how 'critical perspectives' (discussed in chapter 3) and the book's analysis of the empirical case studies (chapters 5, 6, 7 and 8) challenge some of the tenets of traditional approaches.

The traditional perspectives seek to analyse relationships between law and integration by asking 'what role does law play in EU integration?' But this assumes, rather than questions, what law is. Law is regarded as the independent, pre-given variable, while integration is the dependent variable. Moreover, the traditional perspectives draw on a conception of law which is derived from the internal descriptions of the legal field which the formal EU and national legal systems themselves generate. Hence such perspectives emphasise formal and instrumental dimensions of law. Law is also taken to be relatively autonomous and thus to have a significant integrating force which is distinct and separate from the social, political and economic dynamics promoting integration. Traditional perspectives focus on the behaviour of official legal actors when analysing the implementation of EU and national law. I argue that this approach is limited because it focuses on one specific, and thus overly narrow, conception of law in EU integration.

The first section of this chapter outlines the main assumptions which underpin traditional perspectives. These include a modernist perspective of the social world, the idea that there is a specifically legal dimension to EU integration, and that a discussion of law's integrating function does not require us to raise any questions about the nature of law. The second and main section of the chapter then focuses on a key element of the traditional approach towards law and integration which flows from these assumptions. This is a conceptualisation of law as formal, relatively autonomous and instrumental in character. This is typically associated with a focus on the official legal actors who implement law. The third and concluding section draws together the main points of the chapter.

Key assumptions of traditional perspectives on law and integration

The idea of a specifically legal dimension to EU integration

That there is a specifically legal dimension to EU integration is a key assumption which informs traditional perspectives on the role of law in EU integration. This is not surprising, given that from the beginning a legal framework has been key to Western European integration. The point is illustrated by the 1957 Treaties of Rome which established the European Economic Community and the European Atomic Energy Community, as well as the 1951 Treaty of Paris which created the European Coal and Steel Community. Integration was further promoted through a proliferation of secondary legislation agreed by member states in the Council and through the development of jurisprudence by the European Court of Justice, later assisted by the Court of First Instance. Some traditional accounts even consider integration itself to be a legal principle:

The principle of the *progressive integration of the member states* in order to attain the objective of the Treaty *does not only comprise a political requirement; it amounts rather to a Community legal principle*, which the Court of Justice has to bear in mind when interpreting Community law, if it is to discharge in a proper manner its allotted task of upholding the law, when it interprets and applies the Treaties.
(emphasis added, Kutscher referred to in Shaw 1996: 238)

Law and its significance for promoting EU integration is a more recent discovery for political scientists (Dehousse, 2002; Koslowski, 1999: 569).[1] Neo-functionalists,[2] early key contributors to the debates on EU integration, did not pay particular attention to the legal dimension of the EU (Koslowski, 1999). They concentrated mainly on the role of transnational – in particular economic – actors whose common interests across member states were considered to be an important driver of EU integration. This early neglect of the role of law has been acknowledged in later neo-functionalist work and there is now greater recognition of the importance of a specifically legal dimension to EU integration (Schmitter, 2004). From the 1990s onwards interest in a specifically legal dimension of EU integration started to grow among political scientists. For instance, there are now a number of studies which examine the role of the European Court of Justice (Wincott, 2002). It is also argued that we are witnessing 'a move towards law' and hence an increasing legalisation of international relations, including the EU (Goldstein et al., 2000: 386, 388). A range of strong drivers for legalisation are analysed, such as the solution of problems arising from lack of commitment to bargains in international relations, the reduction of transaction costs and an expansion of the grounds for compromise (ibid.: 394). In short, traditional approaches start from the assumption that there is a specifically legal dimension to EU integration. They also make further assumptions about the nature of law.

Assumptions about the nature of law in EU integration

Traditional approaches tend not to concern themselves with inquiry into the nature of law. They do inquire whether and how law contributes to EU integration, but do not properly recognise that a further set of questions needs to be asked about what law actually is. The definitions of law within the formal EU and national legal systems are taken as the basis for a concept of law in general. Analysis of the nature of law is not considered to be an empirical issue. But analysing whether and how law contributes to EU integration – an issue central to the traditional approach – is likely to benefit from making explicit what idea of law is deployed and to distinguish between various theoretical and empirical conceptions of law. Our assumptions about the nature of law will colour our answers to questions about whether and how law integrates. For instance, conceptualising law in instrumental and functional terms paves the way for attributing an integrating function to law. When law is portrayed as a tool of EU politics and as capable of being deployed in a strategic manner, it can then transform its contexts, such as political and economic obstacles to EU integration. Moreover, traditional approaches assume that law is relatively autonomous in relation to its social, political and economic contexts. They rely, for instance, on images projected by specific doctrines of EU and national constitutional law, such as the 'rule of law' and the 'separation of powers'. These doctrines portray formal legal rules as a specific set of social practices that are separate from the sphere of economic and political power. Once it has been accepted that law is relatively autonomous with respect to its social, political and economic contexts, the path is already paved for the argument that there is a specifically legal dimension to EU integration.

To summarise: a traditional view approaches questions about law and integration in a particular way. It does not sufficiently differentiate between empirical questions about the nature of law, on the one hand, and questions about whether and how law integrates, on the other. For some political scientists and EU lawyers, the integrating force of law seems to flow naturally from prior theoretical conceptions of society and law, such as an emphasis on the relative autonomy of law and instrumentality as well as modernist perspectives upon the social world.

Modernist perspectives in a traditional approach towards law in EU integration

Neo-functionalist[3] and neo-realist[4] political science accounts of EU integration as well as the sociological functionalist view on law and integration are informed by modernist perspectives. They refer to an objective social reality which can be rendered visible through empirical research. Where they rely on quantitative research, these perspectives seek to detect relationships between pre-specified independent and dependent variables, with law as the independent and integration outcomes the dependent variable.[5] Since social life is analysed in terms of cause and effect, a rationalist paradigm underpins this understanding of the social world and research methodology (Schmitter, 2004: 48). According to this perspective, social actors pursue their own interests, expressed as preferences (Abbott and Snidal, 2000: 422). These have an objective dimension because interests are seen as flowing from pre-existing social structures within which social actors operate (Snyder, 1989: 173). It is already assumed that 'social actors' exist. How 'social actors' actually come to be 'actors' is not considered to be problematic. For instance, neo-realists in particular start from the idea that the behaviour of 'major actors' – such as powerful member states – and the events which they are assumed to create and shape, such as Intergovernmental Conferences and Treaty revisions, are key to an analysis of EU integration (Schmitter, 2004).

Finally, the traditional approach towards law and integration is anchored in modernist theoretical commitments since it retains the concept of the nation state as a key point of reference for understanding EU integration. Neo-realists emphasise the intergovernmental features of the EU and insist that member states still exercise significant powers, despite the creation of supranational EU institutions such as the European Parliament, the EU Commission and the European Courts. In contrast, neo-functionalists emphasise the declining importance of member states and the increasing role of various supranational institutions, as well as transnational private interest groups, such as trade associations, in EU integration. But later neo-functionalist work, in particular that which has begun to recognise the importance of law in EU integration, still refers back to nation states. Its conception of law draws on images generated by formal EU and state national legal systems. It is informed by liberal legal ideology which also developed with the rise of the nation state in Western Europe in the eighteenth and nineteenth centuries. Here law is the formal 'law in the books'. It is created by public, democratically legitimated institutions and its authority is also guaranteed by formal sanctions at the level of the state.

To summarise: a traditional approach towards law and integration proceeds from modernist assumptions about the nature of the social world. It employs a rationalist perspective, where social 'actors' pursue objective interests and nation states still matter, either in the process of EU integration itself or by informing conceptions of law in EU integration. In the following section I will explain in more detail key elements in the traditional approach towards law and integration. In particular I will argue that the traditional approach perceives law as formal, instrumental and relatively autonomous. It also focuses on official legal actors in the implementation of EU and national law.

The focus on official legal actors promoting EU integration

Though interest in the European Courts only developed in the 1990s among political scientists, the European Court of Justice (ECJ) is now a key point of reference for analysing EU integration (Wincott, 2002; see, for example, Stone Sweet, 2004). Evaluations of the ECJ and the Court of First Instance vary from 'hero' to 'villain', but it is clear that the European courts are considered as a key driving force for EU integration (Haltern, 2004; Goldstein et al., 2000: 388). There are good reasons for this focus on the courts. The early decisions of the ECJ concerning the supremacy and direct effect of EC law visibly and dramatically propelled EU integration forward. Moreover, some political scientists see the ECJ as an authoritative, independent agent with the crucial task of monitoring agreements between member states. This task arises from a limited degree of trust between member states which increases the risk that mutual agreements may not actually be adhered to (Schmitter, 2004: 50).

A good example of this emphasis on the courts is Geoffrey Garrett's debate with Anne-Marie Burley and Walter Mattli concerning neo-realist critiques of neo-functionalist accounts of legal integration. Burley and Mattli's (1993) neo-functionalist study of legal integration examines the preliminary reference procedure under Art. 234 EC Treaty. National courts can refer questions about EC law to the ECJ under Art. 234 EC Treaty. They (Burley and Mattli, 1993: 52) seek to develop a political explanation – 'from the ground up' – of the role of the ECJ in EU integration. They argue that the ECJ created an enduring pro-community constituency of private individuals by giving them a direct role in the implementation of EC law through the doctrines of supremacy and direct effect (ibid.). In contrast to this, Garrett (1995) points to the continued importance of member states who may ignore ECJ decisions or change the EC legal order through concerted action, such as Treaty revision.

The focus on courts as key official legal actors in EU integration has been further reinforced through analysis of interactions between the European and national courts. Judicial integration in the EU involves 'a set of constitutional dialogues between supranational and national judges' (Stone Sweet, 1998: 305). National judges may drive EU integration forward, especially if there are specific incentives to do so, such as opportunities for enhancing their power (through pro-integration jurisprudence) in relation to national executives, parliaments and other judges (Stone Sweet, 2004: 20).

The focus on courts has also been developed through the argument that it is necessary to differentiate between different layers of national courts because they can react differently towards the EU legal order. Higher and constitutional courts in the member states may have an interest in limiting the expansion of EC law into the national legal order, in order to preserve their scope for autonomous action. But lower courts may derive advantages from developing their jurisprudence on the basis of EC law (Burley and Mattli, 1993: 63). Thus, they may be keen to refer to the ECJ questions about EC law that have been raised in cases before them.[6] New EC legal principles – developed through the preliminary reference procedure – will also be binding upon higher national courts. Consequently, courts lower down in the national legal hierarchy may expand their influence in relation to higher national courts (Haltern, 2004: 183).

Through this focus on courts other official legal actors, such as litigants and their legal representatives, are foregrounded in theories of EU integration.[7] For instance, neo-functionalists have highlighted the importance of private litigants as defenders of transnational economic interests (Mattli and Slaughter, 1998). They mobilise EC law through legal actions before national courts. Their cooperation with the ECJ and national courts is thought to create a self-sustaining judicial machinery which promotes EU integration (Burley and Mattli, 1993; Mattli and Slaughter, 1998: 204). Neo-functionalists highlight the importance of a developing common legal profession in the EU (Schmitter, 1996b: 13). The traditional approach, however, is not simply characterised by a focus on official legal actors, but also perceives law as formal, instrumental and relatively autonomous.

The focus on formal law in EU integration

Formal conceptions of law refer to legal doctrine. The latter in turn relies on 'institutionally defined materials of a collective tradition' which are key to determining what the law is. Within this tradition the interpreters of the law speak authoritatively. They elaborate law as an 'application of state power' (Unger, 1983). Formal law usually works through conditional programmes. If various conditions are fulfilled for the applicability of a legal rule, then a particular legal result can be achieved (Teubner, 1983: 257). Thus formal law provides the analytical means for settling disputes about the basic terms of social life (Unger, 1983: 564). It is based on the belief that determinate solutions can be identified to issues of legal choice through deductive methods, such as subsuming social facts under a seamless and rational system of legal rules. According to a more expansive definition, legal formalism can be clearly distinguished from open-ended perspectives concerning the basic terms of social life, such as ideological, philosophical or visionary debates (ibid.: 564). From the perspective of this more expansive definition of formalism, legal reasoning is objective because it relies on 'impersonal purposes, policies and principles' (ibid.).

Accounts of EU integration often rely on this conception of formal law. When researchers refer to 'law' in EU integration, they usually mean formal primary Treaty law and secondary legislation, such as Directives and Regulations, as well as judgments of the European Courts and the law of member states (see, for example, Burley and Mattli, 1993: 43):

... even today, legislative activity is the main parameter by which we measure the growth in the scope of EU activities.

(Dehousse, 2002: 207)

Hence law has been defined here as the 'law in the books' (Snyder, 1990).[8] Given the sheer number and easy visibility of formal legal measures, it is perhaps not surprising that they are a key point of reference for conceptualisations of EU law. While there were only a few dozen EC Directives in the 1960s, by 1986 this figure had risen to over 700 Directives (Cappelletti, Seccombe and Weiler, 1986b). The White Paper for the completion of the Single European Market alone proposed 282 legal measures (Armstrong and Bulmer, 1998: 6, 23). By 1992 European law included 22,445 EU Regulations and 1,675 Directives (Alter, 2000: 493). Moreover, since the EU has been perceived as 'the product of successive treaties between formally (and formerly) sovereign national states', primary Treaty law[9] has featured extensively in discussions of EU law (Schmitter, 2004: 49).[10]

In addition, efforts to constitutionalise the Treaties – by considering them not merely as agreements between sovereign member states governed by public international law, but as the basis for an EU constitution which is binding on member states – further emphasise the significance of primary Treaty law. Similarly, federalist accounts of EU integration stress the importance of formal legal rules in EU integration (see, for example, Pinder, 1991). They place a constitutional settlement based on the rule of law at the heart of EU integration. This would spell out formal legal rights for the member states and define the EU polity through constitutional legal principles (Rosamond, 2000: 24).

Emphasis on formal law is strongest, however, in debates about juridification in the EU. It has been suggested that formal law actually inhibits political processes, thereby creating a 'political deficit' in the EU (Dehousse, 2000: 26). It is claimed that politics are juridified insofar as law increasingly takes over political decision-making processes. For instance, political actors may use litigation strategically for wider political purposes. Such accounts point to the important role which the ECJ plays in resolving inter-institutional conflicts and power struggles between the major EU institutions. The ECJ strengthened, for instance, legal rights for the European Parliament to initiate legal actions before the ECJ in order to challenge the validity of acts adopted by the Council and/or Commission.[11] Moreover, private actors have also been successful in using the ECJ strategically for litigation in order to advance political reform initiatives, such as in the field of sex discrimination (see, for example, Deards and Hargreaves: 2004: 321–352). Hence, juridification and its emphasis on the formal law also mean that political actors have to plan their political strategies with reference to a legal framework which opens up the possibility of legal challenges to political initiatives (Dehousse, 2000: 20).

But formal law has not just been invoked to illustrate the power of the ECJ in EU integration. It is also central to debates concerning the limits of the ECJ's agency. For instance, Daniel Wincott (2002: 3) argues that there are 'strategic contexts' in which the ECJ has to operate. A key element of such strategic contexts is EC law itself which includes the ECJ's previous decisions. Further elements in these 'strategic contexts' are external structures, consisting of official legal actors, such as litigants and legal practitioners as well as educators (ibid.: 18). These contexts restrict how the ECJ can promote integration because its scope of action also depends on litigants' decisions about whether to pursue actions before the courts.

Moreover, neo-realist accounts of EU integration also focus on formal law.[12] They start from the idea that anarchy and intrinsic hostility are an important aspect of relations between states. While states are also capable of cooperating in integration regimes, their main aim will be to enhance their power in inter-state systems. Hence, neo-realists suggest that states seek to avoid limitations on their own power, for instance by limiting EU integration to inter-governmental cooperation (Rosamond, 2000: 131–134; Schmitter, 1996b: 3).

The focus of the neo-realists on formal law in EU integration, such as legal doctrine developed by the ECJ and legislation, becomes particularly obvious in their discussions of how to reconcile the focus on member states' self-interest with the existence of EU supranational institutions. Geoffrey Garrett (1995: 175–177) suggests that member states will try to uphold the validity of a national law which is in conflict with EC law, if an important national interest is at stake. But where a crucial national interest is not at stake, it will be in the interests of member states to support an ECJ decision declaring a national law incompatible with EC law. There is an incentive for member states to support ECJ decisions because they enforce the political bargains which member states have struck when legislating in the Council. Each member state can rely on the fact that not only it but also other member states will be held to these agreements. Hence, the ECJ acts in the interest of all the member states by resolving problems which arise from incomplete contracting between them (ibid.: 172). Moreover, some neo-realists consider formal law to be important for moulding the preferences of member states. Legal doctrine developed by the ECJ is also shaped by the preferences of member states and these, in turn, are influenced by formal law and in particular the legal duty of member states to comply with EC law (ibid.). Moreover, in support of their inter-governmentalist perspective on EU integration, neo-realists have argued that the executives of the most powerful member states control the process of EU integration and they consider formal law as central to this control. Member states exercise significant power through the drafting of Treaties and their revisions, as well as through controlling the process of passing secondary formal legislation.

Neo-realist accounts of EU integration are usually contrasted with neo-functionalist accounts because neo-functionalists emphasise the significance of transnational coalitions often based on economic interests (Rosamond, 2000: 58). Neo-realists, in contrast, consider member states as key drivers of EU integration. But also some elements of neo-functionalist analysis focus on formal law. Neo-functionalism draws on the functionalist idea that social action can be adequately explained through reference to its consequences. Hence, consequences contribute to the causes of human behaviour (Schmitter, 1971: 235, referring to Arthur Stinchcombe). For instance, a particular social action can be analysed in terms of the contribution it makes to the maintenance of a stable society. By working with a utilitarian concept of interests neo-functionalism differs from functionalism which considers actors to pursue common goods or to be unselfish (Burley and Mattli, 1993: 54).

In particular, the neo-functionalist concepts of 'spill-over' and 'spill-around' direct attention to formal law in EU integration. 'Spill-over' means that there is an increase both in the scope and level of integration efforts, while 'spill-around' describes the lateral extension of integration activities without a change in the level of authority (Schmitter, 1971: 242). Member states have employed both these connected strategic options in regional integration efforts. Legal rules have been extended from one policy sector to another and member state competencies have been transferred to the EU supranational institutions, once member states realised that supranational governance in one field can often only be fully achieved when combined with supranational governance in another area.

The logic of 'spill-overs' and 'spill-arounds' captures how EC law has actually been extended to a number of policy fields for which the Treaty of Rome in 1958 did not originally allocate competencies. For instance, the legal rules establishing the internal market have been followed by further EC social law in the fields of environmental and consumer protection in order to harmonise regulatory burdens on businesses throughout the EU and thus to create a 'level playing field'. Formal EC law is also at the heart of another spill-over effect, that from economic, political and social integration to an integration of the member states' different legal systems. An increase in trade in goods and services in the internal market between different member states has spawned EC Regulations and Directives which harmonise standards for products and the supply of services. Moreover, formal law is also central to another spill-over effect in the EU. Actors' expectations change as they start to operate within the framework of legal rules developed by the ECJ. Hence there is a spill-over effect from the legal into the political sphere, where new expectations generated by legal rights can generate demands for further political integration initiatives (Rosamond, 2000: 103). To summarise, neo-functionalist concepts, such as 'spill-over' and 'spill-around', specifically capture the proliferation of *formal* law in EU integration. While a focus on the formal law is a key element of traditional approaches towards law and integration, these approaches also perceive law in instrumental terms.

Instrumental conceptions of law in EU integration

Instrumental conceptions of law regard law as capable of effecting social change, such as the creation of an integrated European Union out of the mere coexistence of twenty-seven diverse nation states. Law is considered as capable of transforming political and economic structures. It is an essential tool for the politics of social engineering and thereby serves individual or social interests (Tamanaha, 2001: 44).[13] Instrumental law is therefore driven by the desired outcomes (Haltern, 2004: 179). It implies that social actors' behaviour can be changed in a direct, causal linear manner, in response to aims clearly specified in the legal rules:

the goal determines the program, the program determines the norm, the norm determines changes of behavior, those changes determine the desired effects.

(Teubner, 1986b: 312)

According to instrumental perspectives law can be deployed for the fulfilment of various functions. First, law is attributed a regulatory function. In fact this has been considered as the essence of modern, goal-oriented law. Political programmes thus define social change as the purpose of law (ibid.: 305). While instrumental perspectives which focus on law's capacity to regulate have been questioned in the context of national law (see, for example, Haines and Gurney 2004; Scott 2003), they still inform conceptions of law in EU integration. In fact, from the perspective of the member states the EU has been described as a new 'regulatory state' which relies significantly on law to implement its regulatory programmes (Majone,1994). While member states are cutting back traditional welfare state provisions – one of the key areas of regulatory, and hence instrumental law – the EU is expanding its activities in education, health care and culture. Moreover, the idea that 'law' in EU integration processes should be understood in instrumental terms, as a tool for regulation, has now been further extended to new forms of law. These new forms of law – sometimes also called social law – arise in the private sphere and thus differ from traditional formal state law. They include, for instance, norms derived from standardisation processes:

It is not the contrast with state law that characterizes the new social law, but *its instrumentalization* for purposes of political regulation, which even goes so far that politics in turn initiates artificial procedures of social norm production.

(emphasis added, Teubner, 1991: 139)

Second, instrumental conceptions of law are not just expressed through the idea that EU and national law can achieve various regulatory purposes. They also rely on the idea that law can be employed as a tool for achieving integration:

That law and the legal system have been among the primary *instruments* for controlling social relationships so as to achieve the desired balance requires little elaboration here.

(emphasis added, Cappelletti, Seccombe and Weiler, 1986b: 4)

The 'desired balance' here deals with a tension at the heart of EU integration, between uniformity of action, on the one hand, and autonomy of individuals as well as diversity of action among culturally different member states, on the other hand. Law is considered to have an integrating function because it can strike the right 'desired balance' between these two aims of the EU polity. Hence, from an instrumental perspective law is perceived as a 'mechanism, tool and technique' of integration (Gaja et al. 1986: 124–126; Cappelletti, Seccombe and Weiler, 1986b: 36).

Instrumental conceptions which emphasise an integrating function of law inform various debates about EU integration. For instance, an instrumental vision of formal primary EU law has underpinned calls for the constitutionalisation of the EU Treaties, even before the drafting of the EU constitution, because the Treaties are regarded as a key tool for achieving social and political integration (Armstrong, 1998: 161).

Sometimes instrumental perspectives have been built into research methodologies. Some studies of EU integration have compared the US and EC legal systems in order to evaluate how well law and its institutions fulfil an integrative function and how well they realise specific policy aims in the field of consumer protection, environmental policy, energy policy, corporate law and capital market harmonisation as well as regional policy (Cappelletti, Seccombe and Weiler, 1986b). But limits to the instrumental function of law are also recognised here. It is acknowledged that sometimes law can only further support already existing social dynamics of integration (ibid.: 46; Cappelletti, 1986: v).

Instrumental perspectives of law also underpin debates among political scientists about whether law or politics is the key driver of EU integration. Liberal intergovernmentalists have argued that politics is dominant because law is merely an instrument of political will (Moravcsik, referred to in Armstrong, 1998: 158). For instance, Andrew Moravcsik sees the ECJ as embedded in a web of member states' interests. The latter are the key drivers for EU integration and hence the ECJ is not an independent legal force. Member states have only delegated legal powers to the Court. ECJ judgments are considered to merely sanction positions for which member states have signalled their approval beforehand (Moravcsik, 1995). Instrumentalism has also been evident in neo-realist perspectives on EU integration. Here again – and sometimes even more strongly than in liberal intergovernmentalist perspectives – politics is taken as the dominant paradigm. It specifies the purposes and direction of EU integration. Law fulfils political interests determined in a political sphere. For instance, Geoffrey Garrett (1995: 172) has argued that the ECJ can be an agent for the interests of dominant member states, such as France and Germany. In later work he has, however, somewhat modified this position by suggesting that the ECJ should be considered as a strategic actor in its own right promoting EU integration, but subject to member states' preferences (Garrett, Kelemen and Schulz, 1998). It is not just some political scientists who perceive law in instrumental terms as promoting integration. The idea that law integrates has also been developed in functionalist sociology.

An instrumental perspective of law: Functionalist sociology's approach

Instrumental accounts of law are further bolstered by sociological functionalism. Functionalist sociologists developed their instrumental perspective on law as an integrative force in the context of societies bounded by a nation state. Their analysis can be seen as potentially strengthening the claim about the integrating function of law in the EU. Functionalist sociologists move the analysis beyond the specific context of EU integration towards a more general claim that law integrates societies. For functionalists the integrative function of law is not just the outcome of a specific political programme within a particular historical context, such as the regional integration project in the European Union. Instead the integrative function of law is associated with the characteristics of modern societies, in particular their high degree of differentiation between various economic, political and social subsystems.[14] Law's integrating function is necessary for achieving a sufficient degree of cohesion and thus for meeting a society's need for some unity, coherence and order.

Functionalists arrive at this conclusion from a particular theoretical perspective. They link an analysis of detailed and specific social phenomena to a macro-sociological view of the nature of society as a whole. Functionalists want to understand how various elements of society fit together and how they form the unity of an integrated society (Cotterrell, 1992: 73). Hence they explain social action by examining how it contributes to the maintenance of a stable society. Functionalists inquire into the consequences of social processes or structures for meeting the needs of various sub-systems in society. They therefore aim to match structures, functions and needs (Devereux, 1961: 50). Integration is regarded as one of the four major functional processes in modern societies. It is defined broadly as 'the process by which order is brought about' or 'the coordination of the diverse elements and units within a system' (Mayhew, 1982: 14, 23).[15] The other three key functional processes in modern societies are the adaptation of social subsystems to their environment, goal-pursuance and latent pattern-maintenance in a social sub-system (ibid.: 23). All four functional processes can be seen in operation in all the various sub-systems in a society. They address fundamental needs common to different sub-systems, such as the economy, as well as the political and social spheres.

Functionalism even further strengthens the claim that law integrates by seeing formal legal systems as the key driver of integration in societies. Both classical functionalists, such as Emile Durkheim (1893), and more contemporary writers, such as Talcott Parsons (1962) and Harry Bredemeier (1968) ascribe an integrative function to formal state legal systems. In fact, an increasing association is identified between the four main functional processes, that is integration, goal-pursuance, pattern-maintenance and adaptation to the environment, on the one hand, and specific social sub-systems, on the other hand (Cotterrell, 1992: 82).[16] Integration is thought to be particularly promoted by the formal legal system. For instance, for Bredemeier (Bredemeier, 1968: 66) and Parsons (1962), law contributes to the coordination, and thus integration, of society because the formal legal state system provides outputs in return for inputs from various social sub-systems. For example, the political sub-system provides standards in the form of legislation according to which courts can adjudicate claims and provide conflict resolution as one output of the legal system (Bredemeier, 1968: 53). Settling disputes, in turn, can adjust or reinforce the organisation of social roles in society. Moreover, the political sub-system provides public policies as inputs for the legal system which, in turn, generates legitimation and interpretation of legislation as outputs. In addition, pattern maintenance and socialisation systems also provide an input into the formal legal system by promoting a willingness among citizens to use courts for conflict resolution and to accept court decisions as final resolutions of a dispute. Harry Bredemeier (1968: 58), however, emphasises that these interchanges between the legal and various other sub-systems in society can be precarious. They are not automatic or inevitable. For instance, policies developed in the political sub-system may be contradictory and thus not represent a clear input into the legal sub-system. Moreover, close connections between a political and a legal sub-system are loosened when judicial decisions are not enforced (ibid.: 59). Hence, functionalist sociology provides a nuanced argument for the integrating function of formal state law in modern societies.[17]

But functionalists further expand the claim that law integrates because they hold that it is not just formal state legal systems which integrate, but also law beyond the 'law in the books'. Law is defined broadly to include not just state law, but also a range of social norms:

Law is not a category descriptive of actual concrete behavior but rather concerns patterns, norms, and rules that are applied to the acts and to the roles of persons and to the collectivities of which they are members.

(Parsons, 1962: 56–57)

Hence, in Parsons' analysis a variety of norms play a key role in the integration of modern societies. Parsons develops this argument by suggesting that all social action involves alternative possibilities. Norms are central because they provide criteria for the choice between alternatives. Parsons sees norms as flowing from human aspirations and values (Mayhew, 1982: 7). He rejects the utilitarian idea that individual choice is founded upon rational calculation of individuals' interests, because norms – as arbiters of choices between different possible actions – have to respond not just to the immediate interests of the individual but also to the need to maintain and coordinate relations between social actors (ibid.: 9). Normative order thus becomes the foundation of social structure. When norms are linked to the ends of social actors, a process of 'institutionalisation' occurs, according to Parsons. This is a key characteristic of modern societies: 'the structure of social systems consists in institutionalized normative culture' (ibid.: 12). Norms then provide the framework for the coordination of relations between institutions. They are not just specific directions for conduct in face-to-face interactions among individual social actors (ibid.: 31).

By recognising a variety of norms, however, Parsons also suggests that the specific normative patterns that each social sub-system can develop and which is specific to its own particular function can be a threat to overall system integration. While the specific normative commitments of particular sub-systems help to stabilise and integrate these sub-systems, their variation also poses an obstacle to the overall coherence and stability of a society as a whole. It is this recognition of variety of norms which turns integration into the central problem for Parsonian analysis. Integration matters because it is an essential response to the fragmentation of modern societies into various sub-systems which also differ with reference to their normative patterns.

Hence functionalist analysis provides important support for an instrumental conception of law which perceives law as an integrating force. It is also a limited perspective, however. First, it makes the case for the integrating function of law from a very specific theoretical perspective, a potentially exaggerated tendency of societies to gravitate towards equilibrium and consensus. Functionalism's strongly normative perspective on social action also makes it more difficult to account for conflict and change in societies. These are, however, key aspects of the integrative processes in the European Union. Second, some aspects of the functionalist claim that law integrates are not entirely clear. Do functionalists go as far as claiming that 'law', including a broad range of social norms, can integrate simply by its own force or does the integrating function of law or even the existence of law depend on some prior integration? The latter perspective seems to capture functionalist arguments more closely. Parsons (1962: 71) suggests that 'law flourishes best where fundamental questions of social values are not at issue or under agitation'. Similarly Durkheim (1893) considers law as the expression of an already underlying organic social solidarity in a society. This organic solidarity is also promoted through shared values, which in turn are reflected in the law. If law, however, is held to be anchored in a pre-established social consensus, the question arises how this consensus is achieved and how and whether it is then possible to identify a separate and independent integrating function of law. Hence, lack of clarity in some functionalist work as to whether law has an *independent* integrating function, weakens functionalism as a support for a traditional perspective on law and integration in the EU which asserts an independent integrating function of law. To conclude: functionalist sociology can provide further support for an instrumental conception of law by arguing that law fulfils a very specific function: it integrates. It also expands the claim that law integrates through a broad definition of law, which includes social norms beyond formal state law. 'Integration through law', however, has also been a key theme in a number of other sociology of law and legal theory perspectives.

Beyond functionalist sociology: Further legal theory and sociology of law support for the instrumental perspective that 'law integrates'

It is not just functionalists who argue that law integrates. A number of perspectives in legal theory[18] and the sociology of law[19] also suggest that law generates social order – and thereby integrates uncoordinated behaviour in societies (Tamanaha, 2001: xi, 208–209). For instance, a social order function of law has been asserted also with reference to the 'evolutionary myth of law' (ibid.: 55). While traditional societies are coordinated mainly through custom, post-traditional societies, rely on positive state law which is taking over the function of binding together the members of a society. State law thus provides what shared values used to deliver in traditional societies.

Today legal norms are what is left from a crumbled cement of society; if all other mechanisms of social integration are exhausted, law yet provides some means for keeping together complex and centrifugal societies that otherwise would fall into pieces.

(Habermas, 1999: 937, referred to in Tamanaha, 2001: 60)

Brian Tamanaha (2001: 68), however, criticises this 'evolutionary myth of law'. He argues that in the case of colonial law in particular, positive state law does not just grow organically out of shared values, but can simply be imposed as the rule of the colonial occupier. Colonial law may even lead to disruption of social order in the indigenous society (ibid.: 209). Hence positive state law which is transplanted from one society to another does not necessarily provide the kind of integrating function which the evolutionary view envisages. Any integrating function which positive state law may have here stems from a repressive imposition of law. This critique of the integrating function of law is powerful because it has been argued that a majority of state legal systems include the imposition of law from other societies (ibid.). Legal transplantation has not just been significant in colonial times, but also occurs in contemporary societies, for instance, through the transfer of the *acquis communautaire* to new central and eastern European member states, after the collapse of their socialist systems of legality.

Also the proliferation of global and transnational economic law questions the close link between positive state law and a society's social practices which underpins one conception of the integrating function of law. The idea that law 'mirrors society' has often been the basis for asserting an integrating function of law (ibid.: xi). Global and transnational economic law, however, reflects to a significant extent only the interests and social practices of a narrow section of a society: its corporations and individual commercial actors.

Moreover, whether law is held to have an integrating function also depends on prior assumptions about the nature of society. Brian Tamanaha (ibid.: 223) argues that an integrating function of law has been exaggerated by those who consider disorder to be the natural state of societies. This order may, in contrast, be the natural social condition of a society, even though it may be 'permeated at various levels with regular episodes of conflict'. In this case state law may not generate integration but presuppose it. It may simply help to contribute to integration (ibid.: 224). An example of pre-existing forms of social cohesion in society is an 'unarticulated substrate' which consists of unthinking rule following and shared habits. This contributes to the coordination of behaviour even though social actors may not be aware of these rules and shared habits (ibid.: 216). Other forms of social cohesion are shared explicit norms and roles, consent, love, altruism, sympathy, group identification and social instinct as well as the threat of and actual coercion (ibid.: 216–223). To conclude: empirical inquiry in particular can shed further light on the question whether law has an independent integrating function or whether integration through law is dependent on some pre-existing social cohesion (ibid.). To summarise: various perspectives in the sociology of law and legal theory argue from an instrumental perspective that law integrates because it possesses a social order function. Instrumental perspectives on law, however, are not just associated with the claim that law integrates. They have also asserted that law is a key resource for the strategic exercise of power and the management of factional interests.

Law (of every kind) should be demystified and understood *as a tool or instrument*, a resource of power and way of doing things that draws upon symbolic connotations of right or good, but with no necessary connection to custom, consent, morality, reason, or functionality in a social arena.

(Tamanaha, 2001: 240)

In the context of the EU, it has been argued, for instance, that the EU legal system and the preliminary reference procedure under Art. 234 EC Treaty, in particular, are a 'powerful' and 'effective tool' for national actors who seek to influence domestic policies. EU law may favour particular positions which domestic actors seek to advance, as in the field of sex discrimination. National courts can be empowered or directed through the Art. 234 preliminary reference procedure to question national policy and law for compliance with EU law (Alter, 2000: 489, 490).

To summarise: traditional perspectives on law and integration in the EU draw on instrumental conceptions of EU and national law. They attribute specific, goal-oriented functions to law, such as a regulatory and an integrative function. Law is regarded as a tool in the hands of social actors, mobilised in order to accomplish specific purposes enshrined in political programmes. Support for the idea that law integrates can also be found beyond the analysis of the historically specific EU integration project by political scientists. Functionalist sociology, as well as a range of other perspectives in the sociology of law and legal theory, argue that law integrates. Traditional perspectives, however, are not just characterised by instrumentalism, they also interpret law in EU integration as relatively autonomous with respect to its social, political and economic contexts.

Relatively autonomous EU law

Formalism and instrumentalism are often but not necessarily associated with a notion of autonomous law. Here law is clearly demarcated from social, economic and political processes. From the perspective of systems theory, for instance, autonomous law is a closed sub-system, differentiated from its environment, and limited in its communication with other sub-systems in complex and highly differentiated modern societies. This systems-theoretical perspective draws on functionalist sociology which regards law as fairly autonomous. For instance, Talcott Parsons (1967) argues that the autonomy of law results from the functional specialisation of modern western societies. Law emerges as an autonomous sphere of social action because societal norms are now a distinct element of normative structures. 'Normative structures' are a key element in Parsons' functionalist sociology. They explain how cohesion in modern societies is possible. They are broadly defined as comprising norms, values, roles and collectivities (Cotterrell, 1992: 84). For Parsons lawyers' law is the most important category of societal norms. Law becomes institutionalised in an autonomous legal system which fulfils the specific function of integrating social systems (Parsons, 1967).

Parsons, however, makes some concessions to the idea that law's social contexts matter and hence that law is not entirely autonomous.

He sees law as linked to social values and allows for the possibility that values can shape the content of societal norms. But while law is interpreted, on the one hand, as reflecting and depending upon society's shared values, it is also considered, on the other hand, as being able – by virtue of being expressed in a specific social-system – to independently shape both political and economic processes (Cotterrell, 1992: 84).

It is not just social theories, such as functionalism, but also political theories underpinning the operation of actual legal systems, that invoke the notion of autonomous law. In liberal legal ideology, law's autonomy is expressed through constitutional concepts such as 'the rule of law' and 'separation of powers'. They delimit boundaries between legal and political action. The legitimacy of law is based on its relative autonomy with respect to political, economic and social action. Autonomous law is associated with the rise of the nation state in the eighteenth and nineteenth centuries and the development of national legal orders.

But the idea that law is autonomous does not quite fit the EU model of a transnational society and its supranational legal order. To start with, a clear concept of 'the state' is still lacking in the evolving EU supranational polity. In addition, the classical concept of liberal democracy does not fully capture the nature of the emerging EU polity. Technocracy, rule by elites and corporatism have also been important influences. Furthermore the tasks assigned to EU law, such as the building of the integrated market and the development of political cooperation under the third pillar under the Maastricht Treaty, make it difficult to disassociate EU law from economic and political processes. Hence a number of accounts have portrayed EU law only as *relatively* autonomous.

For instance, neo-functionalism works with notions of relatively autonomous law in EU integration. Legal integration is seen as different from other forms of EU integration. It is defined as the development of transnational interdependencies in the sphere of law, through international law firms specialising in EU law, networks between European lawyers and, most importantly, through the *acquis communautaire*[20] itself and the more abstract EU legal principle of respect for the rule of law. Legal integration is perceived as 'a quite different form of interdependence' than the transnational economic interdependencies upon which early neo-functionalist accounts focused (Schmitter, 1996b: 13). Similarly, Burley and Mattli's (1993; Mattli and Slaughter, 1998: 196) neo-functionalist account of legal integration also seems to invoke a notion of relatively autonomous law in EU integration. They argue that law serves as a 'mask' and a 'shield' for politics. Just as early neo-functionalist theory suggested that economics was an important domain for promoting EU integration because it could help to avoid a 'direct clash of political interests', law similarly provides a domain through which self-interested supranational and sub-national social actors can promote integration but without direct reference to political interests, thus avoiding potential political conflicts (Burley and Mattli, 1993: 44). Law's ability to integrate is directly related to its being removed from the explicitly political domain:

The strength of the functional domain as an incubator of integration depends on the relative resistance of that domain to politicization.

(Burley and Mattli, 1993: 44)

Similarly it has been argued that the more EU legal provisions resemble traditional law, in the sense of being binding, precise and involving the delegation of dispute resolution to third parties, such as courts, the more likely EU law is going to represent a bulwark against the direct expression of power politics. For instance, it has been suggested that 'the greater the clarity of EU legal texts, case precedent, and legal norms in support of a judgment, the less likely the ECJ is to bend to political pressure' (Alter 2000: 495, referring to Garrett, Kelemen and Schulz, 1998).

Moreover, theories of EU integration which have addressed the inter-relationships between law and politics shed further light on the question of the extent to which EU law can be treated as relatively autonomous. Joseph Weiler's (1981) account of normative and deci-sional supranationalism in EU integration highlights the links between law and politics. But these links occur between law and politics as two conceptually different spheres. Legal processes are not considered as essentially political processes. Joseph Weiler contrasts normative supra-nationalism – ECJ judgments which have promoted EU integration – with decisional supranationalism – the promulgation of harmonising EC legislation by member states in the Council. These two forms of supranationalism, one located in a legal and the other in a political sphere, are portrayed as alternative drivers for EU integration (Burley and Mattli, 1993: 46). Joseph Weiler argues that in the 1970s legal supranationalism filled the vacuum in EU integration created by the decisional gridlock in the Council. Given the requirement of unanimous assent for secondary legislation in a number of EC policy areas, member states were slow to agree in the Council of Ministers on harmonising EC secondary legislation. This hampered, for instance, the elimination of barriers to trade arising from differentiated legal rules in the various member states and thus the development of the single market. Decisional supranationalism was on the decline, but the gap was filled by the ECJ's normative supranationalism, in particular by the EU's doctrine of mutual recognition. This stipulates that goods which are lawfully produced and marketed in one member state have to be allowed onto the market in other member states.[21] Only limited exceptions to this general rule are allowed.[22]

Hence, from this perspective, EU integration is characterised by a 'delicate balance between political process and legal structure' (Cappelletti, Seccombe and Weiler; 1986b: 31). Normative supranationalism could fill the gaps of decisional supranationalism, but the pace of decisional supranationalism could also be adjusted in response to normative supranationalism. Where members states perceived the development of EU constitutional law by the ECJ as interfering too much with their sovereignty, they could resort to the option of slowing down 'decisional integration' by political means, for instance by delaying legislative agreements in the Council. This notion of responsiveness, ultimately implying a separation between a political and a legal sphere, has also been a corner stone in some accounts of EU integration because it helps to explain how tensions between centrifugal and centripetal tendencies in the EU integration process are balanced (ibid.).

In addition to Joseph Weiler, Ulrich Haltern (2004) also seems to retain the idea that law is relatively autonomous. On the one hand Haltern argues that EU human rights law can bridge legal and political approaches to EU integration because human rights protection addresses fundamental questions about the identity of the European polity through the means of formal law (ibid.: 184–185). But on the other hand, he seems to conjure up once again a clear demarcation between a legal and a political sphere. He suggests that 'political imagination'[23] is required in order to address questions – currently central to EU integration – about 'identity, belonging, loyalty and responsibility'. But he then suggests that this is beyond the reach of law (ibid.: 184). He also states that in times of waning political imagination EU integration may be pushed forward by law (ibid.: 194). Hence legal and political processes in EU integration seem to be perceived as alternatives rather than as closely intertwined factors. Moreover, Haltern's suggestion that EU law is non-political seems to be derived from the idea that EU law – as he perceives it – does not embody *his* normative vision of a dynamic political community which transcends the narrow aim of economic integration through the internal market. But the absence of such a broader conception of a developed, vibrant political community in EU law could also be considered as an expression of a different, but nevertheless political, vision of the nature of the EU.

Moreover, Haltern also differentiates between legal and political institutions. He attributes the success of the preliminary reference procedure under Art. 234 EC Treaty to its non-political nature. In his interpretation of Art. 234 EC Treaty it is crucial that judicial rather than political institutions, such as the ECJ and national courts, are involved in deciding how EC law should impact on the law of member states. He considers courts under the Art. 234 procedure as neutral arbiters which bypass political actors such as member states (ibid.: 182). It is surely questionable, however, whether national courts and the ECJ can be described as non-political actors. Neo-realists, for instance, have argued that the ECJ is an agent of the political interests of member states (Garrett, 1995). Moreover, community or national courts are political actors when their judgments affect the distribution of power between EU supranational institutions and member states. In addition, judges effectively become policy makers when they decide disputes before them on the basis of indeterminate legal provisions (Stone Sweet: 2004, 10). To conclude: elements of Haltern's discussion of the relationship between law and politics in EU integration seem to suggest that law can be separated from the political sphere and thus treated as relatively autonomous.

Conclusion

This chapter has outlined key assumptions and elements of traditional perspectives concerning relationships between law and integration. Although these perspectives are important and influential, they are also limited because they are informed by specific and arguably narrow assumptions about the social world and law in particular. Traditional approaches replicate the descriptions of the legal field which formal legal systems themselves generate. They regard law as formal, instrumental and relatively autonomous. They focus on official legal actors for understanding the implementation of EU law. They are informed by 'modernist' social theory. They do not clearly distinguish between the questions whether law integrates and what law actually is. They therefore risk asserting an integrating function of law on the basis of unquestioned theoretical assumptions about the nature of law and society.

Traditional approaches, however, are just one perspective on law and integration. Other perspectives on EU integration have started to question some of its modernist assumptions, for instance by taking on board the 'linguistic turn' in philosophy and social thought. They examine how commonly presupposed notions in the analysis of EU integration, such as 'social actors', 'integration outcomes' and 'law', are themselves socially constructed through language. They question the significance of the 'nation state' in an analysis of EU integration by interpreting the EU as a 'network polity', that consists of a variety of complex links between the public and private spheres. Such perspectives also cast their net more widely in order to capture a variety of social actors – not just official legal actors – who become involved in the day-to-day construction of relationships between law and integration. These include various professional groups, such as scientists, engineers and economists, as well as individual citizens and pressure groups. Hence the next chapter turns to an examination of the potential of such approaches – which I call 'critical perspectives' – for understanding relationships between law and integration.

Notes

1. For early exceptions see Stein, 1981 and Weiler, 1981.
2. Neo-functionalism is the application of functionalism to the study of European integration. Functionalism explains institutions and practices in terms of the functions they perform for the workings of a society as a whole. Neo-functionalists argue that the strengthening of social and economic ties is a key driver for integration in the EU, and that the power of nation states in the EU is declining.
3. Neo-functionalism draws on the functionalist idea that social action can be explained through reference to its consequences. Hence, consequences are important elements of the causes of human behaviour (Schmitter, 1971).
4. Neo-realists assert the continuing importance of sovereign nation states in regional integration. They recognise that EU member states have limited their sovereignty in some policy areas through delegating powers to EU supranational institutions. But neo-realists emphasise that member states are the source of these limited transfers of sovereignty which could be revoked.
5. Stone Sweet (2004), for instance, refers to the data of econometrics.
6. Under the preliminary reference procedure in Art. 234 EC Treaty.
7. But some accounts have gone further and recognise a whole range of actors as important in EU integration, including interest groups, administrators and technical experts (see, for example, Stone Sweet, 2004: 236).

8. The term 'formal law' is also often contrasted with soft law measures, such as policy guidance, circulars and recommendations (Snyder, 1990: 1).
9. Such as the Treaties founding the European Economic Community (EEC), the European Steel and Coal Community (ESCS) and the European Atomic Energy Community (Euratom) as well as the Treaty on European Union (EU), and various amending treaties, such as the Single European Act (SEA) and the Nice and Amsterdam Treaties.
10. For instance, a discussion of the different forms which a future EU polity may take has been based on a detailed analysis of various articles in the Maastricht Treaty (see Schmitter, 1996a: 127–128).
11. See, for instance, Case C-70/88, *Parliament v. Council (Chernobyl)* [1990] ECR I-2041.
12. A number of neo-realists, however, do not pay all that much attention to law in the process of EU integration. There is, for instance, little in Moravcsik's work on the legal dimension of EU integration. But law, and in particular the activities of the ECJ, have been analysed from a neo-realist perspective by Garrett, Kelemen and Schulz (1998) and Garrett (1995).
13. According to Brian Tamanaha (2001: 49) public choice theories of legal processes provide a good illustration of an instrumental conception of law because they perceive legislation, for instance, as the outcome of competition between self-interested groups. Here law is transformed into an instrument of specific interests in a society.
14. A system, in turn, is defined as 'any set of interdependent elements that coheres into a self-regulating whole and is maintained by drawing resources from an environment' (Mayhew, 1982: 24).
15. Some commentators consider integration even as synonymous with 'socialisation, internalisation and institutionalisation' (Mayhew, 1982: 14).
16. For instance, adaptation is particularly linked to the economic sub-system. Goal pursuance is mainly related to the political sub-system and pattern-maintenance occurs especially through socialisation processes, in the family for example.
17. Formal state law is differentiated and thus to a degree autonomous from other sub-systems, such as the political system. Parsons (1962: 59) emphasises that the legal system must not be considered as a political phenomenon, although he recognises that there are close links between the state legal and political system, particularly since the state is key to ultimately guaranteeing legal sanctions and by establishing the legal system's jurisdiction. Moreover, state law is discussed by Parsons (1962: 64–69) with reference to official legal actors, such as lawyers.
18. Such as Hobbes, Hans Kelsen and the Natural Law tradition (discussed in Tamanaha, 2001: 2, ch. 2).
19. Such as Marxism, which suggests that law in a capitalist society maintains social order against a background of class conflict (Tamanaha, 2001: 40), as well as classical sociology of law. For instance, Eugen Ehrlich (2002: ch. 3) argued that the 'living law', not just positive state law, plays an important

role in maintaining social order. Moreover Adam Podgorecki (1974) also argues that law integrates social actors' mutual expectations of behaviour. Order is achieved because mutual expectations of obligation and claim are adjusted and made compatible in exchange relationships. Social order flows from reciprocally structured duties and rights in a way that is consistent with the general values existing in a given social system. This perspective closely links social control with an integrating function of law.

20. This describes the body of common EU law as it applies to all the different member states.

21. *Rewe-Zentrale AG v. Bundesmonopolverwaltung für Branntwein*, Case 120/78, [1979] ECR 649.

22. The exception to this is the 'rule of reason': in the absence of Community harmonisation member states can impose export or import restrictions – applicable both to their own home-produced goods and goods imported from other member states – if they fulfil a 'mandatory requirement' initially defined as effectiveness of fiscal supervision, the protection of public health, the fairness of commercial transactions and the defence of the consumer. This was later extended to include the protection of the environment in *Commission v. Denmark*, Case 302/86, [1988] ECR 4607.

23. Haltern (2004: 195) describes political imagination as a world 'where politics call upon citizens for sacrifice, where the popular sovereign shows itself by displacing interest, and where the most basic imaginative structure of political reality is the transtemporal community'.

3   Critical perspectives on the role of law in EU integration

Introduction

While chapter 2 outlined key assumptions and elements of a traditional approach towards the role of law in EU integration, this chapter focuses on alternative critical perspectives. While there is no single unified critical perspective, some key elements of such an approach can be identified. Critical perspectives do not necessarily assume an integrative function of law. They also start to inquire into the nature of law in EU integration processes. They differ from conceptions of law as formal, instrumental and relatively autonomous state law. They abandon some of the modernist assumptions of the traditional approach and engage with post-modern ideas about the constructed nature of the social world.

This chapter argues that such critical approaches towards law and integration can be further developed. In particular, it is also necessary to explore law's relationship to its contexts, in order to understand to what extent we can really speak of a distinctly legal dimension of EU integration. Are there identifiable boundaries between law and its environments? Do we need to differentiate between macro- and micro-levels in order to answer this question? For instance, can law and its environments be linked on a micro-level? If so, how?

The first section of the chapter outlines key assumptions of certain contemporary critical approaches, while the second section discusses their main elements, in particular their questioning of the conception of law as instrumental, formal and relatively autonomous. The concluding section draws together the main points of the discussion.

Key assumptions of critical perspectives on the role of law in EU integration

Distinguishing questions about the nature of law from questions about the role of law in EU integration

In contrast to a traditional approach towards the role of law in EU integration, critical perspectives distinguish more clearly between questions about the nature of law and its role in EU integration. What law actually is, is not just taken for granted. The nature of law is explicitly addressed. Moreover, critical approaches question the idea whether 'law' does in fact further integration. They discuss the possibility of 'integration without law' or integration through hybrid forms of law, where combinations of traditional state 'hard' law and various forms of 'soft' law generate forms of integration. They recognise the development of new forms of EU governance, such as the increasing resort to proceduralised law, which differ from images of traditional 'hard' law. In short, critical perspectives don't perceive law as an independent, pre-given variable. Finally, critical approaches like these are also an expression of the broadening of theoretical perspectives employed by political scientists for analysing EU integration.

Theoretical commitments of critical perspectives on the role of law in EU integration

This chapter focuses on institutionalist,[1] and constructivist accounts as key examples of critical approaches towards law and integration. Constructivism in particular explores the constructed nature of the social world and thus responds to post-modern challenges to modernist social theory. Some constructivist accounts explore the role of discourse in the construction of the European Union and hence take the 'linguistic turn' on board.[2] But, as this chapter argues, there is also potential for a more critical account of the role of law in EU integration according to the perspectives of neo-functionalist political science and functionalist sociology which draw on modernist assumptions about the social world.

Institutionalist and constructivist accounts also add a sociological perspective to theories of EU integration which places social actors clearly in the context of the institutions and societies in which they operate. Institutionalist accounts, though some of them are grounded in modernist assumptions, provide a sociological challenge to the rationalist paradigm which attempts to trace relationships of cause and effect in EU integration processes and which underpins in particular neo-realist accounts of EU integration. Constructivist accounts also differ from the modernist, rationalist research paradigm of neo-realist and neo-functionalist perspectives which seek to develop parsimonious accounts of the social world that focus on a selected number of variables in order to unravel the causal mechanisms at work in EU integration. Rationalist accounts focus on individual human action or its aggregate as key variables for explaining EU integration processes. Social constructivist accounts, in contrast, consider interactions between social actors and their environments as crucial to how social worlds are built up. Constructivist accounts also seek to capture the complexity of social life by paying attention to small-scale social processes and to the contingency of human practices (Risse, 2004: 161; Koslovski, 1999: 565). They explore how the meaning of these social processes is actively constructed through the interpretative practices of social actors.

Constructivist approaches also differ from modernist theoretical commitments by being less state-centred. The traditional approach towards law in EU integration still focuses on the state as a relevant category for analysing EU integration processes. For instance, intergovernmental perspectives point to the continued relevance of EU member states, while federalism discusses the possible role of a European state and neo-functionalists analyse how the role of nation states has been weakened through supranational institutions. Moreover, it is a particular conception of the state – the state as a legal entity and formal organisation – which informs the traditional approach towards law and integration in the EU.

Constructivist approaches, in contrast, are less state centred. They focus on 'the political practices of actors at all levels' in the EU 'without presupposing the primacy of states' (Koslowski 1999: 565). Thus they can capture, for instance, subnational politics and regionalism as well as consociationalism operating at the European level (ibid.: 563). This approach helps to recognise new forms of institutionalising these political practices, without resorting to the traditional category of the state (ibid.: 562).[3] Moreover, critical approaches assume less clearly defined boundaries for the state and thus emphasise the fragmentation of the latter. The state is understood as a 'an ensemble of normatively constituted practices by which a group of individuals forms a special type of political association' (ibid.: 565). Such critical approaches direct attention to various links between public and private social actors and thus to the networks which organise the EU polity.

Constructivist approaches do not simply take the analytical category of 'social actor' for granted. They problematise how agency is actually achieved. In contrast to this, the traditional approach towards law and integration relies on modernist assumptions and interprets actors' interests and preferences as exogenously pre-given or inferred from a given material structure (Trubek, Nance, Cottrell, 2005: 14). Critical approaches aim to go beyond the neo-rationalist and neo-functionalist emphasis on the pre-given interests and preferences of social actors. They consider *ideas* as crucial to understanding the behaviour of social actors. They are interested in finding out how actors develop their current identities and interests and how they may change. They also ascribe importance to ideas of the 'polity', i.e. ideas which are normative with respect to what constitutes a legitimate political order (Wæver, 2004: 203). Moreover, where critical approaches refer to language, they examine how language shapes and influences actors, but also how actors can use language strategically. Critical approaches which employ discourse analysis examine how a notion of 'social actor' is not pre-given, but is itself an effect of discursive construction. Hence the categorisations and conceptualisations that discourses provide are considered to be significant in constructing the social world. Meaning is established through the classifications provided by discourses.

Key elements of critical perspectives towards the role of law in EU integration

Beyond a focus on official legal actors

Traditional approaches towards the role of law in EU integration focus on official legal actors, such as courts, litigants and formal EU and national legislative institutions, such as the Commission, Council and parliaments. In contrast to this, critical perspectives recognise a whole range of actors which are involved in constituting and interpreting 'law' in EU integration processes. For instance, Harm Schepel's (2005) work on the role of standardisation in the EU highlights the importance of private actors in law-making processes. In fact he argues that private standard-setting processes are displacing public norms in the international and national regulation of product safety. Member states' attempts to reassert public control over national standardisation bodies are unsuccessful in a developing system of 'private "supranationalism"' (Schepel, 2005: 405).

In addition, the burgeoning literature on comitology in the EU illustrates the significance of a range of non-traditional legal actors, often determining the actual scope and meaning of legal obligations through discussion and deliberation of EU law in various EU committees. They include private individuals, such as scientists and consultants, as well as representatives for sectoral interests, such as industry associations. They can also be representatives of member states, such as national civil servants.

Finally, the literature on new forms of EU governance also recognises the importance of other than official legal actors in processes of EU integration. Traditional forms of governance emphasise the role of courts for ensuring accountability and thus legitimacy of EU activities. New forms of EU governance seek to enhance citizen involvement through a 'civil dialogue' and through national parliaments for achieving accountability and legitimacy (Scott and Trubek, 2002: 8). Critical perspectives towards the role of law in EU integration, however, do not just differ from a focus on official legal actors in EU integration processes, they also move beyond instrumental conceptions of law.

Questioning instrumental conceptions of EU and national law in EU integration processes

Chapter 2 associated a traditional perspective on the role of law in EU integration with an instrumental conception of law. Instrumentalism in this sense involves the attribution of specific functions to law, such as a regulatory function or a capacity to integrate a society or various member states in a regional integration project. Critical perspectives differ from such instrumental conceptions of law. First, they question whether law in EU integration can be attributed a regulatory function, by pointing to the amorphous and open-textured qualities of law. They emphasise that the meaning of law can be contested and thus negotiated.

Law's rule is a system of beliefs – a structure of meaning within which we experience public order.

(Haltern, 2004: 192)

A more open-textured conception of law is also evident in EU studies which discuss indeterminacy in EC law (Stone Sweet, 2004: 9). Here EC law is seen as permeated by discretion. It has also been argued that the ECJ operates within a 'zone of discretion' in order to rebut the argument that the ECJ is simply an agent for the interests of the EU's most powerful member states (ibid.: 28). But discretion is not regarded as entirely unlimited. The ECJ's zone of discretion is seen as determined by three interrelated factors. First, the nature and scope of powers delegated to the ECJ, for instance through the Treaty of Rome 1957, circumscribe the court's discretion (ibid.: 23, 24). Second, various control mechanisms further curtail how the ECJ can decide. Indirect controls arise from attempts of the ECJ to respond to what it perceives as the preferences of the relevant parties (ibid.: 26). Third, the ECJ's zone of discretion is delimited by its previous decisions which provide the framework for subsequent decisions (ibid.: 27). Moreover, where law allows for discretion, legal actors, such as the ECJ, can also routinely produce 'unintended consequences' (ibid.: 235). This further relativises the idea of instrumental law in EU integration. For it becomes questionable whether law can achieve specific regulatory outcomes.

Also some institutionalist accounts recognise a 'meaning dimension' within law as an 'institutional structure' (Armstrong, 1998:156). Law embodies specific ideas about the social world. For instance, EU law expresses ideas about relationships between the EU and member states, including interactions between EU and national legal orders (ibid.: 156). Some institutionalists have also anchored their rejection of an instrumental conception of EU law in Habermas's distinction between law as an institution and law as a medium (ibid.: 156). 'Law as a medium' regards law as a functional socio-technological steering-instrument which runs the risk of colonising economic and political sub-systems in society. It can thus be a threat to central areas of cultural reproduction, social integration and socialisation. 'Law as an institution', in contrast, assumes a more modest role. Here law only externally constitutes and guarantees the autonomy of the spheres of the life world. Hence, instrumental conceptions of law are also questioned by institutionalist accounts which hold that law only ensures the existence of an otherwise fairly autonomous social life world. Limitations to law's ability to regulate thus flow from the internal characteristics of law itself. But institutionalists have not merely questioned law's ability to regulate on the basis of law's internal characteristics. They also point to external restraints on law by highlighting path-dependency. This concept implies that the history of decision-making in a particular policy field can steer subsequent decision-making in a specific direction (Maher, 1999: 598; Armstrong, 1998: 168). Previous decisions about the use of law in a policy area restrict choices further down the line. Path-dependency, however, does not imply determinism because institutionalists recognise that actors can shape their own institutional context (Armstrong, 1998: 170).

Moreover, by highlighting complex organisational links in EU integration processes an institutionalist perspective also questions whether law really can be attributed a regulatory function and thus whether it can be conceptualised in instrumental terms. Institutionalists have argued that EU law arises out of complex organisational links. How law can be deployed is also further mediated and complicated by these organisational links. This questions a key element in the notion of law as 'regulatory', in particular the idea that there is a linear sequence from formal law to specific regulatory outcomes.

To give a practical example from the EU integration process: In order to ensure the free movement of goods in the EU internal market, the main policy actors did not deploy legal rules in a straightforward, instrumental manner. Instead organisational links emerged, which – inter alia – also generated legal norms. These organisational links involved the Commission, the Council and the ECJ. In response to the Council's failure to reach agreement on secondary harmonising legislation for product standards, the ECJ also decided through its doctrine of mutual recognition, that products produced and marketed lawfully in one member state have to be allowed into the markets of other member states.[4] The Commission began to take on a mediating role because member states have to notify the Commission of restrictive trade measures they have taken and which may be justified as a 'mandatory requirement' or as an exception to Art. 28 EC Treaty (Armstrong and Bulmer, 1998: 156). Hence, organisational links have mediated how law became involved in the construction of the single market, a cornerstone of EU integration. The notion of 'organisational links' in institutionalist analysis questions the idea that legal rules are always deployed in a linear, instrumental, causal manner in the pursuit of specific regulatory outcomes in EU integration.

Second, critical perspectives question the idea that EU law is an instrument of integration (see, for example, Haltern, 2004). In particular, a critical approach points to the limitations of the functionalist sociological argument in support of the integrating force of law.

Limitations of the functionalist sociological argument in support of the integrative force of law

While a number of functionalist sociological accounts discussed in chapter 2 support the claim that law integrates, some contributors to functionalist sociology also recognise limits to this integrative function in a national context. I argue that these limitations apply with even greater force in the context of EU integration.

For instance, Harry Bredemeier (1968) points to the limits of a legal system's integrating capacity. He (1968: 58) suggests that output/input links between the legal and other social sub-systems are neither automatic nor inevitable. They can be precarious. For instance, the political system does not always provide clear and specific inputs to the legal system. Lobbying by various groups can render public policies contradictory. Lobbying, however, is a crucial part of EU law-making. The fact that it is widespread and intensive was also the reason for the establishment of an EU regulatory framework.[5] Commission Directorates possess limited in-house resources for researching legislative initiatives, in comparison to national ministries which employ larger numbers of staff (Craig and De Burca, 2003: 59). Hence, the advice and information which lobbyists provide, e.g. to Commission Directorates, is an important input into the legislative drafting process.

Moreover, functionalist sociologists argue that law's integrating function is limited because transactions between the political and the legal system can break down. For instance, the political system may not provide enforcement of the decisions of the courts (Bredemeier, 1968: 59). Again, this limitation of law's integrating capacity applies with even greater force in the context of EU integration. The EU Commission can pursue legal actions against member states for breach of EC law under Art. 226 EC Treaty before the Court of First Instance and the European Court of Justice. In case member states do not comply with these declaratory court judgments, the Commission can apply to the ECJ again for the imposition of lump sum or penalty payments under Art. 228 (2) EC Treaty. But the EC Treaty does not provide a mechanism to ensure the actual collection of these fines, if in fact member states are not prepared to pay. The EU institutions and other member states may consider imposing political sanctions on recalcitrant member states, such as the suspension of voting rights in the Council for the non-compliant member state. Hence, what functionalist sociologists identified as a limitation to law's integrating capacity in a national context – a failure of the political system to enforce court decisions – seems to be even more significant in the EU context.

Moreover, Bredemeier (1968: 66) also argues that law's integrating function is threatened when the legal system starts to go its own way and pursue its own goals instead of being closely linked to the inputs from the political sub-system. Again, this limitation to law's integrating function applies in the EU context. Sometimes the European Court of Justice has also promoted its own conception of the aims and direction of EU integration, through its method of teleological interpretation. It has not merely just complemented, but also supplanted its vision of EU integration with that of the political institutions, such as the Commission and the Council.[6]

But the basic element of the functionalist argument that the legal system has an integrating force, because it is linked to other social sub-systems through input/output links, cannot be easily transferred to the EU context. Inputs from the EU political to the EU legal sub-system may be less clear and specific than in a national context because twenty-five member states are likely to generate more diversity and differentiation than political actors in a society defined by a single nation state.

In addition, for some functionalist sociologists, law integrates because it reflects an underlying value consensus in society. For instance, Durkheim (1893) thought that law was directed at the compensation and restoration of a previous situation between disputing parties as an expression of an 'underlying organic social solidarity' in society. He considered this type of law as characteristic of modern western societies. He also attributed an integrative function to it, because it was closely embedded in social life. But this view does not sit easily with EU integration because EU law is often seen not as a natural expression of an already integrated EU polity, but rather as the distinct tool through which such integration may be achieved in the first place (De Burca, 1995: 48).

Finally, according to functionalist sociologists, law has an integrating function because this is necessary in order to achieve some coherence and order in modern societies, which are characterised by a high degree of differentiation between various social sub-systems. But some political scientists who have analysed EU integration actually emphasise the close interconnections between the political, economic and social sub-systems in the EU. William Wallace (1990: 9) defines existing informal EU integration in the following way:

These [intense and diversified patterns of interaction] may be partly economic in character, partly social, partly political: *definitions of political integration all imply accompanying high levels of economic and social interaction.*

(emphasis added)

Hence, it appears questionable to what extent the traditional perspective can rely on functionalist sociology for its argument that law integrates. Critical perspectives further seek to unpack the claim that law integrates by questioning what is meant by integration.

What actually is 'integration'? – Questioning the claim that law 'integrates'

The EU integration literature defines 'integration' in various ways. Definitions range from mere coordination of behaviour to the creation of a federal state. Often, however, integration is understood as the creation of social, political and economic *communities* (Schmitter, 1971: 242). The often quoted definition of Ernst Haas (1958: 16) interprets political integration as:

the process whereby political actors in several distinct national settings are persuaded to shift their loyalties, expectations and political activities toward a new centre, whose institutions possess or demand jurisdiction over the pre-existing national states. The end result of a process of *political integration* is *a new political community*, superimposed over the pre-existing ones.

(emphasis added)

Hence the claim that law integrates is sometimes understood as the more specific idea that law generates political community. This, however, can be contested. Law has also been seen as undermining 'organic' and 'natural' forms of interactions which are considered as a prerequisite for the development of a free political community. In particular the juridification of everyday life is perceived not as promoting integration, but as destroying community:

law is vital. . .but when every relationship in society becomes a potentially legal relationship, expressed in adversary fashion, the very juices of the social bond dry up, the social impulse atrophies.

(Robert Nisbet, 1975: 240, referred to in Cotterrell, 1992: 289)

The potentially divisive nature of law is also highlighted in criticisms of classical liberal rights discourse in EU law. The legal protection of human rights which relies on the idea that one right will trump another can generate adversarial interactions (DeBurca, 1995: 52).[7] Moreover, from a sociological perspective Donald Black (1971) has provided empirical support for his idea that law develops as community declines. In his study of the social organisation of arrest he found that police arrest practices vary with the relational nature of disputes between complainants and suspects. The more remote social relations were between complainant and suspect, the more likely was a suspect to be arrested.[8] Black (1971: 1107) also refers to other research which has shown that relational distance is a major factor in the probability of litigation in private-law contexts, including contract disputes.[9] Hence, one of his conclusions is (1971: 1108):

Law seems to bespeak an absence of community, and law grows ever more prominent as the dissolution of community proceeds.

Moreover, the claim that law integrates in the sense of developing community has been criticised on the basis that communities based on law can be narrow and exclusive. For instance, Zenon Bankowski and David Nelken (1981) argue that the 'pull of the legal solution is always to the rule of the few and the legal solution is the enemy of full participatory democracy'. From this perspective, integration through law generates at most limited and exclusive communities. To summarise: from a critical perspective the idea that law integrates can also be questioned by inquiring further into the meaning of integration itself. Integration is often defined as the creation of community. But a number of legal sociologists argue that legal relationships can actually undermine the bonds of community.

Moreover, the association of law with integration begins to appear questionable when one considers that integration is sometimes defined as only involving a very limited degree of harmonisation. Some definitions of EU integration do not require a new political community as the defining element of an integrated European Union. From this perspective, integration is defined as involving such a slight advance from previously uncoordinated practices in the EU member states that the role of law in bringing about this change may be fairly negligible. David Wallace's definition of informal integration only requires 'intense patterns of interaction among previously autonomous units'. These develop 'without the impetus of deliberate political decisions' by merely 'following the dynamics of markets, technology, communication networks, and social change' (Wallace, 1990: 9, referred to in Armstrong, 1998: 314). This is a much more modest definition of an integration outcome than, for example, the establishment of central political institutions which have binding decision-making powers and exercise new methods of control in the newly integrated political community (Harrison, 1974, referred to in Rosamond, 2000: 12). Some definitions of integration even require only 'convergence' of 'human behavior basic to social life' (Cappelletti, 1986:vi). Here integration is clearly not associated with uniformity, centralisation or even harmonisation (De Burca and Scott, 2000: 2; Cappelletti, 1986: viii). To summarise: where 'integration' is defined as only involving very modest forms of convergence between the activities of EU member states, the claim that law integrates seems seriously weakened. Law would not have to do much here to bring about these modest results of integration, so whether law really performs any integrating function looks highly questionable.

Whether law integrates, however, has been also questioned in the literature on new modes of EU governance (De Burca and Scott, 2006). Here, in the context of discussions about definitions of integration, it has been argued that EU integration can no longer be equated with uniformity and centralisation. Instead, increasingly much looser forms of coordination of activities between member states can be observed. Often EU integration now no longer employs traditional 'hard law' in the sense of formally binding legal EU rules (Scott and Trubek, 2002). A recognition of these new forms of EU governance can form the basis for arguing that there is now integration without law. This matters because new forms of EU governance are not marginal phenomena. For instance, there has been increasing resort by the EU Commission to a variety of 'soft' law[10] measures, such as recommendations, opinions, guidelines, resolutions, Council declarations and Commission communications (Snyder, 1994; Borchardt, 1989: 292). A further important example is provided by open methods of coordination (OMC) which are employed in a range of policy sectors, such as employment policy, social exclusion, pensions and education. Specific OMC procedures and outcomes vary from policy to policy sector. But there are some key characteristics of the OMC which can be identified. It sets only non-binding guidelines and targets for member states to achieve, and not necessarily at the same time. It also aims to achieve a degree of convergence in activities between member states in various policy fields by facilitating mutual learning through the exchange of information. The social dialogue is another key example of new forms of EU governance which was established under the Maastricht Treaty.

Here official representatives of the social partners enter into voluntary agreements in relation to employment matters. These voluntary agreements can later be enacted as Directives by the Council. Hence this form of new EU governance involves the possibility of 'soft' regulation which later, however, may still turn into traditional community 'hard' law (Scott and Trubek, 2002: 4).

These new forms of EU governance are important because they are not just marginal phenomena. They are widely regarded as enduring and central to EU integration processes. They are enduring because they are considered to provide some of the answers to endemic problems in EU regulation which will continue to exist. Soft law tools in particular can deal with 'irreducible diversity', i.e. situations where 'hard' law aiming at the uniformity of legal rules and outcomes across the EU are inappropriate because there is, for instance, a strong tradition of different approaches to regulation in a given policy sector in the various member states (ibid.: 7). Finally, new forms of EU governance are also central to EU integration processes because they are associated with wider regulatory trends and ideologies already in evidence in a number of member states, such as 'new public management approaches' to the reform of the public sector and public service delivery (ibid.: 6).

To conclude, new forms of EU governance question the idea that it is only 'hard' law which contributes to integration. They suggest that various phenomena which do not amount to legally binding rules, such as soft law, benchmarking, simply exchanging information, as well as a variety of combinations between 'hard' and 'soft' law, are actually now promoting processes of EU integration. By pointing to various new forms of governance beyond hard law, like soft law and voluntary policy coordination, the debate about new forms of EU governance has also given rise to the idea of integration without law.

But the traditional claim that law integrates can also be questioned from another angle. Inquiry into the meaning of integration here suggests the idea that integration and disintegration can actually be closely associated. This argument has been made in various ways. First, the emergence of 'differentiated integration' in the European Union, in particular through the Maastricht Treaty, has been seen as evidence of a close link between integration and disintegration through law. While the Maastricht Treaty has promoted integration in some policy areas, it has also lead to 'disintegration' in others by allowing some member states opt outs from harmonisation initiatives (Shaw, 1996). Second, integration and disintegration have also been linked beyond the specific context of EU integration. Some sociologists of law have suggested that integration and disintegration are linked phases in the development of societies. Legal integration is defined here as involving a close match between positive state law and social customs (Podgorecki, 1974). While at some stage a society may be characterised by a high degree of legal integration, it may be characterised by disintegration in other periods. Disintegration occurs in particular during times of social change when positive state law is out of step with social customs. It can be witnessed, for example, during revolutionary change in societies which may then be followed by a new period of integration under a changed legal regime which is in congruence with post-revolutionary values. Hence, integration and disintegration are linked as cycles of change in a society. The notion that law integrates is then questioned on the basis that law can be associated both with integration and disintegration at various stages of a society's development. The traditional approach towards the role of law in EU integration, however, does not just rely on an instrumental conception of law which suggests that law integrates, it also focuses on formal law. Critical approaches question this.

Transcending formal conceptions of law in EU integration

Traditional approaches towards the role of law in EU integration rely on a conception of law as the formal 'law in the books'. Critical approaches, in contrast, work with a broader concept of normativity which includes not just formal state law, but also brings into focus a whole range of social norms originating in the private sphere, including state 'soft' law. 'Soft' law is a further significant source of normativity in EU integration processes. Even though it does not rely on formal, legally binding rules, it may shape the behaviour of social actors. For instance, it has been argued that federal norms may govern political relations in the EU, even though there is no federal state (Koslovski, 1999: 564). Similarly Kenneth Abbott and Duncan Snidal (2000) trace legalisation in international relations, including the EU, with reference to the whole range of legal phenomena from 'soft' law, which can include 'informal understandings' and 'customary practices', to 'hard' law.

Moreover, new forms of EU governance also differ from traditional conceptions of state 'hard' law as key to EU integration. They also consider 'soft' law as central to EU integration, because it can be linked in various ways to traditional 'hard law' in EU integration. There are increasingly 'hybrid' forms of EU law where both 'soft' and 'hard' law are deployed in the regulation of one policy area, such as in employment policy and fiscal policy coordination (Trubek, Cottrell and Nance, 2005). Moreover, EU soft law can also be implemented in member states through 'hard' law (Borchardt and Wellens, 1989: 310). Soft law can even be transformed into hard law, for instance, when soft law measures feed into the development of legal principles by the ECJ or when they provide the basis for formal legislation, or when they are turned into Commission decisions (Snyder, 1994: 214, 216). Moreover, what appears as 'hard' legal provisions may in practice entail law that cannot be considered particularly 'hard'. The EU Commission increasingly resorts to Framework Directives which do not necessarily define clear, substantive standards. Reference to the principles of subsidiarity and proportionality during drafting can mean that member states enjoy broad margins of discretion when implementing these Framework Directives (Scott and Trubek, 2002: 2). Moreover, the literature on new forms of EU governance also recognises the significance of a plurality of norms for EU integration processes. For instance, private standards are analysed as a significant aspect of the creation and regulation of the internal market in the EU. They are even increasingly considered as more important than traditional public state law for the regulation of product safety (Schepel, 2005). This analysis usually draws on legal pluralist ideas. It assumes that there are various self-contained, separately identifiable and clearly delimited normative orders. Private norm setting processes beyond the nation state or the supranational EU institutions have even been described as 'relatively autonomous systems of global law making' (ibid.: 405). Legal pluralism recognises their existence and directs attention to analysing the interrelationships between the norms of official legal systems and these various private normative orders (see, for example, ibid.: 2).

Institutionalist and constructivist approaches also recognise social norms – a further type of 'law' in a broader conception of normativity – as a key element in EU integration processes. Institutionalists emphasise the importance of institutions in EU integration. They draw attention to the fact that 'recurring face to face interactions within established institutions' help to construct and socialise actors within these institutions (Jupille, Caporaso, Checkel, 2003: 32). Hence the social norms which organise the internal operation of these institutions are recognised as important elements in EU integration (Scott, 1995: 196). For instance, normative structures contribute to the way policy problems are framed, managed and finally solved in the European Union (Armstrong and Bulmer, 1998: 259). Hence institutions provide the 'rules of the game' (Armstrong, 1995: 191; Scott, 1995: 196). Moreover, both EU supranational institutions as well as domestic institutions have been regarded as important in shaping the reception, interpretation and enforcement of EC legal norms (Armstrong and Bulmer, 1998: 290).

But social norms receive an even higher profile where institutions themselves are broadly defined. Institutionalist accounts work with a broad definition of institutional actors (Rosamond, 2000: 115). Formal organisations, such as courts, legislatures and bureaucracies, have been taken as examples of institutions. But informal rules and procedures have also been recognised as institutions in their own right (Armstrong, 1998: 166). An even broader and amorphous category of social norms is captured in accounts informed by historical institutionalism. Here social norms also include cultural dimensions of institutions, such as belief systems, rhetoric, ideologies and knowledge (Armstrong and Bulmer, 1998: 51; 52). Even discourses have been considered as institutions (Risse-Kappen, 1996: 69). Hence, these broad definitions of institutions highlight the importance not just of formal law in EU integration, but of a whole range of other normative phenomena, from fully fledged social norms to the normative force of belief systems and knowledge.

According to institutionalists there are various reasons why normativity beyond formal state law is important. First, informal rules can fill the gap left by an absence of trust resulting from the fact that the EU is not yet a developed polity comparable to a national political system. Second, procedural and informal norms which constitute institutions also 'orientate institutional actors to their allotted functions' (Armstrong, 1995: 167). Third, they are also significant for mediating the formation and expression of interests in EU integration (ibid.: 8, 43). Fourth, they 'structure the access of political forces to the political process' and even can be themselves the sources of policy change (ibid.: 52). Fifth, neo-functionalists who have drawn on institutionalist accounts have considered norms inherent in institutions as important because they can help to maintain integration effects (see, for example, Lindberg and Scheingold, 1970). There are always various obstacles to efforts to promote regional integration, such as tensions among social actors in an integrating region and pressures to adopt a range and level of regional organisation which only just meets minimal common objectives. Hence once the difficult task of setting up regional organisations has been achieved, national pro-integration actors will tend to stabilise these institutions by isolating them off from their environment. Regional organisations are strengthened by being turned into a 'self-maintaining set of institutional norms' (Schmitter, 1971).

Hence some of the theoretical departures from formal law are inspired by the theory of social constructivism and go beyond the modernist commitments which underpin the emphasis of a traditional approach on formal law in EU integration. But perspectives associated with the traditional approach, such as neo-functionalism,[11] can also be read in such a way that they could accommodate a broader conception of law which includes soft law. Neo-functionalists have not just analysed the relevance of various types of 'spill-overs' as crucial for the promotion of EU integration, they have also recognised the possibility of 'spill-backs'. 'Spill-back' means that social actors will tone down their commitment to integration because of tensions among them which lead to the withdrawal from the original objectives of integration (Schmitter, 1971). New forms of EU governance seem to be captured by this approach. In some policy areas the EU supranational institutions have retreated from the deployment of traditional formal legal rules. For instance, in EU environmental law and social policy the EU legislature refers increasingly to framework directives, soft law and technical standards which return powers of defining the specific content of the legal obligations to private actors and member states when they implement EC legislation. Hence, the notion of 'spill-back' can capture types of legal rules beyond the prevailing notion of formal, EU 'hard' law that is imposed from the centre upon legal actors in the member states.

Moreover, neo-functionalist approaches can accommodate a broader conception of law because by 'decentring' the state they can recognise private law-making processes such as the drafting of standards by bodies for standardisation. Neo-functionalists decentre the state by arguing that nation states are no longer predominant actors in regional political organisations. Member states transfer real sovereignty in the policy areas in which they initiate regional integration and thus create supranational organisations. Moreover, neo-functionalists regard the state as a fragmented, rather than as a homogeneous and unitary actor. The state here is more akin to a loose organisation of various social interests which allows various sub-national actors to act independently of the nation state as traditionally understood (Schmitter, 1996b: 5). Hence transnational interest groups, such as EU-wide trade and labour associations as well as other non-governmental organisations, are considered as key drivers of EU integration. This neofunctionalist notion of the decline of the nation state directs attention away from traditional state law to the normative practices of these transnational interest groups.[12] The social practices, norms and standards of transnational interest groups can also significantly influence new forms of EU legal harmonisation, for instance through the representation of their interests in the various committees which are increasingly important in EU law-making processes, such as comitology committees.[13]

Only the assertion of transversal cleavages following class, sectoral professional lines across present national boundaries and their transformation into *common, informal practices* within private associations, parties, movements, even individual enterprises and firms will be effective in linking economic to political integration in the long run.

(emphasis added, Schmitter, 1996a: 149)

Finally, it is constructivist accounts of EU law that go furthest in abandoning formal conceptions of law in EU integration. They suggest that there is no 'objective reality out there'. It is simply that social 'realities' are negotiated between the relevant actors. Social constructivist approaches to EU integration have focused on the transformation of identities and the role of *ideas* in policy making. They emphasise *learning* as key to achieving convergence in the EU. Hence, they reject the idea – which underpins some neo-realist accounts – that social actors' exogenously pre-given interests and preferences are key drivers of EU integration. Instead constructivist approaches examine the process through which interests are socially constructed and identities transformed (Christiansen et al., 1999: 529). Hence they pay attention to ideas as well as material factors for understanding the dynamics of regional integration. This reference to ideas renders visible the fluid, changeable, contested and fragile aspects of the social world (ibid.). It also recognises the spatial, and in particular local dimensions, of social action and its limited temporal frame. Moreover, neo-realist and neofunctionalist approaches are interested in parsimonious accounts of the social world which focus on a selected number of variables in order to unravel causal mechanisms in EU integration. Constructivist accounts, in contrast, attempt to capture the complexity of social processes from a more holistic perspective (ibid.: 532).

Constructivist accounts go beyond a concept of formal state in EU integration. They argue that an analysis of a whole range of norms and rules is required for understanding the processes of EU integration. Some constructivists ascribe a central role to small-scale norms because they see them as *constituting* interests, identity and behaviour, and not just as *regulating* behaviour (Martin Marcussen, referred to in Christiansen et al., 1999: 542, Risse 2004: 163). In comparison to institutionalist accounts, constructivists have also emphasised the role of ideas in their analysis of EU integration. Hence they recognise the normative role which ideas, institutions and identities can play in EU integration (Wiener and Diez, 2004:9; Christiansen et al., 1999: 532). They have also analysed culture as something which helps to illuminate the process of policy formation and how the interests and identities of EU actors are constructed and can change (Jupille, Caporoso and Checkel; 2003: 14; Christiansen et al., 1999: 528).

To conclude: formal law has been a key reference point for debates about the role of law in EU integration. But debates about new modes of EU governance as well as institutionalist and constructivist perspectives on EU integration question this focus on formal state law in the process of EU integration. Even elements of neo-functionalist approaches seem to allow for a broader concept of norms which recognises the importance of small-scale social norms in EU integration. But these critical perspectives challenging the exclusive emphasis on formal law in EU integration also suffer from some shortcomings.

Developing further critical alternatives to the emphasis on formal state law in EU integration

While the perspectives discussed above go some way towards abandoning conceptions of formal EU law and national state law as central to EU integration processes, they may not go far enough. For these perspectives abandon reference to the formal state only to a limited extent. For instance, legal pluralist perspectives have informed some of the literature on new modes of EU governance. And here the analytical categories and normative concerns which are central to the operation of official state legal systems sometimes seem to resurface. Thus Harm Schepel (2005: 6) describes standardisation processes as similar to official law-making. Hence a key concern of the analysis is to elaborate the normative principles which guide standardisation. These principles are described – in the language of state law – as the 'internal administrative law' of standardisation. The analysis also addresses normative issues which are key to the operation of official state legal systems, in particular how – from the perspective of constitutional law – the legitimacy of standardisation processes which draw also on private norms can be enhanced (Schepel, 2005: 407). Moreover, some concepts of legalisation in the EU recognise that there are a whole range of different normative phenomena ranging from 'softer' to 'harder' forms of normative obligations. But the criteria which are used to identify these different types of law and to classify them are derived from conceptions of formal state law and expectations of what the 'law in the books' should be like. Normative standards are considered to be more law-like, the more obligatory and precise they are, and if they involve independent third parties, such as courts, for the resolution of disputes over the meaning of normative standards (Goldstein et al., 2000: 387, 390).

Similarly there are limits to the extent to which institutionalists reject state-centred conceptions of formal law. Formal legal member state systems and the formal EU supranational legal system are still considered as very significant in EU integration processes in some institutionalist accounts. The institutionalist perspective here is not employed to challenge the idea that formal legal systems are highly significant in EU integration. It merely suggests that the formal legal system is understood as an institution, is analysed in terms of its institutional structures, and thus that institutional context is seen as shaping legal doctrine (Armstrong and Bulmer, 1998).

Moreover, some critical perspectives still seem to refer back to the state and its formal legal systems; and where they do refer to state law and other forms of normative orders as relevant to EU integration, the relationship between state law and other such normative orders is by no means transparent. What is the relationship between the small-scale social norms, cultures and values which underpin various institutions, on the one hand, and formal law, on the other hand? These questions are raised, for instance, by accounts which examine the legalisation of international relations, including those involving the EU (Goldstein et al., 2000). Here institutions are defined as 'enduring sets of rules, norms, and decision-making procedures that shape the expectations, interests, and behaviour of actors'. Hence 'rules and norms' are an aspect of institutions. It is then acknowledged that institutions vary.

They are 'legalised' to different degrees (ibid.: 387). Legalisation is defined with reference to three criteria: the degree to which the rules are binding, the precision of those rules and the delegation of some functions of interpretation, monitoring and implementation to a third party. Completely legalised international institutions steer the behaviour of states through law. But the question then arises how 'the law' through which international institutions steer the state can be differentiated from the 'rules and norms' that make up the institutions themselves? Moreover, can the 'rules and norms' which constitute institutions shape or even displace what is here understood as formal state law?

In addition, while a number of critical approaches recognise social norms beyond formal state law as significant in processes of EU integration, these social norms are understood as fully fledged normative orders. From a legal pluralist perspective the interest then shifts to various forms of competition and interaction between different types of bounded norms. The emphasis is not on understanding how non-normative contexts, 'the social', feed into the constitution of various types of norms, including private norms and state law (Lange, 2002). Similarly a traditional conception of norms, i.e. that they have a specific normative content, is not questioned. Even 'soft' law is still considered to have a normative content even though it lacks binding legal force as defined by the formal state law system (Trubek, Cottrell and Nance, 2005: 5; Goldstein et al., 2000: 387).

Moreover, normative concerns, especially in relation to legitimacy and accountability, feature strongly in debates about new modes of EU governance (Scott and Trubek, 2002: 8, 16; Snyder, 1994: 218–219). For instance, the question whether procedures for promulgating soft law comply with traditional state constitutional and administrative law standards of transparency, fairness, proportionality etc. has been closely analysed. Whether individuals can derive legitimate expectations from soft law has been another concern (Borchard and Wellens, 1989: 307). Moreover, it has been questioned whether EU soft law coheres easily with the established constitutional architecture of the EU and the specific distribution of powers between the EU and the member states which it envisages.[14] It has been argued that soft law has given rise to a 'competency creep'. It can turn into an important method through which the European Community assumes new competences where the Treaties do not do so. The use of the open-method of coordination in the area of pensions and social exclusion are often seen as examples of this.

Finally, while some critical perspectives start to question traditional conceptions of law as formal state law, their main interest is not in developing a new concept of law in EU integration. For instance, institutionalists stress the importance of small-scale norms in EU integration, but they do not reconceptualise the very notion of EU law on the basis of this insight. They do not seek to develop a conception of EU law which may modify or replace the idea of formal EU law. For instance, Armstrong and Bulmer's (1998) account of the Single European Market project still considers Treaty provisions, secondary legislation and ECJ decisions as central to EU integration. A key issue in rethinking the nature of law in EU integration is to analyse law's relationship to social norms and contexts. If we recognise that not just formal law, but also a broader range of social norms inform EU integration processes, then we need to further analyse how formal EU law 'in the books' and national state law relate to various social norms. These various social norms may arise out of political, economic and social practices. Hence law's relationship to political, economic and social contexts becomes a central question. Consequently questioning formal conceptions of EU 'law in the books' and national state law as key to EU integration processes, requires us to address questions about the relative autonomy of law.

Questioning the idea of the relative autonomy of EU and national law

Whether law is perceived as autonomous is significant not just for debates about the nature of EU law, but is also central to the question whether there is a distinctly legal dimension to EU integration. If law is conceptualised as clearly separate from its social contexts, it is then possible to assert an integrating function of an independent category of law. But where no sharp distinction between law and its contexts is assumed, it becomes harder to identify a specifically legal dimension of integration. Where critical, contextual approaches operate with a broad definition of law which captures a variety of normative phenomena, including state law and social norms, they question – by definition – the idea that there is a separate integrating force on the part of formal EU law 'in the books' and national state law. A close association between state law and its contexts may even suggest that the formal law can only further integrate what is already integrated at the level of social norms (Podgorecki 1974). Within the traditional approach, by contrast, state law and integration are two separate variables. Hence nothing in the traditional approach to the definition of law excludes the possibility that formal EU law 'in the books' and national state law have a distinct integrating function. In fact, this has been the dominant assumption of the traditional approach towards the role of law in EU integration.

The challenge to the notion of autonomous law in functionalist sociology

There are differences within functionalist sociology about how precisely autonomous law is supposed to be. Usually functionalists see law as bounded within a separate, social sub-system, the legal system, which has only limited interchange with other social sub-systems. But Harry Bredemeier (1968) works with a less autonomous conception of law than Talcott Parsons because he constructs a close link between various social sub-systems. He perceives law as dependent, for instance, on inputs from the political system in the form of public policies, if it is to discharge its integrating function. The legal system also relies on inputs from the pattern-maintenance system which includes socialisation processes. For instance, a willingness to use the courts as a mechanism for conflict resolution and to accept their decisions is a necessary input from the pattern-maintenance system into the legal system. It is a precondition of the legal system developing its integrating function. But Bredemeier (1968: 58, 59) still maintains the autonomy of law to a significant degree by pointing to the limits of these close links between law and other social sub-systems. He emphasises that these input/output links can break down, for instance when the political system does not provide a clear, specific input for the legal system and only yields contradictory public policies instead. Similarly, courts may not be used as primary mechanisms for conflict resolution when they suffer from a deficit of legitimacy, for instance in totalitarian political regimes.

Moreover, functionalists as well as legal sociologists and lawyers relying on their work explore interrelationships between law and the social world from a quite specific and thus restricted perspective by focusing on the relationship between law and social values (see, for example, De Burca 1995: 43; Pound, referred to in Cotterrell, 1992: 74; Cotterrell, 1992: 76; Timasheff, 1939: 17; Durkheim, 1984: 329–341). But the idea that law is grounded in shared social values relies on a consensus model of society which does not facilitate analysis of power relations and thus of conflict between irreconcilable differences in the perspectives and interests of social actors (Cotterrell, 1992: 78). Hence there is room for critical perspectives on law in EU integration to explore further relationships between law and the social world and thus to question the idea of relatively autonomous law. To some extent this has occurred in the literature concerning 'EU law in context'.

Challenging the notion of autonomous law in studies on 'EU law in context'

Approaches to 'law in context' stress the importance of analysing law in relation to its economic and social contexts, as well as in relation to political power and interests (Snyder, 1990: 1). Thus from a contextual perspective the analysis of specific substantive areas of EC law has also considered 'relationships among institutions, rules, ideologies and processes'. For instance, it has located EC external relations law in the context of the international political economy, especially trade relationships between developed and developing countries (ibid.: 4). Hence EC law is not analysed here as a self-contained, autonomous legal order. Instead contexts become relevant for understanding what EC law is. For instance, interests generated in the political sphere are expressed in law and influence how the actual meaning of law is socially negotiated. Contexts also supply particular assumptions about the social world which then inform legal ideas, principles, rules and decisions (ibid.: 7). But this analysis only goes so far in abandoning the notion of autonomous law in EU integration. While the importance of context is emphasised, law and context are still considered as conceptually distinct:

[law] is to some extent *distinct from – though not independent of –* political and economic processes and policy decisions.

(emphasis added, Snyder, 1990: 3)

But can 'law' really be considered as conceptually distinct from its economic, social and political contexts? Can economic, social and political contexts give rise to or simply constitute normative orders which should also be recognised as 'law' that plays a role in EU integration? Should social, political and economic dynamics be considered not just as 'factors' in the environment of law, but as building blocks in the constitution of law? 'Context' may not be just a 'factor' which only impinges on the drafting, operation and final implementation of the law, but may constitute law itself or become closely intertwined with formal legal orders. Contexts may fill out the empty shell of 'formal' law. Hence, a consideration of the limits to the autonomy of law may require us to rethink the very concept of 'EU law' itself. Attempts to jettison notions of autonomous law in EU integration can also be found in contributions to the literature on EU integration which recognise close connections between law and politics.

Close links between law and politics in EU integration

Daniel Wincott's account of EU integration identifies close relationships between law and politics and thus questions the notion of fairly autonomous EU law. He argues that law can be open to 'strategic political intervention'. It can become politicised and thus deviate from the 'ideal of law' (Wincott, 2002: 8, 25). Moreover, political institutions – though separate from European law – are considered as part of the strategic context in which the ECJ operates. Hence the ECJ is perceived as subject to political influence, but this is limited by the ECJ's imperative to maintain its ideal conception of a 'legal institution' (ibid.:10). Political institutions are also recognised as important for legal developments in a more general sense. It was the Commission's legal service which first suggested the idea that EC Treaty provisions should be directly effective (ibid.). The ECJ gave formal legal expression to this view through its judgment in the Van Gend en Loos case.[15] There are further examples which illustrate the point that legal systems are not really segregated and impervious structures. For instance, national legal systems in Western Europe have influenced each other not just through the transfer of legal rules, but also through transfers of policy even before the start of EU integration (ibid.: 16).

In addition, institutionalist accounts also question the idea of relatively autonomous EU law because the idea of EU law as an institution highlights close relationships between law and politics. It can explain how forces from outside a legal system are 'mediated through law's institutional structure' (Armstrong, 1998: 156). Institutionalist accounts have also acknowledged close links between the legal and economic dimensions of EU integration. They argue that the Single European Market has an important legal dimension but is also a response to a changing international economy (Armstrong and Bulmer, 1998: 38, 39). To conclude: a number of approaches have started to question the idea of law as relatively autonomous. But they may still not go far enough. For instance, for institutionalists the idea of 'law as an institutional structure' still implies a degree of stability and independence of law from its environment:

the institutionalisation of particular policy solutions may make it difficult for EU institutional actors themselves to control their own systems of governance and regulation.

(Armstrong and Bulmer, 1998: 274)

To summarise: a number of accounts regard law and politics not as alternative drivers but as closely linked in the promotion of EU integration processes. Law is recognised as 'a product of the polity and the polity is to some extent the creature of the law' (Cappelletti, Seccomber, Weiler, 1986b: 4). But two issues need further clarification in accounts which recognise close links between law and politics. First, if law and politics are closely connected, does this mean that we should no longer conceptually distinguish between those two spheres of social action? For instance, law is perceived as 'deeply embedded in politics'. Law is considered as 'affected by political interests, power, and institutions', and 'law and legalization affect political processes and political outcomes' (Goldstein et al., 2000: 387). How far can this image of the close interconnection between law and politics be pushed? Can politics actually 'constitute' law? If not, how and why can 'law' and 'politics' be clearly distinguished? Second, the relationship between law and politics are often examined on a macro-level, as mediated by institutions, for instance (ibid.). This needs to be complemented by more specific and detailed accounts of how law and politics can become linked on a micro-level. Law-making builds on interest positions and interest politics can also be conducted by legal means, for instance through playing for legal rules in strategic court actions (see, for example, Craig and Harlow, 1998). It has even been argued that law's integrating force in the European Union does not rest on law itself, but on the interests of the relevant actors (Christian Joerges, 1996, referred to in Haltern, 2004: 178). Hence what needs to be further explored is how law can become linked to its contexts, such as politics and economics on a micro-level. How do interests and small-scale power dynamics contribute to the construction of legal meaning? The perspective then shifts from an analysis of politics and economics as separate factors in the environment of law to a consideration of political and economic dynamics *within* law. This helps to illuminate an important facet of the 'living law' in EU integration. 'Law in action' approaches are an important springboard for the analysis of the relationships between law and its contexts.

'Law in action' in EU integration

To what extent have approaches to 'law in action' informed studies on EU integration? Some neo-functionalists recognise 'law in action'[16] as significant for EU integration. But 'law in action' is simply used here as a shorthand for implementation deficits of formal law on the ground. The key insight of this 'law in action' perspective is that EU law is often not implemented. Reference to 'law in action' on its own is not, however, enough to encourage the rethinking of the very concept of EU law. The focus is still on the formal 'EU law in the books' as the central vision of what EU law is. Treaty articles as well as EC Directives and Regulations are seen as crucial to fixing EU policy objectives (Schmitter, 1996a: 145).

'Law in action' has also been considered by some sociologists who have discussed the integrating force of law. For instance, Roscoe Pound and Karl Llewellyn have attributed an integrating function to 'law in action'. Llewellyn defined law very broadly to include not just formal state 'law in the books' but also social norms generated and applied in various social groups, such as formal organisations and the family. According to him, this broad notion of law fulfils four functions which underpin the integrating force of law in a society. These four functions are dispute resolution, reorientation of behaviour for conflict avoidance, the allocation of authority in a group and finally, the organisation and harmonisation of activities within a group in order to provide direction and purpose (Llewellyn, 1940). Llewellyn called these functions 'law jobs'. In fact he considered that law always fulfils these functions even across different societies. What varies is only *how* these functions are fulfilled in practice according to the specific social context in which the law operates.

Similarly Pound (Pound, 1954) based his discussion of the integrating function of law on a 'law in action' perspective which seeks to capture how law actually works in society. For lawyers the source of law's integrating function is the *logical* unity of law, as displayed by the ordered structure and rationality of formal legal rules (Cotterrell, 1992: 74). In contrast, Pound argued that law has a *functional* unity which springs from its social engineering function and from the legal values which law applies to the adjudication of conflicting interests. He referred to these legal values as 'jural postulates' of time and place. True to a 'law in action' perspective, he argued that the 'jural postulates' arise from the specific societies in which a legal system is embedded (Pound, 1954). Hence, Pound and Llewellyn began to question the idea that an integrating function of law can only be discussed with reference to the formal 'law in the books'. They began to develop a 'law in action' perspective which draws on a sociological conception of law. It draws attention to how law is embedded in political, economic and social contexts. Pound's and Llewellyn's work raises the issue, but it still requires more detailed analysis of such a sociological conception of law, and in particular an analysis of law's relationships to its environments on a micro-level. Moreover, their analysis is limited through its focus on common law systems and a specific historical context. The next chapter therefore examines further literature on 'law in action' and asks how this can advance critical perspectives on concepts of law in EU integration.

Conclusion

This chapter has argued that it is important to question the focus of a traditional approach on formal, instrumental and autonomous conceptions of law in EU integration. It is important to conduct critical empirical analysis which asks what kind of law EU integration processes actually generate. There are limits to the insights which can be derived concerning the integrating function of 'law' simply from grand social theoretical reasoning, such as functionalist sociology, and major integration theories, such as neo-realism and neo-functionalism. It is also important to analyse on a small-scale level how 'law' becomes linked to its 'contexts' and how contexts can become involved in the constitution of 'law'.

Critical approaches towards conceptualisations of EU law are significant because how we envisage law has implications for how we conceptualise the process of EU integration. For instance, an emphasis on soft law can question the supranational perspective on EU integration. This is particularly well illustrated through various types of soft-law, such as open methods of coordination. But soft law in the form of EU Commission guidelines can also enhance the power of supranational actors, such as the Commission. This process questions intergovernmental theories of EU integration (Borchardt and Wellens, 1989: 292). Moreover, some of the literature on new forms of EU governance interprets deliberation as one way of enhancing the democratic legitimacy which is potentially diminished by strategic bargaining in various EU committees, including comitology committees. Such forms of 'deliberative supranationalism' imply that a purely intergovernmental or supranational account of the EU is no longer appropriate. In fact it has been argued that deliberative supranationalism dissolves the tension between the two (Schepel, 2005: 412). In addition, constructivist approaches have been specifically invoked in support of federal theories of EU integration (Koslowski, 1999). Further inquiry into what law is, rather than relying on traditional conceptions of 'hard' state law as the main conception of law, is also important to move beyond the basic dichotomy between 'integration through law' and 'integration without law'. The theme of 'integration without law' features in the literature on new modes of EU governance. To conclude: empirical analysis into the nature of EU law does not simply matter for developing a socio-legal analysis of integrating law but it also crucially influences how we theorise EU integration processes.

In addition, critical perspectives on law in EU integration help to shift the perspective from normative theorising to analytical approaches. Inquiry into what law actually is, makes it less likely that a particular idea of law is simply taken for granted and then subsequently employed for making normative prescriptions about the process of EU integration, for instance in order to deal with deficits of legitimacy and accountability and to constitutionalise informal legal processes.[17] Chapter 4 argues that 'law in action' approaches in particular are well suited to develop a deeper analysis of the nature of law in EU integration.

Notes

1. Institutionalist approaches emphasise the role of institutions in EU integration. But beyond this focus on institutions, institutionalism is not a coherent label for an easily identifiable approach towards the role of law in EU integration. 'Institutionalism' has been informed by two further perspectives which are usually clearly demarcated. These are neo-functionalism and intergovernmentalism. Some institutionalists draw on neo-functionalism, under the label of 'supranational institutionalism'; others – 'intergovernmental institutionalists' – rely on neo-realist perspectives (Armstrong and Bulmer, 1998: 30). The picture is further complicated by the fact that there are various strands, such as historical, rational choice and sociological institutionalism. Rosamond (2000) suggests that for rational choice institutionalists actors formulate their preferences on the basis of a rational pursuit of self-interest, but preference formation is exogenous to institutions. In contrast to this, historical institutionalists think that institutions structure political processes. Institutions are independent variables which

can entrench path dependent forms of decision-making. Sociological institutionalists work with the idea of a 'mutual constitution of actors and institutions' (Rosamond, 2000: 119). In fact sociological institutionalism has been perceived as an example of constructivist approaches towards EU integration (Risse, 2004: 174; Rosamond, 2000: 120).

2. For instance, Koslowski (1999: 569) draws attention to the different meanings attributed to federalism in various language communities. He suggests that Germans tend to perceive federalism as a power-sharing arrangement based on limited central government, while the British view federalism as the loss of sovereignty to an all-powerful Orwellian state. See also Wæver, 2004.

3. For instance, it has been argued that a constructivist analysis of political practices in the EU renders transparent the development of federal political relationships, which provide a higher degree of institutionalisation than a mere confederation, but do not amount to a federal state (Koslowski, 1999: 562).

4. Case 120/78 Rewe-Zentral AG v. Bundesmonopolverwaltung für Branntwein, ECR 649, European Court of Justice 1979.

5. See, for instance, the Commission Communication of 2 December 1992, 'An Open and Structured Dialogue between the Commission and Special Interest Groups', 93/C63/02.

6. This happened, for instance, when the ECJ turned EC law into a truly supranational legal order through its early rulings on direct effect and supremacy of EC law which did not have a clear basis in the text of the EEC Treaty itself. For later examples of the creative development of the ECJ's own vision of integration, in particular through the development of remedies, see: Cases C-6&9/90, Francovich and Bonifaci v. Italy [1991] ECR I-5357 and C-46/93, Brasserie du Pêcheur SA v. Germany and C-213/89, R. v. Secretary of State for Transport, ex p. Factortame Ltd and others [1996] ECR-I-1029.

7. But De Burca (1995: 52) also points to the principle of proportionality as helping to make rights discourse less divisive and turning rights considerations into a more consensual balancing exercise.

8. This result was particularly clear in relation to felony cases where 88 per cent of suspects were arrested in a stranger relationship between complainant and suspect, while only 45 per cent of suspects were arrested in a family member relationship, and 77 per cent were arrested in a friends, neighbours and acquaintances relationship (Black, 1971: 1097). This scenario applied when complainants stated a clear preference for arrest of the suspect.

9. See Macaulay, 1963: 55–67.

10. Soft law has been defined as 'rules of conduct which, in principle, have no legally binding force but which nevertheless may have practical effects' (Snyder, 1994: 198).

11. See, for example, the discussion of Burley and Mattli's neo-functionalist account of EU integration in chapter 2.

12. Especially in neo-functionalist accounts which draw on institutionalist approaches.
13. These are committees (increasingly referred to in EU law-making processes) where the Council has delegated implementing law-making powers to the Commission, in order to flesh out details of general legal provisions passed in the Council. The Commission can not exercise these powers directly by itself. It has to take into account the advice of a comitology committee. There are various types of comitology committees, consisting, for instance, of representatives for member state administrations or independent scientific experts. See Joerges and Vos, 1999.
14. Soft law has been employed for some time in the EU. It is not an entirely new phenomenon and academic papers discussing it started to appear in the 1970s (Snyder, 1994: 199). But now EU soft law clearly plays an increasingly significant role in the EU.
15. Case 26/62 [1963] ECR 13. Furthermore at the time when the ECJ was considering turning the protection of human rights into a principle of EC law the Council of Ministers made various declarations about the importance of the protection of human rights in the EC (Wincott, 2002:14–15).
16. Also Daniel Wincott (2002: 17) refers to significant gaps between EU 'law in the books' and 'EU law in action'. He also attributes a meaning dimension to law by recognising EU law as a mechanism for the diffusion of ideas, though the focus is mainly on *legal* ideas, such as legal principles, concepts and abstract theories of law from different member states (ibid.: 18).
17. This argument is employed in relation to a non-prescriptive use of federal theory for understanding the EU. How federal theory is actually employed in political practices can help us to understand more about EU politics. Hence federal theory is not simply employed here as an abstract prescriptive device:

> By focusing on federal principles evident in political practice, one can utilise federal theory to analyse political relationships to better understand what politics are rather than what they should be, and to better understand what the European Union (EU) is rather than what it may never become.
>
> (Koslovski, 1999: 562)

4   What is EU 'law in action'?

Introduction

Chapters 2 and 3 discussed traditional and critical approaches to conceptualising law in EU integration. Chapter 3 argued that it is necessary to inquire more closely into the nature of law in the process of EU integration. This chapter therefore examines what sociological accounts of law can offer for understanding the nature of EU law. It focuses on a 'law in action' approach. This, in turn, draws attention to the points of intersection between a legal and a social sphere and how power relations mediate them. The chapter argues that discourse theory can shed new light on 'law in action', specifically how the key legal obligation under the IPPC Directive to use 'the best available techniques' is defined in practice. The first section of the chapter begins by defining the terms 'social' and 'legal'. The second section explores different types of intersection between them. The final section analyses Michel Foucault's contribution to understanding power relations in 'law in action'.

Points of intersection between 'social' and 'legal' worlds at the heart of 'law in action'

What does 'law in action' mean? The term 'in action' draws attention to the 'dynamic' element of legal rules, to the 'living law' and allows us to explore how rules become 'animated' (Selznick, 2003:177; Ehrlich, 1936). In more positivist terms, 'law in action' refers to 'the reality of law' (Brigham and Harrington, 1989: 45). It also implies that normative orders are not just abstract constructs, but have an empirical basis. Hence the concept of 'law in action' suggests that the nature of law is best understood with reference to a social world. Intersections between a 'social' and a 'legal' world are the analytical core of 'law in action'. So what is the 'legal' and the 'social'?

Definitions of 'the legal' have been widely debated in the sociology of law. The question 'what is the social?' has received less attention, despite the fact that systematic study of the social is considered central to the sociological analysis of law (Cotterrell, 1998: 368; Cotterrell, 2002: 635). When sociologists have approached the question 'what is the social?' they have suggested that it[1] is the particular way in which populations think about and act upon their collective experiences (Rose, 1999: 101). It comprises:

the sum of the bonds and relations between individuals and events – economic, moral, political – within a more or less bounded territory,

usually a nation state and national economy which is 'governed by its own laws' (Rose, 1996: 328). In more specific terms, 'the social' has also been defined as 'modes of production, systems of class conflict, forms of social solidarity and phases of rationalisation' (Unger, 1983: 633). Since the mid-nineteenth century a social sphere has been subjected to political programmes, including the management of national economies, which are aimed at 'social justice, rights and solidarity' (Rose, 1996: 329). The welfare state became one of the institutional expressions of a social sphere and the knowledge generated by modernist social science contributed to constituting and stabilising the social sphere (Baudrillard, 1983: 41; Rose, 1996: 327). The concept of 'the social' or 'society' is thus a specific construct which arose as 'the great discovery of political thought at the end of the eighteenth century' (Foucault, 1987: 241). 'Society' came to signify that government did not merely have to deal with a particular spatial domain and subjects, but that there was now a realm of 'the social',

a complex and independent reality with its own laws and mechanisms of reaction, its regulations as well as its possibilities of disturbance.

(Foucault, 1987: 242)

It has been argued that in the late twentieth and early twenty-first century 'the social' is undergoing significant transformation (Rose, 1996; Lash and Urry, 1994: 320; Pavlich, 2001:4). While some have suggested that we may be even witnessing an 'implosion of the social' and an 'end to social relations', it is clear that the notion of a unified, homogeneous social sphere is no longer meaningful (Baudrillard,

1983: 4, 23). The idea that 'the social' can be envisaged as patterned and stabilised through the social order has been questioned. Hence the social has been characterised as 'indeterminate, fluid and heterogeneous and thus subject to variation' (Cotterrell, 2002: 635). It consists of increasingly tenuous social bonds, which arise primarily in local contexts, like the particular commitments which individuals take on with regard to their families and communities (Lash and Urry, 1994: 16; Albertsen and Dieken; Rose, 1996: 327; Baumann, 1988: 800). Moreover, it has now become far less certain what actually constitutes the domain of the social. Clear boundaries between state and civil society are disappearing (Cotterrell, 1998: 379). Hence 'community' rather than civil society has become the new reference point for conceptualising the social. Community can be a matter of 'shared beliefs or values', 'common projects, traditions and history' or 'shared emotional attachments' (ibid.: 389). It is different from the pre-modern 'Gemeinschaft' which established 'static, enclosed and exclusive communities' (ibid.). Hence heterogeneous communities, including imagined and virtual ones, are now the new spaces upon which advanced liberal government acts (Pavlich, 2001: 2; Rose, 1996: 331; Lash and Urry, 1994: 3). Moreover, in the context of globalisation the nation state as the main perimeter for defining the national social sphere is in decline. Transnational communities and networks, sometimes abstracted from specific geographical locations, now represent the changed character of the social sphere (Cotterrell, 2002: 640; 1998: 389).

Two key points emerge from this definition of 'the social'. First, the social is a cognitive construct which expresses how we *think* about our collective experiences. It comprises more than simply the actual behaviour of social actors. The *construction* of concepts of the social is thus important for understanding 'EU law in action' and the intersections between a social and a legal sphere at its core. Second, the social is currently undergoing significant transformation and is thus historically contingent. Contemporary accounts emphasise its fluid, unbounded and unstable aspects. Social structures and the idea of social order are now less central to constituting 'the social'. Moreover, it is important to avoid two pitfalls when defining 'the social'. First, if 'the social' is defined too narrowly a specific perspective on the intersections between 'the social' and 'the legal' may be already implied. For instance, 'the social' has been defined as:

the patterns of human connections and interactions in relation to which law exists and which in some way it expresses and regulates. [...] society's nature is expressed in and through law.

(Cotterrell, 1998: 368)

This definition seems to leave no space for a social world beyond law. 'The legal' and 'the social' are tied together through one specific connection: law constitutes the social. Second, some accounts fall into the trap of reifying 'the social' (Hunt, 1978: 146). 'Law in action' research has explicitly criticised reifications of 'the legal' in 'black letter' doctrinal analysis of law. But ironically it has sometimes relied on reified images of 'the social'. Both post-structuralist and Marxist writers criticise some perspectives in the sociology of law for treating 'the social' as a material and objective 'reality'. The economic and political 'realities' of the social world have been interpreted as highly significant for shaping how law acquires meaning in practice (Valverde, 2003: 6). Law has been even perceived as a tool of social structures. For instance, in some Marxist accounts capitalist relations of production in the social sphere are thought to shape the formal law – a mere superstructure grafted upon the economic base. But also some Marxist writers have detected a problematic 'reification' in some accounts of the 'social'. They have criticised sociological jurisprudence and realism as particularly prone to reifying 'the social' by perceiving society as 'an autonomous social relation', a source of social forces controlling its members' conduct (Hunt, 1978: 146). Inquiry into how law is implicated in the social processes which sustain modern capitalist society is marginalised in this perspective (ibid.: 151). This obfuscates to identify those who exercise social control.

An analysis of 'the social' in EU law in action seeks to respond to these criticisms of reified notions of 'the social' by pointing out the importance of 'discourses' in constructing our perceptions of the social. It also defines 'the social' broadly and thereby avoids defining 'the social' simply as something constituted through formal law. More specifically, 'the social' in the implementation of the IPPC Directive can be defined as the various discourses which are mobilised in debates about what constitutes 'the best available techniques', such as technical, economic and political discourses. It also includes 'social actors', their interactions and institutions (Brigham and Harrington, 1989: 55). Implementing the IPPC Directive involves local permitters, operators, BREF writers, members of Technical Working Groups, the Information Exchange Forum, trade associations, national civil servants and NGO

members. It also involves the groups, networks, associations, companies and bureaucratic institutions through which these social actors are
organised, such as the EU Commission, the EIPPC Bureau, the European
Environmental Bureau, regulatory authorities and national environmental ministries. Having now defined 'the social' for the purposes of
EU law in action analysis, we must proceed to examine the definitions of
'the legal'.

For some sociologists of law the question 'what is the legal?' is not a
key concern. Some realists and critical legal studies researchers in
particular consider legal texts as a naïve formality. Where law is
unmasked as powerless and failing to steer social relations, questions
about the nature of 'the legal' become less relevant (Brigham and
Harrington, 1989). But for some socio-legal researchers 'what is the
legal?' is a key concern. In fact, some research has defined 'the legal'
expansively and turned it into a key organising concept. For instance,
from the perspective of legal pluralism 'law in action' is a form of
'interlegality'. The social sphere is interpreted as being constituted of
various normative orders which interact with the formal law (Santos,
1987: 298).

The definition of 'the legal' adopted in this book for EU law in action
analysis differs from this latter perspective. It does not interpret the
social in highly normative terms. But it does share with legal pluralism
an emphasis on the importance of taking into account social actors'
own definitions of what constitutes 'the legal'. It also emphasises that
social actors mobilise formal legal texts through the construction of
discourse. Hence formal legal texts are not dismissed as irrelevant. But
the definition of 'the legal' adopted here does not insist on drawing rigid
boundaries around a 'social' and a 'legal' sphere. Instead, it seeks to
expose the interchange between a 'legal' and a 'social' sphere in order to
avoid reified and essentialist definitions of 'social' and 'legal'. It is now
necessary to discuss how intersections between legal and social worlds
can be thematised.

Are social and legal worlds dependent or independent?

Sociological accounts of law have generated numerous and complex
accounts of how 'legal' and 'social' interrelate in 'law in action'. Two
themes have been central. The first addresses whether social and legal
worlds are mutually dependent or have to be conceptualised independently. Some definitions of 'the social' are dependent on a definition of

'the legal'. Here the formal law provides the lens through which elements of the social world are captured. Only that aspect of the social world which exists in relation to formal law is brought into focus. For instance, some socio-legal researchers argue that law consists of 'a body of statements and legal action'. Legal action is simply that 'set of organised activities which express or implement the body of statements', such as creating, interpreting, enforcing and adjudicating formal legal rules (Johnson, 1977: 49, 50 referring to Selznick, 1961). Organisational routines and codes for interpreting formal law in public bureaucracies or private regulated organisations are examples of behaviour in the social sphere that is specifically related to formal law (Johnson, 1977: 60, 61). To conclude: where 'the social' is defined as dependent on 'the legal', narrow definitions of the 'law in action' naturally follow. This approach merely captures behaviour in a social sphere specifically related to the creation and implementation of formal law.

Other accounts, however, grant more independence to a social sphere and regard it as a separate source of various normative orders. Here, it is not just those segments of the social world directly linked to the creation and implementation of the formal law which are analysed. Instead, an independent social sphere which can generate its own normative orders is explicitly recognised. For instance, Eugen Ehrlich (1936) referred to the 'living law' in order to argue that people experience a range of normative orders within social groups and associations which may be entirely unrelated to the formal legal rules of an official state legal system. This perspective generates broad definitions of the 'law in action'. In fact some legal pluralists use the term 'law' to refer to these various normative orders which originate from a social sphere (Tamanaha, 2001: 171). Various social norms, such as customs, mores, habits and normative practices, can furnish content for the space of 'the social':

Gray Dorsey observes that man is an ordering creature. His social arrangements quickly assume patterned forms.

(Barkun, 1973: 13)

A key element of the social sphere is communicative interaction. Hence, one example of social norms is conventions and rules of grammar governing communication (Goffman, 2002). It is acknowledged that all 'talk' itself is to be structured in the sense of following rules (Bryman, 2001: 356). Discourse and conversation analysts trace how rules guide the use of language:

The notion of the interpretative repertoire is interesting because it brings out the idea that belief and action take place *within templates that guide and influence the writer or speaker.*

(emphasis added, Bryman, 2001: 362)

Moreover, beyond the rules governing language use, there are also further situational and cultural rules which organise behaviour and interactions between social actors. But a perception of the social world in highly normative terms implies a potentially limiting 'Russian doll' view of the 'law in action'. How formal law acquires meaning is explained with reference to a variety of social norms which can be traced to ever more intricate, small-scale social norms, down to the rules of grammar governing communication. Here the 'law in action' is narrowly defined, as just another normative structure. It becomes difficult to distinguish 'the social' from the 'legal'. This matters not just for analytical but also for normative purposes. The 'social' also disappears as a distinct sphere from which we might envisage resistance to highly normative forms of social life. The idea that the 'law in action' represents a 'human element' in law where 'men [sic], not rules administer justice' is also marginalised (Pound, 1910: 20). To summarise: the theme of the analytical dependence and independence of 'the legal' and 'the social' – whether law can be grasped in terms of the social or whether the social can be grasped in terms of normative orders – is key to discussions of the 'law in action'. The proximity and the distance between a 'social' and a 'legal' sphere are, however, another key theme.

Proximity and distance between a 'social' and a 'legal' sphere

A second key theme in accounts of intersections between a 'legal' and a 'social' sphere invokes spatial metaphors by focusing on the proximity and the distance between 'social' and 'legal'. Distance is emphasised by accounts which highlight 'gaps' between the 'law in action' and the 'law in the books' (see, for example, Johnson, 1977: 50; Frank, 1930; Pound 1910: 14, 30). Here 'law in action' is considered as a transformation of the original formal legal rule. 'Gap perspectives' underpin many socio-legal studies on the impact and effectiveness of legal rules. Here the focus is on assessing whether formal legal rules are actually applied in practice and whether the aims of a legal programme are realised. 'Gap' perspectives suffer from various shortcomings (Lange, 1999; McBarnet,

1997; Feeley, 1976; Sarat, 1985; Brigham and Harrington, 1989). They rely on a modernist understanding of legal texts which assumes that it is possible to determine in abstract terms the meaning of formal legal rules. They then compare this with 'actual behaviour on the ground'. Moreover, some gap accounts tend to perceive 'law in action' statically, as the final, fixed consequence of implementing law. This detracts from the idea of 'law in action' as an ongoing social process which may also be indeterminate. Gap accounts also implicitly privilege 'law in the books' because it is taken as the main reference point for detecting, describing and differentiating 'law in action'. To conclude: the analysis of 'EU law in action' pursued in this book challenges accounts which emphasise the distance between a 'legal' and a 'social' sphere. It seeks to develop accounts of the proximity between a social and a legal world. Three basic versions of proximity can be distinguished.

First, some sociologists of law argue that 'the legal' is pervasive. For instance, they suggest that formal law constitutes the social world: It is 'constitutive of social institutions, practices, ideas and identities' (Cotterrell, 2002: 639; Tushnet, 1980: 30). The pervasive influence of law can also be traced on a micro-sociological level because it 'enters into the construction of routine lines of action' (Grace and Wilkinson, 1978: 161).

Second, other accounts regard 'the social' as predominant. Here the social is constitutive of the legal. The social elements of law become the focus of inquiry. 'The legal' is merely an empty rhetorical shell. Its meaning is derived from social processes. Social contexts supply the meaning for law and the effectiveness of law may even depend on its openness towards its social environment. 'Law in action' – arising at the intersection between the formal law, and its social contexts – far from being an obstacle to the implementation of the formal law may actually help to make the formal legal order work (Selznick, 2003: 178). For instance, through 'law in action' general legal rules can be adapted to specific social circumstances. Formal law becomes thus more flexible and adapts to social change. 'Law in action' can thereby promote equity and fairness (Pound, 1910: 19). It can smooth over shortcomings in the formal law and thereby bolster its status and significance (ibid.).

Third, some accounts seek to avoid interpretations of either 'the social' or 'the legal' as predominant. They result in potentially problematic, theoretical compromises, such as the idea that there is a 'dialectical relationship between 'the social' and 'the legal'' or that the 'social' and 'the legal' are 'mutually constitutive' (Hunt, 1978). For instance, it has been argued that law 'adapts to the contours of society, but also gives directions to its change' (Selznick, 2003: 177). Similarly, social institutions and relations have been considered as important for constituting the law, while legal institutions also 'structure social life and political discourse' (Brigham and Harrington, 1989: 42,46). Beyond these three accounts, however, there are two further more specific ways of envisaging the intersections between a social and a legal sphere.

The non-hierarchical continuum

One of them is the non-hierarchical continuum or a network-like structure (Cotterrell, 2002: 637, referring also to Picciotto and Haines, 1999; 644; Santos, 1987: 299, 298):

> Law, power, ethics, customs and morality do not exist in reality as separate and distinct sets of phenomena. Rather, they all belong to the same continuum with imperceptible transitions leading from one to the other.
> (Johnson, 1977: 51; referring to Weber, 1954)

In order to harness this conception for thinking about the intersections between a 'social' and a 'legal' sphere some points, however, need to be further clarified. First, what really is the continuum? Does it represent social life itself with formal law on the one side, different types of normativity in between, and social life without a specific social order at the other end? Or are social life and formal law end points on a continuum which covers quite different types of social processes? Second, if intersections between a 'social' and a 'legal' world are to be interpreted as a network, what is the nature of this network? Sociological accounts of networks, such as actor-network theory, provide insights that can also be harnessed for an analysis of law in action (Lezaun, 2006; Scheffer, 2003; Latour, 1996). A second key conception from the socio-legal literature for envisaging the intersections between a social and a legal world is the notion of 'law in context'.

Law in context

Here the social is grasped precisely as the context of law. 'Law in context' can mean that 'legal norms and institutions are conditioned by culture and social organization' (Selznick, 2003: 177). There are external forces which – sometimes independently of each other – act upon law and which can bring about internal change in the law (Hunt, 1978: 143, referring to Julius Stone). Law's relationship to its contexts can vary. 'Discontinuities' as well as 'continuities' between law and its contexts have been noted. This, in turn, can help to explain how formal law is stabilised, responds to its social environment or may remain autonomous (Selznick, 2003: 178). For instance, institutions such as public regulatory bureaucracies can create bridges between law and its contexts by integrating legal rules into the decision-making structures of regulated firms (ibid.: 179).

The 'law in context' idea is key to questioning the neutrality and objectivity of law. How far law can transcend its contexts remains open to debate. Some argue that law can be disciplined by its contexts, but contexts can also be transcended by comprehensive principles and ideals of 'legality' which can also govern normative orders in private organisations (ibid.: 177). In order to develop the 'law in context' idea as an analytical tool for understanding the intersections between a 'legal' and a 'social' world, it is, however, important to elaborate theories of that context (ibid.: 180). What do contexts consist of? Do they consist of a separate social sphere or of overlapping economic, political and social contexts?

To conclude: 'law in action' approaches seek to understand the intersections between a 'social' and a 'legal' world. Accounts which focus on the distance between a social and a legal world, such as 'gap' perspectives, suffer from various shortcomings. The EU law in action analysis developed here therefore focuses on an exploration of proximity between a social and a legal world. But accounts of law in action are also shaped by the theoretical assumptions which underpin them. The next section turns to a discussion of these.

Moving away from positivist, behaviouralist and instrumental perspectives on intersections between a 'social' and a 'legal' world

Analysing the intersections between 'social' and 'legal' does not occur in a theoretical vacuum. Sociological jurisprudence and realist scholarship on 'law in action' specifically draw on positivist, behaviouralist and instrumental perspectives. Realism draws on sociological positivism (Hunt, 1978: 42). It aims to generate 'accurate recordings of things as they are, as contrasted with things as they are imagined to be, or wished to be' (Llewellyn, 1931). Hence, realist research starts 'with an objectively scientific gathering of facts' (ibid.: 1237).

It has also a behavioural focus (Brigham and Harrington, 1989: 44). Realists are interested in 'what people are really *doing*' (Llewellyn, 1931: 1224). For realists, it is behaviour and interests – not the formal law – which determine the outcome of court cases (Brigham and Harrington, 1989: 44; Hunt, 1978: 37). In particular, the behaviour of official legal actors, such as judges, law enforcers and those subject to legal regulation, are a key focus for realist 'law in action' studies. Behaviour is also at the heart of Eugen Ehrlich's definition of 'law in action'. He defines the 'living law' as patterns of behaviour from which a rule can be deduced (Ehrlich, 1936). These can be empirically identified through observations of further behaviour, such as the experience of informal social sanctions by those who do not comply with the 'living law'. Moreover, expressions of behaviour, such as a capacity to apply sanctions or otherwise change behaviour, are key for identifying 'law' in a range of socio-legal studies. Here the existence of law is inextricably linked to the evaluation and observation of behaviour (see, for example, Feeley, 1976: 50; Gibbs, 1973: 17–19). Some 'law in action' research also seeks to predict law-related behaviour, for instance how disputes are handled (Brigham and Harrington, 1989: 51; McEwen and Maiman, 1984; Bush, 1984; Sander, 1984). Other 'law in action' studies focus on behaviour by asking how legal actors avoid law, make discretionary decisions, create alternative social norms and hence what behavioural practices mediate the reception of state law in regulated and regulatory organisations (Hawkins, 2002; Hawkins, 1984; Hutter, 2001; Hutter, 1988; Ross, 1995).

Realists also work with instrumental perspectives on law. Research into 'law in action' matters because it can enhance law's effectiveness. Understanding how formal legal rules are transformed into 'law in action' through encounters with the social world is a first step in turning law into a more effective instrument of private and state actors. While realists recognise certainty and determinacy in law as an illusion they nevertheless think of law as a means to social ends (Llewellyn, 1931: 1230, 1241). Moreover, Karl Llewellyn's account of what he calls 'law jobs' reflects an instrumental conception of law (Hunt, 1978: 50). Law serves specific functions. In particular six 'law jobs' which Llewellyn identified help to ensure the existence of human groups, ranging from small groups, such as a business partnerships, to whole societies. These six law jobs comprise conflict resolution, preventative channelling of conduct and expectations, channelling conduct and expectations in order to achieve adjustment to change, allocation of authority and procedures for authoritative decision-making, providing directions and incentives within the group as well as providing juristic method (Twining, 1968). Through the development of these specific 'law jobs' law becomes an instrument for the maintenance of social groups.

In contrast to this, the approach pursued in this book for an analysis of 'EU law in action' seeks to question positivist, behaviouralist and instrumental perspectives on the intersections between a 'social' and a 'legal' world. It does so by taking into account the insights of post-structuralist perspectives which pay attention to discourse in the construction of the 'law in action'. Realists began to recognise that the legal language of statutes and cases allows for various interpretations (Tushnet, 1980: 23). But their analysis can be further developed through close attention to discourses. Discourses also capture the 'knowledges' – not just behavioural strategies, such as threats of coercion – which are key to specific intersections between a 'social' and a 'legal' world. 'Law in action' involves social actors coming to think and perceive of the social world in a particular way. Attention to discourse and not simply to behaviour is also particularly relevant for understanding the implementation of the IPPC Directive. Determining what constitutes 'the best available techniques' involves the construction of knowledges through persuasion, negotiation and exchange of arguments, framed in terms of technical, economic and political discourses, rather than just coercion. Hence, the analysis pursued here challenges purely modernist assumptions by considering both behaviour and discourse as important resources in the inter-subjective construction of 'law in action'. Finally, in order to analyse intersections between a 'social' and a 'legal' world, it is important to understand how power can mediate such intersections.

Power mediating intersections between a 'social' and a 'legal' world

Realist approaches neglect the analysis of power, but power is clearly central to the construction of 'law in action'. For instance, social struggles over rights to determine law illustrate the operation of power in the 'law in action' (Brigham and Harrington, 1989: 50, 55). Moreover, power becomes significant in intersections between the 'social' and the 'legal' if one takes into account law's ideological functions. Law's power to make social actors see and comprehend the social world in particular ways can be an important aspect of relations of domination. Legal categories and structures can be a powerful optic through which social life is perceived (Feeley, 1976: 515). But what concept of power can help us to understand further 'the law in action'?

First of all, does a concept of power need to be distinguished from normativity? Some accounts of power come close to socio-legal concepts of normativity because they include reference to socially structured and culturally patterned behaviour of groups and the practices of institutions as manifestations of power (Lukes, 2005). The exercise of power thereby includes the construction of social practices which are supported also through the consent of those subject to domination (ibid.: 108–151). In particular some legal pluralists recognise social practices as 'law' if the relevant social actors label them as 'law' (Tamanaha, 2001: 200). For some law and power also share common elements. Both are said to involve 'direction and control of human action' and 'subordination to authority' (Johnson, 1977: 51). Even where power and law are not equated, law is at least associated with the presence of power. Legal actors are considered as inherently powerful and recourse to state power is necessary, for instance, for enforcing legal rights (Johnson, 1977: 51).

Some post-structuralist conceptions of power, however, work with a looser link between normativity and power. Foucault for instance, rejects the 'classic, juridical' conception of power where political power of the sovereign is understood in terms of *rights* to carry out certain actions as well as constitutional restraints on these (emphasis added, Foucault, 1980). In the 'classic, juridical' conception, power is a commodity which can be possessed and thus also transferred, for instance through legal acts such as contracting (ibid.: 88). From this perspective power is an individual's or a group's domination over others that is facilitated by normative frameworks (ibid.: 97).

Foucault, however, abandons the idea that power is a commodity possessed by the powerful. He argues that power cannot be identified through observing the behaviour of 'key players' and powerful social actors. Instead it exists in productive networks and circulates throughout society (Foucault, 1987). Power is performative because it can give rise to new forms of behaviour. It cannot just be demonstrated through normatively regulated and thus restrained behaviour. It is an anonymous apparatus, 'a machinery that no one owns' (Mills, 2003; Foucault, 1980: 156). The very idea of 'individuals' or 'subjects' is simply an effect of power (Foucault, 1980: 97, 99). Hence, power is not possessed by social actors, but passes through people. They can become 'elements of the articulation of power relations' (Foucault, 1980: 97; 1987: 247). They are not the point of application of power.

Foucault's idea of power is also different from the concept of power as patterned social practices because he perceives power as less stable, solid and static. Power can exist simply as local, small-scale, contingent tactics and strategies. In fact, power relations may require constant repetition and stabilisation (Mills, 2003: 47). They can fail. They should not be equated with total domination (ibid.: 44, 48). Moreover, Foucault interprets power not as a specific set of patterned social practices which can be located at a particular site, but as social relations which are diffused throughout the whole social body. Power is enacted in every-day interactions (ibid.: 52).

Foucault's concept of power involves reference to normative social practices only in a fairly indirect way. Foucault explains power through the operation of discourses. But for Foucault too, discourse, in turn, involves patterned social practices. Foucault defines 'discourse' in various ways in his work. But it is clear that he uses the concept of 'discourse' in order to inquire into the regularities which underpin knowledge systems about the social world. He therefore defines discourse as 'the *regulated* practices which account for a number of statements' (emphasis added, ibid.: 53). These can involve 'unwritten rules and structures which produce particular utterances and statements' (ibid.: 53). Moreover, Foucault describes the 'épistème', one of the other terms he employs to talk about discursive formations, as an 'ensemble of practices' (ibid.: 62). Disciplinary power, for instance, can 'spatialize, observe and immobilize' social action (Foucault, 1980: 159). In addition, some practices keep discourses in circulation while others suppress them (Mills, 2003: 54). Thus patterned social practices matter for understanding discourse.

Discourse, in turn, is related in various complex ways to power. Discourse can generate power relations and power relations can also work through discourse because discourses structure how we perceive the social world (ibid.: 55). While discourse can both be an instrument and an effect of power, it can also be a site of resistance to the exercise of power (ibid.: 33–34, 54). To conclude: in Foucault's analysis the possibility that patterned social practices are linked to effects of power is not excluded, but rendered more marginal. But how can these abstract ideas about power be harnessed for an analysis of 'EU law in action' in the implementation of the IPPC Directive?

Interests as a pointer to power?

'Law in action' research has often operationalised an abstract concept of power through the medium level concept of interests:

A exercises power over B, when A affects B in a manner contrary to B's interests.
(Lukes, 2005: 37)

Interests feature in various ways in 'law in action' research. For instance, the process of 'creating law', including 'law in action', can be understood in terms of conflicting social interests. Some socio-legal analysis pays attention to the struggles which are waged over determinations of what counts as law (Brigham and Harrington, 1989). Attention has been directed here to how social actors link interests to particular behavioural strategies, such as the 'setting of agendas', shaping 'the rules of the game' and 'structuring decision-making processes' as well as 'exercising power by non-decision making' (Grace and Wilkinson, 1978: 136, referring to Bachrach and Baratz). This focus on the operation of interests in legal processes as an expression of power has also been important because it questions the liberal myth of the neutrality of law.

Foucault, however, does not examine the operation of power through reference to social actors' interests. For him (1980: 96), questions such as 'who exercises power and what are their motivations and conscious intentions?' are unanswerable. For Foucault 'interests' cannot really explain power because, in his view, there are no groups or individuals who use power to further their interests (ibid.: 159; Smart, 2002). Categories such as 'individual', 'group' or 'social actor' are simply effects of power. Hence interests are discursive constructions. They are not the 'real' driving forces of power hidden beneath the surface of discourse. It is the surface of a discourse and hence how interests become discursively constructed which matter for documenting power relations. Discourse analysis does not invoke distinctions between 'appearances' and 'reality'. Discourses are transparent and they do not need further interpretation or meaning to be assigned to them (Foucault, 1987: 57). Hence, interests are a particular way of seeing the world. They are indications of how various actors locate themselves in relation to their social environments and hence mere claims to power. Understanding interests as discursive constructs avoids reifying them as unquestioned and material aspects of social 'reality'. Being part of the surface of a discourse they are not explained with reference to deeper social causes or structures.

Moreover, understanding interests as a way of seeing the social world connects directly with Foucault's idea that knowledge and 'truth' are crucial for understanding power. How something comes to be considered as a 'fact' is ultimately a question about power relations. Foucault (1980) refers 'to power/knowledge' to suggest that knowledge is constructed at the cross-section of power relations and information seeking. Power requires knowledge for its exercise and knowledge engenders power relations (Mills, 2003: 67). It is often imbalances in power relations between people or institutions which give rise to the production of knowledge (ibid.: 69). Being in a position of power is often a prerequisite for enjoying the privilege of speaking the 'truth' and only 'true' statements may circulate as part of a discourse.

Knowledge production is key to the determinations of the 'best available techniques'. Defining BAT draws on various knowledges. They range from 'high' to 'low status knowledges' (Valverde, 2003: 22). They include environmental science and engineering knowledge as well as job-based knowledges, such as how to licence a PPC site, how to negotiate with operators and environmental regulators, how to navigate organisational hierarchies within national regulatory agencies, regulated companies and EU systems of multi-level governance.[2] 'Low status knowledges' also include the local, ad hoc, sometimes elaborate systems of ideas that participants in BAT determinations develop about 'state law' and 'law in action'. Some of these knowledges are more privileged than others. Particular authority may attach to the knowledges generated by environmental regulators in comparison to knowledges about BAT that are generated by operators, environmental NGOs or members of the public. To conclude: from a Foucauldian perspective social actors' interests are not a pointer to the operation of power or 'real driving' forces beneath the surface of social life. Instead they are discursive constructions. Hence, Foucault's approach advocates empirical research into the detailed 'small-scale manoeuvres, tactics, techniques and functionings' of power relations (Foucault, 1987: 57). The operation of discourses is central to understanding these.

Conclusion

This chapter has argued that an 'EU law in action' approach can provide further insight into the nature of law in EU integration. 'Law in action' highlights intersections between a social and a legal world as crucial to understanding the nature of law. It also seeks to move away from essentialist and a priori definitions of social and legal. Social actors can construct and mobilise various meanings of 'social' and 'legal' in communicative processes which involve translation between different professional and language communities, as in the case of the implementation of the IPPC Directive. This chapter defined the social as discursively constructed perceptions of interactions. What we perceive as the social world is historically contingent and thus subject to change. Contemporary accounts recognise patterned social practices and normative orders as one element of the social world, but also emphasise fragmentation and fluidity in social bonds. A legal sphere is defined with reference to social actors' own definitions of what constitutes law. Legal texts still matter. In fact, how they are discursively mobilised is key to the construction of 'the legal'. The analysis developed in this book rejects the assumptions that 'social' and 'legal' are rigorously delimited concepts. It thereby directs attention to the proximity between a social and a legal world. It allows us to explore open exchanges between 'social' and 'legal' in communicative processes.

This chapter has also argued that Foucauldian ideas about power can help to deepen the analysis of intersections between 'social' and 'legal' in 'law in action'. They enable us to ask the following questions: How and what type of power relations are involved in BAT determinations? How and what kind of 'BAT law in action' do they generate? What knowledges about BAT determinations do political, economic and technical discourses generate? How do these knowledges express or conceal relations of power? What according to these discourses are key factors in BAT determinations? What do social actors in the field identify as the relevant 'interests' involved in BAT determinations? How do they link 'interests' to particular BAT determinations? These questions are examined in the following chapters which are based on the empirical data concerning the implementation of the IPPC Directive.

Notes

1. In classical social theory, the 'social' world has been distinguished from the natural and the technical world. See Herrnstein Smith and Plotnitsky, 1995: 380. Some contemporary perspectives, however, hold that the social world interacts with and is even stabilised by its association with the natural and technical domains. See Law and Mol, 1995: 276.
2. Such as interactions between the EU Commission, federal and land environmental ministries as well as regulatory authorities at different levels, such as

Bezirksregierungen as well as *Kreise* and *kreisfreie Städte* on the local level in the German three-tier level of government which can be found in some of the *Bundesländer*. In the UK navigating EU multi-level governance systems has involved interactions between the EU Commission, the national environmental ministry, DEFRA, the main regulator for IPPC sites with a significant pollution potential, the Environment Agency, and local authorities.

5   Talking interests – generating procedure: How political discourse constructs key aspects of BAT determinations in BREFs

Introduction

Chapter 4 argued that in order to understand more about the nature of law in EU integration it is necessary to analyse 'EU law in action'. 'Law in action' draws attention to the intersections between a 'social' and a 'legal' sphere because power relations mediate such intersections. They are also a key aspect of BAT determinations. This chapter therefore traces how a political discourse, especially expressions of interests in relation to what constitute 'the best available techniques', shape BAT determinations at the first level of the implementation of the IPPC Directive, the drafting of BREF documents for the whole of the EU. BREF writing generates 'EU law in action' in various ways. First, the fifth chapter[1] of each BREF lists 'BAT conclusions'. While these are not legally binding, they have to be taken into account by local permitters when they determine BAT for a specific plant. Second, participants who produce the relevant BREFs make numerous suggestions as to what should be considered as BAT during discussions in the BREF drafting process. Central to the generation of 'BAT law in action' is the procedure through which BAT determinations are achieved. This chapter argues that an analysis of a political discourse is key to understanding procedures for determining BAT in the BREFs. It draws attention to the productive nature of power relations by analysing how they construct procedures for determining BAT.

The first section of this chapter explains why power relations in BREF BAT determinations are best captured through an analysis of a political discourse. It also delineates the key elements and characteristics of this political discourse. The second section focuses on the effects of power generated by this political discourse, in particular the procedure for determining BAT during the production of BREFs. The final section discusses how an analysis of power relations in BREF BAT determinations can contribute to wider debates about conceptualisations of power in socio-legal research about 'law in action'.

Capturing power relations through an analysis of a political discourse on BAT determinations

Why does the analysis focus on a political discourse in order to capture power relations in BAT determinations? First, as discussed in chapter 4 analysis of 'law in action' has often focused on behaviour in relation to law. Less research has been carried out on the significance of discourses for mediating the intersections between 'social' and 'legal' worlds. Second, discourse is central to the implementation of the IPPC Directive. Defining BAT is based on the production of knowledge about what constitutes the 'best available techniques'. Arguing, advocating and persuading in written and oral debate are key tactics for defining BAT. All these practices have been deployed in the Technical Working Groups (TWGs) in which BAT determinations are finalised during the production of BREFs and through the Information Exchange Forum (IEF), a second layer of decision-making for BREFs which is intended to focus mainly on wider policy issues in BREF BAT determinations.[2] The statements generated during these debates and the rules according to which they are produced can be captured by the concept of 'discourse' (Foucault, 1972). Moreover, BAT definitions during BREFs are framed in a multi-lingual environment. Participants in the production of the BREFs do not share a common native language. Discussions in the technical working groups are conducted in English without translation facilities.[3] Hence language – one aspect of discourse – is here directly implicated in power relations. Some participants find it easier than others to make and understand complex technical points about what constitutes BAT in English or indeed understand the subtleties of BREF drafting in English.[4] Third, power relations must be analysed through attention to a political discourse because the research data consist of records of talk.[5]

There were various ways in which a political discourse was revealed in BAT determinations. A number of participants in the production of BREFs expressed concerns about the influence of 'politics' on BAT determinations. For instance, a member of the EIPPC Bureau management stated that some participants in BREF drafting were uncomfortable with the term 'negotiation' as a description of discussions about what constitutes 'BAT'.[6] In a later interview he described discussions in the 2nd Technical Working Group (TWG) for the Iron and Steel sector in the EU as follows:

They are not negotiating, they are compromising against arguments being made at the meeting.[7]

But the BREF writer during the same 2nd TWG meeting for Iron and Steel seemed to refer to negotiation when he described a debate about which emission levels should be associated with a potential BAT technique:

We are getting a little bit closer, at least we are at the same decimal point: 0.1; 0.2; 0.3–04 plus 0.5. I don't feel yet like on the market in Delhi or somewhere.

Moreover, a political discourse concerning BAT determinations in BREFs matters because it is pervasive. A member state representative who participated in several TWGs and the IEF suggested that most aspects of BAT determinations are political in character. For instance, he considered determinations of the 'costs and advantages' of techniques according to Art. 2 (11), second indent of the IPPC Directive, not as an application of expert economic knowledge but as a political process which involves negotiations between the member states and the relevant industrial sector. Moreover, a political discourse was thought by some participants to fill the methodological vacuum which was created by the absence of a pre-given, fixed and clearly determined procedure for defining BAT.

But the role of politics in BAT determinations – while acknowledged to exist – was also considered as problematic. A number of participants in BREFs sought to draw boundaries around the political discourse and limit its application by distinguishing it from a technical discourse. In the words of the European Environmental Bureau, a Brussels based environmental non-governmental organisation (NGO) which coordinates activities of member state environmental NGOs:

The EEB felt that there was a basic question as to whether the process was primarily technological or political. The EEB preferred a more strictly technological approach, but felt that if politics could not be avoided then clear rules of procedure and a framework for reaching decisions were needed.[8]

From the perspective of a technical discourse BAT determinations in BREFs are achieved through the application of up-to-date knowledge in engineering and environmental science, rather than through interest-based bargaining. In the technical discourse TWG discussions are portrayed as the consensual and technical argument-based work of a group of experts, some of which happen to have gained their experience through working in industry, while others have gained their expertise from working in the environmental administrations of member states. TWG members were perceived as fellow professional colleagues engaged in open technical, neutral information-based discussion about what constitutes BAT. The political discourse, however, created a different set of actors and roles in BAT determinations. Here TWG members were recognised as negotiating, sometimes as adversaries, especially where representatives already came to meetings with fixed preferences.

A political discourse in BREF writing is problematised by some BREF writers and the EEB because undue emphasis on interests is perceived as lowering the quality of BAT determinations. Exposure to political pressures is seen as potentially in conflict with BREF writers' self-image as technical experts exercising independent judgement:

because they [TWG members] don't have data, so the problem is to collect first data. Otherwise the discussion about BAT is simply going to be only a political discussion and I don't want a political discussion.[9]

To conclude, a political discourse matters for BAT determinations in the BREFs. But what does this political discourse consist of?

Do interests shape BAT determinations?

The political discourse privileges the idea that the expression of 'interests' in TWG and IEF discussions is important for defining BAT. It portrays 'interests' in BAT determinations in the BREFs as multi-faceted, complex and subtle. On the one hand, interests are interpreted as concrete, objective, material phenomena which are determined by the economic and political structures in which actors operate. Interests are also seen as motivating and guiding behaviour. Shared interests are perceived as underpinning the formation of social groups. On the other hand, the political discourse also perceives 'interests' as something constructed and as too fragmented and complex to form the identity of social groups.

The interests of industry and member states in BAT determinations

Various participants in the BREF drafting process perceived member states, the European Environmental Bureau and EU trade associations as pursuing specific interests in BAT determinations. EU trade associations and sometimes individual companies, as well as equipment suppliers were seen to assert their commercial interests. Trade associations and individual companies were perceived as pursuing BAT determinations which would not threaten their competitiveness and would only place limited burdens on industry, in terms of costs and innovation. Equipment suppliers – involved only to a limited extent in the TWGs[10] – were perceived as promoting BAT definitions which opened up sales opportunities for their pollution abatement equipment. Hence 'industry' was perceived as promoting a clearly defined commercial interest. For some actors this was self-evident and did not even require any further elaboration. A member of DG Environment responded as follows to an interview question concerning the role of EU trade associations in the BAT determination process: 'industry, well, we all know what their perspective is.'[11]

According to BREF writers, there were various indicators of commercial interests in the information supplied by industry. For instance, low figures for emissions and costs of operating pollution reduction technologies were considered as an expression of manufacturers' interests to promote their pollution control technologies.

Member states' interests were often described as 'national' interests. They would sometimes pursue a particular BAT definition because it would fit in with the pursuit of national environmental policy priorities. Some member states attempted to replicate their particular national approach towards environmental regulation in the BREFs. Throughout the BREF drafting process Germany advocated BAT determinations which include the setting of emission limit values. The BREFs provide figures for the consumption of raw materials and energy as well as the emission of pollutants by specific processes. Germany wanted these figures not simply linked to the description of BAT techniques, but to be declared as 'achievable levels'. Other participants in the BREF writing process, however, preferred the term 'reference levels' in order to emphasise that these consumption and emission figures for techniques were not to be understood as strict limits. The term finally adopted for use in the BREFs was 'associated consumption and emission levels'.

This suggested that BAT was defined first in general terms, through a description of techniques, and only secondly, through the particular consumption and emission figures which these techniques could achieve. This is different from the German approach which defines strict emission limits first and thereby implies a technique in order to achieve these emission limit figures:

They [i.e. the Germans] have big problems understanding these associated BAT emission levels which we are giving in the documents because they see them as emission limit values.[12]

Moreover, some member states were influenced by national environmental protection targets in their definition of BATs which become applicable to the whole of the EU:

The Netherlands have generated a unique situation. That for cement plants, they have one plant, it is a significant contribution to national emissions of nitrogen oxides and they have calculated it, they need that cement plant to reduce its emissions to 120 and our BAT range is 200–500 and the European average is 1300 and the maximum is about 3000–4000 and the Netherlands are saying but we need our kiln to go to 120, so everybody is saying 'ouch'. That is really maximum application. And then the question is whether this is BAT or whether this is driven by a special force.[13]

Stringent national reduction measures for a number of emissions in response to the EU National Emissions Ceiling Directive (2001/81/EC) coloured the Dutch view on BAT definitions for the cement and lime as well as the iron and steel sector, especially in relation to associated emission levels for nitrogen oxides and sulphur dioxide. Dutch national interests were served in two ways through stringent limits on these emissions through BAT definitions in the EU-wide BREFs. First, strict EU-wide limits could help to avoid a situation where BAT determinations in the BREFs would be less strict than Dutch national provisions, hence potentially undermining Dutch regulators' pollution reduction efforts with Dutch industry. Second, EU-wide stringent reduction levels for nitrogen oxides and sulphur dioxide through BREF BAT definitions could reduce the costs of national emission reduction measures for Dutch industry. Dutch industry would encounter less of a competitive disadvantage if other member states had to comply with similar measures.[14] A political discourse which involved reference to interests was, however, complex in character. It transcended simple classifications of homogeneous 'member state national' and 'industry' interests.

Fragmented and overlapping interests

A political discourse on BAT determinations recognised that member states' interests could be fragmented and could also sometimes overlap with the interests of industry, thus making it more difficult to identify clear-cut power 'blocs', such as 'industry' and 'member states as regulators'. Perceptions of interests in the political discourse transcended the basic idea that industry is exclusively concerned with commercial interests while member states are mainly pursuing environmental protection. For instance, member states were recognised as asserting a variety of national interests. Some of these tallied with the interests of industry:

> There are some member states that are more pro-industry than the industry. I have an example, but I don't want to mention that country. Yeah, some member states from the EU, they are playing games, some playing harder than the industry itself [. . .].[15]

For instance, Italy supported the tanning industry in the TWG for this industrial sector because it has numerous small and medium-sized tanneries.[16] The idea that member state and industry interests could overlap was also reflected in the fact that some member states, such as Italy and Portugal, would sometimes send representatives from trade associations or companies as their member state delegation to TWG meetings.[17] Moreover, according to DG Environment UNICE, the umbrella organisation for EU industry, did not just represent industry's interests in the BREF writing process. It also supported DG Environment's interest by assisting the organisation of BREF writing. UNICE streamlined communication by being the main contact point for DG Environment in talks with 'industry'. UNICE also organised and coordinated the various sector-specific EU trade associations for participation in the TWGs and the IEF. In addition, the European Environmental Bureau was not always considered as a distinct bloc representing 'environmentalists', but its interests were sometimes equated with commercial aims, especially pollution reduction and clean production technology suppliers' interests.[18] To conclude: the drafting of the BREFs generated coalitions of interests which have transcended conventional distinctions between the interests of 'industry' and 'member states' as 'regulators'. Moreover, by pointing to the fragmentation of interests a political discourse also questions the conventional assumption of homogenous power blocs shaping the production of BREFs. For instance, member states could not simply be identified as homogenous power blocs but could be divided. A number of member states opposed Germany's attempts to set emission limit values in BAT definitions in the BREFs. Member states also varied in their views on what BAT is on the basis of different histories of environmental regulation. While Northern European member states have experienced environmental regulation since the 1960s, new member states and some southern Mediterranean member states, like Portugal and Greece, have only recently embraced pollution reduction and clean production technologies.

There is also no homogenous category of 'industry'. BREFs cover a number of very different industrial sectors. The IPPC Directive regulates major EU industrial sectors such as iron and steel as well as chemicals production. These industries are dominated by a few large, often multinational, companies which are represented by strong EU trade associations.[19] But the IPPC Directive also covers the textiles and tanning industry, which has a high percentage of small and medium-sized businesses. For the tanning sector there is also no single EU-wide trade association. Moreover, the IPPC Directive also applies to the agricultural sector, especially intensive livestock farming, which is represented by powerful trade associations.[20] Moreover, there is no uniform approach on the part of 'industry' towards BAT definitions and also no unified expression of an industry interest because different industry sectors have different histories of environmental regulation. The iron and steel as well as the chemicals sector have been regulated for decades by national and EU legislation, especially in relation to air and water pollution. But other sectors, such as tanneries, textiles as well as food and drink, have only been subjected more recently to environmental controls. Moreover, some sectors covered by the IPPC Directive, such as intensive livestock farming, have not worked in open and competitive markets, but have been the beneficiaries of special production support measures, such as subsidies from the EC common agricultural policy.

In addition, industry sectors vary according to the complexity and importance of their production operations. For instance, the chemical sector is a core aspect of EU industry and involves complex production processes.[21] Hence, according to the EIPPC Bureau management, 'thorough preparation' was undertaken before the first TWG meetings were held for the BREFs covering this sector.[22] The chemicals sector, for instance, was considered as different from the food and drink sector which involves simpler and more limited issues for environmental control, such as problems concerning smell and noise. Moreover, industry associations would not necessarily pursue a common interest. Some industry sectors were represented by more than one EU trade association and different associations sometimes had different views on BAT determinations. To conclude: BAT determinations are informed by a political discourse. A key element of this political discourse is the idea that BAT determinations are framed with reference to the 'interests' of various participants. But a political discourse also manifests itself in the way participants talk about small-scale tactics and strategies of power in BAT determinations.

Small-scale tactics and strategies of power: Managing the supply of information

A political discourse also involves talk about small-scale tactics of power which contribute to the social organisation of BREFs without establishing a specific procedure for determining BAT. They are deployed by various participants in the BREF process, not just by those who are considered as structurally 'powerful'. These small-scale tactics and strategies are key to the construction of the day-to-day routine practices of BAT determinations in BREFs. A number of these small-scale tactics and strategies of power revolve around the actual writing of the BREF documents. They relate in particular to managing the provision of information about BAT to TWGs.

Information about techniques is key for selecting the 'best available techniques'. In particular what is considered as 'high quality' information by BREF writers could significantly shape the final text of a BREF document. BREF writers compiled the BREFs under considerable time pressures. Sometimes parts of documents provided by TWG members were scanned into BREFs.[23] Hence supplying information could merge with the actual writing of the BREF. Some member state representatives expressed their concern about industry's role in supplying information to the EIPPC Bureau management. The Bureau replied:

We are not delegating the task [of composing the BREFs] to industry experts but utilising them in a structured way as sources of data and information for us to validate with the assistance of the TWG. However, it is not realistic (and it may be illegal) for us to copy substantial paper documents and distribute them [to Member State representatives].[24]

Since supplying information is key to the writing of BREF documents, controlling information flows is an important strategy for influencing BAT determinations. This occurred in various ways.

The withholding or provision of too much information

Some TWG members 'snow stormed' BREF writers with large amounts of sometimes irrelevant information and numerous, often critical, comments on draft BREF chapters which had been sent out to TWG members for consultation. Sometimes TWG members withheld crucial information.[25] For instance, industry was reluctant to provide information on costs and actual emissions from pollution reduction techniques. According to Art. 2 (11) of the IPPC Directive these were important criteria for the definition of BAT. But member states were also sometimes not forthcoming in supplying monitoring data about techniques collected by national environmental regulators.[26] Monitoring data are valuable because they give an indication of the emission levels which certain pollution abatement techniques can actually achieve in practice.

Sometimes industry or member state representatives in TWGs withheld information by simply assuming 'observer' status. Formally all TWG members are active participants in an information exchange process under Art. 16 of the IPPC Directive. But some TWG members acted as mere 'observers'. They came to meetings to watch discussions and report back to their trade associations on the progress and the direction of the BREF. Others actively contributed to the discussions and supplied information, as originally envisaged for all TWG members. Promoting the roles of either more active or more passive participants was, however, also a small-scale tactic deployed by BREF writers. A full draft of a BREF was made available to all TWG members for comment, usually before the 2nd TWG meeting.[27] Hence this implied equal status for all TWG members. But before that 2nd TWG meeting BREF writers would send draft BREFs to selected 'experts' from inside and sometimes outside the TWG for comments and feedback.[28]

Managing information flows through the strategic production of information

A further small-scale tactic for managing the supply of information involved specially producing information for the BAT determination process. A number of participants, sometimes in collaboration with each other, such as DG Environment, member states and industry, commissioned research and organised discussion related to the exchange of information under Art. 16 IPPC Directive. For instance, through the Commission Directorate 'Joint Research Centre', DG Environment commissioned and financed research on the impact of BAT on the competitiveness of EU industry.[29] The research concluded that plants which had already adopted BAT and were achieving good environmental performance did not suffer a competitive disadvantage. In fact the research suggested that plants which had adopted BAT were 'already strongly competitive'. It also concluded that expansive definitions of BAT could threaten the economic viability of some plants. For these cases a carefully phased implementation of BAT was recommended (Hitchens et al., 2001:16, 17). By associating BAT implementation with high levels of competitiveness of some plants in various sectors of industry, the research questioned some EU trade associations' view of their commercial interests. Applying BAT could not necessarily be considered as a threat to the competitiveness of EU industries.

A further small-scale tactic in the management of information flows was the organisation of workshops. For example, France and an EU trade association organised a workshop in Paris on the determination of BAT for the chemicals sector. The workshop was scheduled before the 1st TWG meeting and hence before the formal BREF writing process began. A number of representatives for industry and different member states participated in this workshop. Its conclusions fed into the 1st official TWG meeting for this sector.

Similarly, the German federal environment agency[30] organised in April 2000 a workshop in Berlin on 'the assessment of cross-media aspects' in BAT determinations. Germany was concerned that a more structured and formalised methodology should be developed for taking into account the impact that the choice of BAT techniques would have on all three interrelated environmental media of air, water and land. One of the key policy objectives of the IPPC Directive is to avoid the choice of a particular pollution reduction technology simply leading to a transfer of pollution, for instance from water courses to land. Thus a BAT technology may involve better waste water treatment through high performance filters but thereby may also generate problematic filter cakes which need to be disposed of in a landfill site. During the BREF writing process Germany had expressed a particular interest in developing methodologies for the consideration of such cross-media aspects.

Several member states and industry representatives participated in this workshop.[31] Similarly, DG Enterprise organised a seminar in association with the independent Belgium De Vito research institute on methodologies for considering costs in BAT determinations.[32]

The organisation of these workshops was also linked to a political discourse. As one BREF writer wrote in an e-mail to another TWG member:

I hope you are not too disappointed by the Berlin workshop! There were too many politicians at the workshop![33]

But these various small scale tactics of power also generated counter-strategies. These counter-strategies focused on questioning the legitimacy of what the European Environmental Bureau called a 'filtering process' which the EIPPC Bureau applied to information submitted to it. Some participants in the BREF writing process therefore called for greater 'transparency' and 'objectivity' in the information exchange process:

The Bureau started in 1997, and 18 months into the work actors in the IEF were requiring more *transparency* and *objectivity*, in particular countries such as the Netherlands, Germany and the EEB.

(emphasis added)[34]

Demands for a clear, specific, systematic, transparent and fair procedure were frequently asserted in the medium of a technical and legal discourse concerning BAT determinations in BREFs.

Moreover, BREF writers also developed counter-strategies for dealing with restrictions on the supply of information. They perceived an informational asymmetry between themselves and other TWG members, such as member states and industry in particular:

Industry, I think, is in the driver's seat. They have the most information, they can control the game.[35]

Where TWG members restricted the flow of information, some BREF writers tried to provoke TWG members into supplying information. Hence BREF writers would draft BREF chapters which contained information on the costs of techniques, for example, which the BREF writer knew to be of limited applicability, by only reflecting costs for operators in one particular member state or from one particular plant. These drafts would then be sent out for consultation to TWG members. BREF writers hoped to provoke them into providing accurate information as a correction to the 'wrong' figures.

Managing time in the provision of information

A further key strategy for controlling the supply of information was the management of time. Curtailing or granting time, for instance, by the EIPPC Bureau management or individual BREF writers for the supply of information was a factor in shaping BAT determinations. For instance, during the second meeting for the BREF for the iron and steel sector, the BREF writer set a time limit of two weeks in which objections to the conclusions agreed at the meeting had to be expressed and supported by further information supplied to him. Information received after this date would not be taken into account in the final BREF draft. TWG members also tried to make the management of time work in favour of their interests. Sometimes they supplied information only at a very late stage of the BREF drafting process in the hope of curtailing critical discussion of this information by the whole TWG.[36]

To conclude: talk about small-scale tactics and strategies employed in the exchange of information is a key aspect of a political discourse in BAT determinations. This talk also generates perceptions of the relationships between the various participants in the BREF writing process and the dynamics of power between them. A political discourse, expressed through talk about small-scale tactics and strategies, thereby allocates roles to the participants which may deviate from the official tasks delegated to them in the BREF writing process, for instance, through the 'IPPC BREF outline and Guide'.[37] In a political discourse BREF writers were not simply neutral coordinators of an exchange of information between industry and member states but became active, interested parties which participated through various small-scale tactics and strategies in the construction of information about BAT techniques. At times their role thus seemed to be comparable to local permitters in member states. One of their main tasks is to obtain 'sufficient' information about a plant in order to determine what 'the best available techniques' for its operation are. The political discourse further allocates roles and thus constructs actors in BAT determinations by portraying BAT determinations in BREFs as the outcome of negotiations.

BAT as the outcome of negotiation

According to a political discourse BAT determinations are achieved through negotiation involving conflict, consensus and compromise. Defining BAT involves 'striking balances' and 'trading off' various aims.[38] For instance, in response to the question how costs informed BAT determinations a BREF writer stated:

it is very much an iterative process, someone will suggest something, someone will suggest something else, a lot of screaming and gnashing of teeth, and saying 'we can't do that', I mean compromise a little bit, that is traditionally also the situation with member state regulators when they are trying to establish what excessive cost is. And because we don't really have any tool at the moment for determining it, it is a somewhat subjective process.[39]

In addition, a number of terms developed by participants in the BREF writing process further expressed the idea that defining BAT involves negotiation. Some TWGs concluded their work with 'split views'. Here no consensus about BAT had been generated.[40] 'Split views' were associated with the process of negotiating BAT. Purely technical discourse was thought to reduce the risk of 'split views':

split views should be avoidable if the data presented were sufficiently well validated and associated with the relevant technical process.[41]

Not just conflict, but also consensus – often achieved through compromises – is foregrounded through a political discourse on BAT determinations. Consensus on BAT was the preferred option for a number of participants in the BREF drafting process. Consensus views were considered to carry more weight and thus be more likely to influence member state permitting practices. Compromises could be achieved through 'balanced considerations'. This entailed BREF writers recognising the influence of particular interest positions on BAT determinations and 'averaging' them out:

We do whatever we can, we cannot do more. So there is subjectivity. But I always said that an addition of subjectivities is much more objective than a single subjectivity. So an addition of subjective points of view is always looking for the average and then the average is closer to the objectivity.[42]

BREF writers and EIPPC Bureau management used the term 'subjectivity' to refer to the influence of interest positions on BAT determinations:

It is to our advantage to provide BREF authors with a framework. I have sympathy for people's view *that the process is too subjective, that it depends on which industry is the best negotiator.*

(emphasis added)[43]

Talk about 'balancing considerations' in BAT determinations was based on the idea that there were imbalances of power to begin with. According to some participants in the BREF writing process member states did not sufficiently counter industry's influence on BAT determinations. Some BREF writers criticised member states for not supplying enough information about the best available techniques in the TWGs. BREF writers suggested that – perhaps due to a lack of resources or unwillingness to take on extra work – member states in some TWGs literally pointed at the industry representative and said 'you are responsible for providing the info'. To summarise: a political discourse generates specific representations of BAT determinations. It suggests that 'interests' inform BAT determinations. It portrays BAT as the outcome of negotiation and compromises. But a political discourse does not just generate mere representations of the social process of determining the 'best available techniques'. It also produces real effects of power. Here this key effect of power is the construction of the procedure for determining BAT.

Talking interests and generating procedure

The IPPC Directive does not provide a pre-given, fixed procedure for determining BAT in the BREFs, apart from a rudimentary framework which is based on the criteria for defining BAT set out in Arts. 2 (11), 16 (2) and Annex IV of the Directive. Hence, procedure is generated through debate and negotiation between the various participants while the BREFs are actually being written.[44] There is no pre-determined procedure which is utilised as a tool by 'powerful actors' in order to further their political interests in BREF BAT definitions. Instead a political discourse – and talk about interests in particular – contributed in two ways to the construction of procedure in BREF BAT determinations. First, it generated the idea that there are specific 'social actors' – members of the Technical Working Groups and the IEF as well as BREF writers – who decide what BAT is. Hence, a political discourse supplies identifiable categories of actors. This is an effect of power of the political discourse against a background of BAT determinations generated by large, not always transparent, networks of people, which extend beyond the official TWG and the IEF, including sub-groups of the TWGs. Within these complex networks it is by no means clear who actually determines what constitutes BAT. Hence a political discourse contributes to the very idea of a specific procedure for BAT determinations in BREFs. Second, a political discourse further constructs the notion of 'procedure' in the determination of BAT by supplying images and characteristics of BAT determinations, such as negotiation and compromise as well as a distinction between technical and political approaches towards determining BAT, a distinction which also comes to be blurred in the process.

Do 'actors' determine BAT in BREFs?

A political discourse privileges the idea that there are 'actors' involved in BAT determinations who take active decisions. It marginalises the idea that BAT determinations are arrived at by default[45] or accident or through complex networks and collectives where contributions of 'individual agents' can no longer be identified. Various aspects of the political discourse suggest the idea that there are 'actors' who decide which technique is 'BAT'. First, a number of participants in the writing of BREFs, such as the EIPPC Bureau management, BREF writers and some EU trade associations, championed the idea of actors, in the sense of active participants, in BAT determinations by questioning the role of scientific methodologies in the choice of BAT. In the words of one BREF writer rejecting Germany's advocacy of a 'more scientific' methodology:

But the Germans say they really want these methodologies, where you can put everything into a big formula and then in the end you get this number out.[46]

There were further assertions of agency despite the continuing search for 'objective methodologies' in particular for an improved consideration of the impacts of techniques on all three interrelated environmental media of air, water and land when defining BAT:

There are some life cycle analysis methodologies. If you read them, you think you get really precise data, precise analysis and you have thousands of sheets in your database of different emissions and whatever. But in the end, the result of this is very statistical. Because you are deciding, *someone is deciding*, you are like weighing different things against each other, so we say, NOX[47] 10 points, SOX[48] 8 points, dust 2 points, *so someone has done this weighing. And the whole analysis depends on what weight you put on different inputs. So, you can have a very clean, nice, precise answer out of it, but it will be a very subjective one. And I don't think there is one* [i.e. methodology] *that everyone agrees on. It depends on what it is used for . . . And it depends on where you are as well and how you weigh the different substances against each other.*
(emphasis added)[49]

A similar point was made by a representative of an EU trade association:

They [name of EU trade association] hoped that the project would address the issue of how environmental investment could most effectively be spent, and *cautioned against putting too much faith in apparently objective approaches involving weighing factors.*

(emphasis added)[50]

The significance of agency in BAT determinations was even more strongly emphasised by the EIPPC Bureau management. It expressed strong reservations about the application of 'objective' methodologies for determining BAT in the BREFs. It suggested that presenting specific methodologies which would identify more precise criteria for defining BAT would encourage TWG members to make strategic arguments rather than to discuss more openly what BAT is. TWG members would try to accommodate their ideas about what constitutes BAT to these more specific criteria. Hence more specific methodologies for BAT determinations would not necessarily structure the process of defining BAT more clearly. Methodologies could not produce BAT determinations since they would simply be reference points for strategic arguments. Hence for a number of participants in BREF writing evaluations could not be eradicated from the process of determining BAT. They were also an inescapable aspect of more 'objective' methodologies for determining BAT. From this perspective, determining BAT involved 'actors' who took decisions:

because what they want is sometimes a methodological formula that could be used in all situations, everywhere. This is not possible. You would still have to have well-educated people in your authorities that can produce an analysis and also take decisions.[51]

To conclude: by reference to the limits of scientific methodologies in the determination of BAT, the political discourse also privileged the idea that 'individual actors' were at the heart of active decision-making processes about what constitutes BAT. The political discourse further develops this idea by identifying specific categories of 'actors'. This matters because an answer to the question as to who actually makes decisions during the composition of BREFs about what constitutes BAT is by no means clear.

The political discourse foregrounded BREF writers as well as 'experts' in the TWGs and the IEF as key actors in BREF BAT determinations. There were also, however, a whole range of – sometimes less obvious – participants in BAT determinations. First, there was a linguist who was first employed in 2000 by the EIPPC Bureau in order to assist various BREF writers whose first language was not English with the drafting of the BREFs in English. He advised BREF writers on appropriate English style and grammar. But his involvement in detailed questions of wording seemed at times to shade into a contribution to defining BAT. TWG debates concerning BAT definitions sometimes focused on the specific wording of a phrase. For instance, should a sentence state that a particular technique 'may' or 'shall' be used? Should a statement in relation to associated emission and consumption levels say that these levels were 'sometimes' or 'usually' 'achieved' or 'achievable'? Not only did the linguist further explain to BREF writers the nuances and subtle differences between some of these expressions from a native speaker's perspective, but he also contributed his own views about which expressions would be appropriate to describe BATs. He advised on whether to use more prescriptive or descriptive, more general or specific expressions.

Second, BAT determinations in BREFs involve a complex and opaque web of sub-groups. A number of TWGs were divided into further groups, called 'shadow groups', 'task forces', 'expert groups' or 'intermediate committees'.[52] Who actually took decisions in these sub-groups was not easy to discern because their working and decision-taking procedures varied. Most importantly their composition varied. Some BREFs, such as those concerned with 'cooling' and 'large volume organic chemicals'[53] had TWG sub-groups which consisted only of experts from industry.[54] Some BREFs sub-groups included both industry and member state delegates.[55] Some TWG sub-groups involved experts who were not members of the TWG, such as academics from national engineering or environmental science research institutes or staff with specialist expertise working for companies in the relevant sector.

Third, it was also difficult to discern who was actually an 'actor' in BREF BAT determinations because TWG sub-groups were not the only sub-groups which contributed to BAT definitions in BREFs. Member states often assembled their own national task forces in order to influence BREF BAT definitions for a particular industrial sector. These sub-groups proposed specific BAT definitions, for instance on the basis of emission limit values imposed in that member state's site licences for plants in this industrial sector. For instance, Germany set up a sub-group on graphite and carbon production[56] which was coordinated by its *Umweltbundesamt* (federal environmental authority). It mirrored the work of the EU-wide sub-group on 'graphite and carbon production' which had been set up by the TWG for non-ferrous metals. The German sub-group incorporated pollution control experts for graphite and carbon production from the environmental regulatory authorities of various German *Länder*. Some member state sub-groups also included representatives from the national industrial sector under discussion. For instance, the German sub-group on aluminium production for the BREF on non-ferrous metals included delegates from the *Länder* working group on air pollution control.[57] This working group, in turn, was made up of delegates from industry.[58] Member state sub-groups contributed in various ways to the European Union TWGs. They supplied reports and documents and also briefed member state representatives in preparation for their contributions to TWGs and the IEF.

Fourth, the web of participants in BAT determinations expanded even further. EU trade associations also sometimes formed their own working groups which worked in parallel with the official TWG and its sub-groups. They proposed their own BAT definitions, submitted documents to the EU TWG and briefed EU trade association delegates for TWG and IEF meetings. For example, the European Apparel and Textile Organisation set up a sub-group for the BREF on textiles production. This group mirrored the writing of the BREF by the official TWG. They also held a 'kick-off' meeting, similar to the first meeting of the official TWG. The BREF writer for the textiles BREF was invited and indeed attended this meeting of the trade association group.

Fifth, it is difficult to identify who actually decides what constitutes BAT and thus to identify 'actors' in the process of writing EU BREFs also because once a final BREF draft has been approved by the IEF, it still has to be approved by the other Commission Directorates in order to be published as an official Commission document, as required by Art. 16 (2) of the IPPC Directive. Hence other Commission Directorates, in particular DG Enterprise – another lobbying point for various EU trade associations – also became involved in the final BAT definitions.[59] This last step in BAT determinations also added a further layer of opacity to BAT determinations because no specific procedure for how inter-service consultations should be carried out for BREF BAT determinations had been developed by DG Environment by the time the first BREFs were to be approved by the IEF.

Against this background of extensive and opaque networks of participants in BREF BAT determinations the political discourse foregrounded 'experts' in the TWGs and BREF writers as key actors. In the interviews participants in the writing of BREFs frequently described BAT in BREFs as the outcome of 'expert judgement'. Some used the term 'expert' widely to refer to all TWG members, including representatives of industry, member states and the EEB. Others, such as the EIPPC Bureau management and BREF writers, however, specifically emphasised and valorised the category of 'expert' by distinguishing 'experts' from 'real experts'. 'Real experts' were TWG members who were considered by BREF writers to have valuable and specific up-to-date knowledge about a particular range of techniques. They were distinguished from TWG members whose technical knowledge of techniques was sometimes felt to be limited, partly because they mainly worked as lobbyists for an EU trade association in an office in Brussels, rather than as technical plant managers in a sector of industry.[60] There were suggestions that 'real experts' were permitted to exercise significant influence on the writing of BREFs, for instance by being granted by BREF writers more opportunities than other TWG members for supplying and commenting on information used as the basis for the BREF. Hence by identifying categories of 'actors', such as 'experts' and 'real experts', the political discourse generated elements of the procedure for determining BAT. This emphasis on 'experts' rather than scientific methodologies as the source of BAT determinations created a procedure that was fluid and flexible. BAT determinations in BREFs were not rigorously structured.

Moreover, the political discourse further develops the procedure for determining BAT not just by identifying categories of actors, but also by implying particular interactions between these actors. It thus constructs the small-scale organisational framework for defining BAT in BREFs. For instance, the political discourse generated both the terms 'BREF author' and 'BREF writer' to describe the role of EIPPC Bureau members who coordinated the production of the BREFs by the TWGs. While some EIPPC Bureau members described themselves as 'BREF authors', others rejected this label and saw themselves as 'BREF writers'. Being either a 'BREF author' or 'writer' implied different relationships with the TWG. 'BREF authors' thought that they were capable of steering significantly TWG debate and thus of contributing to BAT definitions. Some participants in the BREF writing process saw this active steering role of 'BREF authors' as a necessary counterbalance in particular to the influence of EU trade associations.[61] This also involved the deployment of a range of small-scale power tactics by BREF writers as discussed above. 'BREF authorship' was linked to the EIPPC Bureau's assertion of 'neutrality' and 'impartiality'. In the words of a representative of one member state:

We could play the game as well the other way round: the contributions of industry are sent to us and we take them into account. However, we were never asked to do so. Why? In this respect I have to recall that it is the task of the EIPPCB to organise the BAT work and to draft papers on the basis of all contributions. *I wonder how the EIPPCB can play its neutral and compromise-searching role without being the author of the draft BREF.*

(emphasis added)[62]

'BREF writers', in contrast, saw their role as mainly coordinating the exchange of information and the views on BAT expressed by the TWG, without attempting to steer the BREF in the direction of their own view of what constituted BAT. They also distanced themselves from conflicts over BAT definitions in the TWG. Hence the categories 'BREF writer' and 'BREF author' implied different power relations between those who coordinated BREF writing and their TWGs.

But there were also further ways in which the political discourse generated categories of actors which ascribed particular roles to participants in the BREF writing process and thus contributed to the construction of the procedure for determining BAT in BREFs. A number of participants in the BREF writing process referred to both industry and environmentalist groups as 'non-governmental organisations'. Hence, through this terminology, 'state' actors, such as DG Environment and member states were contrasted with NGO civil society actors in BREF writing. This classification of participants in the BREF drafting process gives the impression of a clear distinction between public and private, diverting attention from overlapping interests between member states and sectors of industry. By classifying industry as another NGO, the role of state actors is at least rhetorically enhanced. Hence, the procedure for drafting BREFs comes to resemble an encounter between the different actors of the 'state' and 'civil society', as in the regulatory process of licensing IPPC plants. Finally, the political discourse also generated more formal aspects of the procedure for determining BAT in BREFs. Talk about 'balance of power' in BREF BAT determinations also underpinned the creation of the formal organisational framework for BAT determinations.

Talking about 'balance of power' – generating fluid, flexible and constantly evolving procedures

Talk about 'balance of power' contributed to the formation of a particular organisational structure for BREF writing, consisting of TWGs, the IEF and the 'neutral'[63] EIPPC Bureau[64] as three key organisations.[65]

This organisational framework has also been shaped through a political discourse which included talk about 'balance of powers', 'legitimacy of BAT determinations', as well as 'procedural fairness' and 'transparency'. Hence this political discourse generated effects of power by constructing BAT determination procedures characterised by fluidity, flexibility, continuing evolution and variation between TWGs.

Talk about 'balance of power' underpinned the evolution of the BAT determination procedure from its early stages. Art. 16 (2) of the IPPC Directive requires the Commission to organise an exchange of information 'between member states and the industries concerned'. In response to representations concerning an appropriate balance of interests, DG Environment, however, also involves environmental NGOs in this exchange of information.[66] Moreover, the 'Information Exchange Forum' (IEF) was initially set up as a forum only for member states to decide what should constitute BAT. DG Environment permitted industry a mere observer status in the IEF. But this was subsequently changed when delegates from EU trade associations were allowed to participate in debate in the IEF on an equal footing with member state and environmental NGO delegates. DG Environment, however, then set up another separate forum the 'IPPC Experts Group' (IEG). This group – which consists solely of representatives of EU member states and DG Environment – hosts discussions concerning wider policy issues in BAT determinations and the general implementation of the IPPC Directive.

Talk about an appropriate balance of power between participants in BREF writing also underpinned the evolving role of the EIPPC Bureau. At the start of BREF writing an organisational structure had been envisaged in which the EIPPC Bureau was a 'neutral' coordinator of the work of TWGs focused on technical discussions. But talk about 'balance of power' turned the EIPPC Bureau into a more active participant in BAT determinations. For some participants this meant that the EIPPC Bureau counter-balanced the influence of industry. For others the EIPPC Bureau paid too much attention to arguments from industry:

Germany felt that EIPPCB had exceeded the mandate given to them by the last IEF meeting by making substantial changes to the two drafts. Germany particularly criticized the deletion of the section on monitoring from the iron and steel BREF. They were concerned that, as a result, the given emission levels associated with the use of BAT would in most cases be indicated without any averaging time.[67]

Other aspects of the organisational structure for BREF BAT determinations also evolved further through a specifically political discourse and talk about 'balance of power' in particular. Sometimes sub-groups to TWGs were set up in response to a perceived 'imbalance in power'. For instance, in connection with the horizontal BREF on cooling systems, Eurolectric, an EU trade association, set up a sub-group which consisted only of industry representatives because it was concerned that the TWG was working towards a BAT defintion for cooling which was regarded as very onerous for the electrical industry running power stations.[68] These sub-groups, which were set up ad hoc in response to particular issues in TWGs, contributed to a flexible procedure for determining BAT in the BREFs.

Talk about 'balance of interests' also generated further evolution in the procedures for determining BAT in the BREFs in relation to other TWG sub-groups. 'Balance of interest' arguments underpinned criticisms of 'shadow groups' which included only representatives of EU trade associations. Hence TWG sub-groups formed later on in the process of BREF writing also sought to include both member state and EU trade association representatives.

Finally, there was also variation in BAT determinations between the different BREFs. Thus there was not one, but many procedures for determining BAT.[69] While the EIPPC Bureau had developed in consultation with TWGs an official 'BREF outline' which provided a basic structure for the BREF documents for the various industrial sectors covered by the IPPC Directive, this outline was adapted by BREF writers to the particular circumstances of BREFs in specific sectors. For instance, the BREF outline provided a workable structure for specific sectors of industry, such as iron and steel and non-ferrous metals. But the EIPPC Bureau also produced 'horizontal' BREFs which dealt with issues that cut across a range of sectors, such as 'cooling' and 'monitoring'. For these BREFs the official outline needed to be adjusted.

To conclude: a political discourse generates 'procedures' for determining BAT by foregrounding a number of 'key actors' which are portrayed as decision-makers at the heart of BREF writing. Among these are 'experts' and specific organisational fora, such as the TWGs, the IEF, the IEG as well as the EIPPC Bureau and its BREF 'writers'. These 'actors' are foregrounded against a background of the opaque, labyrinthine networks of a whole range of sub-groups both at EU and member state level which feed into the work of the TWGs and the BREF writers. This broad range of less visible participants in BAT determinations flexibly determined their working procedures as they engaged with their tasks. Moreover, there was not one procedure for determining BAT in the BREFs, but rather various procedures. These were not fixed and static, but open and provisional. Defining BAT in the BREFs did not involve a highly structured bureaucratic form of decision-making. Instead there was a process of continuous redesigning, of changes and variations in the procedures for determining BAT. Redesigning procedures for BAT determinations were a small-scale power tactic. It could be a lever for addressing one of the key difficulties in BREF writing, a device to get member states and especially industry involved in active and constructive contributions to BAT determinations. Accommodating interests through procedural adjustments could facilitate arriving at BAT determinations. A political discourse, however, also generated effects of power by giving rise to a countering technical discourse on BAT determinations. The formal procedure for BREF BAT determinations reflected this tension between political and technical elements in defining BAT. This tension remained unresolved and boundaries between politics and technical issues ultimately became blurred.

How a political discourse generates a technical counter-discourse

The deployment of a political discourse in BREF writing was not without consequences. It generated certain effects of power. Some participants in BREF writing, in response to a political discourse, emphasised a technical counter-discourse on BAT determinations. Here 'objective information' and 'factual knowledge' provided the building blocks for BAT determinations. Here the 'best available techniques' would be defined, for instance, on the basis of precise figures rather than through merely discursive verbal descriptions of techniques. According to one BREF writer, the statement that the associated emissions from a technique were $20 \, mg/m^3$, while another technique emitted $30 \, mg/m^3$ of dust, was 'objective'. In contrast, a statement suggesting that one technique was more polluting than the other was not.

BREF writers were looking for objective, high quality, factual information in order to identify the 'best available techniques'.[70] They considered the 'best available techniques' to have a real and material existence 'out there' in the world of engineering knowledge. BAT was not merely a malleable political concept in their eyes. There were various ways in which BREF writers in particular attempted to keep politics at bay. 'Validating' information supplied by TWG members to BREF writers was a key strategy for finding the 'truth' about what constituted the 'best available techniques'. In fact, 'validating' information was one of the EIPPC Bureau's official tasks:

validation of received information and comments was a crucial task for the EIPPCB. This implied that comments and requests for changes in a document must be backed up with compelling arguments and data.[71]

'Validating information' involved 'looking through' the information and comments on draft BREF chapters supplied to BREF writers. It meant 'seeing through' politicised accounts of BAT in order to find 'real' information. According to the EIPPC Bureau coordinator, BREF writers sometimes removed 'political statements' from documents supplied by industry because they mainly emphasised the industry's environmental protection achievements. They did not necessarily provide a clear and open picture of techniques employed in the sector and their associated emission levels:

The classic function of a writer, author is: he is given this nice report from industry, they go through it with a pen, striking out all these political statements, 'how wonderful is our industry', 'we are doing this and this and this for the environment'. Right let's get down to it, let's cut out the crap.[72]

'Validating information' could also involve naming companies which had supplied data about achievable emission limits in order to check the data and 'to establish their credibility'.[73] It could also mean seeking out further information in order to conform with standards of scientific reporting. Sometimes BREF authors received information which did not define emissions of pollutants from techniques in sufficient detail. Important parameters were left unspecified. These could be the conditions under which measurements had been obtained, such as temperature, gas pressure and normal or abnormal operating conditions, with the latter including peak releases of pollutants. Sometimes the time periods for which emission levels were reported, such as half hourly values or annual releases, had not been specified. At other times the actual measurement methods for recording emission levels were not specified in detail. In some cases cross-media pollution effects had not been quantified.

Some BREF writers sought to 'validate information' by maximising the variety of sources from which they obtained data about the performance of clean production and pollution abatement techniques. For instance, a number of BREF writers actually visited plants covered by their particular BREF. They wanted to obtain information about the performance and costs of techniques directly from the operators or to check data supplied on this to the BREF writer by the EU-wide trade association for the sector.[74] Some BREF writers asked for the local environmental protection agency's inspector for the site to be present in person during these site visits. To conclude: validating information was an important aspect of a technical counter-discourse on BREF BAT determinations. The formal organisational framework for determining BAT in BREFs also reflected attempts to balance political with technical approaches. But ultimately distinctions between politics and technical issues in BAT determinations became blurred.

Blurring distinctions between a political and a technical discourse

DG Environment set up a basic organisational structure which tried to separate technical from political issues in BREF BAT determinations. There were the TWGs, one for each BREF, which consisted of representatives for EU trade associations, member states and the EEB.[75] Representatives for member states were often staff from national environmental regulators who had experience in permitting plants in the sector under discussion or had been involved in BAT policy work. Delegates for the TWG were nominated by IEF members. The IEF was the second major forum in BREF writing. It was also composed of member state, industry and environmental NGO representatives. Member state delegates were usually higher ranking civil servants from the central state environmental ministries.

DG Environment envisaged a clear distribution of tasks between TWGs and the IEF. TWGs were to collate 'good quality' information about what constituted 'best available techniques' for the particular industrial sector under discussion. They were also meant to discuss BAT conclusions within the framework of a technical discourse. The IEF, in contrast, was to support BREF drafting through advice on wider policy questions which emerged during debates in the TWGs, such as disputes over the correct interpretation of terms used in the text of the IPPC Directive.[76] The IEF's main task was to debate final draft BREFs and to decide whether to approve them, so that DG Environment could publish them as a Commission document.[77] This attempt to clearly demarcate the TWG as the forum for a technical approach towards BAT definitions and the IEF as the political forum is also illustrated by the following quote:

The meetings of the TWG are chaired by the Bureau to stress *the important difference between the technical elaboration of a draft BAT. The political approval* of BAT is chaired by DGXI in the Information Exchange Forum.

(emphasis added)[78]

The initial discussions about how BREF writing should be organised and the creation of a dedicated EIPPC Bureau for hosting BREF writers who would coordinate the work of the EU-wide Technical Working Groups also reflects these attempts to separate technical from political issues in BREF writing:

What can IPTS[79] offer: EIPPCB at IPTS must remain *neutral* from all above-mentioned interest groups and deliver to the 'IPPC IEF' well documented techno-economic data about BAT candidates. The whole 'secret' for successful work is to carry out an effective technology watch in order to detect all important recent technological progress that can be used to improve previous BAT definitions. To this end a climate of confidence with the information providers needs to be established and maintained. The fact that EIPPCB does not participate actively in the work of 'IPPC IEF' is of key importance and protects EIPPCB from being involved in *political debates* of the actors involved. However, IPTS must be extremely careful to protect the *neutrality* of the technical work of EIPPCB from efforts of the different interest groups to influence it preferentially.

(emphasis added)[80]

This distinction between technical and political issues in support of the credibility of BAT technology standard development was also supported by industry. Two major EU trade associations, UNICE and CEFIC, supported the hosting of the EIPPC Bureau at IPTS in order to preserve its 'neutrality'.

But the differentiation between a technical and a political approach towards BAT definitions in the TWG and the IEF was effectively blurred in practice.[81] Participants in BREF drafting attempted to turn the IEF into an appeals forum where technical decisions taken in the TWG, and with which they disagreed, could be reopened. Moreover, policy issues such as how descriptively or prescriptively worded accounts of BAT techniques should be were also discussed in TWGs. TWGs were not just engaged in technical deliberations. The key term used by participants in BREF writing in order to describe how TWGs defined BAT was 'iterative expert judgement'. This welds together political and technical dimensions of BAT definitions, such as the subjective evaluation of techniques through ongoing negotiation between all interested parties – 'iterative judgement' – and the reasoned application of structured and documented scientific and engineering knowledge – 'expertise' – for choosing the best available techniques.

To conclude: a political discourse in BREF BAT determinations generates real effects of power. It contributes to the construction of procedures for determining BAT. These were fluid, flexible and constantly evolving. They were also characterised by a blurring of distinctions between technical and political issues. But what can this tell us about the nature of power in BREF BAT determinations?

What concept of power is implied in a political discourse concerning BAT?

As discussed in chapter 4, some 'law in action' research has invoked modernist conceptions of power as mediating relations between a 'social' and a 'legal' world. But a political discourse in BREF BAT determinations was multi-faceted. It contained elements of both modernist and post-structuralist conceptions of power. From a modernist perspective, power is understood as a commodity possessed and wielded by 'powerful actors' and 'key players'. Hence power is personalised. In response to accountability and transparency issues raised in BREF writing, a political discourse also provided certain categories of 'actors' in BAT determinations. In modernist terms power is also understood as a structuring device and hence as a restraint on other actors' agency. Here power is a relationship between those who have it and those who don't (Minson, 1986 : 111).

Modernist conceptions of power, and especially relationships between power and interests, have informed some socio-legal studies of EC law-making (see, for example, Snyder, 1989). Some of these studies are informed by a macro-sociological analysis of 'objective' interests which flow from structures. Such interests are considered as important determinants of law-making processes even though they may not be specifically articulated by actors (ibid.: 184). Class interests are considered as a key example of such 'objective' interests (ibid.: 182). 'Objective' interests are seen as an important analytical advance over the notion of merely 'subjective' interests which are expressions of 'individual consciousness' (ibid.: 182). Social structures are emphasised here as one important factor in shaping social processes (ibid.: 191).

In contrast, post-modernist accounts of power are less interested in questions such as: Where does power come from? Who is powerful? What economic and political structures shape actors' behaviour? Instead, for post-structuralist analysis the key question has become: 'What are the effects of power?' (Smart, 2002: 77). In particular, power is not merely considered as restraining, but also as productive. 'Actors' and 'subjects' are constituted by relations of power (Wickham, 1986: 155). Power can actually enhance the forces of those subjected to power, through discourses of resistance, for example (Minson, 1986: 109). Post-modernist accounts of power make an important contribution to 'law in action' research. Often these focus on modernist conceptions of power by analysing organisations' internal rules as an important element of the 'law in action'. Such internal rules and procedures are thought to create effects of social control, considered as a key aspect of the 'living law'. This social control version of power in 'law in action' emphasises the restraining rather than the constitutive effects of power. Here power is the capacity to dominate other social actors. It presupposes that there are 'subjects' or 'actors' which possess power and can exercise it over other social actors. But what characteristics of power did the political discourse invoked by participants in BREF drafting emphasise?

The idea that modernist power structures are at play in BAT determinations is expressed in particular through the notion that there are specific, identifiable, unified, homogeneous power blocs influencing BREF BAT determinations. For instance, participants in BREF determinations were often identified as 'representatives for EU trade associations',[82] 'member states' and the 'environmental NGO', the EEB, or simply as 'industry' and 'regulator'. Reference to 'industry' and 'regulator' was a shorthand for commercial and environmental protection interests in BAT determinations. Participants in BREF writing also sometimes referred to 'North' and 'South' as power blocs influencing BAT determinations. Some expressed concerns that BAT determinations were overly dominated by the regulatory approaches and perspectives of Northern EU member states. The EIPPC Bureau was thought to host too many BREF writers from Northern European countries. Moreover, member states such as the Netherlands, Sweden, Austria, Germany and the UK were perceived as particularly vociferous and influential in TWG discussions. Hence political and economic power structures were also considered as significant in BAT determinations through the interests to which they gave rise and which were expressed in

BREF writing. Interests were here regarded as flowing from power structures and hence implied a conceptualisation of power in material terms.

But such a conceptualisation of power in structural terms served further purposes in BAT determinations. It was part of a discourse of resistance to existing BAT determination procedures. Structural conceptions of power were often invoked by those who perceived themselves as less 'powerful' in the BAT definition process, such as Southern EU member states and the EEB. The identification of specific power structures was often part of a discourse of critique aimed at changing BAT determination procedures towards 'fairer', 'more balanced' and 'transparent' procedures.

But the concept of power invoked by participants in BREF BAT determinations also went beyond modernist conceptions. It did not just refer to the restraining effects of power but also referred to the constitutive and productive effects of a political discourse. A political discourse included talk about various small-scale tactics and strategies of power which were utilised not just by traditionally 'powerful actors' but by a whole range of participants in BREF writing. In addition, talk about shifting interest coalitions and the fragmentation of interests questioned the idea of stable and fixed power structures. Moreover, reference to the sheer variety and complexity in BAT determinations across various BREFs put in question a notion of clear power structures shaping BAT determinations. For instance, BREF writers suggested that 'industry' had significantly shaped BAT determinations for some sectors of industry. But TWGs for other sectors of industry were portrayed as heavily influenced by individual BREF writers striving to enshrine ambitious BAT standards in the BREF.[83]

Conclusion

This chapter has analysed power relations in BREF BAT determinations by reference to a political discourse. This discourse matters. It generates effects of power. It constructs procedures for determining BAT which are evolving, flexible and characterised by blurred distinctions between political and technical issues in defining BAT. Technology standards in EU Framework Directives can be conceptualised as procedural norms (see e.g. Scott, 2000). The micro-level analysis developed in this chapter suggests that procedures for BAT determinations could be unsettled.

The political discourse invoked by participants in BREF BAT determinations is complex and multi-faceted. It highlights the subtleties of power relations in BAT determinations. It contains elements of modernist conceptions by personalising power as a commodity wielded by powerful 'experts' in BAT determinations. But it also chimes with some aspects of post-structuralist perspectives by drawing attention to small-scale tactics and strategies of power also invoked by those who are not 'structurally powerful' and by pointing to fragmented and overlapping interests. Moreover, some BREF writers regarded interests merely as specific and malleable *perceptions* of actors' relationships with their social environments, rather than as objective and material social facts determined by external social structures and attributable to specific groups of actors, such as 'industry' and 'member states'. This analysis contributes to existing accounts of 'law in action' which often invoke modernist conceptions of power as mediating intersections between a 'social' and a 'legal' sphere.

Notes

1. All BREF documents for specific industrial sectors, the so-called vertical BREF documents, have a standard structure. This comprises an executive summary, a preface and a brief introductory chapter 1 containing general information about the industry sector regulated by the IPPC Directive. Chapter 2, entitled 'Applied Processes and Techniques' describes the production processes currently employed in the particular industrial sector. Chapter 3 reports current levels of emissions to the environment from these production processes and levels of consumption, e.g. of raw materials. Chapter 4 which used to be called 'BAT candidates' discusses 'techniques to consider in the determination of BAT'. Hence this chapter lists the range of techniques which may be considered as BAT. Chapter 5 lists those techniques which have been identified as '*the* best available techniques'. Chapter 6 discusses 'emerging techniques', which are novel pollution prevention and control techniques. Chapter 7 presents the conclusion. See http://eippcb.jrc.es/pages/Boutline.htm
2. See chapter 1 for a further description of the process of writing BREFs.
3. Debates in the TWGs were held in English without translation facilities, partly because of cost considerations.
4. The Commission finally decided that the executive summary of all BREFs would be translated in all of the official EU languages. Some member states financed at their own expense the complete translation of the BREFs into their own language. For instance, some BREF documents have been translated into Polish, Spanish and Lithuanian (Entec Report, 2006: 74, 170).
5. These were generated through transcripts of interviews, notes of informal conversations between the researcher and various participants in BREF writing and extracts from the EIPPC Bureau's background files on BREF drafting.

6. During a discussion of the detailed wording of the 'standard preface' which introduced each BREF document the following statement was made: 'the term "negotiation" seemed to cause some difficulty'. Quote from the official minutes of the 5th IEF meeting, 18–19 February 1999.
7. Quote from interview no. 12 with EIPPC Bureau management.
8. Quote from the official minutes of the 6th meeting of the IEF forum, 29–30 September 1999.
9. Interview no. 2 with BREF writer.
10. See official minutes of the 18th meeting of the IEF, 4 October 2006.
11. Interview no. 13 with member of DG Environment.
12. Interview no. 8 with BREF writer.
13. Interview no. 12 with EIPPC Bureau management.
14. There were also references to the impact of other national environmental policy priorities on BAT determinations in BREFs, such as a member state's 'very sensitive landfill policy'. Moreover, national environmental policy preferences were recognised as shaped by national taxes, fees and subsidies, as well as cost and availability of water and energy.
15. Interview no. 4 with BREF writer.
16. 65 per cent of the production of cattle and calf leather originated from Italy in the EU of fifteen member states.
17. The nomination of experts from industry to Technical Working Groups by some member states continued to be perceived as a problem by the EIPPC Bureau; and the IEF, which confirms members of TWGs, was invited to address this issue (see official notes of the 18th meeting of the IEF, 4 October 2006).
18. Alliances between the EEB and industry were considered as unusual. This is also illustrated through an entry in the official minutes for the 7th IEF meeting, 28–29 February 2000 which reads: 'In an unprecedented move that triggered widespread laughter, the EEB gave its wholehearted support to UNICE in their criticism of the procedure' [for determining BAT].
19. There are 41 integrated iron and steel works left in the old EU. Corus – one of the operators – has plants in the UK, the Netherlands, Germany, France, Norway and Belgium.
20. EU-wide representation of farming interests could also build on strong national lobbying organisations such as the National Farmers Union (NFU) in the UK and the *Deutscher Bauernverband* in Germany. Also in response to lobbying from the UK NFU, the UK regulator adopted a system of 'standard rules' rather than a BREF note in order to define BAT for UK intensive livestock operations. These 'standard rules' are less detailed than a BREF note and can reduce compliance costs for operators in the sector.
21. The IPPC Directive subdivides the sector into organic and inorganic chemicals production, as well as fertiliser, basic plant health and biocides production, production of basic pharmaceutical products and explosives production (Annex I, Article 1, No. 4).
22. See official minutes of the 7th IEF meeting, 28–29 February 2000.

23. For instance, sections of the text of the German Engineers Association (VDI = *Verein Deutscher Ingenieure*) on BAT for graphite production was scanned into the draft BREF for the non-ferrous metal sector. The VDI is the main association representing German engineers. It also contributes to environmental policy and rule-making in Germany (see: http://www.vdi/de/vdi/english/index.php). Sections of the Dutch national BREF note on iron and steel making were also transferred to the draft BREF for the iron and steel sector.

24. This issue was raised specifically by a member state representative in relation to the flow of information in sub-groups of the non-ferrous metal TWG. He was concerned that some technical documents were exchanged only between industry representatives and the BREF writer, excluding member state representatives (e-mail exchange print-out in EIPPC Bureau background file).

25. Restrictions on the supply of information by industry was often referred to by BREF writers as 'game' playing. In the words of the EIPPC Bureau management: 'Process secrets can be revealed if they go into details of how they recycle dust, *they have their little tricks* to hide this information' (emphasis added).

26. Official minutes of the 7th IEF meeting, 28–29 February 2000.

27. There were usually two main meetings of the full Technical Working Group for the drafting of each BREF. The first, kick-off meeting and the second and final meeting in which the text of the whole BREF document was agreed.

28. The construction of 'active' and 'passive' members of TWGs was also promoted through extensive strategies of informal information management by BREF writers. BREF writers would choose with whom to consult informally – beyond the official 1st and 2nd TWG meeting – in order to discuss draft BREF chapters. They relied on informal communications through e-mails, telephone calls, site visits and lunches with a number of experts whom they considered as providing helpful input into the process of writing the BREFs.

29. The study focused on the cement and lime, non-ferrous metals as well as pulp and paper sectors covered by the IPPC Directive. These sectors were some of the first for which BREFs had been written.

30. The *Umweltbundesamt* (UBA). It does not carry out regulatory functions, but its main task is to provide scientific knowledge and advice to the German federal government in connection with the development of environmental policy and law. For further information see the UBA's website at http://www.umweltbundesamt.de/.

31. For a copy of the conference proceedings see the EIPPC Bureau webpages at http://eippcb.jr.es/pages/doc/Stuttgart.pdf.

32. The De Vito Institute had been involved in writing national BAT guidance documents covering certain sectors of Belgian industry.

33. Copy of e-mail from BREF writer to another TWG member, dated 16.2.1998, in EIPPC Bureau background files for BREFs.

34. Quote from interview with EIPPC Bureau management. In the EIPPC Bureau's background files for the different BREFs there were also records of submissions from various trade associations asking for more 'transparency' and 'objectivity' in the BREF writing process.
35. Quote from interview no. 1 with BREF writer.
36. This occurred, for instance, in the BREF for the pulp and paper sector where data were submitted to the BREF writer after the second TWG meeting (see official notes of 5th IEF meeting, 18–19 February 1999).
37. http://eippcb.jrc.es/pages/Boutline.htm.
38. Official minutes of the 6th IEF meeting, 29–30 September 1999.
39. Quote from interview no. 1 with BREF writer.
40. These were officially recorded in the BREFs. For an example of 'split views' see the conclusions about NOx (nitrogen oxides) and dust abatement for the cement industry in the cement and lime BREF, at http://eippcb.jrc/es/pages/FActivities.htm.
41. Statement by an EU-wide trade association representing the whole range of EU trade associations [UNICE], Official notes of the 5th IEF meeting, 18–19 February 1999.
42. Interview no. 4 with BREF writer.
43. Extract from a discussion about ways to achieve greater consistency between BAT definitions expressed in various BREFs for the different industrial sectors (from EIPPC Bureau background files on BREF drafting).
44. For instance, BREF writers replied to some interview questions about the procedure for writing BREFs that they had already asked themselves the same questions.
45. For instance, strategies of time management could mean that simply the lack or availability of time would shape what BAT definition would be adopted. Moreover, failures in complex communication networks which were generated by BAT determinations were another example of BAT determinations by default.
46. Quote from interview no. 8 with BREF writer. Also Germany's and the Netherlands' contribution to the ammonia production pilot BREF suggested that especially at the beginning of the BREF writing process these two countries wanted to apply a full scientific and structured methodology approach to BAT determinations.
47. Nitrogen oxides emissions.
48. Sulphur oxide emissions.
49. Quote from interview no. 8 with BREF writer.
50. Quote from official minutes of 6th IEF meeting, 29–30 September 1999.
51. Interview no. 8 with BREF writer.
52. One exception to this was the horizontal BREF on monitoring for which no sub-groups had been organised.
53. The European Chemical Association organised eight sub-groups which covered different aspects of large volume organic chemicals production. Here the BREF writer had only limited involvement with these sub-groups.

54. Interview no. 3 with BREF writer. In some BREFs EU trade associations asked for member state representatives to chair meetings of the sub-groups in order to ensure a 'balance of interests'. But sometimes member states declined to do so and did not attend further sub-group meetings in Brussels beyond the plenary TWG meetings, partly because of financial and staffing resource implications.

55. Such as all of the sub-groups for the non-ferrous metals BREF. Also the horizontal BREF for cross-media and cost issues involved three sub-groups which included both industry and member state representatives.

56. *Unterarbeitsgruppe Kohlenstoffproduktion.*

57. *Länderarbeitsgruppe Immissionsschutz* – states' working group for protection against emissions. This was a national German working group which comprised staff from environmental regulatory authorities from the different *Länder* and from companies who specialise in air pollution controls. The group had been set up in order to coordinate air pollution control work across the different *Länder* in Germany. Similar groups also existed for water and waste pollution issues.

58. Austria similarly set up national sub-groups which mirrored EU-wide TWG sub-groups and which also included representatives from industry.

59. At the beginning of the BREF drafting process DG Enterprise suggested that it would carry out 'cost-benefit' analysis of some BAT standards in the draft BREFs in order to counter the 'environmentally driven' BAT determinations in the EIPPC Bureau (extract from notes on EIPPC Bureau background files).

60. DG Environment distinguished between two types of 'experts' associated with the EIPPC Bureau in BREF writing: First, experts who had experience in BAT licensing from having worked in national regulatory authorities, and who would be employed by the EIPPC Bureau as BREF writers, who coordinate the work of the TWGs. Second, there were also experts who would provide more specialised expertise and who could contribute specific sections of a BREF. These experts would be more likely to be found in industry and could be recruited for a shorter period of time, such as a couple of weeks. They were not necessarily based in the EIPPC Bureau in Seville (see official minutes of the third IEF meeting, 3 July 1997). The EIPPC Bureau's background files contained notes of approaches from the EIPPC Bureau management to EU trade associations for the recruitment of such experts. The financial arrangements suggested by the EIPPC Bureau management were 'normal EC terms for invited experts'. This meant that the Bureau would pay travel and subsistence and the EU trade association would pay the consulting fee for the expert. Another e-mail suggested that the consulting fee could be shared between different companies in the sector. Such a recruitment of industry experts, however, seemed to occur only to a limited degree. An industry expert, for instance, was employed for a short period of time by the EIPPC Bureau for the BREF on non-ferrous metals.

61. See, for example, calls by Germany for an 'active role' to be played by 'an author' in the information exchange (official minutes of the 17th IEF meeting, 17–18 November 2005).
62. E-mail dated 10.07.1998 from member state to BREF writer, extracted from the EIPPC Bureau's background files on BREF writing. In its response to this member state's concerns, the EIPPC Bureau management insisted that they actually were 'authoring' the BREFs.
63. Various expressions were used to refer to this 'neutrality' of the EIPPC Bureau, including the terms 'independent of outside influences' (official minutes of the 3rd IEF meeting, 3 July 1997). See also the – later slightly modified – official 'Overall Organisation and Working Procedures for the Exchange of Information under Art. 16 (2) IPPC Directive': 'The Bureau is a neutral entity that provides technical and administrative support to the TWGs'. 'The Bureau collects information from all TWG members and other sources, and compiles this into (elements of) draft BREFs that can iteratively be assessed by TWG members.'
64. The EIPPC Bureau was established early in 1997. It was a project within the Institute for Prospective Technological Studies (IPTS) in Seville, Spain. In fact the EIPPC Bureau was a sub-project of the 'Technologies for Sustainable Development' group within IPTS. IPTS, in turn, is a part of the DG Joint Research Centre of the Commission. DG Environment put out an open call for tenders for the EIPPC Bureau for which all the eight different Institutes from the Joint Research Centre could bid.
65. Initially a number of different options for organising the 'exchange of information' were discussed. Once IPTS had been successful in the tendering procedure for the EIPPC Bureau, various staff from IPTS presented different ideas for the organisation of the Bureau. One idea was that during the first year of the operation of the EIPPC Bureau there would be two Bureau coordinators. Each of the Bureau coordinators would be responsible for 2 BREFs. External contractors, such as consultants, would assist these coordinators in the writing of the BREFs (draft note from a member of staff in IPTS to the IPTS Director, extracted from the EIPPC Bureau background files).
66. The Commission also continued to reimburse travel expenses for EEB representatives to attend TWG meetings in Seville after it had abolished these reimbursements for member state and industry representatives on account of limited resources.
67. Quote from the official minutes of the 6th IEF meeting, 29–30 September 1999.
68. TWG sub-groups were formed for a number of reasons, often for that of managing the sheer complexity and comprehensive scope of BREF writing. For instance, the BREF for the non-ferrous metal sector covered BAT techniques for ten different metals, such as copper, zinc, nickel, aluminium, mercury and others. In order to facilitate sufficiently detailed discussion within limited time sub-groups were formed for seven of the metals.

69. For instance, there were difficulties in agreeing the official 'BREF Preface' which explains the status and nature of the BREFs and is included as standard introductory text for all BREFs. It took the EIPPC Bureau a long time to get this official BREF preface approved and there were several attempts by TWG members to reopen debate about the wording of the BREF preface.

70. One BREF writer stated that he was looking for 'tatsächliche, nachweisbare Sachen' (factual matters that can be proved). Quote from interview no. 11 with BREF writer.

71. Quote from official minutes of the 5th IEF meeting, 18–19 February 1999.

72. Quote from interview no. 12 with EIPPC Bureau management.

73. In this particular case certain paper mills were identified: quote from the official minutes of the 5th IEF meeting, 18–19 February 1999. The shadow group on coke making for the iron and steel industry also initially suggested that no names of companies and countries should be mentioned in the final BREF and that presentation of emission data or specific performance should remain anonymous (from EIPPC Bureau background files on BREF drafting).

74. For instance, 60 site visits were carried out for collecting and 'validating' information for the BREF on non-ferrous metals production (see official minutes of the 16th IEF meeting, 23–24 June 2005 and official minutes of the 7th IEF meeting, 28–29 February 2000).

75. The EEB coordinated the participation of delegates for various national environmental NGOs, such as Friends of the Earth UK as well as Dutch and German environmental groups.The EIPPC Bureau publishes the complete lists of membership of TWGs for each BREF on its website, including the names and organisational affiliation of each member. For further information see http://eippcb.jrc.es/.

76. For example, there was often debate about the interpretation of the capacity thresholds for various industrial activities spelt out in Annex I to the IPPC Directive. These capacity thresholds were sometimes unclear and required further interpretation. Their interpretation decided whether the legal obligations of the IPPC Directive applied to a particular process or not. Another policy issue was the interpretation of the term 'directly associated activities' in Art. 2 (3) of the IPPC Directive which expands on the concept of 'installation' to which the IPPC Directive applies.

77. As required by Art. 16 (2) of the IPPC Directive.

78. Quote from EIPPC Bureau background file for BREF writing.

79. Abbreviation for the Institute for Prospective Technological Studies, a sub-unit of DG Research, based in Seville, Spain.

80. Extract from background file from EIPPC Bureau. A number of member states were concerned about the participation of industry in BREF drafting when the initial organisational structure for BREF writing was discussed. For instance, the Netherlands advocated staffing the EIPPC Bureau solely with civil servants seconded from member state environmental ministries (note from EIPPC Bureau background file).

81. See also the following statement in the official minutes of the 16th meeting of the IEF, 23–24 June 2005: 11: 'The Commission also stressed that technical discussions could not take place in the context of the IEF at this late stage of the elaboration of the BREF.'
82. Such as, for instance, EUROFER representing EU iron and steel industries at http://www.eurofer.org/.
83. For instance in the pulp and paper and cement and lime BREF.

6 Variation in open and closed BAT norms

Introduction

Chapters 2 and 3 analysed how law is conceptualised in the various contributions to the literature on EU integration. Chapter 2 identified a traditional approach which draws in particular on images of law generated by official supranational and national legal systems themselves. This perspective interprets law as formal, instrumental and relatively autonomous in relation to its social contexts. Chapter 3 examined critical perspectives which suggest that EU law has now assumed various forms. I argued that these critical perspectives abandon instrumental and relatively autonomous conceptions of law only to a limited extent. Even if the term 'law' is employed to refer to a variety of norms beyond official EU and member state law, law is still regarded as a clearly delimited domain with a specific normative content, although, in the case of soft law, this content is not formally legally binding.

This chapter further develops the discussion about the nature of EU law. It argues that implementation of the EU Directive on Integrated Pollution Prevention and Control in practice generates various types of EU law. It generates open and closed BAT norms. According to the IPPC Directive's key legal obligation operators of mainly industrial installations have to employ 'the best available techniques'.[1] Sometimes, there is a clear and specific definition of what the 'best available techniques' are, either for a whole industrial sector or for a specific installation. But at other times there is no specific, clear outcome to BAT determination processes.

This empirical discovery of variation in open and closed BAT norms is significant. It questions three key assumptions of traditional and of some critical approaches to conceptualising law in EU integration. It queries the idea of relatively autonomous law because open norms are not entirely abstracted and differentiated from a social sphere. It questions the notion of instrumental law because a focus on a discrete outcome such as a specific prescription of techniques, is lacking in open BAT norms. It also questions the equation of EU law with formal law because variation in open and closed BAT norms suggests that *implementation practices* can be an important source of norms. Law in EU integration is not just the law which can be found in the 'law books'. In practice social actors' views of what constitutes a norm are another source of law, in addition to the procedures which the formal legal system provides for identifying authoritative sources of 'law'.

The first section of this chapter explains why variation in open and closed BAT norms is an interesting empirical finding. The second section defines the term 'variation' in 'open' and 'closed' norms. The third and main section discusses the role of technical and political discourses in generating variation in open and closed BAT norms. The final section summarises the chapter's argument.

Why does variation in open and closed BAT norms matter?

The idea that the IPPC Directive does not produce highly specific, determinate normative obligations is nothing new. Mere analysis of its text suggests that the Directive is 'open' because it defines its legal obligations only in outline (Hey and Taschner, 1998: 30). Since the IPPC Directive is a Framework Directive it does not impose its own specific limit values for emissions of pollutants to air, water or land. Instead Art. 3 (a) of the Directive requires member states to ensure that installations are operated in accordance with 'the best available techniques'. It is for local permitting authorities to determine in an IPPC licence what emission limit values – if any – should be achieved by the installation. Art. 18 (2) of the IPPC Directive only requires that emission limit values imposed in IPPC licences must at least achieve those specified in a range of other existing EU environmental Directives.[2]

It is also clear from the text of the Directive that – as a technology norm – BAT is to some degree open to a social sphere. It draws on a range of social actors' practices in the field. First, BAT determinations draw on actual practices of operating technologies at installations, including management and maintenance routines. Second, the way an installation is run often reflects earlier social practices of regulatory decision-making by operators and regulators. Third, BAT determinations are linked to the social practices of technological innovation. New techniques developed by equipment suppliers may be considered as BAT. Fourth, Art. 2 (11) of the IPPC Directive also opens up BAT definitions to social practices. The costs of techniques are taken into account when deciding whether a technique is 'available'. Hence the social practices of economic accounting for production processes are a factor in BAT determinations. But the analysis developed in this chapter differs – in three ways – from these first initial impressions of an open legal framework generated by the text of the IPPC Directive. First, it moves beyond an examination of the Directive text alone by drawing on detailed qualitative empirical data on the practical implementation of the IPPC Directive. Second, the chapter discusses not just open, but also closed BAT norms. Third, the chapter does not just highlight the existence of both open and closed BAT norms. It also explores *how* and *when* specific technological operations and management practices acquire a normative, prescriptive dimension by being recognised as '*the* best available techniques' and how and when such final BAT determinations are not achieved. To summarise: an analysis of variation in open and closed BAT norms matters because it counters an initial impression of an open legal framework generated by the text of the IPPC Directive.

But variation in open and closed BAT norms is also an empirically puzzling finding. Open BAT norms were pervasive, although participants in BAT determination processes expressed clear expectations that there should be at least some degree of closure in BAT determinations:

This sentiment was echoed by France, who suggested that a BREF without any selection or hierarchy [of techniques] would be pointless.[3]

Hence identifying the 'best available techniques' in the BREFs was understood as a process of whittling down a whole range of possible BAT candidates to one or a few specific BAT techniques:

From these 200 you go down to about 50. And that means that here on average maybe you have 4 types of techniques for each process. And then my idea will be to challenge those techniques and to try, if it is possible, to really define which is the best one. Yes, the star technique is the BAT.[4]

This expectation of closure and the perception of BAT determinations as a process of selecting a specific or at least a limited range of BAT techniques is also enshrined in the structure of the BREFs. Chapter 3 of each BREF describes all techniques that are currently used in the EU for reducing emissions in a particular industrial sector. Chapter 4 then contains a smaller selection of the better performing techniques, previously described as 'BAT candidates', now referred to as 'techniques to consider in the determination of BAT'. Chapter 5 contains an even more narrowly defined selection of techniques, *the best* available techniques', called 'BAT conclusion'. There is thus an assumption that BAT norms in BREFs are gradually closed, not by being just site specific, but also by providing standards for all installations in an entire industrial sector.

At the local implementation level clear expectations were also expressed that there should be a degree of closure in BAT norms in IPPC permits. Where there was a degree of openness in BAT norms, such as in UK site licence conditions which asked the operator to carry out improvements to the installation, there were attempts to reintroduce a degree of closure. For instance, the EA's internal work instructions suggest that improvement conditions should be specific, rather than open and vague:

Where an improvement condition is to be included, it should be *clear in its intent* and be *explicit in the end result required*. Where the requirement is for investigation into alternatives (and recommendations) and subsequent implementation the subsequent phases *should be split into separate improvement conditions*.

(emphasis added)

Open BAT norms are also an empirically puzzling finding because there is no shortage of legal standards which could be used to close BAT norms. There are now many legal provisions and guidance which can help to find a specific conclusion to a BAT determination. First, there are EU Directives, national primary and secondary legislation as well as tertiary rules, such as the technical instruction air (TA *Luft*) in Germany. Second, a range of BAT guidance documents are available, such as the EU-wide BREFs, UK national guidance notes as well as BAT guidance developed by industrial associations, such as the European Fertilizer Manufacturing Association and the European Cement Association. Third, there are also private self-regulatory norms, such as industry sector voluntary agreements. They concern, for instance, the phasing out of mercury[5] and solvent emissions as well as lead stabilisers in PVC production.[6] Fourth, both the UK and German regulatory authority have developed internal organisational rules for how to achieve BAT determinations. So, why – despite this thicket of legal rules, formal guidance and policy – do BAT norms still sometimes remain open ? Before further addressing this question, I would like to clarify what I mean by 'open' and 'closed' BAT norms.

Defining variation in open and closed BAT norms

Variation in open and closed BAT norms suggests that the practical implementation of the key legal obligation under the IPPC Directive – namely that operators must use 'the best available techniques' – generated a *variety of different types of norms*. The term 'best available techniques' in the IPPC Directive text refers to a technology norm. But in practice social actors invoked the BAT concept in order to refer to a range of different normative phenomena. So what do I mean by 'open' and 'closed' BAT norms?

Defining open BAT norms

In the case of open BAT norms a closed, self-contained determination of what actually amounts to the best available techniques for a whole industrial sector or a specific installation does not finally crystallise. There is no identification of '*the best* available techniques'. No specific techniques are abstracted and singled out from the whole range of possible techniques. In EU and national guidance documents open BAT norms are merely a *description* of the social world – of a whole range of operating practices currently adopted in an industrial sector. Social actors in the field also consider open BAT norms as lacking prescriptive force. I use the term 'BAT norm' to refer to BAT determinations which are legally binding because they are enshrined in member states' statutes, secondary legislation, tertiary rules[7] and in IPPC site licence conditions. But I also use the term 'BAT norm' for BAT determinations which have simply the *potential* to be legally binding,[8] such as BAT determinations in BREFs and UK national guidance documents.[9]

Here is an example of an open BAT norm at the local installation level. The Environment Agency (EA) often inserts improvement conditions into IPPC licences for existing sites.[10] These improvement conditions do not specify a particular BAT norm. Instead they may require the operator to collect further information about a particular aspect of his/her installation and then to outline to the regulator various BAT options for preventing or minimising emissions:

An improvement condition requires assessment for reduction in emissions of nitrogenoxides, particulates and nitrogendioxide.[11]

For that aspect of operations dealt with through the improvement condition a specific BAT norm will only be inserted at a later date, once the information has been gathered and the various BAT options have been assessed. In contrast, a specific, closed BAT norm may require the achievement of a precise emission limit value for nitrogen oxides of $20\,mg/m^3$ of air flow. Improvement conditions are an example of open BAT norms because they project BAT determinations into the future.[12]

BAT norms can be open to varying degrees. First, they vary in the extent to which they identify specific pollutants to be controlled. Some improvement conditions, such as the one above, already identify particular pollutants for control. But other improvement conditions could be even more open and unspecified. For instance, emissions to sea from the same IPPC installation were regarded as complex.[13] For these emissions the specific pollutants which needed to be controlled through BAT techniques had not yet been identified. The IPPC permit simply contained an improvement condition which required the operator to carry out a Direct Toxicity Assessment in order to find out more about these emissions.[14] Second, BAT norms vary in how open they are, depending on whether there is a timetable for their implementation. Some improvement conditions did not contain a timetable by which the BAT norm had to be implemented. In one Decision Document this was referred to in the following terms:

The operator has said that improvements in burner arrangements/configurations were planned over the next several years and this is where reductions in NOx emissions from ammonia plant were to come from. There were no step changes, but only gradual improvements over time, and the company could not at this stage give commitments to reductions and timings.[15]

Other improvement conditions simply asked the operator to come up with a timetable for the implementation of the BAT norm. At other times the improvement condition already contained a timetable for implementation which had been negotiated between the operator and the EA.

Rendering BAT norms open by projecting BAT determinations into the future also occurred during IPPC licensing activities in the German regulatory authority. Sometimes specific emission limit values for pollutants were inserted into site licences, though – in particular for new sites – the precise quantity of actual emissions from the process was not yet known. Hence the BAT norm remained open because it was not clear whether actual practices at the plant would conform to this abstract BAT standard. While the German regulatory authority inserted conditions into the licence which required the operator to provide emission data once the process had started, it could take some time before such actual measurement data were forthcoming.[16]

Defining closed BAT norms

BAT norms are closed when a specific conclusion is reached in response to attempts to pin down, specify and render concise what 'the best available techniques' for an industrial sector or a particular installation are. For instance, a closed BAT norm prescribes a particular pollution abatement technology for an installation, such as a bag filter for limiting dust emissions to air. It also imposes a specific emission limit value in the site licence, such as $10 \, mg/m^3$ of dust, which has to be achieved during the operation of the dust filter. A closed BAT norm also includes reference to an agreed, validated measurement procedure for determining in practice the quantity of emissions.

BAT norms can be closed to varying degrees. A closed BAT norm does not necessarily imply that just one particular technique has been identified. This is particularly unlikely in the case of BAT determinations for a whole industrial sector, such as in the EU-wide BREFs or in national guidance notes or binding rules. Sometimes sector-wide BAT determinations refer to just one or two techniques. Often they involve reference to a number of techniques. These are, however, specific and limited, since they are the techniques which are employed in the environmentally top performing installations in a sector:

It is not *the* best available technique because that would not be accepted, but it is the top 10% of the installations.

(emphasis in the original)[17]

Moreover, in contrast to open BAT norms, closed BAT norms are to some extent abstracted and differentiated from a social sphere. They are therefore also considered as having more of a prescriptive force. In particular BREF writers associated BAT norm closure with BAT techniques being applied to all or most installations in a sector. To refer to a technique as BAT means that it is no longer just one example of a particular abatement technology used at a specific plant.[18] Instead it becomes the norm for other installations in that sector. The possibility of BAT norm closure was expressed in various ways. Some BREF writers said that it was sometimes simply 'obvious' what the BAT for a sector or an installation is.[19] Moreover, some participants in BAT determinations suggested that they sometimes intuitively[20] recognised that a particular technique was the BAT for a sector or an installation. They knew a BAT when they saw one.[21]

Recourse to technology norms which had been defined and closed under previous environmental regulatory regimes were another source of closed BAT norms. Most IPPC licensing work[22] consists of bringing existing installations into the IPPC regime, also by applying BAT to the site. A lot of German and UK existing sites had been regulated under previous pollution control regimes which also applied technology norms. In the UK, according to section 7 (2) (a) of the Environmental Protection Act 1990 operators are required to employ 'the best available techniques not entailing excessive costs' (BATNEEC). In Germany operators were required according to paragraph 5 (2) of the BimSchG to employ the 'Stand der Technik', i.e. state of the art technology.[23] There are some differences between the legal definitions of 'Stand der Technik' and BATNEEC on the one hand, and the new IPPC BAT concept on the other hand.[24] But both German and English permitting officers suggested that IPPC BAT was 'basically the same'[25] as the previous national concepts. Hence BAT determinations for existing IPPC installations would often refer back to the closed technology norms and emission levels through which the site had been regulated under previous pollution control regimes.[26] To summarise: this section has defined the terms 'variation in open and closed norms'. But is it really possible to distinguish 'open' from 'closed' BAT norms?

Can open and closed BAT norms really be distinguished ?

Literature on the indeterminacy of law argues that legal rules can be 'open', even if they seem to have been phrased in a precise manner in a legal text (see, for example, Endicott, 2001). So, why refer to 'open' as well as 'closed' BAT norms in order to capture a key finding of empirical research into the implementation of the IPPC Directive? It is clear that there are limits to any attempt to draw sharp distinctions between open and closed BAT norms. As discussed above, BAT norms could be open or closed to varying degrees.[27] Moreover, openness and closure in BAT norms is not necessarily mutually exclusive. For instance, some elements of BAT norms in the EU BREFs and UK sector guidance notes can be closed, while other elements of the BAT definition can remain open. A BAT norm may identify a specific or limited range of BAT techniques, and hence be closed. But it may be opened up again through a very wide range of emissions being associated with the specific technique or limited range of techniques. For example, a fabric filter may be considered as the BAT for the reduction of dust emissions, but the range of dust emissions to be achieved can be very wide, ranging, for instance, from $10\,\mathrm{mg/m^3}$ to $500\,\mathrm{mg/m^3}$. Thus while some elements of a BAT determination are closed, others are open.[28]

Moreover, there were ongoing debates about how closed or open BAT *should* be, for instance in the Information Exchange Forum during the drafting of the BREF documents.[29] Hence it appears that for actors in the field too there is no sharp differentiation between open and closed BAT norms. Some BREF writers did not strive to produce a fully closed BAT determination. They suggested that a 'good' BAT determination is not about identifying a single BAT technique for a sector or inserting a 'general, bureaucratic figure [for emissions] in the BREF'. Instead good practice – in their view – required them to pay attention to specific, local circumstances and to provide enough information about these in a BREF in order to specify more precisely an abstract, general and thus closed BAT norm which aims to be applicable to a whole industrial sector.[30] But BREF writers also expressed concern about this potentially slippery slope which starts with 'good BAT determinations' – sensitive to local contexts and thus qualified – but ends with the kind of very open BAT norms advocated by some industry associations.

Finally, I do not refer to 'open' and 'closed' BAT norms as sharply differentiated concepts because clear distinctions between open and closed BAT norms also became blurred in the actual discursive strategies employed in BAT determinations. For instance, arguing for open BAT norms was also a tactic for achieving some degree of closure of BAT in BREFs. From time to time DG Environment and the EIPPC Bureau management emphasised that BAT determinations in BREFs were not necessarily fully closed norms, but could be open to some degree through qualifications of BAT conclusions, for instance. This view of BAT norms was intended to facilitate agreement and hence achievement of a BAT conclusion among participants in BREF drafting. Moreover, member states were considered to be more likely to deviate from EU BAT norms in their national IPPC implementation strategies, if very specific, closed BAT determinations were written into the EU BREFs:

And the narrower the ranges we agree on that are BAT, I think the more likely that various regulators would choose a national approach. The wider the range and the more qualification, that is really site specific, the less likely that people try to use another approach.[31]

Hence the EIPPC Bureau management considered a degree of openness in BAT norms – seemingly paradoxically – as facilitating some BAT norm closure, and thus EU-wide harmonisation. To conclude: I use the terms open and closed BAT norms not to imply that these are two sharply differentiated concepts, but to highlight that BAT norms can be envisaged as situated on a sliding scale with various degrees of openness and closure. While there may not be fully closed BAT norms – as the perspective of radical indeterminacy suggests – it is clear that participants in BAT determinations identified BAT norms which varied in their degree of openness. Some were less open than others. But why are there different types of BAT norms?

Why and how are open and closed BAT norms generated during the implementation of the IPPC Directive?

BAT determinations involve discursive processes. Language, in the form of written and oral communications, is crucial for specifying BAT. For instance, BAT definitions in the BREFs are the outcome of drafting detailed and sometimes lengthy documents running to several hundred pages.[32] Identifying BAT is achieved through close work on the text of these BREF documents, something which is also required in order to resolve differences of opinion:[33]

If the differences of opinion here could be solved by merely changing the words used, an effort should be made to do this.[34]

Participants in BAT determinations actively develop and construct BAT discourse. The text of the IPPC Directive provides the basic vocabulary for arguments about what BAT is. But beyond this a whole range of new terms were developed.[35] For instance, some participants in BAT determinations sought to clarify and thereby close BAT norms by distinguishing 'the best available techniques' from 'emerging techniques'. Emerging techniques were ones that are not yet widely applied in a sector. They were often advanced techniques which could deliver especially high standards of environmental protection. They were still regarded as experimental and thus not BAT. Participants in BAT determination processes also invented the concept 'obsolete techniques' in order to delimit the meaning of BAT. Here 'the best available techniques' were distinguished from older, more outdated technologies with lower environmental performance.

Given the proliferation of new terms[36] in BAT discussions, participants in BAT determinations constantly sought to clarify and define key terms.[37] But there was no authoritative source for settling definitional disputes, and hence the meaning of key terms appeared malleable:

[member of EIPPC bureau management] said that he was puzzled by the fact that some delegations felt that the text had been weakened whereas others felt that it had been toughened. He affirmed that the sole purpose of the changes was to reflect the discussion at the last IEF meeting and to make the text clearer. He suggested that the phrases 'benchmark' and 'reference point' were synonymous in the context used, but the former phrase seemed to have caused problems in earlier discussions.[38]

Hence, the development of new terms and the ongoing, never fully resolved attempts to clarify and define them were a key element of this dynamic BAT discourse. Whether a technique was considered as BAT could depend simply on whether the label BAT could be made to stick – as an adequate description – to a particular technique or a specific set of techniques. This could be subject to negotiation:

Walter[39] says it's *BAT*, Richard[40] says, it's an *emerging technique*.

(emphasis added)[41]

Similarly an industry association suggested that 'dioxin and furan abatement are *emerging* techniques' for the operation of electric arc furnaces in the iron and steel sector. According to the BREF writer:

dioxin and furan abatement are already *existing*, for instance in [name of plant in Italy] and [name of plant in Germany].[42]

The idea that concepts and terms were malleable was a further resource for BAT determinations. Some advanced BAT definitions were clearly in conflict with the text of the IPPC Directive. For instance, an industry association suggested in a technical working group discussion that BAT only applied to new, not existing plants.[43]

Portraying BAT determinations as a discursive process highlights the fluid and unstable aspects of defining BAT. BAT is not simply determined by social structures. Technical issues and political interests in BAT determinations are actively constructed through discourse. BAT determinations are not interpreted here as shaped by technical 'facts' and 'frameworks', or by static political groupings whose interests are externally determined by neo-corporatist power structures in the European Union.[44] Instead what actually counts as technical and political issues is actively constructed in ongoing conversations about what BAT is. Technical and political discourses are also fluid in the sense that there can be exchanges and overlaps between them. For instance, political points could be made in the language of technology. Sometimes the complexity of installations was referred to as a reason for not determining one specific and thus closed BAT norm. 'Complexity' invokes a technical discourse, but can also help to make a political point. It could advance some industries' interests in avoiding specific and thus more prescriptive, potentially costly BAT norms. In one Technical Working Group, an industry association argued that non-ferrous metal production sites in Europe were working with very different combinations of metallurgical processes. Different processes were even used for the production of the same metal. This technical argument was invoked in order to support the industry association's interest that no limits should be set for overall emissions or discharge loads for pollutants, not even as a recommendation in the BREF.[45] Similarly economic points could also be made in the language of the technical discourse. Some open BAT norms were justified with reference to a lack of sufficient high quality information about techniques. But the technical reason for insufficient performance data about techniques could express an economic argument. Researching further information could cost more time and thus money for BAT determinations.

To summarise: the IPPC Directive supplies the key terms of 'best available techniques' and some further criteria for their determination. But beyond this starting point, the discursive process of determining BAT develops a dynamic of its own, sometimes only tenuously linked to the conceptual and terminological framework of the Directive. BAT determinations involve a highly developed, independent discourse and hence more than simply an 'interpretation' of pre-given legal rules on BAT or a process of 'bargaining' about the meaning of BAT 'in the shadow' of the IPPC Directive. It is through this fluidly constructed discourse that a range of BAT norms are generated which vary in their degree of closure in practice. Moreover, discourses can be strategically deployed by social actors in the generation of open and closed BAT norms. But BAT determinations are also embedded in particular perceptions and views of the social world which discourses mobilise independently of actors' strategic behaviour. Hence social actors are influenced by the discursive universe in which they operate, but they also strive to assert agency in that universe through actively generating discourse. The next section illustrates in more detail how discourses generate variation in open and closed BAT norms. It focuses in particular on the contribution of political and technical discourses to generating open and closed BAT norms.

Technical and political discourses could also find themselves in tension with each other. On the one hand, participants in BAT determinations seek to identify an objective 'truth' about installations, their emissions and techniques for limiting them. Hence within the technical discourse social actors try to pin down and specify precisely the meaning of words used to make arguments about what BAT is:

[these points] were merely intended to clarify some of the different concepts available. The importance of getting behind the labels and to agree on underlying concepts was emphasised.[46]

On the other hand, participants in BAT determination processes recognise that defining BAT is not just a matter of the disinterested application of technical, objective knowledge to installations. Finding 'the best available techniques' also involves mediation between conflicting interests, hard and soft bargaining and hence the assertion of regulatory and commercial power. This political discourse finds expression in the strategic use of words, often deployed in an attempt to broaden, change and extend the meaning of concepts used in discussions about BAT. Hence variation in open and closed BAT norms needs to be examined in the context of the discourses which establish a particular view of the social world within which social actors operate.

BAT discourse leaving tensions between key dimensions of BAT unresolved

There are various ways in which discourses generate both open and closed BAT norms. First, discourse generates open BAT norms by rendering *the concept of BAT* open. The way participants in BAT determination processes talked about BAT obscures a core conceptual meaning of BAT. There were conflicting views and thus no clear specification of three key dimensions of BAT. They also remained unresolved during discussions in Technical Working Groups and the Information Exchange Forum.

Firstly, there was no agreement on whether BAT in the BREFs had a purely *descriptive* or also a *prescriptive* dimension. According to Art. 16 (2) of the IPPC Directive, BAT determinations in the BREF documents are simply the result of an 'exchange of information' between member states and industry. The Directive, however, opens the door for BAT determinations in the BREFs to be more than purely descriptive. Art. 2 (11) in connection with Annex IV No. 12 requires member state local permitters to take BREF notes into account when determining BAT for a specific installation. Local permitters, however, do not have to follow the BREF documents. They can deviate from them in their BAT determinations. Hence while these provisions in the IPPC Directive clarify the formal legal status of the BREF documents, they do not themselves resolve how prescriptive or descriptive BAT determinations in the BREFs should be formulated. There was ongoing discussion about this during the BREF drafting process.

For instance, it was asked whether BAT in the BREFs should be expressed simply as factual statements about techniques currently being used, or whether there should be definite evaluations of techniques resulting in the identification of the 'best' techniques for pollution control in a sector:

By contrast, terms such as 'achievable', 'expectation' and 'aspiration' expressed a judgement about what was reasonable rather than a statement of fact. In the process of drafting BREFs, the EIPPC Bureau had attempted to identify for each sector the best performance world-wide.[47]

Some participants in the 4th IEF meeting suggested that BAT in the BREFs was less prescriptive than BAT determinations in UK guidance notes issued by the EA. DG Environment nevertheless argued that BAT in BREFs should have a certain normative dimension:

In response to a comment from CEMBUREAU, the Commission stressed that if a technique is not currently widely applied in a sector it does not follow that it cannot be considered as BAT and included in chapter 5. If this were the case the BREFs would merely serve to ratify the status quo and would not provide a tool to drive environmental performance.[48]

The question whether BAT determinations in BREFs were only purely descriptive or also possessed a prescriptive dimension was particularly clearly raised when BREFs were written for industry sectors which were also regulated by other formal, binding EU environmental standards, like those contained in other Directives. If BAT determinations in the BREFs were considered as prescriptive, the question then arose about how a conflict with prescriptive standards in other EU legislation could be avoided. But even in this situation there was no real clarification as to how prescriptive or descriptive BAT determinations in BREFs should be considered. For instance, large combustion plants are covered by the IPPC Directive and hence have to comply with the 'best available techniques' standard. But they are also regulated through the EU Directive on Large Combustion Plants (2001/80/EC) which imposes specific binding emission limits on plants. They require the installation of specific techniques in order to ensure compliance. The Large Combustion Plant Directive was revised by the Commission while the BREF for this sector was being written. The question whether BAT in the BREF on large combustion plants was prescriptive was now clearly raised, partly in order to avoid a potential conflict with the binding standards from the Large Combustion Plant Directive. But the issue was fudged:

[The EIPPC Bureau management] underlined that the BREF 'Large Combustion Plants' does not require any legal obligation and insofar it may not be an alternative to the LCP Directive. Nevertheless it is a relevant tool for decision makers as permitters and operators.[49]

But BAT remained conceptually open not just because there was an unresolved tension between prescriptive and descriptive dimensions in the BAT concept. BAT, secondly, also remained conceptually open because there was an unresolved tension between *generality* and *specificity* in BAT determinations. Some participants in the BREF drafting process suggested that determining BAT requires us to give a very specific account of techniques. Others argued that only general statements about techniques could count as a BAT determination. For instance, BAT in a BREF could only represent a general standard which would be rendered more specific through BAT determinations with respect to a site licence. These would take the particular technical and financial circumstances of a plant into account.[50] For instance, some TWG members argued that reference to a bag filter for controlling dust emissions to air from an installation was too specific for a BAT definition in a BREF. In their view only a general reference to various air pollution abatement measures, including both bag filters and other techniques, such as electric precipitators, could represent BAT in a BREF. Others insisted that BAT in BREFs should be a specific standard.

Finally, a third dimension of BAT was also unspecified and hence left the BAT concept open. BAT is also characterised by a tension between *consistency* and *flexibility*. While some argued that BAT definitions should be consistent, for instance, between different industrial sectors covered by the IPPC Directive, or between different types of plants within an industrial sector,[51] others perceived BAT as flexible. While consistency in BAT definitions meant that previous BAT decisions were taken into account, flexibility allowed some departure from previous BAT definitions and permitted BAT to be adapted to the specific geographical, financial and technical circumstances of an installation. At the EU level arguments for consistency in BAT determinations were also advanced by the EIPPC Bureau management. It strove to introduce a degree of consistency in the BAT definitions applied by the different Technical Working Groups across the whole range of BREF notes for all the sectors covered by the IPPC Directive.[52]

To conclude: the way actors talked about BAT in BREF writing turned the very concept of BAT into an open one. Discussions in the Technical Working Groups and the Information Exchange Forum suggest that the BAT concept is characterised by unresolved tensions between a prescriptive and a descriptive dimension, between generality and specificity, as well as between consistency and flexibility. In the absence of a clear BAT concept at the EU level, generating the closure of BAT norms in specific instances in member states could be more difficult. Moreover, at the local level the conceptual openness of BAT was further promoted through norm differentiation.

Norm differentiation as a further means of opening up a BAT concept

Norm differentiation captures the further fragmentation of the meaning of BAT through the creative development of new quasi-BAT concepts. New BAT terms were developed for various reasons. Sometimes they could help to manage the difficulties of some existing installations in complying with IPPC BAT. For instance, a UK permitting officer developed new concepts such as 'indicative target' and 'flow band' for one particular UK inorganics site in order to deal with the situation that the installation could not meet 'indicative BAT' as set out in the UK sector guidance note. 'Indicative target (IT)' is defined in the Decision Document for the site as:

the highest level of emission of a substance that would normally be experienced at an emission point. Occasionally, and not normally greater than about 5% of the time, emissions higher than this can be expected as a natural feature of the activity concerned. A brief exceedance of an IT is not considered a Regulatory breach. In case an exceedance of an IT is caused by anything other than natural variation, all exceedances of ITs are investigated by the Operator.[53]

The concept of 'indicative target', however, does not help to focus or clarify the meaning of BAT. It is another normative phenomenon couched in the language of BAT. 'Indicative targets' share features with established uses of the BAT standard but also introduce new elements. 'Indicative targets' are set – as BAT standards usually are – with reference to both what the installation can achieve in practice and what UK sector guidance on BAT expects installations in the sector to achieve.[54] But the 'indicative target' also adds a new feature to BAT. It introduces some flexibility into the BAT standard by abandoning the idea of an absolute standard. It allows exceedances of the 'indicative target' in about 5 per cent of the time not to be counted as a 'regulatory' breach. Such breaches are dealt with by a self-regulatory regime where the operators themselves investigate these exceedances.[55]

The BAT standard was also rendered even more flexible for this installation through the concept of 'flow bands'. Usually an installation emits pollutants into the environment from various release points. How much pollutants are emitted from each point can vary significantly. Some emission points have low flows, some medium flows and some high flows. A 'flow band' combines various specific emission points, and hence can include low, medium and high flow emission points. 'Indicative targets' were set both for specific emission points, but also for a 'flow band' consisting of various emission points with different intensity flows. By also setting 'indicative targets' for whole flow bands, which included low, medium and high flow outlets, further flexibility in the BAT standard was achieved. The indicative target set a total limit for the combined outlets. Hence an exceedance of an indicative target for a low flow could be compensated by the emissions remaining well below the indicative target for a high flow outlet.[56] The reasoning behind this was that by definition the low flow outlet only released small amounts of pollutants to the environment. Hence an exceedance of the indicative target for the low flow outlet would have only an insignificant impact on the environment. Often the indicative target for various emission points was set at a level less than that which would be required to comply with the indicative target for the sum of the emission points. This was intended as an incentive for the operator to reduce emissions from specific emission points.

But BAT norm differentiation did not just occur through new concepts such as 'indicative target' and 'flow band'. It was also promoted through a whole range of other new concepts. While these sought to capture specific aspects of BAT, they also made it more difficult to establish a definitive, unified, core meaning of the BAT concept. They thereby rendered the BAT concept even more open. For instance, some EA PPC permitters stated that they had been advised by their legal department that there were two types of BAT. One BAT was the BAT which plants had to meet at the time of licensing. But there was also a 'future BAT'[57] which existing plants only needed to meet 'in a couple of years time'. In addition, the meaning of BAT at the local level was further differentiated, rather than treated as closed, through distinctions between terms such as 'indicative BAT' and 'installation or site specific BAT'.[58] UK sector guidance[59] provided by the EA used the term 'indicative BAT' to refer to BAT for a whole industrial sector. 'Installation or site specific BAT' might be different from 'indicative BAT' because of particular technical, economic or geographical conditions, such as local pollution hot spots. Site specific BAT could also be an adaptation of the 'indicative BAT' laid out in the national sector guidance notes in response to what a particular installation could comply with. Site specific BAT could involve emission limit values above the levels that were described as BAT levels in the UK sector guidance notes:

The current emission levels from line 1 may exceed the benchmark levels, average emission levels are in line with the benchmark but maximum levels may be higher. Previous work has been carried out by the applicant to identify potential reductions and some improvements made to reach near benchmark levels. This work has been previously discussed with the Agency and it has been determined that the controls in place represent BAT *for the site*.

(emphasis added)[60]

During EA permitting practice the term '*express BAT* conditions' was also developed. These were general BAT conditions set out in the EA permit template. They were automatically inserted into all IPPC site licences, except those applying to landfill sites. Here is an example for an 'express BAT condition':

The Operator shall use BAT so as to prevent or where that is not practicable to reduce emissions of noise and vibration from the Permitted Installation, in particular by: equipment maintenance, e.g. of fans, pumps, motors, conveyors and mobile plant.[61]

'Express BAT conditions' introduced a new dimension to the BAT concept. They signalled that for some issues of pollution control BAT can be very *general*, in fact so general that one BAT condition can be applied to installations across a range of different industrial sectors. This is a departure from 'installation specific' BAT determinations.

Finally, the BAT concept was also opened up through a further type of norm differentiation at the local level. BAT was defined here not just in terms of pollution reduction technologies and associated emission limit values, but BAT was expressed in terms of a variety of plans for the operation of an IPPC installation. UK PPC site licences frequently included reference to site closure, energy efficiency, noise and odour management plans, as well as site protection and monitoring programmes.[62] Hence, BAT was expressed here not in terms of fixed legal limits, e.g. for the emission of odour or noise, but as a management practice at the site.[63] So far this section has discussed how talk about what counts as BAT rendered the very concept of BAT open, generating a range of different BATs and hence reducing the possibilities for BAT norm closure. The next section discusses how discourses generated variation in open and closed norms by providing justifications for open and closed norms.

Generating variation in open and closed norms by providing justifications

Justifications for specific outcomes of BAT determinations matter because they can stabilise, normalise and legitimise variation in open and closed BAT norms. In this sense they generate variation in open and closed BAT norms. Justifications are important because open BAT norms can also be interpreted as incomplete or even as failures of BAT determination processes. For instance, where BAT determinations for existing sites were postponed through improvement conditions[64] to a date after 1 October 2007,[65] member states were potentially in breach of the IPPC Directive. Justifications, however, can counter the narrative of failure and portray open BAT norms as 'normal' and routine aspects of BAT determinations in practice. Both a political and technical discourse were key to generating such justifications. Within the political discourse variation in open and closed BAT norms was regarded as deriving from interest positions.

Accounting for variation in open and closed BAT norms in a political discourse

From the perspective of the political discourse a BAT determination is the outcome of negotiation between various interested parties. It involves the assertion of regulatory and commercial power. Both BREF writers[66] and other participants in Technical Working Groups, as well as German and UK permitting officers, frequently referred to BAT determinations in terms of 'negotiation'. The emphasis on negotiation of BAT which is characteristic of a political discourse was sometimes contrasted with BAT determinations as an application of the law, as illustrated by the following extract from a UK judicial review challenge to an IPPC licence:

the fact is that Mr. Hosker and Mr Durham [i.e. officers for the regulatory authority who worked on the IPPC permit] saw the process as in part a negotiation. That lies outwith any of the processes required or permitted under the Directive or the Regulations.[67]

In the political discourse closed BAT norms represent the outcome of a successful negotiation process. In contrast to this, open BAT norms derive from irreconcilable interests and views – between participants in BREF drafting at the EU level or between operator and regulatory authority at the local level – concerning *the best* available techniques. Hence a political discourse on BAT determinations began explicitly to manifest itself where large numbers of participants with heterogeneous interests deliberated on BAT. A political discourse surfaced in particular during discussions of the EU-wide Technical Working Groups and the Information Exchange Forum, as well as in national working groups implementing the IPPC Directive into UK and German law. During these debates it became clear that some participants saw open BAT norms as something which promoted their interests.

Open BAT norms in BREFs as an interest position of some industry associations and member states

A number of industry associations and some member states expressed an interest in avoiding clear and specific BAT conclusions in the BREFs. Some industry associations and member states argued for flexibility and thus for the opportunity to choose between various different techniques. They did not want to be tied down to a specific BAT standard.

This argument was particularly strongly urged by industry associations in relation to existing plants. Here, they suggested, BAT could only be decided on a 'case by case' basis:[68]

Here, we have to distinguish between two categories of installations: the new installations where the BAT utilisation is possible and the existing ones where the application of BAT must be done, 'case by case' – either for technological reasons or for economical [sic] reasons.[69]

Some industry associations also argued for open BAT norms in BREFs by advocating broad, rather than specific and potentially more prescriptive ranges of emissions to be associated with BAT techniques.[70] For instance, during the first IEF meeting some industry associations suggested that BAT techniques should be connected with a very broad range of emissions, including high levels from older, existing plants as well as much lower levels from new plants with high performance pollution control.[71]

Not just trade associations, however, but also some member states[72] advocated open BAT norms in BREFs. For instance, some member states advocated open BAT norms by arguing for broad ranges of emissions associated with BAT:

There was an extensive discussion on the suggested difference between 'achieved levels' and 'levels associated with BAT'. *The Netherlands...supported by Germany, Sweden, Austria, EEB and at the end also the UK, proposed to widen the range of 'levels associated with BAT' by including in general all shown achieved levels*, unless the whole TWG agrees that certain levels are to be considered as a real exception and thus excluded from 'levels associated with BAT'. *The Commission replied that narrow ranges are preferred where possible to reflect BAT* and illustrated this by making a reference to the dust issue in the cement and lime BREF. The Commission was of the opinion that current wording accurately described the process of going from achieved levels, via the 'BAT test' including economic consideration and expert judgement by the TWGs, to levels associated with BAT in a general sense for the sectors concerned.

(emphasis added)[73]

Open BAT norms were also championed by some member states for particular types of BREFs, such as horizontal BREFs which dealt with cross-sector issues.[74] For instance, the Netherlands expressed reservations whether a BAT conclusion could be achieved for the horizontal BREF on cooling. It suggested that it was only possible to provide pointers for local permitters on how to determine BAT.[75]

Open BAT norms preserved more powers for member states to choose their own particular national approach towards implementing the BAT concept. This could help to maintain national cultures of environmental regulation or provide support for an industry sector central to a member state's economy. Open BAT norms in BREFs were also sometimes interpreted as a more general expression of member state sovereignty in this EU legal process. For instance, early on in the BREF writing process Germany challenged attempts by DG Environment to arrogate to itself the power to determine BAT and thus to bring about closure of BAT norms at the EU level, in case Technical Working Groups and the IEF found it difficult to achieve consensus. But the political discourse also helped to generate variation in open and closed norms by accounting for closed BAT norms.

Accounting for closed BAT norms through a political discourse

Successful negotiation at EU, national or local level could generate specific BAT determinations accepted by a wide range of actors as 'the best available techniques'. For instance, in an IPPC site licence a specific technique, such as selective non-catalytic reduction, may be prescribed for the control of dust emissions to a level of $300 \, mg/m^3$ of oxides of nitrogen emissions for a cement plant. Closed BAT norms could also be achieved through hard bargaining. For instance, DG Environment suggested to industry associations that in case of difficulties in reaching agreements on BAT determinations in the BREFs, it might consider invoking its powers under Art. 18 (2) of the IPPC Directive. Under this provision the Commission can propose legislation for legally binding emission limits for installations and substances covered by the IPPC Directive. These binding measures would remove some of the flexibility involved in emission limit-setting under the BAT approach in the absence of legislation passed under Art. 18 (2) of the IPPC Directive.

Closed BAT norms were also regarded as promoting the interests of some industry associations, in particular those of equipment suppliers. Their advocacy of documenting generally applicable techniques, rather than just specific examples of 'good' techniques, in the BREFs introduced a degree of closure in BAT norms. Sometimes environmental technology suppliers even advocated the applicability of particular pollution control techniques, for example, for dust, across different sectors.[76]

Moreover, a few industry associations[77] suggested that closed BAT norms are in their interests because they promote fair and open competition in an internal market with a level playing field. According to this view, individual companies should not be able to gain a competitive advantage by negotiating a lenient PPC permit with a local regulator in a specific member state. Moreover, a degree of BAT closure in the BREFs was considered advantageous from a commercial perspective because clearer standards in the BREFs could facilitate the planning of investment decisions. Some industry associations also emphasised the opportunity for a common, specific EU wide approach to BAT to be exported to regulatory regimes outside the EU, thereby enhancing the competitiveness of EU industry. To summarise: a political discourse generates variation in open and closed norms, also by helping to account for open and closed BAT norms. It thereby also explains, justifies and normalises variation in open and closed BAT norms with reference to interest positions. But the political discourse also provided more specific justifications for variations in open and closed BAT norms. One such approach was to justify open BAT norms by portraying BAT as a procedural norm.

BAT as a procedural norm

The political discourse also helped to legitimise inconclusive outcomes of BAT determinations by foregrounding the idea that BAT is a procedural norm.[78] Here BAT prescribes only a political governance structure for *how* a determination of the best available techniques has to be achieved. From this perspective BAT is a reflexive norm which is expected to be open to some degree. For instance, even after lengthy discussions EU Technical Working Groups could not always agree on what constituted BAT for the sector. In this case 'split views' were recorded in the BREF.[79] They represent the different views held by various working group participants on what should be considered as BAT for the sector. The executive summary[80] – contained in all BREF documents and agreed by the IEF – explicitly recognises the possibility that no consensus on BAT may actually be achieved. It therefore requires that each BREF shall report the level of consensus associated with its BAT determination. But the political discourse did not simply justify open BAT norms through talk about procedures which dealt with inconclusive deliberations on BAT. It also helped to justify open BAT norms through reference to environmental regulators' policies.

Justifying variation in open and closed BAT norms through a political discourse on environmental regulators' policies

Regulators' organisational policies represent a further element of a political discourse which could help to justify open BAT norms. For instance, the Environment Agency also justified open BAT norms associated with improvement conditions annexed to IPPC permits through reference to its organisational aims, such as 'risk regulation'. 'Risk regulation' involves the targeting of EA resources at those activities which pose the greatest environmental risks.[81] Some BAT determination issues were not considered serious enough to take up time during the PPC permitting process. Such issues were more likely to be dealt with through improvement conditions, which the operator has to address after the IPPC licence has been issued. Environmental management issues not deemed serious enough for a BAT determination during IPPC licensing could also be hived off to area inspectors. They were thus declared to be a task for ongoing supervision and enforcement work at the site.

But it was not just 'risk regulation', but also other EA regulatory policies which chimed with and hence served as justifications for open BAT norms. Within the spirit of 'new public management' the EA increasingly seeks to regulate industrial sectors through environmental performance targets. These are based on information about the quantity of emissions generated per ton of product by a particular installation. Hence environmental performance targets allow an assessment of how well one installation is reducing its emissions in comparison to other installations in the same sector. In the world of environmental performance targets the norms of closed, 'hard' state law are becoming peripheral. Open BAT norms which request the operator to move towards compliance with an environmental performance target – for instance through improvement actions – are considered as sufficient for achieving environmental improvements in this regulatory approach. Environmental performance targets turn site regulation into an ongoing process of continuous environmental improvements. In this approach, fixing specific, determinate legal obligations at a particular moment in time is no longer central. The political discourse, however, did not just generate variation in open and closed norms through reference to a range of justifications for open BAT norms. From the perspective of the political discourse striving to open up BAT norms was also a matter of various tactics and strategies.

Tactics and strategies for achieving open BAT norms in the political discourse

First, where BAT determinations failed to materialise, this could also be justified by lowering the threshold for determinations, reducing a BAT norm to simply a 'BAT approach' or 'philosophy':

In cooling we have gone one step further, we have tried to describe *an approach, a philosophy, because BAT is very difficult to define, it is a very specific thing*. If you say this is BAT, you may have BAT for one situation or for two, maybe. But for the other hundreds of thousands of situations you have not. So, it is very difficult to say, this is BAT in a horizontal BREF. But you can say there is a *BAT approach*, to the issue of finding a technique where you can say, well, come on *this is BAT*.

(emphasis added)[82]

Second, industry associations sometimes argued that it was not possible to distinguish between techniques and therefore to select 'the best ones'. For instance, an industry association for the non-ferrous metal sector stated that there was a 'photofinish' between the techniques in chapter 4 of the BREF which lists the 'BAT candidates'. Therefore it was not possible to narrow down the range of techniques to a smaller segment in chapter 5 of the BREF, the 'BAT conclusion'. All of the techniques listed in chapter 4 were to be transferred to chapter 5 as well and thus considered as 'BAT'.[83]

Third, some industry associations and member states suggested that a specific BAT could not be determined because the 'BAT candidates' in chapter 4 of the BREF were not representative for plants across the EU. They only reflected specific and isolated cases of particularly high environmental performance, techniques encountered only in a few plants in the EU. Only techniques used in a wide range of plants and thus representative of EU installations could be described as BAT.[84] Often this more clearly policy-oriented argument was allied with the 'photofinish' strategy of mitigating against closed BAT norms. For instance, an EU trade association argued that the available environmental performance data, in this case concerning energy consumption, did not really allow us to discriminate between different techniques and thus to identify '*the best* available techniques':

The quoted energy consumption figures already show in [name of EU trade association] eyes small differences to start with. The above considerations [i.e. only a few EU plants employed this technique] reduce these differences in [name of EU trade association] opinion to insignificant ones.

Fourth, a further key tactic for achieving open BAT norms was to avoid making selections between techniques in the BREFs by simply 'adding on' techniques. BREF writers stated that industry associations and member states seldom suggested in their comments on BREF drafts that particular techniques should be deleted from the text.[85] Instead members of the Technical Working Groups often asked to have techniques simply *added* to draft BREFs.

Fifth, BAT norm closure could also be made more unlikely by restricting information about closed BAT norms and supporting the dissemination of information about a wide range of techniques. Some member states and industry associations deployed this strategy by arguing against merely translating chapter 5 of all the BREFs into the various community languages. Since the BREFs are written in English, some member states had asked for a translation of the BREFs into other official community languages. According to DG Environment there were insufficient EU funds for translating all five chapters of the BREF for all of the different industrial sectors. This gave rise to a discussion about which parts of the BREFs should be translated. Italy and UNICE argued strongly against the EU Commission's suggestion that only chapter 5 – the 'BAT conclusion' – should be translated. They also wanted to see a translation of chapter 4. Chapter 4 lists the 'techniques to consider' in the determination of BAT. This would discourage a focus on and the dissemination of knowledge concerning only the narrower range of BAT conclusion techniques in the BREFs. By also arguing for the translation of chapter 4 any prescriptive force which may have been attached to the narrower range of techniques in chapter 5 would be weakened.[86]

Sixth, a further strategy for countering BAT norm closure was to reopen BAT conclusions. This occurred during the drafting of the BREFs at the EU level, but also at the local permitting level. For instance, industry associations and member states would sometimes try to reopen in the Information Exchange Forum (IEF) a BAT conclusion which had been reached in a Technical Working Group. They did so on the basis that their interests had not been sufficiently considered in the original BAT conclusion.[87] This also sometimes turned the IEF into an appeal forum on technical decisions reached in TWGs. The distinction between the EU Technical Working Groups as a forum for the discussion of mainly technical issues, on the one hand, and the Information Exchange Forum, as the arena in which mainly policy issues were discussed, on the other hand, was blurred as a result.

Reopening BAT determinations also occurred in UK EA area offices. PPC permitting had been moved from area offices to four central strategic permitting groups. Some area officers were concerned about this loss of control over IPPC licensing in particular in light of the fact that area officers were still responsible for the supervision of IPPC installations and hence for the enforcement of IPPC licences. They had to make these licences work in practice. Hence area offices would sometimes reopen BAT determinations achieved by strategic permitting groups which they did not agree with. This is possible through the power to vary PPC permits under reg. 17 of the PPC Regulations 2000 which is retained by area offices.

Seventh, some strategies for opening BAT norms also sought to capitalise on the opportunities presented by the multi-level governance system through which BAT determinations are achieved. At least temporarily open BAT norms could be the result of 'passing up, passing down or passing on' decisions about what should be considered as BAT among the various levels of government through which the IPPC Directive is implemented.

Grasping opportunities for avoiding norm closure in a multi-level governance system: 'passing up', 'passing down' and 'passing on' BAT determinations

BAT determinations involve different levels of decision-making within the EU multi-level governance system. The drafting of the IPPC Directive text and the BREF guidance documents involves decision-making at the EU level. National implementing legislation and further BAT guidance occur at the national level. Finally, BAT is also determined at the local level when regulatory authorities issue IPPC site licences. BAT norm closure could be avoided through passing decisions on, up or down in this multi-level governance system. Some actors saw it as in their interests to avoid making a BAT determination at a particular level since being associated with a specific, closed and potentially controversial BAT norm could cause significant political costs for the decision taker. For instance, members of EU Technical Working Groups sometimes argued that a specific aspect of a BAT determination, such as the narrowing down of emission ranges associated with BAT, should not really be decided at the EU level, but only by a national or local member state regulator.[88] This occurred in particular when there was significant conflict in the group about what should be considered as BAT.[89] Such arguments for 'passing down' BAT determinations were sometimes further justified by TWG members through reference to member state sovereignty and by DG Environment with reference to subsidiarity. It was suggested that BAT norm closure in the BREF usurped powers which the IPPC Directive had bestowed on member state environmental regulators, not on the EU Technical Working Groups and the IEF.[90]

Similarly the EIPPC Bureau management suggested that BAT determinations in BREFs should not trespass on the decision-making powers allocated to local permitters under the IPPC Directive. The EIPPC Bureau management, for instance, was concerned that the executive summary of the BREF should not be used by itself for determining BAT in a local PPC permit. Permit-writers should conduct their own BAT determination, with reference to other parts of the BREF, and not simply transfer BAT determinations from a BREF executive summary into a local permit.[91]

Open BAT norms, however, could be generated not just by 'passing down' decisions but also by 'passing up' decisions about what BAT is. Sometimes local permitters suggested that they could not decide an outstanding BAT issue for a particular site without getting some clear direction from a higher level in the environmental regulatory bureaucracy. Sometimes local permitters argued that a BAT determination involved a fundamental policy issue in the implementation of the IPPC Directive which needed to be decided on the EU level.[92]

Finally, BAT decisions could remain initially open not just because they were passed 'up' or 'down' between EU, national and local permitting levels, but also because they were 'passed on' between different organisational units at the local IPPC permitting level. For instance, in the UK both central strategic permitting groups and local area teams were involved in the PPC permitting process. The EA had set up four central strategic permitting groups (SPGs) which covered installations for the whole of England. Staff in these strategic permitting groups focused solely on writing PPC permits. The strategic permitting groups had been set up in order to manage the additional workload which the implementation of the IPPC Directive generated. They were also meant to ensure that the UK would implement the Directive in time in compliance with legal deadlines.[93] But area offices still retained some involvement in IPPC licensing. First, they were involved in pre-application discussions with operators. Second, and most importantly, some aspects of BAT determinations which were not resolved during permit-writing were passed on to area offices. There were frequently references in Decision Documents for UK PPC permits which contained statements such as 'this should be pursued by area inspector as a potential improvement.'[94] Sometimes these issues would be flagged up in a written and more official form in so-called 'handover documents'[95] for area offices which accompanied IPPC licences drafted by staff from a central permitting group. 'Passing on' decisions from the SPG to the area office meant that there was no longer an attempt to formulate a norm.[96] Instead the BAT determination was turned into a matter of pollution control through enforcement practice by an area officer.[97] To summarise: a political discourse was key to generating variation in open and closed BAT norms. Open and closed BAT norms were justified with reference to interest positions, and more specifically through reference to BAT as a procedural norm and regulators' policies. Finally, the political discourse also generated talk about how to open up BAT norms. A variety of tactics and strategies were regarded as generating open BAT norms. But it was not just a political, but also a technical discourse which generated variation in open and closed BAT norms.

Generating variation in open and closed BAT norms through a technical discourse

Variation in open and closed norms is also generated through a technical discourse on BAT determinations. From the perspective of the technical discourse BAT determinations are a matter of collating objective, high quality, validated technical and scientific information about the characteristics and performance of process and pollution reduction technologies. BREF writers and local permitters in particular characterised BAT determinations within a technical discourse as a process of finding the 'truth' about techniques. This could also involve cutting through a thicket of politically motivated and interest-based submissions by participants in BAT determination processes on what should be considered as BAT for an industrial sector or a specific installation.[98] Where within the technical discourse sufficient high quality technical information was available, which allowed, for instance, a clear identification of the best performing pollution reduction techniques, the technical discourse generated closed BAT norms. But the technical discourse also generated a range of justifications for open BAT norms and thus contributed to variation in open and closed BAT norms.

Insufficient 'information' about techniques

According to participants in BAT determination processes BAT norms sometimes remain open because there is insufficient information about techniques and installations. Sometimes participants did not have 'enough confidence in the technical data' in order to define closed BAT norms. Hence open BAT norms are justified with reference to open technical facts. For instance, information about costs and sometimes also environmental performance of techniques was not always forthcoming during the BREF writing process.[99] At the local level both German and UK permitting officers frequently received applications for IPPC licences from operators which did not contain sufficient or correct information.[100] Hence improvement conditions in UK PPC licences, particularly for existing sites, often require the operator to collect further information about the nature and quantity of emissions from an especially complex or not yet fully researched aspect of the site. Sometimes the improvement condition would also require the operator to come up with information about possible techniques which could be used for the reduction of emissions to a BAT standard.

Information could also be lacking because measurement techniques had not yet been developed for some emissions. And sometimes, measurement techniques compliant with quality control standards, such as MCERTS in the UK, were not yet available.[101] Hence in the technical discourse BAT norms could remain open at the stage of issuing IPPC licences because both regulator and operator had insufficient understanding of some aspects and emissions from a site.[102] Sometimes information was lacking for regulators because an entire sector was new to pollution control regulation, such as for instance the food and drink as well as farming sectors.

Time pressures, particularly for both German and UK local permitting officers, could contribute further to the lack of information promoting open BAT norms. For instance, UK permitting officers suggested that formally requesting further information from the operator under schedule 4, paragraph 4 of the PPC Regulations (England and Wales) 2000 – before the conclusion of the permitting process – could be time consuming. The completion of the PPC permit could thus be delayed.[103] Permits, however, had to be issued in compliance with internal EA deadlines. Existing sites also had to meet the final EU legal deadline of 1 October 2007 imposed by the IPPC Directive itself. Simply requesting further information through an improvement condition annexed to the IPPC licence could help to avoid further delay in the issuing of the licence.[104] This meant that at the stage of IPPC licensing there could be insufficient information for achieving BAT norm closure. But it was not just insufficient technical information, but also the complexity of techniques and installations which justified open BAT norms in a technical discourse.

Complex techniques and installations

Where production technology varied widely between different installations it was considered difficult to determine an abstract, general BAT for the whole sector and hence to achieve closed BAT norms in the BREFs or UK guidance notes. For instance, the BREF writer for the textiles sector which is dominated by small and medium-sized businesses in the EU stated:

I don't expect to arrive at the end and to say o.k. I found *the* BAT. Because the BAT can be BAT here and not BAT in another situation. And in such a *complex sector* where you have little standardisation, every company in a way is working with its own recipes and ways of working, it is even more difficult to say 'this is the one', so it will be quite a big one and hard work, hard work to define what is BAT. I hope, I don't know, I won't be obliged to write this is the BAT, the best, probably there will be more, different ways of reaching BAT.

(emphasis in the original)[105]

In contrast, some sectors involved a large number of different production processes because there were small, medium-sized as well as large multinational companies operating in the sector. They chose different production technologies appropriate to the size of the company. The argument concerning the complexity of technical processes was also invoked during the drafting of the BREF for large volume organic chemicals. Industry associations and the BREF writer[106] argued that production was here especially complex because sites usually had upstream and downstream processes which needed to be integrated in the manufacturing of specialist chemicals.[107]

It was not just the EU, but also at the local permitting level that complexity of operations featured as a justification for open BAT norms. For instance, changes in product patterns at a site could lead to fluctuations in energy and water consumption. The need to adapt to such changing production patterns was referred to in order to justify openness in BAT norms in the site licence in relation to energy and water use. More generally open BAT norms were justified in a technical discourse through the idea that BAT is a dynamic technology standard.

BAT as a dynamic technology standard

A degree of openness in BAT norms was thought to be inextricably linked to the further dynamic development of BAT techniques. Some industry associations argued that closed BAT norms would act as a brake to further research and investment into new pollution control techniques. Where BREFs would select only a limited and specific number of techniques as BAT, this would curtail the industrial operator's flexibility and reduce incentives to choose and develop other techniques.

Moreover, the idea of BAT as a dynamic technology standard suggests that pollution control and production techniques are developing and improving all the time. What can be the BAT today may be an outdated technology tomorrow. This is also recognised in Art. 11 of the IPPC Directive which states that member states shall ensure that their regulatory authorities follow or are informed of developments in the best available techniques.[108] Art. 13 of the IPPC Directive requires member states to take the necessary measures 'to ensure that competent authorities periodically reconsider and, where necessary, update permit conditions'. Hence, Regulation 8 (14) of the PPC Regulations (England and Wales) 2000 and para. 5.1.1. of the TA Luft (air)[109] impose a duty on environmental regulators to keep abreast of developments about what constitutes the best available techniques in an industrial sector. The UK sector guidance notes specify for each sector when permits should be periodically reviewed.[110] Moreover, standard condition 4.1.6. from the EA permit template – which is inserted into every non-landfill PPC permit – provides powers to the EA to serve a notice on operators which requires them to review whether their installation is still operating according to BAT. Similarly para. 17 (1) BimSchG imposes a duty upon the German regulatory authority to change an existing IPPC permit if the existing permit does not provide sufficient protection of the public or the installation's neighbours against disadvantageous environmental impacts, other dangers or significant nuisances.

A further element of the idea that BAT is a dynamic technology standard was the notion that BAT might further depend on implementing measures at an installation. By being dependent on further implementing steps BAT norms can remain 'open'. The specification of an emission limit value as the BAT norm is not sufficient on its own to achieve closure. Further implementing actions – not necessarily specified in the BAT norm itself – may be required. For instance, maintenance routines, such as the regular cleaning of dust filters, sometimes have to be carried out in order to achieve operation of the installation according to BAT and hence compliance with a particular emission limit value for dust. Finally, limits to closing off BAT norms could also arise from changes in the priority accorded to environmental issues. Moves in air quality control to restrict increasingly smaller particles, such as PM2,5 not just PM10,[111] require new BAT reduction technologies and thus render BAT for air pollution control much more open. To conclude: this section has argued that political and technical discourses, often perceived as in tension with each other, generate variation in open and closed BAT norms.

Conclusion

This chapter has argued that EU law in action can involve a variety of norms. The practical implementation of the IPPC Directive generates variation in open and closed BAT norms. The chapter has focused on political and technical discourses generating variation in open and closed BAT norms. Legal discourses, such as formal legal dispute resolution procedures, are marginal to the majority of BAT determinations. Appeals and judicial review procedures were perceived by some UK PPC permitting officers also as an opportunity for clarifying BAT and for obtaining an authoritative view on the validity of specific PPC permit conditions.[112] But most UK permitting officers tried to avoid the invocation of formal legal procedures and preferred to resolve conflicts about BAT determinations at an earlier stage through negotiation.[113] Very few appeals are lodged in the UK by operators to the Secretary of State for the Environment in relation to PPC licence determinations by the EA or local authorities. This is particularly the case with the process industries covered by the IPPC Directive. Most appeals against permit conditions, revocation notices and refusals of permits are generated in one sector, namely the waste management industry, for two specific reasons. First, the EA has rejected a number of PPC permit applications for landfills because the sites' engineering has been too basic to comply with the requirements of the Landfill Directive[114] which is implemented through the IPPC regime. Moreover, compliance with a BAT technology standard constitutes new and potentially challenging environmental regulation for the waste management industry. Process industries subject to IPPC have already been regulated for about fifteen years through a BAT type technology standard, such as BATNEEC[115] under section 7 (2) of EPA 1990.[116] Hardly any applications for PPC permits from process industries were rejected by the EA.[117] Second, waste management operators lodged appeals against notices revoking existing licences for landfill sites for strategic reasons. Under regulation 27 (6) of the PPC Regulations (England and Wales) 2000 an appeal against a revocation notice implies that the original licence will remain in force. The application of the revocation notice will be suspended until the appeal is decided. This provides an opportunity for the operator to draw up a site closure plan under the less onerous, previously applicable waste management regulation regime under section 39 of EPA 1990.[118]

In addition, there has only been one UK judicial review case challenging the issuing of a PPC licence so far.[119] This concerned the granting of a PPC permit for a glass manufacturer, Quinn, by a local authority, Chester City Council. The case contributes to BAT norm closure by establishing that the range of nitrogenoxides emissions indicated as achievable for new plants in the UK sector guidance notes and the EU BREF were to be considered as BAT for the glass manufacturing process. An alternative technology, the so-called Oxyfuel process, should have been considered in the BAT determination.[120]

Similarly, in Germany formal appeals from operators[121] against BAT ('Stand der Technik') determinations play a limited role in practice in BAT determinations. The number of such appeals has increased since the new TA Luft came into force on 1.10.2002 also because operators want to test their interpretations of BAT determinations contained in the new TA Luft. But formal appeals against BAT determinations only address specific points raised by the particular facts of an individual case. Moreover, most appeals lodged by German operators against BAT determinations do not question the imposition of specific emission limits but the procedures for the measurement of an installation's emissions. Hence, appeals are lodged against requirements to measure continuously rather than through spot samples and against licence requirements for particular technical specifications of the instruments used for measuring emissions. Hence legal discourses, in the form of formal legal dispute resolution procedures, contribute only little to BAT norm closure.

So what is the analytical significance of variation in open and closed BAT norms? First, this finding suggests that social actors in the field work with various concepts of law. My focus on discourses as generating open and closed norms suggests that conceptualisations of law are a matter of perception rather than fact. Closed BAT norms resemble traditional, 'hard' state law. Open BAT determinations simply generate promises of norms which may not materialise. Thus, from an empirical perspective, various norm concepts coexist rather than merely compete. This differs from some theoretical accounts which suggest that conceptualising EU law involves choosing between competing conceptions of law (see, for example, De Burca and Walker, 2005).

Second, recognition of open norms can advance debates about the nature of EU law by adding a new perspective to the theme of 'norm variety', which has already been raised by inquiry into new forms of EU governance and legal pluralism. Legal pluralism is becoming increasingly influential in the analysis of EU and international legal orders (Schepel, 2005; Griffiths, 2005; Twining 2000). It highlights the fact that transnational legal orders often involve a variety of public and private norms which interact in complex networks. The legal pluralism theme chimes with some aspects of the practical implementation of the IPPC Directive. BAT determinations draw on a range of norms, such as EU as well as national primary and secondary public law norms, but also on private norms, such as industry agreements for the phasing out of specific polluting substances in production processes. Norm variety is also a key theme in the literature on new forms of EU governance. This literature highlights the coexistence of various forms of hard and soft law in some areas of EU policy, such as fiscal coordination and employment. The emphasis on private actors in new forms of EU *governance* also fits the IPPC Directive. Various private actors – especially industry associations and environmental NGOs – participate in BAT norm formation.

But the finding of open BAT norms adds a new angle. The legal pluralism literature emphasises the coexistence of and the interactions between various types of *closed* norms, such as private and public legal rules. New forms of EU governance, by virtue of being a governance and regulatory mechanism, are also usually understood to have a specific normative content. Open BAT norms question this perception of normative orders as clearly bounded and expressing specific prescriptions. The analysis in this chapter has drawn attention to precarious, fragile and unfinished social processes in the formation of law. Micro-sociological insights into how standards fail to materialise and hence how law remains normatively open, in turn, provide a starting point for questioning assumptions of the inevitability, naturalness and integrative nature of law. Such micro-sociological analysis can add another dimension to existing macro-sociological perspectives, like those of the Marxist tradition, which question whether law is 'a necessary consequence of social life itself' (Hunt, 1978: 141). They are an important step in developing a critical sociology of integrating law.

So what does variation in open and closed BAT norms tell us further about the nature of law in EU integration? Open BAT norms help to question three elements of traditional conceptions of law in EU integration. First, open norms question the idea that law is a normative order which can be clearly demarcated from its social contexts. Second, open norms question the idea that EU law can be wielded in a strategic manner in order to achieve specific purposes and outcomes. In the case of open norms it becomes difficult to identify a core normative meaning which could be deployed as a prescriptive challenge to existing patterns of behaviour. Hence, whether law can be employed in an instrumental manner, as a tool of behavioural change, becomes questionable. In the case of open norms there may be no automatic association of law with either government or governance.

Third, EU law is often taken to be the formal law, the 'law in the books', which can be identified as arising from specific legal sources. The official supranational or state legal system provides authoritative criteria for determining what can be considered as 'law' in a legal system. Such tests which spell out what counts as valid 'formal law in the books' are prescribed not negotiated (DeBurca and Walker, 2005: 13). Open norms – one important facet of EU law in action – suggest that legal process also works through law which cannot simply be captured in terms of the 'formal law in the books'. Open norms may not even fulfil the criteria which the formal legal system provides for the recognition of 'law'.[122] Moreover, EU law in action can be shaped by the specific settings in which negotiation occurs. Hence, the empirical finding of variation in open and closed norms suggests that *implementation practice*, not just formal sources of law, can give rise to a variety of norms.

To summarise: this chapter has argued that variation in open and closed norms is an empirically puzzling and theoretically significant finding. It challenges the expectation of closure in legal norms and sheds further light on the nature of EU law. This chapter has focused on how political and technical discourses, often perceived as in tension with each other, generate variation in open and closed BAT norms. The next chapter will explore how economic discourses also become relevant for BAT determinations.

Notes

1. Art 3 (a) IPPC Directive.
2. Listed in Annex II to the IPPC Directive. The emission limit values of other EU Directives apply as minimum standards for emission limit values associated with the 'best available techniques' as long as community-wide emission limit values have not been specified under Art. 18 (1) of the IPPC Directive. This has not yet occurred. In fact DG Environment has suggested that it is unlikely to propose new legislation under Art. 18 (1) of the IPPC Directive. Hence, the IPPC Directive is 'open' because it also relies on standards from other EU Directives. It does not specify its own emission limit values for the pollutants it controls.
3. Extract from official notes of IEF 5th meeting, 18–19 February 1999. Similarly a BREF writer stated: 'I think a good BREF is a BAT reference document that focuses on chapters 4 and 5. So that really focuses on the message of BAT'. Interview with BREF writer, no. 5.
4. Interview with BREF writer, no. 4.
5. For instance, the World Chlorine Council, which represents the chlorine industry, has set limits for mercury in chlorine production which the EA refers to in some of its Decision Documents for IPPC licences.
6. For instance, the site which was party to an industry agreement on phasing out lead stabilisers in PVC production had an improvement condition imposed for the phasing out of lead from their production process. Hence, the private self-regulatory norm did not automatically generate BAT norm closure at the site.
7. Such as the technical instruction air (TA *Luft*).
8. According to Art. 3 (a) of the IPPC Directive, member states have to ensure that installations are operated according to BAT. Art. 2 No. 11 in connection with Annex IV No. 12 of the IPPC Directive requires that competent authorities shall take into account BAT determinations in BREFs, but they do not have to follow them. Hence where the competent authorities of member states follow the BREFs, BAT determinations in BREFs can have normative force.
9. These were written by analogy to the EU BREF guidance documents, by the main environmental regulator in the UK, the Environment Agency. Like the EU BREF documents, they cover BAT determinations for the different sectors regulated under the IPPC Directive.
10. In contrast to new sites which were yet to be built and operated as a new process after the required implementation of the IPPC Directive in the member states by 30 October 1999.

11. Decision Document no. 2, p. 2. Open BAT norms in improvement conditions were also sometimes inserted when the operator had not yet carried out a full BAT assessment for a pollution control issue (Decision Document no. 2, p. 16).

12. If improvement conditions were not complied with, this rendered BAT even more open. Since non-compliance was in practice a significant issue, the EA had developed a standard condition for IPPC licences to address this. Standard condition 1.4.2. from the permit template obliges the operator to inform the EA if he/she fails to comply with an improvement condition by the required date (see EA internal work instruction on the PPC permit template).

13. As recorded in the Decision Document no. 2 for the site. EA official guidance states that 'the Decision Document explains how the applicant's permit application has been determined and why the specific conditions in the permit have been imposed. It is a record of the decision-making process to show how all relevant factors and legislative requirements have been taken into account'. In practice Decision Documents provided limited information about reasons for particular BAT determinations and presented a very brief, formalised account of the BAT decision-making process.

14. Decision Document, no. 2, p. 22.

15. Decision Document, no. 2, p. 6.

16. In one case, two years after the issuing of the IPPC licence no measurement had yet been submitted by the operator.

17. Interview no. 8, with BREF writer.

18. Interview no. 4 with BREF writer. For an example of a closed BAT norm in a BREF see, for example, the BREF for non-ferrous metals. It defines BAT for controlling dust emissions from non-ferrous metals as involving two pollution abatement technologies: fabric filters and wet scrubbers. Fairly specific emission levels are associated with the use of these technologies in the definition of BAT: 1–5 mg/Nm^3 was the associated emission level for dust for fabric filters and less than 5 mg/Nm^3 of dust if the wet scrubber was used. This applied to the production of all 42 non-ferrous metals, ferro-alloys, as well as carbon and graphite production.

19. The BREF on economics and cross-media effects also clearly envisages the possibility that in a number of cases BAT will be obvious. It states that the methodologies set out in this BREF for costing techniques and assessing their cross-media impacts need not to be applied 'where there is an obvious conclusion, or where there is broad agreement as to which alternative is the preferred option for implementation': p. xiv BREF on economics and cross-media effects, May 2005 at http://eippcb.jrc.es/pages/FActivities.htm.

20. As one BREF writer put it: 'You know by intuition'. From interview no. 4 with BREF writer.

21. BREF writers used expressions such as 'it falls naturally into place' (interview no. 8 with BREF writer) and 'one has the right feeling that something is BAT' (interview no. 12 with EIPPC Bureau management).

22. The First EU Commission Report on the Implementation of the IPPC Directive lists for the reporting period of 2000–2002 for the fifteen old EU member states 43,943 permits being issued for existing installations, 4750 permits being issued for substantially changed installations and 795 permits being issued for new installations (EU Commission, 2004: 29).

23. The amended BImSCHG which implements the IPPC Directive into German primary law refers to 'Stand der Technik' in order to implement IPPC BAT. This is exactly the same term which was used in the BimSchG before its amendment to implement the IPPC Directive into German national law. 'Stand der Technik' is also the German technology standard which was previously used in national pollution control law, although this had a slightly different content than IPPC 'Stand der Technik' from a legal perspective. For instance, the German 'Stand der Technik' concept did not refer explicitly to costs as one criterion for determining the 'Stand der Technik' in a licence for a specific installation.

24. BAT under IPPC deals with a wider range of issues in pollution control, including energy efficiency, prevention of waste, an assessment of the consumption and nature of raw materials used as well as accident prevention and site restoration. The BATNEEC concept under sect. 7 (2) of EPA 1990 did not grant powers to the regulator to deal with these issues. Moreover, the concept of emissions is more broadly defined under Art. 2 (5) of the IPPC Directive to include emission of noise and vibration which were not included in the definition of polluting substances in sect. 1 (3) and (13) of EPA 1990 under the previous UK IPC regime.

25. Interview with UK PPC permitting officer, no. 1.

26. Moreover, reference to existing operational practices at an installation could represent another route to closed BAT norms (see Decision Document, no. 2). In this case experience of operating practices at a plant provides the basis for a closed BAT determination. For instance, emission values actually achieved by the operator and techniques already employed for pollution abatement can form the content of a BAT determination. If operational practices deviate to a limited extent from BAT definitions in national legislation or guidance notes, accepting an operator's justifications for this discrepancy might present another route to a closed BAT determination without the regulator having to impose an improvement condition.

27. Especially in complex sectors with lots of different production and therefore different pollution reduction techniques, the identification of six techniques as BAT represented a significant degree of closure, while in a simple sector with one or a few production techniques, six techniques could be considered as a fairly open BAT determination.

28. Similarly, in one case a member state, Sweden, argued for a clear, closed BAT norm for a sector in one BREF and thus opposed wide ranges in the emission levels associated with the BAT technique. But Sweden accepted that some aspects of this BAT determination – such as the details of measurement procedures – could only be determined at the site

level: 'Sweden expressed the view that the final draft was well-balanced and that they could agree to it subject to further comments. They said, however, that ranges are sometimes a little too wide. Furthermore, they stressed that some things can only be addressed at the site level' (extract from official notes of 7th IEF meeting, 28–29 February 2000).

29. For instance, an extract from the official notes of the 6th IEF meeting, 29–30 September reads: 'The penultimate bullet point in the outline for chapter 4 put too much emphasis on local conditions.'

30. Interview with BREF writer no. 2 and BREF writer, no. 3.

31. Extract from interview with EIPPC Bureau management, no. 12.

32. The BREF on pulp and paper, for instance, was 509 pages long. The BREF on iron and steel production contained 383 pages. The chlor-alkali BREF was 178 pages long and the BREF for the cement and lime industry was 127 pages long.

33. This is also illustrated by the following extract from the official notes of the 6th IEF meeting, 29–30 September 1999: '[Name of EU industry association] requested more time to react to the comments made by member states. [Name of sector specific EU trade association] expressed concern about the reference to the "sector as a whole", while [name of other sector specific EU trade association] supported keeping the word "many" that Sweden had inserted'. Deletion of the words 'sector as a whole' could help here to avoid BAT norm closure, because BAT would then only apply to the plants for which it was described, rather than to 'the sector as a whole'. The BAT determination would then not be applicable to other plants in the sector. It would only be considered as BAT for those plants which were already operating these techniques.

34. Intervention by the EIPPC Bureau management during a debate in the Information Exchange Forum about the official BREF outline. Extract from official notes of 7th IEF meeting, 28–29 February 2000.

35. For instance, terms such as 'candidate BAT', 'general BAT', 'sectoral BAT' and 'European BAT' were invoked. In addition participants in TWGs referred to 'local BAT', 'specific BAT' and 'individual BAT' when referring to BAT determinations for a specific installation in a member state.

36. Numerous other terms were also developed during BAT determinations at the national and local permitting level, such as 'indicative BAT', 'express BAT conditions', 'future BAT', 'European BAT', 'local BAT' and 'sector BAT'.

37. There were numerous examples where participants in BAT determination processes tried to pin down the meaning of words, for instance in discussions during the BREF writing process. The EIPPC Bureau background file on the non-ferrous metals BREF referred to attempts by the EIPPC Bureau to clarify terms such as 'emerging techniques' which were to be distinguished from the 'best available techniques'. The Bureau introduced the concept of 'emerging techniques' in the following way: 'information on promising novel pollution prevention and control techniques that are under development. Information will include the potential efficiency of the

technique, a preliminary cost estimate and an assessment of the time scale before the techniques will be "available".' There was also an attempt in this file to further clarify the meaning of the word 'available', a term used and defined in outline in Art. 2 (11) second indent in the IPPC Directive. 'Available' techniques were distinguished from 'emerging' ones, given the fact that only 'available techniques' could be considered as BAT according to the text of the IPPC Directive. The entry in the file read:

> 'Available' refers to whether an operating company, following issue of a commercial invitation to tender to a metallurgical engineering design contractor for the construction of a full scale plant, could expect to receive an offer capable of acceptance, including technical and commercial performance guarantees. If such an offer was unlikely to be forthcoming the process/plant should be considered as 'emerging'.

38. Extract from official notes from 7th IEF meeting, 28–29 February, 2000.
39. Fictitious name of technical working group member used to replace actual name given in the extract from the file.
40. Fictitious name of technical working group member used to replace actual name given in the extract from the file.
41. Extract from EIPPC Bureau background file on iron and steel BREF.
42. Extract from EIPPC Bureau background file on iron and steel BREF.
43. Extract from EIPPC Bureau background file on iron and steel BREF. Art. 5 of the IPPC Directive requires member states to ensure that existing installations are operated in accordance with the requirements inter alia of Art. 3 of the IPPC Directive. Art. 3 (a) of the Directive requires member states to ensure that installations are operated in such a way that 'all the appropriate preventive measures are taken against pollution, in particular through application of the best available techniques'.
44. For an insider's account of BAT determinations from this perspective see, for example, Hey, 2000.
45. Extract from EIPPC Bureau background file on the non-ferrous metal BREF. After the statement of the industry's position on this point the following text appeared, re-emphasising the use of a technical discourse for making this point: 'Attached is a note from [name of staff member] of [name of non-ferrous metals company] which demonstrates, in numerical terms, the validity of the above.'
46. Extract from 4th IEF meeting, 16–17 February 1998.
47. Extract from official notes from 5th IEF meeting, 18–19 February 1999.
48. Extract from official notes from 5th IEF meeting, 18–19 February 1999.
49. Extract from EIPPC Bureau background file on the BREF for large combustion plants. Similar statements could also be found in the background files for other BREF documents. The following is an extract from the EIPPC Bureau background file for the iron and steel sector: 'The BREF documents are not legally binding, but they have considerable de facto importance.'

50. In one TWG discussion this point was made in relation to BAT for iron and steel production. Southern member states argued that a particular technique that had been suggested for BAT could not properly represent BAT for them because they did not receive high quality scrap as input into iron production like northern member states.

51. Such as electric arc or blast furnaces in the iron and steel sector.

52. 'As coordinator of the Bureau I have the task of promoting consistency in our technical approach and of the product documents across the whole series of notes. We welcome the response of the IEF to date in recognising that different documents need to reflect the different subjects but there also needs to be a coherence between all our products' (Interview with EIPPC Bureau management, no. 12).

53. Decision Document, no. 3, p. 13.

54. Indicative targets were set at the levels which the UK sector guidance proposed as 'indicative BAT' where the operator could achieve this. Where the operator could not achieve this, 'the most reasonable level, achievable by the process is set'. Decision Document, no. 3, p. 13. Where the actual performance by the operator deviated too far from the standards required in the UK sector guidance note, improvement conditions would usually insist on measures to bring down the installations' emissions.

55. In fact only those breaches were to be investigated by the operator which were not the outcome of 'natural' and routine process fluctuations. Decision Document, no. 3, p. 13.

56. Hence an indicative target was also set for each individual outlet for emissions.

57. There is no reference in the IPPC Directive to the term 'future BAT'.

58. The following is an example for reference to *site specific BAT*: 'Second stage scrubber reduces HCL [hydrogen chlorine gas] emissions below benchmark – BAT. Rapid quench reduces possibility of dioxin formation, thermal oxidation, shown to be site specific BAT for VOC [volatile organic compounds] and dioxin reduction (Decision Document no. 1)'.

59. So-called sector guidance notes, written for each of the sectors to which the IPPC Directive applies. For a further explanation of these see chapter 1.

60. Decision Document no. 1.

61. Condition 2.9.1. from the EA permit template. The list of activities through which BAT should be achieved continued with a number of other noise abatement measures.

62. Site protection and monitoring programmes provide plans for monitoring pollutant release from an IPPC installation in order to avoid land contamination. See EA internal work instruction on PPC permitting: 'Determination of an application for a PPC permit (non Landfill) under the PPC Regulations 2000 (SI 2000 No. 1973)'.

63. The definition of 'techniques' in Art. 2 (11) first indent of the IPPC Directive includes 'both the technology used and the way in which the installation is designed, built, maintained, operated and decommissioned'.

64. Improvement conditions were not just a technique used in the UK to manage the application of the BAT standard under the IPPC Directive. This is also illustrated by early references in discussions during the BREF writing process where other member states also seemed to indicate that the application of the BAT standard could be open in the sense that it would be projected into the future for some installations: 'The objective should be to always apply the General BAT in each individual case. Sometimes this is possible immediately and sometimes this can take a number of years. In certain cases it might not even be possible at all to apply the General BAT, anyhow not within a foreseeable future. In the latter case a programme for taking steps towards the full application of the General BAT could be required in the permit'. 'If the General BAT is not applied it should be explained why, e.g. in the permit and/or in the exchange of information required under Art. 16.1.' (Extract from Swedish position paper, 15 May 1999, filed in the EIPPC Bureau background file for the non-ferrous metals BREF.)

65. Art. 5 of the IPPC Directive imposes this deadline.

66. Interview no.7 with UK permitting officer.

67. Para. 132, *R. (on the application of Rockware Glass Limited) v. Chester City Council*, 2005 WL 3048992.

68. Similarly a comment made by an industry association on the draft for the non-ferrous metal BREF read 'This draft allows practicable pollution prevention and control on a site by site basis dictated by local constraints' (extract from EIPPC Bureau background file for the non-ferrous metal BREF).

69. Extract from EIPPC background file for the iron and steel industry.

70. Sometimes industry associations advocated associated emission levels for techniques which would vary by a factor of 1000, e.g. from $5\,\mathrm{mg/m^3}$ of a particular substance to $5000\,\mathrm{mg/m^3}$.

71. Official notes for 1st IEF meeting, 4 December 1996.

72. There was variation, however, in relation to the particular pollution control issue discussed. While the Netherlands here argued for broader ranges of associated emissions for techniques, they argued for a closed BAT determination in relation to the first ammonia pilot BREF, where they strongly argued that only one particular plant technology could be considered as BAT for the production of ammonia, not all three of the production technologies that had been discussed during the drafting of the guidance note for this sector.

73. Extract from official notes from 6th IEF meeting, 29–30 September 1999. A preference for a degree of BAT norm closure in the BREFs was also expressed by a member of DG Environment in an interview: 'We expect them [i.e. BREFs] to contain clear BAT conclusions, we expect them to reflect state of the art technology in an accurate way' (from interview no. 13 with member of staff, DG Environment).

74. Horizontal BREFs were BREFs which were written not for a specific industrial sector covered by the IPPC Directive but to cover issues which were

relevant for a number of different industrial sectors, such as cooling and monitoring systems.

75. For instance, an extract from the official notes from the 6th IEF meeting read: 'On cooling, NL agreed with the EIPPC Bureau position that the BREF should not contain BAT conclusions, but rather a BAT tool kit. By contrast Austria and EEB expressed the view that it should be possible to come to BAT conclusions. Germany stressed the need for concrete conclusions, including specific recommendations where possible.'

76. 'FEAD/EURITIS [i.e. European trade associations] emphasised the need to consider the potential for transferring techniques used in one sector to other sectors. UNICE clarified that the representatives from FEAD and EURITIS (which had been separately invited by the Commission) were not part of the UNICE delegation and had not discussed their comments before hand' (extract from 6th IEF meeting, 29–30 September 1999).

77. A significant number of trade associations for the large industrial sectors also advocated open BAT norms in BREFs in order to avoid the imposition of high costs on the worst performers in a large, heterogeneous industry sector through the designation of very advanced pollution reduction techniques.

78. Regardless of whether the view that BAT in the IPPC Directive is a proce-dural norm is accepted, preamble 17 to the IPPC Directive clearly states that there should not be a prescription of one specific technique or technology.

79. See, for example, the split views on BAT on energy issues in the BREF on Waste Incineration (16th meeting of the IEF, 23–24 June, 2005, p. 2).

80. See: http://eippcb.jrc.es/pages/FActivities.htm.

81. Interview no. 4 with UK PPC permitting officer.

82. Interview no. 5 with BREF writer.

83. Extract from EIPPC background file for the non-ferrous metal BREF.

84. The field data provide numerous examples of industry associations using this argumentative strategy of suggesting that particular techniques could only be applied to some plants and hence could not be considered as BAT for the whole sector. The following is an extract from the EIPPC Bureau background file for the BREF for the non-ferrous metals sector: 'There are options available for salt free melting for some types of feed materials.' The statement 'for some types of feed materials' is added by industry. It is amended in the file by a comment from the BREF author which reads 'for most types of feed materials'.

85. Interview with BREF writer, no. 11.

86. 'Italy and UNICE opposed the approach whereby BAT chapters would be translated by the Commission, but not chapters on techniques to consider' (extract from official notes, 7th IEF meeting, 28–29 February 2000). The EU Commission finally decided that the executive summary of all BREFS would be translated into all of the official Community languages.

87. For instance, the industry association for the pulp and paper industry tried to reopen BAT decisions in the IEF.

88. Sometimes participants in BAT determinations in BREFs would argue that a particular process to be regulated in a sectoral BREF involved specific aspects which could not be regulated at the EU level. Hence the BAT determination at the EU level would have to remain open. It was argued, for instance, that the choice of fuel for operating a process which could vary was a reason for an open BAT norm in a BREF. But energy efficiency is one criterion which according to Art. 2 and Annex IV No. 9 of the IPPC Directive should be taken into account when determining BAT. There is no indication from the text of the IPPC Directive that energy efficiency measures are only to be considered during BAT determinations at the local level.

89. Statement by BREF writer in EIPPC background file for the BREF for the non-ferrous metal sector.

90. Interview no. 5 with BREF writer.

91. Interview no. 12 with EIPPC Bureau management.

92. For instance, the definition of plants which come within the ambit of the IPPC Directive in Annex I of the IPPC Directive is unclear. Annex I contains a list of installations and capacity thresholds for deciding whether a particular installation is regulated through the IPPC Directive. Annex I is not very clear and hence in some cases local permitters did not know whether a particular installation was meant to be covered by the IPPC Directive.

93. At the beginning of the implementation of the IPPC Directive in the UK teams were also writing IPPC licences in addition to their day to day site supervision work. It was found that the licensing of sites took rather long under this system and that legal deadlines for the implementation of the Directive were in danger of not being met.

94. Decision Document no. 2, p. 15. For instance, minor issues in the determination of BAT were passed on for further decisions and actions to be taken by the inspector for the site based in the area team. At one site waste minimisation issues were to be further pursued by the area inspector.

95. The hand-over document was a brief document of usually just a few A4 pages in which the key environmental pollution issues of a site were listed so that these could be further dealt with during site inspections and enforcement work by area officers.

96. Both minor and more major issues in BAT determinations for a site could be passed on to area inspectors. For instance, while at one site minor issues about waste minimisation at the site were handed over to the area inspector, at another site energy use was 'highlighted for the area inspector'. Energy use according to Art. 2 (11) in connection with Annex IV No. 9, is one criterion which should be considered in the determination of BAT for an installation. The particular site had a high energy use, but had not produced an energy efficiency plan. This was handed over to the area team as a matter to be dealt with during inspection practice. Similarly for another site which had not been regulated before under IPC, minimising energy consumption for a particular aspect of the production process was not dealt

with through the BAT determination in the licence, but was an issue
flagged up for the area team in the hand-over document (Decision
Document, no. 4, p. 13).

97. Decision Documents declared some issues at sites as 'inspection topics' or
'improvement action'. (Decision Document, No. 2, p. 35). These terms
seemed to indicate the absence of an imposition of norms.

98. UK area officers and German licensing officers were blunt in suggesting
that operators would sometimes try to 'pull the wool over the regulatory
authority's eyes'.

99. 'I will be able, I hope, but that will be a very hard job to identify already the
better performances and the best performances. This is what I hope I can
do because if they say that they don't have numbers I don't know how
without numbers I could distinguish between the good and the better
performances, but anyway, this is, my, you know, objective'. Extract from
interview no. 2 with BREF writer. See also the statement by an EU trade
association which suggested that member states had only provided limited
information in the TWG for the BREF for the Waste Treatment Industries
(official notes of 16th meeting of the IEF, 23–24 June 2005, p. 4). The BREF
writer uses the term 'they' here in order to refer to the members of the
Technical Working Group, including industry associations for the sector
and member state representatives which are meant to provide information
to the BREF writer about the performance of techniques so that the BAT for
a sector can be identified.

100. For instance, some Decision Documents stated that there were discrepancies between the figures which operators supplied in the PPC licence
application in order to describe their emissions and the figures of the EA
for emissions from the operator as a result of standard reporting conditions imposed upon the operator under the previous IPC Authorisation
(see Decision Document, no. 5, p. 14).

101. For instance, the EA usually required measurement instruments
employed at installations to be certified to its MCERTS standard. MCERTS
is the Environment Agency's Monitoring Certification Scheme. It
provides a framework within which environmental measurements are
made in accordance with the Agency's quality requirements. The scheme
covers a range of monitoring, sampling and inspection activities. But
sometimes MCERTS-certificated instrumentation was not yet available
for measuring substances emitted from the site. Hence the site licence
would refer to non-MCERTS equipment to be used, but laboratory per-
sonnel carrying out the monitoring may have been already MCERTS
qualified.

102. The following is a good example of an open BAT norm in a UK PPC licence
due to a lack of technical information about the process:

> Monitoring carried out on 1/11/2004 calculated the particulate emission
> concentration to be 32.7 mg/m^3. This does not compare favourably with
> the benchmark range of 5–20 mg/m^3 (Table 3.1. TGN). *Based on the limited*

monitoring available, an ELV has not initially been set in the permit, however, provision has been made to include an ELV on completion of improvement condition 8. This specific improvement condition will require that operator to characterise the particulate and lead emissions and identify the measures required to achieve the benchmark figures, where appropriate. The inclusion of an ELV for particulate matter at a later date has been highlighted for follow up in the handover document.

(Decision Document, no. 4, p. 15)

103. According to para. 7.6. of the the DEFRA IPPC: A Practical Guide suggests that duly made applications should be normally determined by the regulatory authority within four months of submission. Paragraph 10 (6a) BimSchG requires German regulatory authorities to decide IPPC licence applications within 7 months. The German regulator can extend this time limit by 3 months.

104. See also the EA internal work instruction on this point: 'A Schedule 4 notice should only be issued where the missing information is essential for permit determination and all the missing information should be requested through one notice. Multiple notices can create delays and add administrative effort, particularly where consultation with each statutory consultee is required.' 'Other missing information, if needed, should be obtained via the Improvement Programme.'

105. Extract from interview no. 2 with BREF writer.

106. Interview no. 1 with BREF writer.

107. In fact the TWG for 'Large Volume Inorganic Chemicals – Solids and Others' did not reach generic BAT conclusions, but only BAT conclusions on 'cornerstone' and 'illustrative products' from the sector (see, official notes of the 18th meeting of the IEF, 4 October, 2006, pp. 2–3). Complexity in the operation of installations could also result from the fact that different installations in a sector could also use different raw materials. Hence what could be efficient BAT techniques for one installation, might not be so for a different installation. Hence BREF writers sometimes argued that this required closure of the BAT norm at the local level on the basis of detailed knowledge and experience possessed by local inspectors about the site and the BAT techniques that could be applied to the site (extract from EIPPC Bureau background file for the non-ferrous metal sector).

108. Preamble 22 to the IPPC Directive also suggests that authorisation conditions must be periodically reviewed and if necessary updated, and that in any case they will be re-examined.

109. Para. 5.5.1. of the TA *Luft* (air) states that in case new BREF documents are published by the EU Commission the rules of the TA *Luft* shall still remain in force. But in this case a committee has to be established by the German federal environmental ministry which will examine whether the new BREF documents contain more onerous obligations than the existing rules of the TA *Luft*. If the committee decides that the 'Stand der Technik' has

moved on, local environmental regulators are no longer bound by the TA *Luft* but have to take into account the more advanced provisions of the new BREF documents.

110. For instance, the UK sector guidance note for inorganic chemicals states that installations previously not subject to IPC or Waste Management Licensing should have their IPPC permits reviewed within 4 years. Installations which have been previously regulated under IPC or Waste Management Licensing shall be reviewed 6 years after the issue of the IPPC permit (p. 8, Guidance for the Inorganic Chemicals Sector, version 20 May 2004). These review periods are flexible and the EA may shorten or extend them. Moreover, condition 4.1.6. in the permit template allows the EA to give the operator 6 months notice of a requirement to submit a report which assesses whether all appropriate measures continue to be taken against pollution at the operator's site, in particular through the application of BAT. One of the purposes of this standard condition was to provide the EA with the information which is necessary in order to conduct permit reviews to keep abreast of developments in BAT.

111. Particulate matter of an aerodynamic diameter of up to 10 μg and 2.5 μg respectively.

112. Interview no. 8 with UK permitting officer.

113. Interview no. 6 with UK permitting officer.

114. Council Directive 1999/31/EC, OJ L 182/1, 16.07.99.

115. Best Available Techniques Not Entailing Excessive Costs are referred to in section 7 (2) EPA 1990.

116. The provisions of Part I EPA on IPC came into force on the 1 April 1991 for new plants and on the 1 April 1996 for existing plants.

117. In March 2006, seven years after licensing under IPPC started and approximately one year before the end of PPC licensing on the 1 October 2007 less than 10 sites in the process industries had been refused a PPC licence (interview with UK permitting officer, no. 8).

118. Interview with UK permitting officer, no. 8.

119. *R. (on the application of Rockware Glass Limited) v. Chester City Council*, 2005 WL 3048992.

120. The successful judicial review proceedings were brought by a competitor, Rockware, which was aggrieved about the fact that the Council's PPC permit allowed Quinn to operate a technology which Rockware did not regard as BAT, also because of its higher emissions of nitrogenoxides. The case establishes that permitting authorities have to consider available alternatives when considering whether an operator's proposed technology constitutes BAT. They also have to apply appropriately national and EU BREF guidance on emission levels achievable by a technique when determining BAT for a new plant. They should not set emission levels for a process on the basis of irrelevant considerations, such as what other existing installations in the sector are achieving.

121. *Widerspruchsverfahren* according to paras. 68–73 *Verwaltungsgerichtsordnung* (administrative court order).
122. For instance, when some elements of BAT determinations in UK PPC licences were handed over to area teams as a matter of enforcement practice.

7   What does it cost? Economic discourse in the determination of 'the best available techniques' under the IPPC Directive

Introduction

Chapter 6 discussed how technical and political discourses generate variation in open and closed BAT norms, a key characteristic of the implementation of the IPPC Directive. It is not just political and technical discourses, but also economic discourse which plays an important role in the search for 'the best available techniques' during the implementation of the IPPC Directive. This chapter explores how cost arguments feature in discussions about what counts as BAT either for a whole industrial sector or for a specific installation. According to Art. 2 (11) second indent of the IPPC Directive, costs are a criterion for determining what constitutes 'the best available techniques'. The text of the Directive, however, does not provide a methodology for determining the 'costs' and 'advantages' of techniques. It is therefore important to examine how participants in BAT determinations actually talk about costs. What does an analysis of cost arguments in BAT determinations reveal about the nature of EU law? Does it confirm or question the picture of EU law as relatively autonomous in relation to its political, economic and technical contexts, or as capable of being wielded in an instrumental manner, and as something to be found 'in the law books'?

This chapter argues that an economic discourse is central to how BAT is defined. It also suggests that this economic discourse overlaps with political and technical discourses on BAT. Consequently EU 'law in action' questions images of EU law as relatively autonomous with respect to its political, technical and economic contexts. The close connection between law and its contexts delineated in this chapter also questions the notion of instrumental EU law. Contexts import meaning from a social sphere into the law. Hence it appears questionable whether law is capable of transforming its contexts and thus of steering political, economic or technical processes. Where contexts enter into the construction of law, it becomes debatable whether EU law can be employed directly as an instrument for achieving abstract pre-specified purposes and outcomes, such as the 'policy aims' of EU environmental legislation. Finally, this chapter also suggests that talk about costs is more wide-ranging and central to the definition of BAT standards than an initial reading of the IPPC Directive suggests. Hence a conception of EU law as the 'law in the books' – expressed in the formal legal text of the Directive – is only a limited pointer to what EU law actually entails.

The chapter develops these points about the nature of EU law through a discussion of three key characteristics of an economic discourse employed in BAT determinations. The first section discusses the broad scope, pervasive nature and sometimes low visibility of an economic discourse in BAT determinations. It ranges from very general, pragmatic and basic assertions about costs to more elaborate, detailed cost calculations informed by economics as a theoretical discipline.

The chapter's second section traces two functions of an economic discourse in BAT determinations. First, an economic discourse contributes to an IPPC permitting process which is characterised at the local level between a highly bureaucratic approach towards determining BAT, on the one hand, and a discretionary approach which involves an unregulated sphere of 'expert judgement', on the other. Second, an economic discourse which draws on developed and detailed cost calculations also helps to distinguish an economic from a political discourse. General and vague statements about costs were often considered by participants in BAT determinations as mere expressions of interests. Establishing the identity of a separate, distinct economic discourse underpinned the second function of an economic discourse. Since it could then be utilised for rebutting purely political arguments in BAT determinations. To begin with it is necessary to define what constitutes an 'economic discourse' in BAT determinations.

Defining a broad-ranging economic discourse

An economic discourse refers to a specific way of addressing the question concerning the 'best available techniques'. It focuses on cost arguments as a key criterion for selecting 'the best available techniques' from a whole range of possible techniques. In practice an economic discourse is broad in scope and hence pervasive in character. It includes general statements about the relationship between the economy and the environment.[1] For instance, BAT discussions involved arguments about whether environmental protection measures conflict with or can be reconciled with economic policy aims. The Directorate General 'Environment' of the EU Commission, in particular, sought to advance the idea of compatibility between environmental protection measures and a competitive EU economy. But an economic discourse also involves more specific talk about detailed costings of particular production and pollution reduction technologies. In practice a wide concept of cost was invoked which further broadened the scope of the economic discourse. A whole range of costs were considered. First, costs for operators of IPPC installations and industrial sectors were taken into account.

Costs of IPPC implementation for operators and industrial sectors

Discussing costs of IPPC implementation for operators and industrial sectors is central to an economic discourse. These costs are also referred to in the text of the IPPC Directive as well as in legal texts concerned with German and UK implementing measures.[2] Art. 2 (11) of the IPPC Directive provides:

available techniques shall mean those developed on a scale which allows implementation in the relevant industrial sector, under *economically* and technically *viable conditions, taking into consideration the costs and advantages*, whether or not the techniques are used or produced inside the Member States in question, as long as they are reasonably accessible to the operator.

(emphasis added)[3]

Art. 2 (11) also requires that special consideration should be given to a number of technical and environmental considerations listed in Annex IV of the Directive.[4] There is further reference to costs in the introductory sentence of Annex IV. It requires that 'the likely *costs and benefits* of a measure and the principles of precaution and prevention' are to be considered when the specific technical and environmental factors from the Annex IV list are taken into account in BAT determinations.

In German environmental law the costs of BAT techniques for specific sites are specifically considered through the application to BAT determinations of the general administrative law principle of proportionality[5] (Winter, 1999: 69).[6] But for new plants there is, according to German permitting officers, limited scope for considering costs in individual BAT determinations. The German technical instructions, such as the TA *Luft* (air) and the technical appendices of the waste water regulations,[7] are formally binding legal rules which permitting officers have to apply to a *new* installation. Hence permitting officers have limited discretion in determining BAT for new installations. Costs are not a separate and additional factor which can be taken into account when assessing whether a particular technique constitutes BAT (see also Winter, 1999: 69).

But there are three types of situations in which costs can also enter German BAT determinations as a separate, additional factor. First and most importantly, where the technical instructions list various techniques as BAT options, costs can be taken into account in order to decide which BAT technique should be applied to a new or existing site. Second, when licensing *existing* sites, the German environmental administration is not bound by the technical instructions and the costs of techniques can therefore be raised here as a separate argument by operators. Paragraph 17 subsection 2 of the Federal Air Immissions Control Statute (BimSchG) clearly states that improvement orders for existing installations have to be proportionate, though operators carry the burden of proof in showing that excessive costs may render the BAT technique a disproportionate measure (Jarass, 2002: 390; Winter, 1999: 69). Third, if local environmental quality standards require measures beyond BAT, cost considerations are permitted to enter the decision as to which techniques should be chosen.

Cost considerations are mainly taken into account during the German implementation of the IPPC Directive in the period when the various technical instructions are drafted. German industry associations affected by the IPPC Directive and large individual operators advanced cost arguments about BAT, for instance, during the revision of the TA *Luft* (air). But industry associations were not just involved during the initial drafting process. They also later lobbied members of the German Parliament and the federal environment ministry (BMU) when the latter put a formal draft of the technical instruction before the upper chamber of the German Parliament, the Bundesrat, in order to pass formally the TA *Luft* as legally binding tertiary rules. Moreover, the public administration has to prepare a general cost statement which assesses the cost impacts of new legal rules, such as technical instructions, upon the federal and *Länder* public administration itself and the industrial sectors concerned, not unlike compliance cost assessments in the UK (Hansmann, 2004:10).

Cost considerations were also taken into account during the drafting of UK national guidance documents on BAT. Moreover, proportionality considerations also informed cost assessments in the UK:

The BAT approach ensures that the cost of applying techniques is not excessive in relation to the environmental protection they provide. It follows that the more environmental damage BAT can prevent, the more the regulator can justify telling the operator to spend on it before the costs are considered excessive.[8]

But in contrast to Germany there is more scope at the local site licensing level for UK permitting officers to take cost considerations into account in BAT determinations. In the UK the issuing of an IPPC licence is a discretionary decision in which permitting officers can weigh up various factors, including costs. The UK Department of Environment, Food and Rural Affairs guidance states that a best technique which operators could obtain[9] should not be regarded as BAT if its costs are too high:

This means that a technique may be rejected as BAT if its costs would far outweigh its environmental benefits.[10]

Cost considerations figured in particular as a justification for BAT determinations for existing, rather than for new sites[11] when these BAT determinations deviated from what is described as 'indicative BAT' in the UK national sector guidance notes.[12]

To summarise: costs of BAT techniques for operators and industrial sectors are one factor that is considered in the determination of BAT, as envisaged in Art. 2 (11) of the IPPC Directive. But a much wider notion of costs is actually invoked in practice in BAT determinations and can include the costs of operators actually preparing a formal IPPC application. Operators, for instance, seek to limit the costs of applying for IPPC permits by curtailing the amount of information which is collected and analysed for the formal written IPPC application. Both German and UK permitting officers suggested that a significant number of formal IPPC applications are of poor quality. Operators seldom outline various BAT options for their process or justify in detail the particular BAT option they have chosen. In particular operators of existing installations simply suggest through brief statements that the techniques which they currently employ are BAT. Regulators tried to counter these indications of cost considerations in BAT determinations. They tried to convince operators – with limited success – that the information collected for IPPC applications could also be efficiently used for internal company reporting purposes and could help to identify savings on energy and waste disposal costs.[13] Limited information in IPPC licensing applications meant that conversations about BAT between operators and regulators started from a limited basis for the exploration of the most advanced BAT techniques. Similar information deficits were also noted by BREF authors during the drafting of BREF documents at the EU level and EA officers during the determination of BAT in UK national sector guidance notes.

In addition, the cost concept invoked in BAT determinations is also a broad one because it includes for existing IPPC installations the costs of production and pollution reduction controls for operators which have been considered in the past. In the case of existing installations – which form the main bulk of IPPC permitting – cost arguments often hark back to previous cost arguments. For existing installations the question as to what constitutes BAT is not approached against a blank canvas. Instead operator and regulator start from a given production technology and existing pollution reduction equipment. These are the result also of operator's and regulator's previous decisions about the affordability of techniques for the site. Hence a history of low investment in environmental protection technology at a site may also help to build arguments that upgrading to BAT standards involves considerable and potentially disproportionate cost. Hence for a specific existing site cost arguments can develop cumulative force in so far as, in relation to IPPC BAT, they draw on a history of cost arguments made for that site in the past. But it was not just past and present talk about costs of IPPC licensing for operators which shaped BAT determinations. An economic discourse was also broad in scope because it included the additional costs of IPPC licensing for regulators.

Costs of IPPC permitting for regulators

That permitting costs can also shape the regulator's BAT determinations is already recognised in UK DEFRA guidance: IPPC: 'A Practical Guide' (2004: 30):

The Secretary of State expects regulators to apply the PPC Regulations proportionately to the environmental risk presented by the operation of the installation. [...] The *regulatory effort needed to determine an application* and any permit conditions should be appropriate for the complexity of an installation and its environmental effects.

(emphasis added)[14]

There is no comparable specific guidance for German permitting officers which explicitly addresses the costs of licensing for the regulatory authority itself. Instead there is a general requirement from § 24 (2) of the German Administrative Procedure Act which stipulates that the regulatory authority has to investigate the matters about which it makes decisions. But the scope and manner of these fact finding processes are determined by the regulatory authority itself according to § 24 (1). In both the German and UK permitting authorities, however, costs of administrative activity had become an issue also in the context of new public management reforms for efficient public services. For instance, according to one German permitting officer, administration reforms had generated a saving of 10–20 per cent of jobs in the regulatory authority, while the implementation of the IPPC Directive had roughly doubled the permitting workload of the regulatory authority.[15] Limited resources could restrict the degree to which BAT determinations were carried out. According to a German permitting officer, in previous financially better resourced years detailed waste audits had been carried out in order to gather information about the quantity and types of waste produced at installations. This helped to determine BAT techniques for the prevention and reduction of waste arising at facilities in accordance with Art. 2 (11) and Annex IV No. X of the IPPC Directive. Requirements to reduce the costs of IPPC permitting meant that such waste audits were now only carried out for the most significant waste producers in an industrial sector.[16]

The costs considered in permitting included not just the direct cost to the regulatory authority, such as the costs of staff time spent on IPPC permit writing, but also opportunity costs. Time spent on permitting is time lost for other regulatory tasks. This became particularly clear in the German regulatory authority where the high number of IPPC licence applications significantly restricted the time available for enforcement work. Consideration of opportunity costs also occurs through the EA's policy of risk regulation. It sets priorities for various regulatory activities and the resources to be spent on them. In contrast to the specific case of the German regulatory authority, it signals – according to an EA permitting officer – a shift to greater priority for ongoing supervision of sites and enforcement of permits in comparison to permitting work. Hence prioritisation of work tasks – a strategy employed in both the German and the UK regulatory authority for controlling the direct and opportunity cost of writing IPPC permits – also shaped BAT determinations. But what other strategies do regulatory authorities pursue in order to limit the costs of IPPC permitting? How do they shape BAT determinations?

First, the costs of BAT determinations can be reduced for regulators and the regulated alike through the imposition of standard rules under Art. 9 (8) of the IPPC Directive. Art. 9 (8) gives powers to member states to draft 'generally binding rules' for whole sectors covered by the IPPC Directive. They generically define BAT for a whole sector and thus cut down on time and thus costs for regulators and the regulated which would otherwise have to be spent on defining BAT for each installation in a sector. By February 2004 no 'Generally Binding Rules' had yet been issued by the UK Secretary of State for the Environment, Food and Rural Affairs. But the EA has developed 'Agency Rules' which set out a general BAT standard for the intensive livestock sector and low impact installations. They seek to accomplish the same objectives of simplification and cost efficiency in BAT determinations, even though they do not have a statutory basis:

[the Standard Rules] contain standard permit conditions which, if an individual operator is prepared to accept them, allow the permit application to be dealt with more simply and *at a lower cost* than may otherwise be the case.

(emphasis added)[17]

In Germany the various technical instructions, such as the technical instruction for air (TA *Luft*) as well as for noise (TA *Lärm*) and for waste (TA *Abfall*) which provide BAT determinations, can be considered as 'generally binding rules'. They are binding upon permitters and provide BAT definitions applicable across a range of sectors. There are also further administrative provisions which guide BAT determinations in Germany across a number of sectors, such as regulations for installations which handle substances which may be toxic to water[18] as well as guidance about odour nuisances.[19]

Second, the EA has developed a permit template which requires permitting officers to impose standard BAT conditions on general issues such as noise or odour control[20] into every IPPC permit which they write. The permit template provides cheap 'off the shelf' BAT determinations for general aspects of IPPC installations. It does not, however, determine BAT for the core of a specific production process. This is still decided for each site by permitting officers.

Third, both the German and the UK regulatory authority seek to control the costs of issuing IPPC permits by setting time limits for the writing of IPPC permits, including BAT determinations.[21] For instance, the EA work instruction 'Pre-application discussions and charging for IPPC' specifies that PPC permitters may spend 15 hours on discussions with operators prior to the operator formally submitting his/her application. Any further time spent by those who are usually EA area staff on advising operators on putting the IPPC permit application together will be charged by the EA to the operator. Most importantly, the EA seeks to control the time spent on IPPC permitting through the allocation of a budget for the writing of each IPPC permit. The size of this budget is determined according to an environmental risk assessment methodology.[22] The budget is financed by the fees that operators pay to the EA for the IPPC licensing of their installation. How much the operator has to pay is based on the installation's EPOPRA (environmental protection operator and pollution risk appraisal) score. This takes into account the technical complexity of the process, its environmental impact and its record of compliance with environmental regulations. The EA requires permitting officers to deliver PPC permits 'to budget'.[23] This means they have to be written within the number of hours that are paid for by the operator's EPOPRA fee.[24]

German operators also pay the regulatory authority a fee for obtaining an IPPC licence and for ongoing supervision of their sites.[25] This fee is calculated with reference to the investment costs of the production and pollution abatement technology to be installed and permitted. The higher the operator's investments costs, the higher the fee payable to the German regulatory authority. To conclude: an economic discourse in BAT determinations also includes the costs of IPPC licensing for regulators. Both the German and the UK regulatory authority had developed various techniques for limiting the time and thus the costs spent on IPPC permitting. This economic discourse shaped BAT determinations because less time for conversations about BAT could also mean skewing BAT determinations towards known and already existing techniques, rather than exploring the latest cutting edge technology in pollution control. Time constraints made it more likely that the regulator would simply accept the BAT option which the operator had chosen and advocated in his PPC permit application.

Fee-charging systems, however, may not merely function as a limit on BAT discussions. They can also broaden the range of techniques to be considered in BAT determinations. For example, German IPPC installations which discharge into surface waters pay the water regulatory authority a fee for their discharge (Kloepfer, 2004: 1184). Permitting officers suggested that the regulatory authority generated considerable income from these discharge consent fees, because a number of large industrial installations were located in their area. The regulatory authority's water protection branch also used these fees to commission research projects for the development of advanced BAT techniques. To summarise: an economic discourse in BAT determinations is broad in scope because it considers various types of costs, including the costs of permitting for operators and regulators. The latter is not referred to in the text of the IPPC Directive. But the economic discourse is not simply broad in scope; it is also pervasive because cost arguments can be raised at various different points in the BAT determination process.

Multiple opportunities for talking about costs

In practice BAT determinations provide numerous formal and informal entry points for cost arguments. These open and flexible BAT determination processes differ from the image of structured BAT determinations projected by the text of the IPPC Directive itself[26] and various official UK and German guidance documents. According to the image of a structured BAT determination process there are specific factors[27] which feed into BAT determinations at specific stages, costs being one of these factors. Moreover, the notion of the structured BAT determination process implies that there are only specific entry points for the consideration of costs in BAT determinations. This suggests that cost arguments are thereby contained and that their influence is limited in BAT determinations. For instance, according to DEFRA guidance, IPPC: A Practical Guide (2004: 44) cost considerations should only be a *second* step in BAT determinations:

Once the options have been ranked, that which minimises environmental impact from the installation will be BAT unless economic considerations render it unavailable.

EA guidance[28] further structures BAT decision-making into six sequential modules. Module 4 provides for a comparison of BAT options and their ranking in terms of their best overall environmental performance. Only in the later modules 5 and 6 – and hence as a subsequent step – are costs to be considered in order to decide what constitutes BAT.[29] But attempts to clearly structure BAT determinations into a distinct sequence with costs being considered later on in the decision-making process already break down when we consider a range of formal guidance documents. The draft EU BREF on economics and cross-media starts with a replication of the EA guidance on costs as a secondary consideration in BAT determinations quoted above. But later on it suggests that costs are a central factor and hence may matter right from the beginning of BAT determinations:

The cost effectiveness of a technique is crucial to the determination of BAT and, in this respect, it is useful to find out which technique offers the most value (environmental benefits) for money (costs). (p. 51)

Moreover, in practice cost arguments are mobilised in a variety of ways in BAT determinations. Sometimes they are raised early on in the process of BAT decision-making and this clearly conflicts with the idea of costs being considered later on in the decision-making sequence. In addition, there are multiple and cumulative entry points for the consideration of cost arguments in BAT determinations. First, cost arguments about BAT can be made at EU, national and local levels. EU industry associations raise cost arguments during the writing of the EU BREF documents. National industry associations and large companies also raise cost arguments during the writing of the UK sector guidance notes[30] and the German technical instructions.[31] For instance, both UK and German permitting officers suggested that a few large companies in the iron and steel sector had also shaped BAT determinations for the sector on cost grounds.[32] Moreover, there are also opportunities for industry associations and large individual companies to raise cost arguments during the drafting of sector permitting plans by the Environment Agency. These sector permitting plans discuss the state of environmental protection measures in a sector and how they can be improved. They can also present objectives for environmental protection to be achieved within specific time frames as well as indicators for measuring performance in environmental protection.[33] UK permitting officers refer also to these sector permitting plans when writing individual PPC permits. Hence cost arguments which have been taken on board in the sector permitting plan can also feed into BAT determinations for site licences. Finally, cost arguments are also raised by operators at the local level when their particular installation is licensed by the regulatory authority.[34]

These various levels at which arguments about the costs of techniques can be raised, are not alternative options. In practice cost arguments are raised at all three levels. Costs are thus considered cumulatively in BAT determinations. For instance, the costs and benefits of techniques are considered when the UK sector guidance notes are drafted. But operators can still raise cost arguments when their specific installation is licensed, usually in order to justify departures from 'indicative' BAT in the UK sector guidance note:

where the techniques differ from those contained in the TGN these should be summarised here, together with an explanation of what the concerns are and how they have been addressed including economic justification for any lower cost options or for use of the Improvement Programme.[35]

But such departures from 'indicative BAT' in the UK sector guidance note are only possible as long as European environmental quality standards are not breached. To conclude: an economic discourse is pervasive in BAT determinations because cost arguments are raised – cumulatively – at various levels, such as the EU, national and local permitting level.

But an economic discourse is also pervasive because there are various *informal* entry points for costs in BAT determinations. The drafting of EU BREFs, national implementation of the IPPC Directive and the licensing of specific sites are first formal entry points for cost arguments in BAT determinations. But there are also more informal opportunities for cost considerations. These arise from the involvement of a whole range of private and other technical associations and committees in the drafting of BAT technology standards.[36] For instance, permitters in the German regulatory authority also consulted reports published by technical-scientific associations[37] and standardisation committees, such as the DIN[38] institute, especially when EU legislation or national legal rules did not provide specific BAT guidance for the particular technical installation or pollutants concerned. The technical–scientific associations include technical experts, academics, representatives from the German *Länder* environmental ministries and also industry representatives.[39] Hence the BAT guidance work of these associations provides another, more informal opportunity for cost arguments in BAT determinations. Technical standard-setting organisations also play a role in UK BAT determinations. Sometimes UK permitting officers refer to health and safety standards developed by the UK Health and Safety Executive in order to decide what constitutes BAT. Moreover, some UK sector guidance notes refer to German DIN norms. Finally, an economic discourse is also wide in scope and thus pervasive in BAT determinations because it encompasses a whole range of different types of cost arguments.

From basic assertions of costs to detailed cost calculations

Cost arguments include both very general, vague and unsupported assertions that some techniques are 'too costly'[40] and more detailed, developed, rigorous cost calculations which are informed by theoretical economics. Within the scientific framework of expert economic discourse[41] costs are economic facts which should help us to arrive at an objective and thus 'right' decision on what constitute 'the best available techniques'. Cost arguments are evaluated here with reference to scientific conventions of validity. For instance, the draft EU BREF on economics and cross-media issues suggests that 'cost data should be gathered from a number of independent sources, if possible' and that the origin of the data and any uncertainty regarding them should be recorded.[42] Moreover, this discourse generated an expectation that cost arguments should be sufficiently developed and detailed. For instance, costs were broken down into installed capital costs of BAT techniques, operating costs and annualised total costs.[43] This discourse of economic experts sometimes drew on specific models for the calculation of 'costs' and 'benefits' of techniques, such as the European Environment Agency 'Guidelines for Defining and Documenting Data on Costs of Possible Environmental Protection Measures', or the German VDI[44] guideline 3800.[45] Finally, a discourse of economic experts in BAT determinations is characterised as rational because it is meant to be 'structured, documented and auditable',[46] and is intended to enhance 'objectivity, clarity, consistency and transparency' in BAT decision-making processes.[47]

But an economic discourse in BAT determinations also includes vague, general and unsupported assertions of allegedly low or excessively high costs of BAT techniques. This discourse was in fact prevalent in BAT determinations. According to UK and German permitting officers, only a few operators engaged in an in-depth analysis of the costs and benefits of techniques.[48] IPPC permit applications prepared by consultants for UK and German operators would sometimes include pay-back times for environmental protection investments at installations. This limited economic discourse in BAT determinations was justified as 'pragmatic'. Cost information was not supposed to be 'overambitious'.[49] For instance, developed techniques for calculating 'costs' and 'benefits' of pollution reduction techniques, such as shadow-prices and benchmarks,[50] were described as 'too complex and sophisticated'.[51] BREF writers also suggested that exact cost/benefit figures for techniques were not always essential for BAT determinations. Knowledge of the general order of magnitude of costs and benefits could be sufficient to identify BAT. Moreover, abstract cost information was not considered as necessary, especially when 'real world' experience was available which showed that an industrial sector had in fact been able to absorb the costs of particular pollution control requirements. Some BREF writers considered techniques as affordable for a sector if member state regulators had required the installation of these techniques in the past and sectors had been financially capable of installing them:

It should be possible in the BREFs to look at the more obvious trade-off decisions. This could be done without an exact quantification of the costs and benefits of using a technique, but should be based on real-world experience.[52]

Sector-specific BREFs usually include operating costs and payback periods for BAT techniques where applicable.[53] Where no individual cost data are available, a BREF may simply state how many plants operate under economically viable conditions while employing a specific technique.[54]

In addition, a further element of this basic, vague and pragmatic economic discourse was a lack of clarity as to precisely what costs should matter in BAT determinations. In particular there was no clarity within an economic discourse whether the 'costs' and 'benefits' of techniques were to be assessed on a sector-wide or site-specific basis. According to Art. 2 (11) of the IPPC Directive, whether a technique is 'available' is to be assessed with reference to the 'relevant industrial sector'. The first sentence of Annex IV of the IPPC Directive refers in more general terms to the 'costs and benefits of a measure' which should be considered – among a range of other factors – in the determination of BAT. Not taking site-specific cost factors into account was also sometimes justified with reference to policy reasons. For instance, permitting officers in the German regulatory authority were also keen to encourage technology transfer. They tried to convince operators that a reduction technique which worked in one sector for a particular pollutant should be employed for the control of the same pollutant in another sector. Some operators tried to rebut such technology transfers with the argument that these techniques were too costly for their particular installation.

In contrast, UK national implementing measures seem to point to opportunities for operators making site-specific economic arguments about BAT techniques. For instance, the UK national guidance note for the inorganic chemicals sector states that the cost data obtained for the sector were 'very general' and not particularly recent, dating back to 1997.[55] Hence the note suggests that:

the costs of abatement on individual installations may be significantly different and to demonstrate BAT, it is the operator's responsibility to develop robust cost estimates that correspond to its own specific processes and circumstances.[56]

But DEFRA's 'IPPC: A Practical Guide' suggests that 'profitability of a particular business' should not affect a BAT determination. The guide, however, also explicitly acknowledges that in some cases the regulator may set BAT standards which deviate from those described as BAT in the sector guidance note. 'Particular local environmental and/or technical circumstances of a particular installation' are recognised as valid justifications for departures from BAT as described in the sector guidance note.[57] But the consideration of specific local environmental or technical circumstances of a plant can reflect cost arguments. For instance, the particular existing technical layout of a plant may make the installation of new BAT pollution abatement equipment difficult and thus potentially expensive. Local pollution hot spots may require the installation of more advanced and therefore expensive pollution abatement equipment. Hence 'local environmental and technical circumstances' which could be considered as legitimate reasons for site-specific BAT arguments could also involve cost considerations. Moreover, in practice some EU industry associations and some operators argued that costs of BAT techniques can only be established at a local level in relation to specific sites. Site-specific cost arguments were sometimes accepted by German and UK permitters. For instance, at a UK integrated iron and steel works the operator argued successfully with reference to costs that no coke side abatement should be installed, although the UK sector guidance note considered this as BAT and other integrated iron and steel works in the UK had coke side abatement installed.

Finally, on the margins of this basic, vague and pragmatic economic discourse we also find cost considerations characterised by regulators as lacking in rationality. Here cost arguments were divorced from information about costs. According to a UK permitting officer,[58] some operators in the inorganics sector who applied for IPPC licences were 'doers' rather than 'thinkers'. They had very little information and understanding of the chemical and financial aspects of their operations. They did not know whether their operations were profitable, let alone what the cost impact of environmental protection techniques on their operations would be. In the words of the UK permitting officer: 'They are just trying to stay in business.' Similarly, a BREF writer suggested that some industry associations contribute 'myths' to TWG debates about the costs of BAT techniques, such as the suggestion that the costs of BAT techniques are likely to put operators out of business. According to the BREF writer, research conducted in Sweden had shown that plant closures could not be attributed to regulatory require-ments for investment in environmental protection technologies.[59] But it was also the regulators' economic discourse which could be perceived as lacking in rationality and not just that of the operators and industry associations. For instance, according to UK permitting officers the EA's permit template seeks to save time and thus cost in PPC permitting. But it also generates new costs. Ongoing technical and commercial develop-ments at IPPC production sites could supersede the very detailed, pre-scriptive requirements for the production process in the IPPC permit template. In that case a formal permit variation under regulation 17 of the PPC (England and Wales) Regulations 2000 would be necessary. These take up further time and thus can add further costs to PPC permitting, beyond those which can be recovered through the fee which operators have to pay for a PPC licence variation according to regulation 17 (3) of the PPC (England and Wales) Regulations 2000.[60] To conclude: an economic discourse is broad and pervasive in BAT deter-minations because it covers a range of different types of cost arguments. It ranges from basic, vague, pragmatic, sometimes even 'irrational' cost arguments to complex, sophisticated, subtle and detailed cost argu-ments based on economics as a science. There is, however, one further characteristic of an economic discourse in BAT determinations which needs to be discussed. While an economic discourse can be broad, it can sometimes also be opaque or barely perceptible.

Pervasive but not necessarily perceptible costs

While cost considerations were considered as crucial by participants in BAT determinations,[61] they were not always clearly visible in BAT decision-making processes. Cost arguments could be expressed in opaque and indirect ways. Sometimes no specific cost information was provided. EU industry associations, operators and also member states were reluctant to provide cost data during EU BREF drafting and the permitting of individual IPPC installations. This is puzzling. Lobbying, specifically with reference to explicit economic arguments, is often considered as a key aspect of the formation of environmental regulation (Falkner, 2001: 161; Newell and Grant, 2000:230). Moreover, some participants in BREF determinations expected explicit cost arguments:

Now industry has the chance to put figures on the table, to tell us how expensive it is for them to install these techniques, but they don't.[62]

So, why were cost arguments not always visible in BAT determinations? Sometimes participants in BAT determinations consider that what constitutes BAT is 'obvious'. Hence costs are not considered as a necessary criterion for distinguishing between various techniques and hence for selecting the BAT. But costs can still play a role in this 'default' choice of BAT. Tacit agreement on what are 'too costly' or 'affordable' techniques can provide the basis upon which regulators and operators recognise 'obvious' BAT techniques for a site or a whole sector.[63]

So what facilitates tacit agreements between an operator and a regulatory authority on what is an 'affordable' technique? First, tacit agreements may arise from an ongoing history of environmental regulation at existing sites. Usually there are continuous discussions between operator and regulator about how to phase in environmental improvements at a site over a number of years. For instance, for some existing sites EA area offices have entered into informal agreements with operators about how environmental improvements at a site will progress and when upgrades will occur. Such longer term planning of environmental improvements provides the framework for cost considerations when a new IPPC licence is required. These histories of ongoing site regulation can make explicit cost arguments superfluous. Second, tacit agreements on costs can be facilitated by shared understandings of cost arguments. Both UK and German permitting officers expressed empathy for cost pressures facing operators when interviewed.[64] For instance, permitting officers from both the UK and German regulatory authority referred to structural economic changes in the area in which they were situated as a significant economic context for industry regulation in their area. In the locality of both the UK and German regulatory authority traditional heavy manufacturing industries had been in decline. Moreover, some German permitting officers expressed concerns about competition for operators from new EU member states such as Poland, specifically on the basis of lower labour costs. In the UK regulatory authority, some Asian countries were referred to as increasing competitive pressures on regulated industries. Empathy for the economic pressures facing operators were voiced in the UK regulatory authority in particular by staff from area offices.[65] They had often worked in the regulated industry before they joined the EA area office. Hence some area officers saw it as their role to 'filter' BAT conditions contained in PPC licences written by strategic permitting groups.[66] 'Filtering' can take several forms. Area offices can vary IPPC licences under regulation 17 of the PPC (England and Wales) Regulations 2000, when they perceive BAT conditions imposed in a PPC licence as too costly. More informally, area officers can interpret BAT permit conditions during their routine enforcement and supervision activities at sites in a manner that is sympathetic to operators' concerns over the costs of implementing these conditions. For instance, where no specific time scale for the implementation of a BAT condition has been set in an IPPC permit, area officers can adjust this timing with reference to operators' cost considerations. Sometimes permitting officers responded to economic pressures facing operators by facilitating the issuing of IPPC permits. UK permitting officers, for instance, would ask questions, such as 'how can we build confidence to be able to permit the site?' They also sought to facilitate the permitting of IPPC sites by trying to bring installations up to BAT standards through the imposition of pre-operational conditions, for new sites, and through improvement programmes.

Especially EU BREF documents and UK sector guidance notes can also sensitise permitting officers to industrial sectors' economic concerns and thus facilitate tacit agreements on appropriate costs for BAT techniques. UK guidance notes contain a section entitled 'economics'.[67] EU BREFs include a section in chapter 1 on the economic situation and the commercial pressures which the whole industrial sector covered in the BREF is facing. Further information on the affordability of specific techniques is provided in the sections of the BREF document which discuss those techniques. Sometimes this information gives very clear guidance to permitting officers on costs and this can make explicit and detailed cost discussions less important for a specific BAT determination. For instance, the fact that a significant number of small and medium-sized businesses are operating in a given sector, such as the inorganic chemicals sector, could be flagged up. Smaller operators are considered as having potentially less capacity than large companies to absorb environmental improvement costs. Sometimes the economics section signals that an industry, such as the refineries sector, is operating in markets with limited competition and hence could fairly easily absorb environmental protection costs. Hence guidance notes used in the implementation of the IPPC Directive can sensitise permitting officers to cost considerations in choosing BAT techniques. This, in turn, can facilitate tacit agreements between operators and regulators which can render explicit and detailed cost discussions less important. But an economic discourse can also function invisibly when cost arguments are raised in the language of a technical discourse.

Raising cost arguments in the language of a technical discourse

Sometimes cost arguments are raised, but not explicitly presented as cost arguments. Views about the costs of techniques can also be expressed in the language of a technical discourse. Such technical discourse focuses on engineering knowledge about techniques, including their environmental performance. For instance, the technical discourse addressed what emission ranges should be associated with specific techniques. Should a bag filter at a lime production plant be required to deliver emissions of 20–60 mg of dust per m^3 or 10–100 mg per m^3? This discussion raised technical issues about the performance of bag filters, but it also contained implicit cost arguments:

However, it was agreed in the meeting that the exact numbers are not critical to the technologies involved, but these ranges might be useful as an indication of different economic situations.[68]

Wide ranges of emissions[69] also encompass higher emissions from a technique. Higher emissions, in turn, can be the result of saving costs on operating a technique by using a lower grade filter or saving on maintenance routines. Hence wide ranges of emissions associated with a technique – a point expressed in a technical discourse – can also reflect implicit cost arguments raised by an industry association or an operator. Moreover, in some BAT determination debates – both at the EU BREF drafting level[70] and at the local level of permitting individual sites – 'process control' was advocated as a key BAT technique. This involves running an installation in such a way that its production processes are properly understood and managed by staff operating the site. The key idea is that emissions can be better controlled and potentially mini-mised if the production process itself is well controlled. Good process control can mean, for instance, less uneven and peak emission of pollutants. But the technical argument for 'process control' as a BAT technique also contains an implicit cost argument. 'Process control' is usually a cheap way of abating emissions which does not require expen-diture on additional pollution control equipment.[71]

Finally, BAT determinations usually involve a technical debate about what counts as 'the installation' to which BAT techniques have to be applied. Art. 2 (3) of the IPPC Directive provides a basic definition of an 'installation',[72] but in practice application of this definition to specific sites usually raises questions about what exactly is captured by it. These technical debates are another example of implicit cost argu-ments in BAT determinations. Decisions about what constitutes 'the installation' have significant financial consequences for operators, sometimes even more so than the actual choice of BAT techniques. The costs of implementing BAT vary according to how widely or narrowly the regulatory authority defines 'the installation' which will be covered by the IPPC permit. A broad definition of the 'installa-tion' captures a number of activities all of which then will have to comply with the BAT standard. In contrast to this, a narrower defini-tion of an 'installation' limits the scope of the operator's activities defined by the BAT obligation. But in the case of complex and large production processes, such as in the organic and inorganic chemicals sectors, a narrow definition of the 'installation' concept could mean that the operator's production process would consist of a number of 'installations' all of which would require IPPC permits.[73] In the case of changes to the production process[74] the operator then would have to apply for variations of a number of IPPC permits. Under Regulation 17 (3) of the PPC (England and Wales) Regulations 2000, permit variations require the payment of another fee to the EA. Hence a wider definition of 'installation' for large and complex operations can be less costly because there is no need for further fee expenditure on IPPC permit variations. To summarise: an economic discourse in BAT determina-tions matters, but is not always visible as such because cost arguments can be made by reference to a technical discourse on what constitutes BAT. Finally, an economic discourse in BAT determinations could also remain invisible, in particular when cost arguments were made sim-ply through reference to the timing of compliance with the BAT standard.

Raising cost arguments through reference to time

According to Annex IV No. 8 of the IPPC Directive, 'the length of time needed to introduce the best available techniques' is one of the criteria to be considered when determining BAT 'generally' at sector level or, 'in specific cases', at site level. In practice the timing of BAT conditions is a key strategy for implicitly addressing cost considerations, especially for existing installations. In the UK this is achieved through improvement programmes. They are annexed to PPC permits and require an operator to take steps towards the implementation of BAT. Hence a completion of BAT activities occurs at a future date, not at the time the PPC permit is issued. Usually operator's commercial considerations, such as the scheduling of refits and rebuilds according to the plant's investment cycle, are taken into account if a date for the installation of BAT at the site is specified in the improvement programmes. Hence costs of BAT techniques for operators are taken into account by avoiding require-ments to intall new environmental protection technologies before investments for existing techniques are written off.[75]

For the German regulatory authority the timing of the introduction of BAT techniques is also key to taking operators' cost considerations into account without engaging in detailed cost calculations and arguments with the operator. This could occur through conditions at the heart of German IPPC licences or through subsequently issued improvement orders. For existing installations BAT requirements are usually imposed through improvement orders (nachträgliche Anordnungen) issued under paragraph 17 BimSchG. These improvement orders usually include a time limit by which the required actions have to be carried out (Jarass, 2002: 388). As in the UK, it is clearly recognised that the timing of an improvement order can address proportionality concerns, including costs (Jarass, 2002: 388). To conclude: references to the timing of com-pliance with BAT requirements can represent another way in which cost arguments are implicitly raised. But what precisely lead to such invisible economic discourse in BAT determinations?

Implicit cost arguments can raise operators' chances of having their cost arguments accepted by regulators. While the IPPC Directive explic-itly provides for cost arguments to be considered in BAT determina-tions, cost arguments were also considered by regulators as potentially undermining the environmental protection objectives of the IPPC Directive. According to a UK permitting officer, 'costs should not really play a role in BAT determinations'.[76] Similarly, a member of the

German regulatory authority suggested that some operators shied away from making open cost arguments because they saw this as potentially incompatible with their attempts to build a reputation for taking environmental protection seriously.[77] Talking about economic considerations in the language of a technical discourse could reduce the cost of such risks to reputation. This mattered in particular when building credibility with the regulatory authority and citizens in the neighbourhood of a PPC installation was important for facilitating IPPC licensing because of local opposition to the plant. Sometimes operators and industry associations justified the withholding of information about costs in order to keep data about their industrial production processes confidential. They feared competitive disadvantages if they disclosed cost data about their production and pollution abatement techniques.[78] Moreover, permitting officers also suggested that operators withheld cost information about their installations in order to make control of their process by the regulatory authority more difficult. Hence an economic discourse could be closely linked to the expression of interests and thus to issues of power in BAT determinations.

Links between an economic and a political discourse in BAT determinations

Very general, vague and basic assertions of costs specifically help to move an economic discourse closer to a political one. Here costs can be expressions of operators' or regulators' interests in the BAT determination process, rather than 'objective facts' which deliver the 'right' answer to the question as to what constitute 'the best available techniques':

In making the step from quantified emission reduction to environmental advantage, it is here that there are both scientifically based *and more political expressions of advantage*. It is not foreseen that 'taking account of costs and advantages' means that a full cost benefit analysis must be carried out using monetary values for environmental advantage.

(emphasis added)[79]

Cost arguments were sometimes considered as 'political' because they were perceived to involve trade-off decisions between various social goals:

On *affordability*, it was said that sometimes it *is a political issue*, looking for a balance between employment and environment, amongst other factors.

(emphasis added)[80]

Hence cost arguments raised by operators can also trigger debate about how this would affect regulators' interests.[81] In some sectors demands for investment in environmental protection techniques could be politically disadvantageous for regulators. For instance, in the refineries sector costs of pollution control can be passed on to consumers of oil-based products, such as car drivers. Hence regulatory requirements could generate public opposition.

Moreover, cost information can be malleable and therefore transformed into a means for the expression of interests. Operators, industry associations and equipment suppliers are the main sources of information about the costs of techniques. In comparison to regulators they therefore have considerable control over information about the costs of techniques, more so than over technical information.[82] Regulatory authorities have limited means for independently verifying cost information supplied by operators, industry associations or equipment suppliers.[83] This control can enhance operators' power when negotiating with a regulatory authority. For instance, managers of IPPC installations also adapt the presentation of cost information for internal accounting purposes. They choose how much of the costs for BAT techniques will be counted as an 'environmental cost' and therefore be charged to the installation's environmental budget, and how much of the costs for BAT techniques will be considered as a general production cost, charged to a different internal budget.[84] Regulators also choose how to present costs of BAT techniques. Stating the maximum amount of costs for BAT techniques was the preferred technique, especially when the regulatory authority also made public statements about its achievements in raising expenditure on environmental protection techniques.[85]

Close links between a political and an economic discourse are also revealed when political conflict resolution procedures rather than scientific economic arguments are invoked in order to settle disputes about the costs of BAT techniques. Negotiation was one way for resolving debates about costs between operators and permitting officers:

The agency wants him to go so far, but the operator says no, it's going to cost me too much, and they meet in the middle ground.[86]

Voting also featured in debates about economic aspects of BAT. The EU Technical Working Group for the BREF on economic and cross-media issues finally voted in order to reach a decision on what should be considered as the five most important factors which affect the economic viability of a technique in a sector.

To conclude: an economic discourse in BAT determinations is broad in scope and thus pervasive. This discourse might sometimes be invisible. It could also find itself linked to a political discourse. These characteristics shed further light on the 'microphysics of power' in EU law in action. Control over cost information is key to the exercise of power by the regulated in their interactions with the regulators. Macro-sociological explanations of EU law have suggested that within capitalist economic systems corporate actors do not always need to raise cost arguments because it is taken for granted that the financial implications of legal regulation for the regulated will be considered (Snyder, 1989: 184–185). This section has discussed some of the strategies and tactics that participants in BAT determinations adopt on a micro level in order to consider costs. The discussion here adds a further twist to a Marxist analysis of the creation of legal regulation. It is not just costs for operators, but also those for regulators which feature in BAT determinations. Moreover, an economic discourse does not follow the straightforward rationality of serving the interests of the regulated. Actual economic discourses invoked in BAT determinations have been wide-ranging and have included not just sophisticated, detailed economic arguments, but also vague, general and sometimes irrational statements about costs. Hence the following section further pursues a micro-level analysis of the functions of this economic discourse.

Functions of an economic discourse in BAT determinations

As discussed above, an economic discourse in BAT determinations is broad in scope and comprises different types of cost arguments ranging from vague, basic and general cost statements to detailed, nuanced cost arguments drawing on the science of economics. The latter type of cost arguments in particular support the idea that there is a *distinct* economic discourse in BAT determinations. This idea of a distinct economic discourse in BAT determinations fulfils a specific function. It is used to rebut the influence of political considerations in BAT determinations. Sometimes, UK and German permitting officers felt the need 'to defend themselves'[87] against cost arguments made by operators.[88] For instance, the German regulatory authority sought to rebut political cost arguments made by the operator by recourse to detailed expert cost calculations obtained from the technical environmental advisory branch of the environmental administration, the *Landesumweltamt*.

The EU draft BREF on economics and cross-media issues also develops a more detailed economic discourse by spelling out four factors which affect the affordability of a technique in a sector:[89]

This advice would be particularly useful when the BAT proposal is contentious, i.e. such as instances when there are disagreements about whether a technique is 'too expensive'.[90]

Hence a developed, elaborate economic discourse is often invoked in response to conflicts about whether a particular technique is 'affordable':

Although an assessment of economic viability is an inherent part of determining BAT, a detailed assessment is expected to be carried out only to resolve a claim that a technique (or a combination of techniques) is too expensive to be BAT. That claim is considered most likely to come from the industrial sector concerned and this chapter sets out a framework within which the arguments can be presented. The burden of proof in such an argument rests with those who object to the proposed BAT.[91]

Moreover, a developed, elaborate economic discourse is considered to enhance transparency in cost discussions, rendering political points in cost arguments at least more visible and thus potentially more open to critical evaluation. According to the draft EU BREF on economics and cross-media issues, a developed economic discourse should be the first step, with a political evaluation of the significance of cost considerations for the BAT determination representing a subsequent step:

Once the critical issues for the sector have been analysed and exposed in the assessment, then it is expected that the Technical Working Group can debate these critical issues and decide whether, or how they should influence the determination of BAT.[92]

A more elaborate and developed economic discourse is also considered to enhance transparency by generating cost information which can be 'validated' and 'audited'.[93] To summarise: one of the functions of a wide-ranging economic discourse in BAT determinations is also to supply more detailed, elaborate economic arguments which can be employed to rebut political cost arguments. But an economic discourse in BAT determinations also fulfils another key function. It generates a BAT determination process which is characterised at the local permitting level by a tension between a highly regulated, bureaucratic approach to permitting and an approach that relies on unregulated 'expert judgement'.

Bureaucratic or expert judgement permitting?

As discussed above, an economic discourse in BAT determinations is wide-ranging and deploys a broad concept of cost. It includes the costs of IPPC permitting for regulators. This contributes to a bureaucratic approach towards BAT determinations. The EA's general PPC permit template is meant to be a cost saving device which limits the scope for discretionary decision-making in routine aspects of BAT determinations. In Germany the technical instructions also generate a bureaucratic approach to BAT determinations. They provide lengthy and detailed prescriptions of a number of BAT techniques for various types of installations. The TA *Luft*, for instance, covers in 250 pages BAT techniques for the control of emissions to air in particular.[94] For BAT determinations in relation to discharges to water, the technical appendices to the waste water regulations[95] provide detailed rules. But an economic discourse deployed in BAT determinations is multi-faceted. It can also find itself linked to a political discourse through an expression of interests. These aspects of an economic discourse introduce a highly discretionary element into BAT determinations, where voting and negotiation also assist in the evaluation of cost arguments. This discretionary element – sometimes associated with political features of an economic discourse – is, paradoxically, also referred to as 'expert judgement'.[96] It can be contrasted with determining cost arguments by reference to economic 'facts'. Economic methodologies:

cannot make the decision, but can support *subsequent expert judgement* and provide a more consistent basis for the ultimate decision.

(emphasis added)[97]

Hence despite attempts to regulate in detail BAT determinations through various binding legal rules and guidance documents, in practice IPPC permitting sometimes involves the exercise of significant discretion by permitting officers in evaluating economic cost information. As a UK permitting officer put it:

I always say, it's down to a judgment call, and it's opinion based, really. I mean, however much guidance you have, how you assess it, how you quantify it matters.[98]

The importance of 'expert judgement' for BAT determinations was also emphasised at the EU BREF drafting level:

When the expert considers the return on investment to be positive, it is concluded that the candidate BAT is always economically feasible. Exact financial figures are not required.[99]

Hence a broad-ranging economic discourse that includes different types of cost arguments generates an IPPC permitting procedure characterised by a tension between a highly regulated, bureaucratic approach, on the one hand, and a discretionary, more unregulated 'expert judgement' approach, on the other. This discourse can be shaped by social actors. It can be adjusted to specific situations. It further contributes to a flexible IPPC permitting procedure at the local level. Economic considerations in BAT determinations are best conceptualised as a fluid discourse rather than as a rigid, static external social structure which determines the meaning and operation of law, in this case the key legal obligation under the IPPC Directive 'to employ the best available techniques'. This also sheds light on the relationship between law and its various contexts, and hence on the relationship between law and a social sphere. Various types of costs were considered at numerous entry points and levels. 'Economics *in* law' describes the relationship between the key legal obligation under the IPPC Directive and its economic context. Hence contexts are intrinsically bound up with the construction of the legal obligation to 'employ the best available techniques'. They are mobilised in various ways by participants in BAT determination processes. They do not resemble static structures 'out there' impinging on a separate and distinct phenomenon of 'law'. Moreover, possibilities for overlap and exchange between different discourses, such as economic, political and technical discourses, suggest that law's contexts themselves may not have clear, tight conceptual boundaries. Instead the boundaries of law's social contexts can be fluid. Hence technical and economic discourses on what constitute 'the best available techniques' may not always simply be perceived as in conflict with each other. A technical discourse may also accommodate and express economic arguments on BAT.

Conclusion

Economic relations are a key element of the 'social sphere'. This book analyses 'EU law in action' by tracing how a social sphere intersects with a legal sphere. Hence this chapter has examined how talk about costs in BAT determinations becomes relevant for defining and thus putting into effect the key legal obligation under the IPPC Directive that installations have to employ 'the best available techniques'. Chapter 4 argued that relations of power are key to understanding concepts of 'law in action'. This chapter has traced the microphysics of power in the implementation of the IPPC Directive by discussing overlaps and exchanges between economic, technical and political discourses. The chapter argues that an economic discourse is broad in scope and thus pervasive in BAT determinations. It involves a broader range of cost arguments than formal legal texts, such as the IPPC Directive, seem to envisage. A notion of EU law as the formal 'law in the books' must therefore be questioned. The chapter also argues that an economic discourse in BAT determinations does not resemble a static social structure. It appears flexible and fluid, involving different types of cost arguments. It is tied into the construction of what constitutes BAT. This also questions perceptions of EU law as relatively autonomous in relation to its contexts. Finally, the discussion in this chapter also questions whether EU law can be wielded in a simply instrumental manner. Where contexts – such as economic ones linked to technical and political contexts – constitute law, law's capacity to influence and transform its social environments must itself appear limited.

Notes

1. For instance, the writer for the BREF on non-ferrous metals argued for the compatibility of economic and environmental considerations in the determination of BAT. He suggested that 'many installations in the industry had made significant improvements to processes in the period since 1990. These process improvements were generally driven by the need to reduce costs and increase efficiency and yield of metal and they also resulted in significant reductions in environmental impact.' Extract from EIPPC Bureau background file for the BREF on non-ferrous metals.
2. Though it is clear that some of the costs of pollution control incurred under the IPPC Directive are not borne by operators of IPPC installations but are passed on to purchasers of their products.
3. The *best* techniques are defined in Art. 2 (11) third indent of the IPPC Directive as those which are most effective in achieving a high general level of protection for the environment as a whole.
4. Such as 'the use of low-waste technology', 'the nature, effects and volume of the emissions concerned' and 'the length of time needed to introduce the best available technique' among others.
5. These proportionality considerations are ultimately grounded in the requirements of constitutional law. Art. 14 of the German Constitution guarantees the right to property and thus limits the powers of the

environmental administration to interfere with operators' property rights (Jarass, 2002: 389).

6. Proportionality considerations and cost arguments were also closely associated during BREF drafting at the EU level, as illustrated in the following statement by a BREF author: 'These are the economic efficiency considerations then, the proportionality considerations in the specific case' (Interview no. 11 with BREF writer).

7. *Verordnung über Anforderungen an das Einleiten von Abwasser in Gewässer*, of 15 October 2002.

8. DEFRA guidance: 'IPPC: A Practical Guide' (2004: 40).

9. Techniques that are available in proven pilot plants are included here.

10. 'IPPC: A Practical Guide' issued by DEFRA, February 2004 at p. 41, www.defra.gov.uk/environment/ppc/envagency/pubs/index.htm.

11. Interview no. 2 with UK permitting officer. Similarly DEFRA guidance: 'IPPC: A Practical Guide' (2004: 47) suggests that 'new installations will normally be expected to comply with or go beyond indicative BAT. However, site-specific factors may justify a different conclusion from the normal understanding of what technique is BAT in particular cases.'

12. Operators have to provide justifications for deviation from the UK sector guidance note. Such justifications can be that work was being planned for the reduction of emission levels. See the following extract from Decision Document no. 1 for an existing IPPC installation: 'The current emission levels from line 1 *may exceed the benchmark levels*. Average emission levels are in line with the benchmark but maximum levels may be higher. Previous work has been carried out by the applicant to identify potential reductions and some improvements made *to reach near benchmark levels*. This work has been previously discussed with the Agency and it has been determined that *the controls in place represent BAT for the site*' (emphasis added). Operators sometimes also successfully justified emissions above benchmark levels on the basis that their emissions contributed little extra emission in relation to existing background levels of pollution.

13. EA guidance document 'Environmental Assessment and Appraisal of BAT', p. 5.

14. This message is repeated in the Environment Agency's internal work instructions on 'Pre-application discussions and charging for IPPC permits', issued to IPPC permitting officers. This suggests that permitting should be carried out in a 'cost effective manner'.

15. These time pressures were partly managed through an extension of time periods for permitting. The German regulatory authority sought to issue permits within 7 months but permitting procedures now took on average about a year in the German regulatory authority. Interview no. 1 with German permitting officer.

16. Interview no. 2 with German permitting officer.

17. DEFRA guidance: 'IPPC: A Practical Guide' (2004: 31).

18. The 'VAwS': *Verordnung über Anlagen zum Umgang mit wassergefährdenden Stoffen und über Fachbetriebe.*
19. The *Geruchsimmissionsrichtlinie.*
20. The permit template drafted by the EA's policy unit contains different types of colour coded text. Black text contains suggested permit text which can be amended where it does not fit the particular circumstances of the site. Plain red text contains permit text where choices still have to be made. Italic red text indicates sections of the permit where information has to be added by the permitting officer according to the EA's internal work instructions. Pink text in the permit template contains further information and guidance for permitting officers. The permit template even contains standard improvement conditions, such as 'a report shall investigate techniques by which the releases of the substances may be further reduced and shall propose a plan and time scale for implementation'. A similar colour coded template has also been provided by the EA's policy unit for the drafting of Decision Documents for PPC licences.
21. There is also a specific control system for keeping track of the time it took to draft IPPC permits. Time taken for work on IPPC permits is logged in the EA's 'national time recording system'.
22. The so-called EPOPRA methodology as set out in EPOPRA Methodology, version 3.1, April 2006. For further information see www.environment-agency.gov.uk/commondata/103599/ep_opra_v3.1_1_728689.doc, site last visited 2 April 2006.
23. UK permitting officers suggested in interviews that IPPC permits were not always delivered to budget, especially when unforeseen technical or political controversies arose during the permitting process.
24. Team leaders have to ensure that their teams of permitting officers deliver IPPC permits within specific time frames. The key performance indicator set for team leaders requires that no IPPC permit application should have been lodged longer than 12 months with the EA before work on it commences and that 75 per cent of all IPPC permits should be issued in under 8 months. The DEFRA 'IPPC: A Practical Guide' document even suggests that all IPPC permits should be issued within 4 months.
25. Each of the German *Länder* has its own statute which specifies the amount of fees which have to be paid for certain administrative acts (*Gebührengesetz*).
26. For instance, through the list of criteria in Annex IV to the IPPC Directive.
27. See the definition of BAT in Art. 2 (11) of the IPPC Directive and the list of factors to be taken into account in Annex IV.
28. 'Environmental Assessment and Appraisal of BAT'.
29. Module 5 deals with the step of 'evaluating costs to implement each option', while Module 6 deals with an identification of options which represent the Best Available Technique by calculating environmental benefits against costs. Moreover, 'Environmental Assessment and Appraisal of BAT' (2004: 74) portrays also costs as a secondary consideration in the following

description of BAT options appraisal: 'Once the options have been ranked according to environmental performance, the option that results in the lowest impact on the environment as a whole will usually be BAT, unless economic considerations mean that it is unavailable.'

30. As the EA guidance document 'Environmental Assessment and Appraisal of BAT' (p. 3) states: 'Indicative BAT provided in IPPC Technical Guidance Notes or BREFs is based on an analysis of the costs and benefits for typical or representative plants within that sector.'

31. *Technische Anleitungen* (TA).

32. For instance, the influence of a large operator in the iron and steel sector had contributed to the inclusion of wet quenching as BAT for the cooling of coke oven gas when the new TA *Luft* 2002 was drafted. While the 1986 version of the TA *Luft* recommended 'dry cooling' as BAT, the 2000 version also refers to 'wet quenching'.

33. Sector permitting plans indicate priority pollutants for control in a sector. Sometimes they also identify the percentage contribution that particular companies make to releases in a given sector. They thereby identify priority polluters on which to focus pollution reduction measures.

34. In the UK costs of BAT techniques can be considered at various stages in the local PPC permitting process. First, cost arguments can be raised during the determination of BAT in the draft permit written by a member of the Strategic Permitting Group. Second, draft permits have been passed to area offices for comments. Sometimes comments of area offices will relate to the costs of BAT techniques.

35. EA internal work instruction 'Determination of an application for a PPC permit (non Landfill) under the PPC Regulations 2000 (SI 2000 No. 1973)'.

36. Some of these committees and associations are not specifically set up for the implementation of the IPPC Directive. They have therefore been involved in the drafting of technology standards similar to BAT well before the IPPC Directive was passed.

37. *Technisch-wissenschaftliche Vereinigungen* such as the ATV = *Abwassertechnische Vereinigung*.

38. *Deutsches Institut für Normung*.

39. For further info see www.dvt-net.de/satzung.html.

40. Examples of very general and vague assertions of costs were statements by operators, such as 'I can't afford this' or 'This is too expensive. My sector is under considerable economic pressure'. The following is an example of a very general cost argument made in response to the Draft BREF on the iron and steel sector by an EU industry association: 'Typically the capital is written off over long timescales. Upgrading of existing plant to BAT standards is economically impossible and recognition of this fact is important when using this Note.' This argument, however, is not compatible with the text of the IPPC Directive which requires all plants, including existing plants, to operate to BAT standards by 31 October 2007.

41. For instance, the UK and German regulatory authority would occasionally seek advice from in-house specialist economists in order to provide assessments of an operator's cost calculations.
42. EU BREF on economics and cross-media effects (p. 33). Also the EA guidance document 'Environmental Assessment and Appraisal of BAT' (p. 7) suggests that a 'sensitivity analysis' should be carried out for cost arguments in order to highlight uncertainties and assumptions in the calculation of costs and environmental benefits of techniques.
43. For instance, the section on 'economics' in the UK sector guidance note for inorganics recognises that it is necessary to further differentiate the costs of BAT techniques according to the precise pollutant emitted, the scrubbing medium and operating conditions. Hence there are limits to providing a typical annualised cost for a particular BAT technique. The EA guidance document 'Environmental Assessment and Appraisal of BAT' also asks operators to provide detailed cost information if various BAT options need to be evaluated. Information should relate to capital costs of equipment purchase, installation costs and average changes in annual operating and maintenance costs.
44. Abbreviation for *Verein Deutscher Ingenieure*, the Association of German Engineers.
45. VDI Guideline 3800 'Determination of costs for industrial environmental protection measures'. For further information see www.vdi.de/vdi/vrp/richtliniendetails/index.php?ID=9233139.
46. EA guidance document, 'Environmental Assessment and Appraisal of BAT' (p. 2). See also p. ii of the EU BREF on economics and cross-media issues.
47. Notes for interim meeting for the BREF on economics and cross-media effects, 30–31 January and 1 February 2002 (pp. 2 and 4).
48. For instance, one UK permitting officer suggested that in eight years of permitting sites he had only been involved on two occasions in engaging in detailed discussions about costs with an operator. German operators of *new* installations have to provide fairly detailed cost information at the IPPC permit application stage because the fees charged by the regulatory authority for issuing the permit are based on the building costs of the installation. But the building costs do not usually provide information about the extra costs caused by pollution reduction techniques or the impact of pollution reduction techniques on profits per product.
49. Dutch presentation in notes of kick-off meeting on economics and cross-media issues, 25–26 May 2000.
50. The costs of environmental techniques are compared here with reference to shadow prices which have been established for the emission of pollutants. For instance, a shadow price of £50 could be attributed to the release of one ton of CO_2. This can then be compared to the cost of abating one ton of CO_2 emissions through a specific technique, which may, for instance, be £60.
51. Notes for interim meeting for the BREF on economics and cross-media effects, 30–31 January and 1 February 2002 (p. 7). But the EU BREF on

economics and cross-media also seeks to raise the level of cost arguments being made in BAT determinations. It lists eight guidelines for dealing with cost arguments in BAT determinations. For instance, guideline eight develops a specifically economic discourse through reference to methodologies for dealing with exchange rates between different EU currencies, inflation, discounting and calculating annual costs of techniques.

52. Extract from 5th IEF meeting, 18–19 February 1999.
53. Economic data are usually reported in the chapter on 'BAT candidates' in the BREF.
54. Frank Farrell, 2001, 'How Economic Issues were dealt with in the Non-Ferrous Metals BREF', March 2001, IPTS, Seville, p. 6.
55. P. 18 UK Sector Guidance Note for the inorganic chemicals sector.
56. P. 18 UK Sector Guidance Note for the inorganic chemicals sector.
57. Notes on DEFRA 'IPPC: A Practical Guide', p. 45. The EA guidance document 'Environmental Assessment and Appraisal of BAT' (2004: 3) also suggests that deviation from BAT techniques as set out in UK sector guidance notes is possible in exceptional circumstances for only three reasons: the technical characteristics of the installation concerned, its geographical location and local environmental conditions.
58. Interview with UK permitting officer, no. 5.
59. Interview no. 8 with BREF writer.
60. The EA is seeking to further control the time and thus money it spends on PPC permit variations. The new PPC permit template will contain reference to generic agency guidance on particular issues, instead of imposing specific requirements on the operator. Hence when the EA updates and changes its guidance on a particular aspect of IPPC operations, it will not be necessary to formally vary the existing PPC permit under regulation 17 of the PPC (England and Wales) Regulations 2000. Instead the permit will be automatically updated through cross-reference to the updated version of the EA guidance.
61. Interview no. 1 with BREF writer and interview no. 2 with UK permitting officer.
62. Interview no. 4 with BREF writer.
63. There were limited references to costs in the EIPPC Bureau background files, the official tape recording of the 2nd TWG meeting for the iron and steel sector as well as in the EA Decision Documents in relation to the permitting of IPPC sites in the UK and the official background files kept by the German regulatory authority for the licensing of individual IPPC sites.
64. This took, for instance, the form of permitting officers saying that they would understand operators' objections against particular techniques on the basis that these pollution abatement techniques might slow down production processes and output.
65. For instance, a member of an area team questioned in an interview whether the environmental assessment levels which the EA had drawn up were appropriate for BAT determinations. They were considered by some area

officers as setting too strict criteria for the determination of the significance of emissions from installations, thus potentially requiring fairly costly BAT abatement measures. Similarly, a German permitting officer considered as too onerous the legal rule of the TA *Luft* according to which installations whose emissions exceed 3 per cent of the TA *Luft* immission values can be required to install technical measures which go beyond BAT. These can be fairly costly.

66. Interview no.1 with UK permitting officer.
67. In the case of the UK SGN for the inorganic chemicals sector this was a 6-page section out of a 260-page document. For instance, in relation to the economic fate of the fertiliser businesses the UK SGN (at p. 16) states:

> Western European fertilizer production and consumption have declined by at least a third since the end of the 1980s. The availability of cheaper imported fertilizers, particularly ammonium nitrate and particularly from Russia and former Eastern Bloc countries, had a disastrous effect on prices with consequential closure of a significant proportion of EU production capacity. It is possible that the European fertilizer environment is now stabilising, albeit at a lower demand level, and that the oversupply situation is improving – but it is not absolutely clear. It seems unlikely that much new investment will occur in the near future – though there will be opportunities for environmental improvements as existing plant is revamped.

In Germany there is no formal source for this type of economic information about a sector but permitters have referred in interviews to similar types of available information from public media about the state of the regulated sector.

68. Extract from the EIPPC Bureau background file on the BREF for large combustion plants.
69. For instance, in the description of techniques in the EU BREF documents or the UK sector guidance notes.
70. For instance, a number of BAT techniques discussed in the EU BREF for the non-ferrous metal sector rely on 'process control'. 'Process control' mattered in particular in sectors with complex and changing production processes, such as chemicals production.
71. Process control, for instance, was employed as an argument against the installation of coke side abatement at an integrated iron and steel works in the UK. The operator argued that there were no emissions of uncarbonised coal from coke (so-called 'black pushes') because the temperature and heating of the coke were fine-tuned and thus the coke making process was well controlled. In fact the operator argued that the installation of coke side abatement technology would provide an invitation to reducing attention on process control.
72. 'Installation shall mean a stationary technical unit where one or more activities listed in Annex I are carried out, and any other directly associated

activities which have a technical connection with the activities carried out on that site and which could have an effect on emissions and pollution'.

73. According to permitting officers, operators, however, would sometimes carry out detailed cost analysis for themselves before deciding which installation definition they recommended to the regulator in the PPC permitting process.

74. Such as the production of a new chemical or a new reaction path for producing existing products.

75. DEFRA 'IPPC: A Practical Guide' (2004: 47) suggests that cost and proportionality considerations should be taken into account. This means that an existing plant which is already operating close to BAT should not be required to upgrade to full BAT if it produces only a small increase in environmental protection. The regulator should only require this when the operator plans a major upgrade in any event. Section 5.5. of the EU draft BREF on economics and cross-media issues also considered the timing of equipment upgrades as a key tool for addressing cost concerns of operators of existing installations.

76. Interview no. 4 with UK permitting officer.

77. The expression used in the interview was that arguing that some environmental protection techniques were too expensive was considered 'ehrenrührig' (dishonourable).

78. For instance, at the EU level of BREF drafting some industry associations complained that no 'rules of the game' had been established setting out how the EIPPC Bureau would handle the information supplied by them.

79. Litten, Vito Conference Proceedings, 2000:3.

80. Dutch presentation in the notes of kick-off meeting for TWG on economic and cross-media issues, 25–26 May 2000.

81. Interview no. 4 with BREF writer.

82. This was also starkly expressed by participants in the drafting of national BAT guidance documents who suggested 'Never trust industry data. 'Never trust suppliers' data': see P. Vercaemst and R. Dijkmans, 'Integrating Economic Aspects when Determining BAT – a Framework', in Vito Conference Proceedings, p. 11.

83. For instance, UK permitting officers would frequently ask operators for cost information about BAT techniques. This occurred by inserting conditions into the improvement programme for an IPPC licence.

84. Interview no. 12 with EIPPC Bureau management.

85. Schaerer, Vito Conference Proceedings, 2000, pp. 1, 7.

86. Extract from interview no. 6 with UK permitting officer.

87. Interview no. 1 with German permitting officer.

88. Cost arguments could be difficult to rebut for German permitters as long as the operator's suggested BAT techniques were compliant with the provisions of the technical instructions. Once the formal conditions for obtaining an IPPC permit are fulfilled by German operators, they have a right to be issued with a licence (*Gebundene Ermessensentscheidung*). In contrast to the UK,

German permitting officers have no further discretion to decide whether a permit should be issued or not and how cost considerations should influence this decision once the formal permitting conditions according to para. 5 of the BimSchG have been fulfilled.

89. These were market structure (including competition), industry structure, resilience in withstanding competition, return on investment, profit margins, price elasticity and speed of implementation.
90. Notes on interim meeting for costs and cross-media effects, 30–31 January and 1 February 2002, p. 4.
91. EU BREF on economics and cross-media issues, p. iii, p. 76.
92. Ibid., p. 76.
93. Ibid., p. iii.
94. There are also of course always some cases which are not fully determined by the rules in the technical instructions. For instance, there may be new types of installations which have been developed since the drafting of the technical instructions, such as biological and mechanical waste treatment plants (*mechanische biologische Abfallbehandlungsanlagen*).
95. *Technische Anhänge der Abwasserverordnung*.
96. EU BREF on economics and cross-media, p. 51.
97. Ibid., p. iii.
98. Extract from interview no. 6 with UK permitting officer.
99. Vercaemst and Dijkmans, Vito Conference Proceedings, 2000:5.

8   Does 'law' integrate? Licensing German and English coke ovens under the IPPC Directive

Introduction

This chapter further develops analysis of the relationships between law and integration. Chapter 2 argued that a range of political scientists and lawyers consider positive state law – closed legal rules differentiated from their social, political and economic environment – to be central to EU integration processes. Hence 'integration through law' has been a key theme in the literature on EU integration. Chapter 3 critically analysed this theme with reference to the literature on new forms of EU governance. This literature draws attention to 'integration without formal state law' because EU institutions increasingly resort to 'soft' law as well as combinations of 'soft' and 'hard' law. Soft law includes various forms of non-binding guidelines, recommendations, opinions, circulars, benchmarking and exchange of best practices, as practised in open methods of coordination. Increasing resort to Framework Directives has also been considered as an element of new forms of EU governance. Framework Directives do not seek to impose specific, detailed, prescriptive 'hard' EC law obligations upon member states, but only spell out legal obligations for member states in outline. Chapter 5 further questioned the argument for 'integration through law' on the basis of empirical data. I suggested that the implementation of the IPPC Directive in fact not only generates traditional, closed 'hard' state law, but also open BAT norms, which do not conform to the image of law invoked in the literature on 'integration through law'.

This chapter provides further critical empirical analysis of the claim that closed 'hard' state law norms are central to EU integration processes. It does so by examining how a harmonised definition of the key legal obligation under the IPPC Directive – that operators of mainly industrial installations have to utilise the 'best available techniques' (BAT) – was actually achieved during the licensing of a German and UK coke oven. Coke ovens produce coal that is usually intended for the production of iron and steel. Is the harmonised definition of BAT for elements of coke production an example of integration through the IPPC Directive? Did non-legal factors, such as political interests, economic considerations or simply technical constraints, generate this integration result? How did formal legal texts and law's contexts get linked here in the construction of 'EU law in action'? What techniques did participants in EU integration processes develop on a micro-level for mobilising contexts in the interpretation of formal legal texts? Can a distinctly 'legal' dimension to the EU integration process be identified here? If not, where does this leave the distinction between 'integration through law' and 'integration without law'?

The first section of the chapter discusses how specific forms of legal, economic, political and technical discourse became relevant to the definition of BAT for the German and English coke oven plant. The second section then examines whether it was actually the integrating force of a legal discourse which led to the choice of the same BAT technology at the English and the German plant for the cooling of the coke.[1] It argues that the intersections between a legal and technical discourse as well as a political and economic discourse can help to explain why the same BAT technology was chosen for the cooling of the coke at the English and German plant. The third section summarises the main findings of the chapter.

Defining and tracing an integration effect in the context of IPPC licensing for coke ovens

The first point that needs to be addressed is whether the definition of BAT for the English and the German coke oven plant can be considered as an integration effect.[2] The literature on EU integration provides various definitions of EU integration. They range from loose forms of mere cooperation between member states to the complete harmonisation of particular policy sectors. For instance, Ernst Haas – one of the first to theorise cooperation in Western Europe – defined integration as:

The process whereby political actors in several distinct national settings are persuaded to shift their loyalties, expectations and political activities toward a new centre, whose institutions possess or demand jurisdiction over the pre-existing national states. The end result of a process of political integration is a new political community, superimposed over the pre-existing ones.

(Haas, 1958: 16)

Neither this nor other definitions of EU integration[3] require complete uniformity of activities in a particular policy sector in order to detect effects of integration. According to Haas's definition, the passing of the IPPC Directive itself is already an example of integration. But in the case of the licensing of the German and the UK coke ovens an even stronger harmonisation effect occurred. The UK and German licences refer to the same technology as BAT for the cooling of the hot coke.[4]

But what actually is coke? Coke production starts with pulverised coal being heated in a coke oven under the exclusion of air at temperatures between 1000 and 1100 degree Celsius for 14 to 24 hours.[5] The coke is then pushed from the coke oven into the quenching tower, where the coke is cooled down. Hence coke cooling is a key aspect of coke production. Coke can be cooled in two ways. First, there is coke dry quenching (CDQ) where the coke is dropped into the top of the quenching tower. It then passes through an inert gas as it falls to the bottom of the tower. As the coke descends it emits heat into the counter-flowing gas and is thereby cooled to a temperature between 150 and 200 degrees Celsius. The heat which has been transferred from the coke to the gas is absorbed into a waste-heat boiler which is used for the generation of steam and ultimately electricity.[6] Second, hot coke can be cooled by water being sprayed onto it.[7] This is called wet quenching. Emissions-minimised wet quenching is a further development of wet quenching. It generates fewer dust emissions than traditional wet quenching.[8]

Dry quenching shows better environmental performance in particular in relation to dust emissions than traditional wet quenching. Traditional wet quenching can generate coke-dust, air, and remaining coke-gas and water-mist plumes which evaporate from the quench tower into the surrounding air. But there are different views about how exactly coke dry and emissions-minimised wet quenching compare in their emissions performance. According to the EU BREF document for the production of iron and steel there is no significant difference in dust[9] and carbon monoxide emissions between dry quenching and emissions-minimised wet quenching.[10] According to figures of a German *Landesumweltamt* (environmental protection agency of the *Land*), produced during the IPPC licensing procedure for the German coke oven, dry quenching involves considerably fewer emissions of total dust and fine particulates than emissions-minimised wet quench-ing.[11] Dry quenching also provides the added environmental advantage of energy reuse through heat recovery from the hot coke for steam generation.[12]

According to Art. 3 of the IPPC Directive member states must ensure that all installations referred to in Annex I are operated in accordance with the Directive's legal obligations. This includes the requirement in Art. 3 (a) of the IPPC Directive that installations must employ 'the best available techniques'. The IPPC Directive itself provides only general criteria for the definition of the 'best available techniques'. It is the EU-wide guidance document on the production of iron and steel which specifies the 'best available techniques' for coke ovens, including coke cooling. According to this BREF dry and emissions-minimised wet quenching with emissions of less than 50 g particulate matter per ton of coke produced are considered 'the best available techniques' for cooling coke.[13]

At the end of the IPPC licensing procedure both the German and the English coke ovens plants received permits for wet quenching of the coke, with the German plant operating emissions-minimised wet quenching. This constitutes an integration effect, in the sense that the same technique was employed as BAT for coke cooling. This also repre-sents an integration effect in the sense that coke ovens in Germany had previously used coke dry quenching.[14] This plant was one of the first to be licensed for emissions-minimised wet quenching.[15] The technical instructions for air (TA *Luft* 1986), which bind German permitters and list dry quenching as a key BAT technique, still applied[16] at the beginning of the German IPPC licensing procedure for the coke oven.[17] Hence the German licensing authority initially believed that emissions-minimised wet quenching could *not* be considered as 'the best available technique'.

In contrast, both the English operator and licensing authority were agreed from the start of the PPC licensing procedure that wet quenching can be regarded as BAT.[18] Hence, in contrast to the German operator, the English operator did not apply for any changes in the coke cooling technique when applying for a PPC licence. In fact the integrated iron and steel works, in which the coke oven was located had been already licensed under the previous UK Integrated Pollution Control regime in Part I of the Environmental Protection Act (EPA) 1990. UK national guidance under Part I of EPA 1990 had considered wet quenching as BAT for coke ovens. When the IPPC licence for the English iron and steel works, including the coke oven plant, was prepared there was still only a draft version of the Environment Agency's new IPPC guidance for the iron and steel sector available. The latter had taken careful account of EU BREF note for the production of iron and steel which referred to both emissions-minimised wet quenching and dry quenching as BAT.[19] Hence the English regulatory authority, an area office of the EA,[20] did not have to consider whether a technique different from the one already employed, such as emissions-minimised wet quenching, could be taken as BAT.

Despite these different starting points, both the English and the German coke oven plant were permitted for emissions-minimised wet quenching as BAT for coke cooling. How can this integration effect be explained? Was this the result of the integrating force of the IPPC Directive? In order to answer this question the key issue to address is why and how the German regulatory authority changed its conception of what constitute the 'best available techniques' and why the Environment Agency continued to maintain that emissions-minimised wet quenching is BAT for coke cooling.

The role of law in shaping perceptions about what constitutes BAT for coke cooling

So what role did law play in shaping perceptions of the German and English regulatory authority about what constitutes BAT for coke cooling? As chapter 4 argued, in order to understand how and whether law contributes to integration effects, it is necessary to understand law in action. Law in action captures how legal, technical, economic and political discourses intersect in creating different views of what constitutes BAT. Discourses are central to BAT determinations in IPPC licensing procedures because debates about what constitutes BAT are conducted through oral discussions, through the exchange of letters and memos between the licensing authority and the operator, and through the writing and discussion of internal and external consultants' reports. Debates about BAT have a significant technical content, but verbal formulations are still key to these discussions. Technical discourse includes graphs and figures. It also pays close attention to language because finding precisely the right words to express technical findings is crucial. For example, a German technical consultant's report presented dust emission figures from coke quenching as 'a true value'.[21] It also discussed 'average mistakes in the whole range of emission values'.[22] Yet, according to the *Landesumweltamt*, which scrutinised this report on behalf of the IPPC licensing authority, there was no 'true value' for emission figures. Moreover, the term 'average mistake in the whole range of emission values' was considered to have no clear meaning because there was no mathematical equation for calculating this average deviation in the emission figures. This extensive discourse, including legal, economic, political and technical perspectives, on what constitutes BAT for coke cooling was compiled by the German licensing authority in an official file (accessible to the public) about the licensing procedure.[23] In the UK a shorter Decision Document[24] was written by the regulatory authority which contained some background information as to how the BAT determination had been arrived at for the integrated iron and steel works. So what did the discourses in these files entail?

Legal discourse on what constitutes BAT for coke cooling

A specifically legal discourse refers to the legal provisions which participants in the IPPC licensing procedures have actually invoked.[25] Various legal texts, such as EU law, as well as primary, secondary and tertiary national legal rules were mobilised for constructing arguments about what the 'best available techniques' for cooling coke really were. Participants in the German licensing procedure invoked both national and EU law as well as the EU BREF,[26] while participants in the UK licensing procedure relied mainly on national law and the EU BREF. The legal discourse for the German licensing procedure included a range of complex arguments exchanged between the operator, his lawyer and the regulatory authority over a two-year period. In the development of this legal discourse one key point crystallised which shaped subsequent debate about what constitutes BAT for the German coke oven plant. The German regulatory authority insisted that emissions-minimised wet quenching had to be comparable in its environmental performance to dry quenching in order to be considered as BAT for the coke oven. But how did this point emerge in the legal discourse?

In its legal arguments the German operator drew on the directly effective provisions of the IPPC Directive[27] and the EU BREF document on the production of iron and steel.[28] Germany was late in formally incorporating the IPPC Directive into national law. The *Artikelgesetz* of 27.07.2001 amended the Federal Air Immissions Control Act

(*Bundesimmissionsschutzgesetz*, BimSchG), the Federal Water Protection Law (*Wasserhaushaltsgesetz*) and the Federal Waste Management Law (*Abfallwirtschafts- und Kreislaufgesetz*). The IPPC Directive was implemented into German law through this *Artikelgesetz*. But it entered into force only halfway through the coke oven licensing procedure. Subsequently the legal discourse referred specifically to the amended §§ 5 and 6 BimSchG.[29] According to § 6 (1) the German licensing authority *has* to issue a permit if the duties listed in § 5 BimSchG and in further secondary regulations passed under § 7 BimSchG are complied with.[30] Hence according to § 6 BimSchG the German licensing authority is not exercising a discretionary power when it issues IPPC licences for new installations. Instead the operator has a right to obtain the licence once he has fulfilled the relevant statutory requirements, in particular those listed in § 5 BimSchG (Kloepfer, 2004: 1224).

§ 5 (1) BimSchG states that plants which require a permit have to be built and operated in such a way that a high level of protection for the environment as a whole is guaranteed. In order to achieve this high level of protection, two further requirements have to be fulfilled. According to § 5 (1) No. 1 the operator has to ensure that the general public and the immediate neighbours of the installation are protected from detrimental environmental impacts and other dangers, and from significant disadvantages and nuisances. Second, according to § 5 (1) No. 2 BimSchG the operator has to employ precautionary measures in accordance with the 'Stand der Technik' in order to avoid detrimental environmental impacts and other dangers, as well as significant disadvantages and nuisances.[31] Finally, § 5 (1) No. 3 also requires that waste must be prevented from arising, where reuse is not possible. In case reuse is not feasible waste must be disposed of without causing detrimental effects to the well-being of the public. Moreover, § 5 (4) BimSchG stipulates that energy must be used in a prudent and efficient manner at licensed plants.

Hence the key question within the legal discourse was whether the German operator had fulfilled the duties arising from § 5 BimSchG. According to the German licensing authority – which also relied on technical information generated by the *Landesumweltamt* – emissions-minimised wet quenching generated higher emissions of dust and other pollutants. Could emissions-minimised wet quenching still then be considered as compatible with the obligation imposed upon the operator by § 5 (1) No. 1 BimSchG – namely not to cause detrimental environmental impacts? This question was also debated within the legal discourse through reference to the technical instruction air (TA *Luft*).[32] The TA *Luft* is a general administrative rule[33] which the environmental administration has to follow when licensing new or existing IPPC installations.[34] It further defines undetermined legal concepts[35] in the BimSchG, such as the 'Stand der Technik', the German version of the 'best available techniques'. Two points from the technical instruction concerning air were debated in particular. First, according to No. 3.1.7 of the TA *Luft* in the 1986 version emissions of organic substances[36] must be minimised with reference to the principle of proportionality. Second, No. 2.5. of the TA Luft in the 1986 version spelt out standards for air quality. If the operator could show that these were complied with, the installation would be deemed not to cause detrimental impacts on the environment.

So what precise difference did the increased pollution from emissions-minimised wet quenching make to the overall air quality in the area?[37] The coke oven plant was located in an industrial area which already had a significant level of background pollution. Would the extra emissions be so significant that the operator would not comply with the duty not to cause detrimental environmental impacts? The operator's lawyers argued that local air quality would only deteriorate by 0.1% through the extra dust emissions caused by emissions-minimised wet quenching. They also argued that the extra emissions from emissions-minimised wet quenching should be considered irrelevant and therefore could not be regarded as causing detrimental impacts on the environment. Moreover, the lawyer contended that the closing down of one of the operator's old coke ovens with dry quenching under an agreement with the *Land* environmental ministry would improve air quality in the area. For the same reason the extra dust emissions from the new coke oven plant with emissions-minimised wet quenching could not be considered as causing detrimental impacts on the environment.

But it was not just the requirement of paragraph 5 (1) No. 1 BimSchG which had to be complied with for an IPPC license to be issued for the German coke oven. The second criterion of § 5 (1) No. 2 also had to be fulfilled. § 5 (1) No. 2 requires that operators of installations have to take measures according to the 'Stand der Technik' in order to guard against detrimental impacts on the environment. Again the technical instruction for air was referred to here because it specifically interprets the general concept 'Stand der Technik'. According to staff in the German licensing authority, the TA *Luft* in the 1986 version envisaged dry quenching as the 'Stand der Technik' – BAT – for the cooling of coke in coke oven plants:

Procedures have to be chosen for an emissions-minimised cooling of the coke, for example coke *dry quenching*; dust emissions in the plumes from the coke dry quenching have to be limited to 20 mg/m3.

(emphasis added)[38]

The operator argued, however, specifically with reference to the directly effective provisions of the IPPC Directive and the EU BREF, that emissions-minimised wet quenching should be considered as BAT. For instance, the German operator's lawyers suggested that German statutory provisions as well as secondary and tertiary rules had to be interpreted in the light of the requirements of the IPPC Directive since the time limit for the implementation of the Directive had expired during the coke oven licensing procedure. No German legal measures had yet been adopted at that stage for the transposition of the IPPC Directive into national law. The operator's lawyer argued that the TA *Luft* requirement to employ an emissions-minimised coke cooling system[39] was in practice an 'indeterminate legal concept'[40] which had to be rendered more specific. This could be done through reference to the EU BREF which referred to emissions-minimised wet quenching as one of the BAT techniques and to qualified dry quenching as a BAT technique in relation to the higher costs associated with it.

Furthermore, the operator's main argument was that the TA *Luft* should no longer be considered as the main point of reference for determining BAT, but that the EU BREF document with its reference to emissions-minimised wet quenching should be taken into account. The TA *Luft* with its reference to dry quenching could no longer be considered as binding on the licensing authority. It had now to be interpreted in accordance with EU law. The operator further sought to strengthen this argument by suggesting that in case of a legal challenge to the licensing authority's decision before a German administrative court, the court would examine whether new developments in science and technology had overtaken the provisions of the TA *Luft* from 1986. Hence it would be likely that a court would also no longer consider dry quenching as the BAT technique.[41]

Permitters in the German regulatory authority sought to resist the operator's cost arguments by suggesting that costs could not be considered in the BAT determination. According to permitters, costs had been already considered when the German federal legislature discussed and adopted the TA *Luft*. Staff in the licensing authority still considered themselves bound by the TA *Luft*. They also questioned whether emissions-minimised wet quenching could be considered as BAT because dry quenching permitted the reuse of waste heat from the hot coke. This was considered significant because § 5 (1) No. 4 BimSchG imposes a duty on operators to 'use energy in a prudent and efficient manner'. The operator's lawyers, however, argued that this duty was too general and had to be specified in more detail through secondary regulations which had not yet been issued. To conclude: a legal discourse for the licensing of the German coke oven plant included the operator's insistence, specifically through reference to EU law and guidance, that emissions-minimised wet quenching was BAT for coke cooling. The German regulatory authority maintained that emissions-minimised wet quenching could only be considered as BAT if it was comparable to dry quenching in its environmental performance. Hence the legal discourse brought no final resolution to the question of what constitutes BAT for coke cooling. It nevertheless fulfilled an important function for it declared the issue of the comparability of emissions from dry and emissions-minimised wet quenching to be central to further debate on what BAT is.

The legal discourse for the English coke oven plant was briefer and simpler. The IPPC licence application referred to existing coke ovens which were part of an integrated iron and steel works. Emissions from the coke oven plants were considered by the permitter as relatively insignificant in comparison with emissions from the other plants on the site, such as the blast furnace, the rolling mills and the sinter plant. In contrast to the German legal discourse, there was no reference to statutory provisions. The Pollution Prevention and Control Act 1999 merely provides the bare bones of the PPC regime in the UK. The key provision directly referred to in the English legal discourse was the UK guidance note for the production of coke, iron and steel.[42] This guidance note – which had been drafted with close reference to the EU BREF[43] – provides further detail about the 'best available techniques' for the operation of coke ovens, including coke cooling. It suggests that wet quenching is BAT.[44] EA licensing officers also referred directly to the EU BREF note, especially in order to justify improvement conditions for the English coke oven. One of the improvement conditions required the operator to conduct a further investigation into how much dust was actually emitted from the wet quenching of the coke.

The UK and EU BREF guidance were the key legal materials referred to in the English legal discourse. But which further points specified in the legal discourse helped to generate the actual emission limit values imposed in the English IPPC licence for the coke ovens? Proportionality considerations were referred to – including reference to DEFRA's 'IPPC: A Practical Guide'[45] – in order to justify the emission limit values imposed in the licence. The guide is not legally binding and has no statutory basis.[46] But it does further expand on how to interpret the PPC Regulations. As paragraph 7.1 of the DEFRA guide suggests, the conditions which the EA imposes on the operator should be proportionate to the environmental risks to be regulated. Finally, the EA licensing officer also invoked a notion of precedent in the legal discourse in order to explain why emissions-minimised wet quenching was considered to be BAT. Both the national guidance issued under the previous pollution control regime[47] and the current UK guidance for the PPC regime consider emissions-minimised wet quenching as BAT. Hence for the EA licensing officer – in contrast to the German regulatory authority – there was a 'historic justification'[48] for considering emissions-minimised wet quenching to be BAT.

If it was needed, it would be something that we'd done before … but, as I said, for an existing process, because it's been in existence and effectively regulated under a very similar regulatory regime, what I didn't expect, or what we weren't going to do was suddenly say it's not BAT, you know, because if it wasn't BAT when we did the PPC permit determination it would have struggled to have been BAT under the old integrated pollution control regime. So it wasn't like it was the first time we'd looked at the process and assessed against what we thought was normal or acceptable.[49]

This 'historic justification' turned the EA's past decisions into an important point of reference for BAT determinations for existing processes under the new IPPC regime. But BAT determinations both for the German and the English coke oven plant were not simply arrived at through reference to a legal discourse. An economic discourse also played a significant part.

What is BAT for coke cooling? The perspective of an economic discourse

That cost considerations matter in BAT determinations is also clear from the IPPC Directive text:[50]

available techniques shall mean those developed on a scale which allows implementation in the relevant industrial sector, under *economically* and technically *viable conditions, taking into consideration the costs and advantages.*

(emphasis added)

This definition of available techniques is reproduced in regulation 3 (1) (a) of the PPC Regulations (England and Wales) 2000. It is also implemented in German national law through the concept of 'Stand der Technik' referred to in § 5 (1) No. 2, and defined in § 3 (6) BimSchG and its annex. The IPPC Directive and its implementation in German and UK national law primarily refer to a specific and potentially narrow cost-benefit[51] analysis as the key element of cost considerations in BAT determinations. In the German licensing procedure an economic discourse in practice referred to a comparison of the costs of dry quenching with those of emissions-minimised wet quenching. The German operator suggested that the installation and operation costs for emissions-minimised wet quenching were significantly lower than those for dry quenching. This was one of the main reasons why the operator had applied for a new licence for the coke oven plant with emissions-minimised wet quenching. While the operator did not raise cost arguments explicitly at the beginning of the German licensing procedure, he did so with increasing force and clarity in later stages also in response to the reluctance of the German licensing authority to abandon its view that dry quenching was the 'Stand der Technik' for coke cooling. For instance, in letters to the licensing authority the operator suggested that the investment costs of a coke dry quenching plant would be about 200 million Deutschmark[52] higher than for an emissions-minimised coke wet quenching plant. The operating costs were calculated to rise by 15 Deutschmark[53] per ton of coke in the case of dry quenching in comparison to emissions-minimised wet quenching.[54] This cost argument was supported by the submission of further figures. The operator suggested that over twenty years the coke dry quenching plant would cause losses of 700–800 million Deutschmark[55] for the company.[56] This economic information was presented as 'facts'. In order to enhance its credibility the operator had also commissioned an external economic consultant[57] who assessed the validity and veracity of these cost data. The report, which was submitted to the licensing authority, concluded that the operator's cost calculations were 'plausible', 'verifiable'[58] and 'complied with generally accepted principles of micro-economic analysis'.

Costs of the various coke cooling techniques were also considered in the English licensing procedure, but in no great detail since both the operator and the regulatory authority were agreed that emissions-minimised wet quenching is BAT for coke cooling. There is no direct reference in the Decision Document for the installation to the costs of different quenching techniques. There is simply a note that the coke ovens 'conform to BAT'.[59] There is also no direct reference in the UK guidance note for the production of coke, iron and steel to the respective costs of dry and wet quenching. But in the Decision Document for another integrated iron and steel works there was a clear admission that dry quenching was considered too expensive in comparison to emissions-minimised wet quenching. Moreover, the investigation of BAT techniques other than wet quenching was also considered too costly by the UK licensing officer on the basis of proportionality considerations. The EA licensing officer suggested that emissions, including dust emissions from the coke cooling process, were considered insignificant in comparison to emissions from other points at the coke making plant and other activities at the integrated iron and steel works, such as the blast furnace, the rolling mills and the sinter plant.[60] The limited emissions from the coke quench chamber were thought not to warrant the consideration of different, more expensive coke cooling techniques, such as coke dry quenching or tighter emission limit values. Moreover, according to the UK licensing officer proportionality considerations also militated against spending too much time on the question on what constitutes BAT for the cooling of the coke. In fact, an efficient organisation of PPC licensing work was a significant factor in how the BAT determination for the English coke oven was achieved. Initially, there was a whole team of officers each with responsibility for a specialist area of regulation, such as air and water pollution, who wrote specific sections of the PPC licence for the integrated iron and steel works. But this teamwork approach was eventually found to be inefficient and highly time-consuming. Air or water specialists who had not earlier been involved in enforcement work for the site required some time to get to know the site and identify key issues with regard to its regulation. Hence the team approach was abandoned and the enforcement officer for the site was principally responsible for writing the PPC licence. He had also drafted the previous IPC licence for the site which had also considered emissions-minimised wet quenching as BAT. Hence, in contrast to the German licensing procedure, there were fewer actors involved in discussing and raising questions about what constitutes BAT for the English coke oven. Proportionality considerations also militated against reopening the question whether emissions-minimised wet quenching really is BAT for the English coke oven plant. These considerations were not just an element of a legal discourse, but also captured costs of IPPC licensing for the regulator in terms of an economic discourse.[61]

To summarise: from the perspective of an economic discourse emissions-minimised wet quenching represents BAT for coke cooling because it was significantly cheaper than dry quenching. This was presented as an uncontested 'fact' and finally accepted by the German licensing authority. In the licensing procedure for the English coke oven plant proportionality considerations also promoted the continued acceptance of emissions-minimised wet quenching as BAT and militated against reopening and reconsidering BAT technology and emission levels for the coke ovens. But the harmonised BAT definition of emissions-minimised wet quenching for the German and English coke ovens was achieved here not merely through reference to a legal and an economic discourse. A specifically political discourse was also deployed.

What is BAT for coke cooling from the perspective of a political discourse?

The political discourse consisted of talk and text about what should be considered as BAT with reference to the interests of various participants in the licensing procedure.[62] Points about what should constitute 'the best available techniques' were presented here not as 'objective facts', such as elements of the economic and technical discourse, but as issues for negotiation. A political discourse was generated by the licensing authority and the operator as well as by official political actors.[63] A key political actor in the German licensing procedure was the environmental ministry of the *Land* in which the licensing authority was located. Its role at the apex of the *Land* environmental administration is to shape and develop environmental policy. It thereby also steers the activities of the lower levels of the *Land* environmental administration, such as district licensing authorities.[64] The *Land* environmental ministry's influence can be significant because it forms the top layer of a hierarchical three-tier system of environmental administration. For the German operator, it was the general management, rather than the technical staff,[65] which advanced arguments about the company's interests in this BAT determination, by talking directly to the German licensing authority and the *Land* environmental ministry.

In this IPPC licensing procedure an agreement between the German operator and the *Land* environmental ministry was the decisive expression of a political discourse in the BAT determination. Once it became clear that the German licensing authority was reluctant to issue a licence for a coke oven with emissions-minimised wet quenching, the operator approached the ministry. The environment minister and the operator finally entered into a formal legal agreement.[66] The operator undertook to stop operating one of his installations, thus reducing the overall level of air pollutants in the area of the planned new coke oven plant. The operator also agreed to invest 120 million Deutschmark[67] in new pollution abatement measures at its other plants in the area of the coke oven plant, in order to reduce even further the level of air pollutants in this locality. In return, the *Land* environmental ministry asked the licensing authority to give serious consideration to the operator's application for a coke oven plant with emissions-minimised wet quenching. Under German law the contract between the operator and the *Land* environmental ministry, on the one hand, and the actual licensing of the coke oven, on the other hand, are two separate legal procedures. They cannot be linked. But, in practice, the emission reduction measures which the German operator had undertaken to carry out would reduce overall air pollutant levels in the area of the planned coke oven plant. This, in turn, would make it more likely that the licensing authority would accept that the extra emissions generated by emissions-minimised wet quenching from the coke oven plant did not cause detrimental impacts on the environment according to 5 (1) No. 1 BimSchG. Given these contractually agreed pollution reduction measures, it was more likely that the additional emissions generated by the new coke oven plant would be judged 'irrelevant' with reference to the provisions of the TA *Luft* 1986. Hence this political agreement between the German operator and the *Land* environmental ministry was crucial for facilitating the acceptance of emissions-minimised wet quenching by the licensing authority as the 'best available technique' for coke cooling.[68]

Given the fairly uncontroversial nature of the licensing process for the coke ovens at the English integrated iron and steel works, little specifically political discourse was generated here. The operator and the EA did not express sharply contrasting interests in relation to the question what should be considered as BAT for coke cooling. Hence in the English coke oven licensing procedure – in contrast to the German situation – there was no involvement of high-level political actors. But a political discourse was also deployed in the English licensing procedure in relation to the licensing of other plants at the integrated iron and steel works. For instance, previously issued consents for discharges to water[69] were reviewed as part of the PPC licensing process. The EA mobilised a political discourse here by referring to agency policies when setting emission limit values. Agency policy expressed the specific interests which the EA pursued in relation to particular environmental protection issues, such as the enhancement of the quality of water courses. There was a legal background to some of these policies because they were an aspect of the implementation of EC water protection legislation. But they were invoked as part of a political rather than merely legal discourse because they expressed the EA's specific policy choices about how exactly general legal EU provisions should be implemented in England and Wales. Moreover, the UK licensing officer suggested that a political discourse was also invoked in other IPPC licensing procedures. 'Political games' would soon begin if the EA proposed imposing IPPC licence conditions which could threaten the continued commercial viability of an installation.[70] But what did a technical discourse add to the quest for BAT in the licensing of the coke ovens?

A technical discourse on what constitutes BAT for coke cooling

A technical discourse consists of talk and text about the details of coke cooling technologies. This kind of discourse was generated by engineers and scientists who worked for the licensing authorities and the *Land* environmental protection agency (*Landesumweltamt* – LUA), which functions at arm's length from the licensing authority. It was also generated by engineers and scientists working for the operator and external consultants. During the German licensing procedure in particular technical reports from the LUA assumed specific importance. These reports scrutinised technical information submitted by the operator, including independent technical consultants' reports commissioned by the operator.[71] An elaborate technical discourse was constructed during the German coke oven licensing procedure. Since the operator had proposed a new technology for coke cooling – emissions-minimised wet quenching – there was considerable debate, for instance, about the construction of the quench tower. There was also extensive debate about the quantity of various pollutants actually emitted from coke dry quenching and emissions-minimised wet quenching. For instance, emission levels were debated for coke dust, sulphur dioxide, carbon monoxide and carcinogens, such as polyaromatic hydrocarbons (PAHs),[72] and especially benzo(a)pyren and benzol. Mathematical equations were invoked in order to identify and measure the velocity of gas flows in the quench tower. This was intended to determine the quantity of pollutants actually emitted from the new emissions-minimised wet quenching technology. A further element of the technical discourse was provided by references to articles about coke cooling techniques in the technical engineering and trade press,[73] especially in letters and reports from the operator submitted to the German licensing authority.

The technical discourse explicitly pursued a 'true' technical perspective on coke cooling. Ideas about what constitutes BAT were presented as 'truthful and objective facts'. For example, a German technical report advocated a particular measurement procedure and a specific way of calculating dust emissions from the quench tower in order to determine the 'true value'[74] of these emissions. Co-production of such a technical discourse by the regulator and the operator promoted further the idea of a technical discourse as 'objective'. During the German licensing procedure different figures were marshalled by the operator and the LUA for dust emissions from emissions-minimised wet quenching.[75] A clear statement, however, about the actual dust emissions from emissions-minimised wet quenching was essential in order to come to a conclusion on the question whether emission-minimised wet quenching was comparable to dry quenching. Hence it was decided that the operator would commission an independent technical consultant's report to develop a professionally validated measurement procedure for dust emissions. But this was to be done 'in consultation with the state environmental protection agency'. Once the report had been prepared there were meetings between the independent technical consultant and the LUA in order to critically evaluate the figures for dust emissions which the consultant had presented.

Given the fact that the English operator did not propose a new coke cooling technique, less technical discourse was generated in this context. There was less involvement of external consultants in comparison to the German coke oven licensing procedure. A limited technical discourse was generated during the licensing of the English coke oven by the operator, in particular by environmental managers and technical staff from the integrated iron and steel works, and the parent company's in-house consultants. The EA licensing officer as well as other EA staff with specialist expertise in particular areas of pollution control, such as waste and air quality[76] also contributed to the construction of a technical discourse. As with the technical discourse for the German coke oven plant, the technical discourse in relation to the English plant also pointed to uncertainties and gaps in knowledge about the operation of coke ovens. According to the EA licensing officer a key aspect of writing the PPC licence lay in identifying what additional information had to be obtained in order to facilitate further regulation of the coke ovens through further BAT conditions in the licence. Hence improvement condition no. 20 in the PPC licence requires that the:

operator shall undertake an investigation into particulate matter (including PM10 and PM 2.5) emissions from wet quenching of coke. The investigation should compare the emission reduction measures and emission performance against the techniques and achievable emission levels referred to in the Iron and Steel BREF note. A report of the investigation shall be sent to the Environment Agency.

To conclude: in both the German and English coke oven licensing procedures a technical discourse did not generate a conclusive answer to the question of what constitutes BAT for coke cooling. While the technical discourse presented itself as a search for an objective 'truth' about coke cooling technologies, it also pointed to a lack of certainty in knowledge about the performance of these technologies. Hence none of the discourses which were mobilised provided on their own a conclusive BAT determination. It is therefore necessary to analyse the interactions between the different discourses. Economic, political, technical and legal discourses represent different perspectives on what constitutes the 'best available technique' for coke cooling. These discourses, however, occurred in conjunction with one another, rather than in isolation. In fact, controlling the boundaries of discourses was a key argumentative strategy for defining BAT. Managing discourse boundaries could also result in opening discourses up to each other. For instance, political and economic perspectives about what constitutes BAT could be linked with a legal and technical discourse about BAT. Hence the argumentative strategy here was not to displace a technical and a legal discourse in favour of a political and economic one. Legal requirements and technical data were still important. One way to open up a legal and a technical discourse to economic and political discourses was by deploying a language of purpose and relativity.

Opening up a technical discourse through a language of purpose and relativity

The key point of the legal discourse generated during the German licensing procedure was that emissions-minimised wet quenching had to be shown to be 'at least equivalent'[77] in its environmental performance to dry quenching in order to fulfil the statutory 'Stand der Technik'

(BAT) definition in the Federal Air Immissions Control Statute (BimSchG). This point framed the debate about what should be considered as BAT for coke cooling at the German coke oven.

In order to determine whether emissions-minimised wet quenching was really equivalent to dry quenching, accounts of how much and what pollutants[78] were emitted from each of the two coke cooling techniques were constructed.[79] Hence comparing the environmental performance of emissions-minimised wet quenching with dry quenching relied principally on a technical discourse. Technical 'facts', presented in terms of graphs, diagrams and calculations were a key resource for constructing accounts of the character and quality of emissions caused by coke cooling. The technical discourse generated 'evidence' that dry quenching would lead to smaller emissions of dust and fine particulates, such as PM 10,[80] than emissions-minimised wet quenching. So how could the latter technique be considered as 'at least equivalent' to dry quenching in the light of these 'data'? The technical discourse developed over nearly two years during the licensing procedure. It was opened up to considerations based on interests through recourse to a language of intentions and relativity.

A language of intentions

A language of intentions helped the German operator to portray emissions minimised wet quenching as 'equal' to dry quenching. It introduced direction and a notion of certainty into the technical discourse. This helped to foreground the German operator's interests. For instance, a letter from the operator's lawyer to the German licensing authority summarised the technical discourse about dust emissions from emissions-minimised wet quenching in the following way:

a *prognosis* is possible that 10 mg dust per ton of coke can be *definitely* complied with.[81]

This statement arises from a recognition within the technical discourse that the actual level of dust emissions can only be hypothetically indicated through a prognosis because the quench tower with emissions-minimised wet quenching has not yet been operated in production on an industrial scale. But the statement then moves on to project the certainty that a specific emission limit value can be achieved by emissions-minimised wet quenching. Compliance with this limit value indicates that emissions-minimised wet quenching is equivalent to dry quenching and thus constitutes BAT.[82] Hence the German operator commissioned an independent technical consultant (TÜV)[83] to develop a new validated measurement procedure which could show that emissions-minimised wet quenching would emit no more than 10 mg of dust per ton of coke. In its final report the TÜV summarised the brief it had been given by the operator:

The measurement procedure should be able prove that emissions of dust from emissions-minimised wet quenching are smaller than 10 mg/t of coke, this corresponds to a dust concentration of roughly 10 mg/m^3 of plumes.

(emphasis added)[84]

Hence the consultant was asked not to develop *any* procedure through which emissions from the quench tower could be measured. The operator asked for a measurement procedure which could accomplish a specific task, namely that of showing that emissions-minimised wet quenching was 'at least equivalent' to dry quenching. Hence a language of purpose steered the technical discourse in a specific direction so as to promote an outcome of the IPPC licensing process which favoured the operator's interests.

There are further examples of a language of intentions opening up a technical discourse to a political discourse of interests. It was not just independent external consultants, such as the TÜV, which were commissioned, but also an in-house technical institute. Technical reports from a consultancy owned by the operator also contributed to the IPPC licensing procedure. Some of the publications referred to in these consultants' reports also adopt a language of purpose which helped to open up a technical discourse to a specifically political one. For instance, the consultant referred to journal articles with titles, such as

Improved Environmental Protection through modern coke making technology, as exemplified by the new coke oven plant at [location of the operator's proposed plant].[85]

In some of its letters to the operator the LUA expressed concerns about the accuracy of some of the figures supplied by the operator. There were discrepancies in the figures provided by the operator to the licensing authority during the formal licensing procedure and the figures on emission values provided by the operator to the *Land* environmental ministry during the political negotiations, which were pursued independently of the formal licensing procedure. Hence opening up a technical discourse to a political discourse rather than replacing a technical with a political discourse, was also a strategy to promote the acceptance of emissions-minimised wet quenching as BAT by the IPPC licensing authority.

Not only the operator, however, but also the German environmental administration invoked a language of purpose which helped to open up a legal discourse to a political one. The political discourse referred not just to the operator's interests, but included the interests of the *Land* environmental ministry – the top level of the *Land* environmental administration. These lay in facilitating the licensing of the coke oven plant with emissions-minimised wet quenching, specifically in light of the fact that the operator of the coke oven plant was a large company in the integrated iron and steel sector and hence a significant local employer and taxpayer. So how did the German environmental administration invoke a language of purpose here? According to the German permitting officer the contract between the operator and the *Land* – while legally not connected to the licensing procedure – clearly indicated a *direction* for the licensing of the new coke oven plant by the licensing authority.[86] But participants in the licensing process not only invoked a language of intentions; they also deployed a language of 'relativity' in order to open up a technical and a legal discourse to a political one.

A language of relativity

The legal discourse generated during the German licensing procedure stipulated that emissions-minimised wet quenching could only be considered as BAT if its environmental performance was 'at least equivalent' to dry quenching. In relation to the key emission of dust this meant that the operator had to show that emissions-minimised wet quenching could achieve 10 mg or less of dust per ton of coke produced. There was also debate about how much carbon monoxide, carbon dioxide and sulphur were emitted through emissions-minimised wet quenching, on the one hand, and dry quenching, on the other. Hence a technical discourse about emissions from the different quenching technologies became key to deciding what constituted BAT. This was also opened up to a political discourse through a language of relativity. A language of relativity turned 'technical facts' into uncertain constructs. It was particularly likely to prove persuasive here because the quench tower for the emissions-minimised wet quenching had not yet been built at the site of the new coke oven plant. Hence figures about pollutants released from emissions-minimised wet quenching were inevitably hypothetical rather than firmly based on actually measured emissions.

One way of relativising emission figures discussed during the German licensing procedure was to relate them to specific coke oven plants. Lower emissions of some pollutants from dry quenching were questioned by being considered merely as the achievement of some specific plants. The operator argued that other coke oven plants with dry quenching may actually emit more pollutants. Comparing these other plants with emissions-minimised wet quenching could favour the conclusion that emissions-minimised wet quenching was 'at least equivalent' to dry quenching. Another way to relativise emission figures was to interpret them with reference to the specific technical features of a given plant. For instance, a report by the German operator's in-house technical consultant, suggested that the higher dust emission figures for emissions-minimised wet quenching should be evaluated with reference to the fact that the quench tower for emissions-minimised wet quenching was higher than in the case of dry quenching. Hence the higher dust emissions from emissions-minimised wet quenching were relativised because they would be dispersed over a wider area by a higher quench tower.

Moreover, a language of relativity also helped the operator to argue that there was actually no straightforward answer to the question of what dust emissions were caused by coke dry quenching. There were a number of German coke oven plants with dry quenching systems. The operator tried to argue that dust emissions from dry quenching were specific and thus relative to particular plants. Which plant was the right comparator for making the case that emissions-minimised wet quenching was at least equivalent to dry quenching?[87] Some coke oven plants utilised old dry quenching systems and hence did not work at full capacity. Their dust emissions were considered as 'too low' by the operator.[88] Moreover, the operator raised the question whether emission limits stipulated in permits for dry quenching could be equated with actually measured values for emissions-minimised wet quenching. Here the operator attempted to question whether 10 mg of dust per ton of coke produced – routinely inserted as an emission limit value in permits for coke oven plants with dry quenching – was a realistic figure to which emissions minimised wet quenching should be held. The operator suggested that 10 mg of dust emissions per ton of coke was just an emission limit value on paper and that actual emissions may be higher. Such actual higher dust emissions from dry quenching would be the right comparator in order to determine whether emissions-minimised wet quenching was 'at least equivalent' to dry quenching. The LUA invoked a language of relativity by arguing that the operator had used data for dust emissions from old dry quenching techniques which reported levels that were 'too high' in comparison to 'normal' dry quenching figures.[89]

A language of relativity was also invoked by the operator in relation to the discussion of carbon dioxide emissions from the plant. The operator sought to suggest that carbon dioxide emissions could not be considered in absolute terms, but only in relation to the amount of coke produced and in relation to the overall carbon dioxide emissions from the whole integrated iron and steel works. The operator suggested that emissions-minimised wet quenching produced a better quality of coke. Hence less coke was needed in the blast furnace. Therefore less carbon dioxide emissions would be generated from the whole of the integrated iron and steel works.[90] The LUA contested this view, also by invoking a language of relativity. It argued that only carbon dioxide emissions from the cooling tower of the coke quenching plant could be considered for determining whether emissions-minimised wet quenching was BAT. According to the LUA, emissions-minimised wet quenching actually generated higher carbon dioxide emissions from the cooling chamber.[91]

A language of relativity, however, was not merely invoked in relation to the question which plant furnished the right comparator for concluding whether the environmental performance of emissions-minimised wet quenching was at least equivalent to dry quenching. Such language was also invoked in order to draw attention to the fact that emission levels varied not just from plant to plant, but also according to how a plant was operated. The German operator argued – by relying amongst other things on an in-house technical consultant's report – that there were no clear figures for the emission of carcinogens[92] from coke cooling because they varied according to how the coke oven plant was operated. The less well the coke would be heated, the higher the emissions would be. Hence carcinogen emissions from coke cooling were portrayed here as dependent on the coke cooking process and thus on operational controls which could be adjusted. Now it became possible to provide a number of answers to the question whether emissions-minimised wet quenching was at least equivalent to dry quenching. The German operator argued that operational controls could be adjusted so that carcinogen emissions from emissions-minimised wet quenching were comparable to dry quenching.

To summarise: a language of relativity was invoked by both the German environmental administration and the operator. It helped the operator to open up a technical discourse concerning higher figures for various emissions and in particular dust emissions, from emissions-minimised wet quenching in the direction of a political discourse. This helped to promote the German operator's interest in obtaining a licence for a coke oven with emissions-minimised wet quenching. Hence a technical discourse was not simply displaced through a simple assertion of the operator's interests. Instead an important aspect of determining BAT was the opening up of the technical discourse to a political discourse. This meant that within the technical discourse – which initially invoked 'true technical facts' about lower emissions from dry quenching – a debate developed which opened up new perspectives on the question whether the environmental performance of emissions-minimised wet quenching was at least equivalent to dry quenching. This helped to pave the way for considering emissions-minimised wet quenching as BAT.

In the English licensing procedure a language of relativity, and especially reference to proportionality, also helped to open up a legal discourse to a political and economic one. The legal discourse here included reference to the fact that dust emissions from the integrated iron and steel works contributed to a breach of the 24-hour Environmental Quality Standard for small dust particles, the so-called PM 10s.[93] Hence dry quenching – according to figures debated during the German licensing procedure – may have addressed this problem by reducing dust (including PM 10) emissions, from the coke cooling process. Dust emissions from coke cooling at the site were considered an issue. A specific improvement condition in relation to this was inserted into the licence for the integrated iron and steel works. Hence aspects of the legal discourse suggested that dust emissions from coke cooling were considerable and thus potentially a problem. But emissions-minimised wet quenching with its potentially higher dust emissions was considered as BAT by the UK licensing officer by invoking a language of relativity, and especially considerations of proportionality, which allowed the commercial interests of the operator in a cheaper abatement technology to be taken into account. The emissions from the English coke oven plants were considered as too significant in comparison to emissions from other elements of the integrated iron and steel works to warrant expenditure on emissions-minimised wet quenching.

There are further examples of a language of relativity and especially of considerations of proportionality opening up a legal discourse to a political and economic discourse on what constitutes BAT. The EA licensing officer and the English operator referred to considerations of proportionality in order to justify deviations in the PPC licence from BAT definitions in the UK sector guidance for the production of iron, steel and coke. For instance, the UK sector guidance states that 'operators of existing coke ovens without desulphurisation and new plant should submit plans for installing it by 2007'.[94] But there was no requirement in the PPC licence for the English coke oven plants – which operated without desulphurisation – to submit plans for the installation of this abatement technique by 2007. Instead the operator submitted a 'BAT Assessment of Desulphurisation of Coke Oven Gas' along with the application. This short report had been compiled by an external firm of environmental consultants. It argued that the installation of coke oven desulphurisation would be a *disproportionate* response in relation to the environmental risk posed by sulphur emissions. The report stated that since there was no breach of air quality standards for sulphur in the locality of the integrated iron and steel works, coke oven gas desulphurisation was not a priority.[95] The report concluded that using less sulphur-rich coal was a cheaper and more proportionate method for reducing sulphur emissions from the site:

The BAT assessment indicates that any small environmental gain achieved by desulphurisation of coke oven gas is achieved at substantial cost, and that the base case, incorporating the improvements already made, therefore represents BAT for the site.[96]

The consultant's report invoked further considerations of proportionality by suggesting that other sectors, such as refineries, general industrial production and power generation, as well as domestic users of power, could reduce sulphur emissions more cost effectively than the iron and steel sector. The report also argued that since the iron and steel sector only contributed to a limited extent to national SO_2 emissions, the cost of coke oven desulphurisation would be disproportionate. Hence a language of relativity, especially arguments of proportionality in the consultant's report, which were accepted by the UK licensing officer, reopened the BAT assessment for coke oven desulphurisation. A BAT assessment had been already carried out at the national level and enshrined in the sector guidance note for the production of coke, iron and steel. The latter had concluded that coke oven desulphurisation was

BAT for the sector, even when the costs of this for the sector had been taken into account.

To conclude: a language of purpose and relativity helped both in the English and the German coke oven licensing procedures to open up a legal and a technical discourse to a political and economic discourse on what constitutes BAT. A language of purpose helped to narrow down the debate about what BAT is by reducing uncertainties and fixing meanings in the technical discourse with reference to political and economic considerations. In the German licensing procedure in particular it moved the debate towards an acceptance of emissions-minimised wet quenching as BAT. A language of relativity in the English licensing procedure invoked general and wide-ranging arguments of proportionality in order to justify emissions-minimised wet quenching as BAT for coke cooling. The discourse generated here was less extensive, detailed and technical than in the German licensing procedure, especially since it was never questioned that emissions-minimised wet quenching constituted BAT. In contrast, the German licensing procedure generated an extensive discourse, including significant technical debate about whether dry or emissions-minimised wet quenching could be considered as BAT. Hence during the German licensing procedure a language of relativity was employed to question 'technical facts' about lower emissions, especially of dust, from dry quenching. Consequently a technical discourse was opened up to interest positions and cost considerations.

Conclusion

This chapter develops a perspective based on 'EU law in action' which sheds light on how BAT norms were constructed in practice in a coke oven licensing procedure in the UK and Germany. The analysis focuses on the role of discourses in the construction of 'EU law in action'. These discourses provided the cognitive framework within which debates about BAT were conducted. They regulated what arguments about BAT would succeed or fail. They thereby also constituted who was a contributor to debates about BAT. It was the interplay between a whole range of discourses – legal, political, economic and technical – which generated BAT determinations both for the English and German coke oven plants. For instance, at the end of the German IPPC licensing procedure emissions-minimised wet quenching was not just considered as BAT on the basis of an economic argument that it was cheaper than dry quenching. Nor was it considered as BAT just because the German operator – also through high-level political channels – had made a clear case that this was in his interests. The interplay of legal, economic, political and technical discourses meant that the operator had to do more than pay lip service to the legal discourse and standards of credibility required by the technical discourse. But while discourses regulated BAT determinations they also opened up a space in which participants in BAT determinations creatively and actively employed discursive strategies in order to shape arguments about what constitutes BAT. Thus uncertainties were not just an inherent characteristic of the technical discourse. They were actively produced through a language of relativity.

This inquiry into how a legal, economic, political and technical discourse was invoked in BAT determinations suggests that a neat distinction between legal and extra-legal contributions to integration effects becomes difficult to uphold. The chapter has argued that through discursive strategies, such as a language of purpose and relativity, a legal and a technical discourse could be opened up to economic and political discourses. Hence law's contexts become relevant to the construction of legal obligations in EU integration, in this case to the requirement from the IPPC Directive to employ 'the best available techniques'. Law's contexts can become constitutive of law. Consequently in order to understand the role of law in EU integration, it is important to move beyond the dichotomy between 'integration through law' and 'integration without law'.

Notes

1. Coke cooling is also called 'quenching'.
2. Since they are listed in Art. 1 No. 1.3 of Annex I of the IPPC Directive, coke ovens are subject to its obligations.
3. See, for example Lindberg, 1963: 5–6 and Wallace, 1990:9.
4. There were, however, differences in the emission limits which were set for various pollutants from the coke ovens. For the English coke oven plant 1 the release of NO_2 was limited to 2200 mg/m^3. For English coke oven plant 2 the limit for NO_2 was 450 mg/m^3. Dust emission limits were not defined as mg/m^3 but were based on 'continuous obscuration monitor readings'. A daily (discrete 24-hour period) maximum limit of 50% average obscuration was applied. The assessment of the PM 10 content of the dust emissions from the quench tower is part of the IPPC improvement programme for the English coke ovens. There was no emission limit value in mg/m^3 set for SO_2 emissions from the English coke oven plants. SO_2 emissions were limited through

restrictions on the sulphur content of the coal used for coking. Dust emissions at the German plant were limited at $10\,mg/m^3$. SO_2 emissions during mixed fuel combustion were limited to $200\,mg/m^3$ and to $275\,mg/m^3$ in the case of coke gas as a fuel. Nitrogenoxides emissions were limited to NO_2 to $500\,mg/m^3$.

5. Water and fugitive (*flüchtige*) gases are driven off the coal when the coal is heated under exclusion of air. The carbonisation process principally generates a solid residue – coke – as well as gases and liquids. Coke and powdered coal form carbon monoxide and are thus used as the basic reducing agent for the iron oxides from which liquid iron is produced in the blast furnace. Coke and powdered coal are also used as a heat source in the blast furnace. The liquid iron which is produced in the blast furnace is then transported to a basic oxygen furnace where the carbon content of the liquid iron, usually 4%, is reduced to less than 1%. This produces steel. For further information see chapter 6 of the Iron and Steel BREF, December 2001, at http:// eippcb.jrc.es/. The German coke oven plant was licensed in its own right through an IPPC permit. This is rather exceptional because coke oven plants are usually sited in integrated iron and steel works. Hence IPPC licences are usually issued for the whole integrated iron and steel works, with a section of the licence containing conditions specifically related to the coke ovens. This was the case for the English coke oven.

6. The inert quenching gas which circulates around the quench chamber is isolated from the atmosphere so that the coke does not combust while being cooled. The gas is kept cool through a heat exchanger which can also be used to recover thermal energy.

7. In coke wet quenching water is usually sprayed on top of the hot coke. An improved system for coke wet quenching – called emissions-minimised wet quenching (CSQ) – was applied at the German coke oven plant. Here the coke is also injected with water from the bottom of the quench chamber.

8. Emissions-minimised wet quenching may involve a different construction of the quenching tower, specifically involving the fitting of 'lamella stack baffles'. These are plastic louvre-shaped grit and dust arresters which are fitted on top of the quench tower. They hold back some dust and grit emissions when the water and dust mist plumes escape from the quench tower.

9. Including fine dust particles of a diameter of PM 10 (and PM 3.5). During dry quenching coke dust is removed from the cooling gas. The scrubbed gas is then emitted into the atmosphere through a chimney.

10. See BREF Document on the Production of Iron and Steel, December 2001: 138.

11. On total dust the environmental protection agency of the *Land* (LUA) stated that dry quenching achieves 13.2 g/t of coke and emission minimised wet quenching achieves 21.5 to 25.7 g/t of coke. In relation to sulphur dioxide emissions the LUA suggested that emissions-minimised wet quenching generates lower emissions than dry quenching. But through further sulphur dioxide abatement dry quenching leads to considerably lower SO_2

emissions. Hydrogen sulphide emissions were considered by the LUA as significantly lower for dry quenching than for emissions-minimised wet quenching. Since hydrogen sulphide, however, turns into sulphur dioxide after a few hours, total sulphur is a better indicator of sulphur emissions from a coke oven. Emissions-minimised wet quenching, according to the LUA, produced lower emissions of carbon monoxide than dry quenching. There were no clear values for carcinogens, such as benzo(a)pyren and benzol which are emitted from both emissions-minimised wet quenching and dry quenching.

12. See BREF Document on the Production of Iron and Steel (December 2001:138).

13. See BREF Document on the Production of Iron and Steel (December 2001: vi, 168). Reference to dry quenching as BAT is qualified by the statement that energy prices in Europe are lower than in some other parts of the world, such as Japan, where dry quenching is widely employed. Thus energy recovery from dry quenching is financially less attractive in Europe. The more detailed description of quenching techniques in chapter six of this BREF also notes significantly higher investment and operation costs for dry quenching in comparison to wet quenching.

14. In fact the operator had already been issued with a licence under the German *Bundesimmissionsschutzgesetz* (BimSchG) before the IPPC Directive was passed for a coke oven with dry quenching. The operator, however, had not actually built the coke oven in accordance with this licence. Instead it continued to seek to persuade the German licensing authority to issue a licence for a coke oven with wet quenching. After the implementation of the IPPC Directive it succeeded in obtaining such a licence.

15. Since 1986 the German technical instructions for air (TA *Luft*) – which bind the licensing authority in its decisions – had required the installation of emissions-minimised quenching techniques in coke ovens, coke dry quenching being a key example of these. The concept of the 'best available techniques' from the IPPC Directive has been implemented in German national legislation, in the BimSchG as 'Stand der Technik'. The purpose of the TA *Luft* is to define in more detail indeterminate legal concepts, such as the 'Stand der Technik'. No. 3.3.1.11.1 TA Luft 1986 specified under the heading of 'coke cooling': 'Procedures have to be chosen for an emissions-minimised cooling of the coke, for example coke dry quenching; dust emissions in the plumes from the coke dry quenching have to be limited to 20 mg/m^3.'

16. The TA *Luft* 1986 was in force until 23 July 2002.

17. A new, revised TA *Luft* came into force on 24 July 2002.

18. In the German licensing procedure an IPPC permit was issued for just the coke oven plant itself. In the UK the coke oven plant was licensed as merely one aspect of a PPC licence issued for an entire, already existing integrated iron and steel works, which also contained a sinter plant, a blast furnace and hot rolling mills.

19. The English licensing procedure formally began with the submission of the operator's application on 30 August 2001 and the final licence was provided by the Environment Agency on 25 June 2004.

20. Iron and steel works were amongst the first installations to be licensed under IPPC and hence the licensing procedure discussed in this chapter was carried about by an area office of the Environment Agency before the four central strategic permitting groups had been set up for IPPC licensing.

21. In German: 'der wahre Wert'.

22. In German: 'der mittlere Fehler in dem Wertekollektiv'.

23. This publicly accessible file, consisting of several A4 lever-arch folders, also formed the basis for the public consultation procedure which the German authority had to conduct for the coke oven licensing procedure under § 10 BimSchG.

24. The Decision Document for the whole English integrated iron and steel works, including the two coke ovens, is 104 pages long. Access is available to members of the public on request under the Environmental Information Regulations 1992 (SI 1992/3240).

25. For instance, there was only limited discussion of desulphurisation for the coke ovens in the English PPC licensing procedure although this is actually a BAT requirement according to UK national sector guidance for coke, iron and steel.

26. The application for the licence for the German coke oven was submitted on 11.04.2000 and the licence was issued on 28.02.2002. The application from 11.04.2000 was in fact an application to vary an existing permit for a coke oven with dry quenching to allow the use of emissions-minimised wet quenching instead according to §§ 4 and 6 BimSchG. The operator had made its original application for a coke oven with dry quenching on 27.02.1997, supplemented through a letter of 30.01.1998.

27. Environmental ministries of the German *Länder* advised licensing authorities through *Runderlaße* (internal administrative orders) about the indirectly and directly effective provisions of the IPPC Directive in German national law.

28. In the version of December 2001.

29. The BimSchG applied because § 4 (1) of the *Vierte Verordnung zur Durchführung des Bundesimmissionsschutzgesetzes* (4. BimSchV) specifies that the installations listed in the Annex to the 4. BimSchV require a permit under the BimSchG. Coke ovens are listed in the Annex in column 1 (Spalte 1) No. 1.11. The IPPC Directive was implemented in Germany through the *Artikelgesetz* of 27.07.2001. Hence Germany had failed to implement the IPPC Directive in time by 31 October 1999. The Directive was passed on 24 September 1996. Art. 21 of the IPPC Directive stipulates that member states had to implement the Directive into their national laws 'no later than three years after its entry into force'. Art. 22 of the Directive specified that the Directive entered into force 'on the 20th day following its publication'. The Directive was published in the Official Journal of the EU on 10 October

1996. A number of German *Länder* therefore issued a *Runderlaß* which clarified which sections of the IPPC Directive had direct effect in German law. This covered the period until the German central government initiated a federal legislative process for the incorporation of the IPPC Directive into German federal law. The IPPC Directive was finally implemented in German law not through an amendment of Germany's main environmental laws, but through a separate *Artikelgesetz*. This contained various amendments of specific articles in all the various media-specific environmental laws, such as the law for air pollution control (the *Bundesimmisssionsschutzgesetz*), water protection (*Wasserhaushaltsgesetz*) and waste management (*Abfallwirtschafts- und Kreislaufgesetz*). The *Artikelgesetz* also incorporated provisions from the changed EU EIA Directive and some other EU environmental directives into German law.

30. § 6 (2) adds that the licence has to be issued if no other public law provisions or health and safety legal requirements prohibit the building and the operation of the installation.

31. The German version of § 5 (1) reads:

> Genehmigungsbedürftige Anlagen sind so zu errichten und zu betreiben, daß zur Gewährleistung eines hohen Schutzniveaus für die Umwelt insgesamt:
>
> 1. Schädliche Umwelteinwirkungen und sonstige Gefahren, erhebliche Nachteile und erhebliche Belästigungen für die Allgemeinheit und die Nachbarschaft nicht hervorgerufen werden können;
>
> 2. Vorsorge gegen schädliche Umwelteinwirkungen und sonstige Gefahren, erhebliche Nachteile und erhebliche Belästigungen getroffen wird, insbesondere durch die dem Stand der Technik entsprechenden Maßnahmen;
>
> 3. Abfälle vermieden, nicht zu vermeidende Abfälle verwertet und nicht zu verwertende Abfälle ohne Beeinträchtigung des Wohls der Allgemeinheit beseitigt werden; Abfälle sind nicht zu vermeiden, soweit die Vermeidung technisch nicht möglich oder nicht zumutbar ist, die Vermeidung ist unzulässig soweit sie zu nachteiligenden Umweltauswirkungen führt als die Verwertung; die Verwertung und Beseitigung von Abfällen erfolgt nach den Vorschriften des Kreislaufwirtschafts-und Abfallgesetzes und den sonstigen für die Abfälle geltenden Vorschriften;
>
> 4. Energie sparsam und effizient verwendet wird.

32. The old TA *Luft* from 1986 was still applicable during the licensing procedure for the coke oven. The new version of the TA *Luft* from 24 July 2002 came into force on 1 October 2002, after the IPPC permit for the coke oven had been issued.

33. *Allgemeine Verwaltungsvorschrift* is a tertiary rule.

34. The TA *Luft* was passed under § 48 BimSchG.

35. In German: 'unbestimmte Rechtsbegriffe'.

36. Such as the polyaromatic hydrocarbons which are emitted from emissions-minimised wet quenching and dry quenching.

37. In German: 'Immissionssituation'. 'Emissions' refers under German environmental law to the pollutants which are emitted from a specific source, such as a chimney stack. 'Immissions' refers to the sum of all emissions in a particular area constituting the local air quality.
38. No. 3.3.1.11.1 of the TA *Luft* 1986. In German: 'Kokskühlung. Es sind Verfahren zur emissionsarmen Kühlung des Kokses einzusetzen, z. B. die trockene Kokskühlung; die staubförmigen Emissionen im Abgas der trockenen Kokskühlung dürfen 20 mg/m^3 nicht überschreiten'. TA *Luft* 1986 No. 3.3.1.11.1 GMBL 95, ber. 202. in Hans D. Jarass, 2002, Bundesimmissionsschutzgesetz – Kommentar, 5th edn, München, Verlag C. H. Beck.
39. According to No. 3.3.1.11.1 of the TA *Luft*.
40. The operator's lawyer also advanced the idea that the requirement of an 'emissions-minimised quenching system' in No. 3.3.1.11.1 was an undetermined legal concept which needed further interpretation with reference to the EU BREF note, which in turn referred to emissions-minimised wet quenching without qualification as BAT (letter from operator's lawyers to the German licensing authority of 25.01.2001).
41. The operator's lawyer also argued that the reference to the specific technique of dry quenching in No. 3.3.1.11.1 of the German TA *Luft* was in breach of preamble 17 of the IPPC Directive, which states that 'emission limit values, parameters or equivalent technical measures should be based on the best available techniques, *without prescribing the use of one specific technique or technology*' (emphasis added). The preamble, however, has no binding legal force.
42. 'IPPC – Guidance for the Production of Coke, Iron and Steel', Sector Guidance Note, IPPC S2.01, p. 53. Interview no. 2 with UK EA licensing officer. The licensing procedure for the integrated iron and steel works began on 30.08.2001 and the licence was finally issued on 25.06.04. Licensing officers referred to the draft UK PPC guidance from February 2001 during the licensing procedure. The final approved UK guidance note entitled 'Integrated Pollution Prevention and Control (IPPC) – Guidance for the Production of Coke, Iron and Steel', Sector Guidance Note IPPC S2.01, was issued in June 2004. For a copy, see www.environment-agency.gov.uk/business/444304/444369/673298/?version=1&lang=_e.
43. Some standards in the UK national guidance were taken from the EU BREF note. For instance, the requirement for coke oven gas desulphurisation was referred back to 'BREF EP. 6'. The fitting of 'selective catalytic reduction (SCR)' – if local NOX air quality standards were threatened – was inserted with reference to the EU BREF. See UK Sector Guidance Note for Coke, Iron and Steel, p. 50.
44. The note also refers to the fitting of lamella stack baffles in the quench tower for arresting dust emissions.
45. See 'Integrated Pollution Prevention and Control: A Practical Guide', Third edition, 2004, at www.defra.gov.uk/environment/ppc/ippcguide/ippc_ed3.htm.

46. I.e. this guide is not issued under regulation 37 of the PPC Regs. 2000.
47. The IPC regime under Part I EPA 1990.
48. Quote from interview no. 2 with UK EA licensing officer.
49. Ibid.
50. Art. 2 (11) second indent of the IPPC Directive.
51. Here costs clearly cover the costs of purchasing and installing the techniques themselves for an IPPC installation. But the text of the Directive is unclear on whether the costs of remedying environmental damage caused by failure to install techniques are also covered.
52. These figures were quoted before the introduction of the euro in Germany. They amount to approximately £678,226.
53. This amounts to approximately £5.
54. This figure included already the savings which could be made through the recovery of energy from the heat of the coke during the dry quenching system.
55. Approximately £237, 423–271, 361.
56. From licensing files of coke oven plant.
57. *Wirtschaftsprüfungsgesellschaft*.
58. In German: 'nachvollziehbar'.
59. Decision Document No. 6, p. 21.
60. Such as fugitive emissions which arose from pushing the coke into the oven and the stack emissions from the flue gases which arose from the heating of the coke ovens.
61. An economic discourse in relation to BAT determinations in relation to coke cooling for both the German and the UK plant also included reference to competitive pressures that operators faced from other steel producers inside and outside the EU, such as China and the US.
62. For instance, a letter from the youth organisation of the German Social Democratic Party (SPD) of 17.04.01 to the licensing authority expressed concern that the operator had 'exerted significant political pressures' in the coke oven licensing procedure through informal talks with the 'political level of the administration', in particular the *Land* environmental ministry and the 'Staatskanzlei'. The 'Staatskanzlei' is comparable to a cabinet which assists the Prime Minister for the *Land* in the realisation of government policies. The letter also suggested that the operator had tried to pursue its cause through a public political campaign.
63. A comprehensive web of political actors became involved in the German coke oven licensing procedure and this was considered controversial. It included for instance the youth organisation of the German Social Democratic Party (Jusos), the city administration of the area in which the coke oven plant was to be situated, the *Land* environmental ministry and the Staatskanzlei. Letters to the licensing authority from interested parties were also sometimes copied to members of the *Land* Parliament and the Prime Minister of the *Land* government.

64. For instance, through *Erlaße* (internal administrative orders which can direct in a detailed manner the activities of subordinate administrative authorities).
65. Such as environmental managers at the site who were also involved in the IPPC licensing procedure.
66. An *öffentlich rechtlicher Vertrag* was concluded in spring 2001. This public law contract is defined in § 54 of the German Administrative Procedure Act (*Verwaltungsverfahrensgesetz*) as a public law contract which can also be used in place of an administrative order (*Verwaltungsakt*).
67. Ca. 60 million euros.
68. Interview no. 1 with German licensing officer.
69. Issued under the Water Resources Act 1991.
70. Interview no. 2 with UK licensing officer.
71. In fact there were two key reports from the *Land* environmental protection agency (LUA) during the licensing procedure. The first report of 16.11.2000 addressed in more general terms the fact that in its new application the operator wanted to switch from dry quenching to emissions-minimised wet quenching. Hence this report discussed whether dry quenching could be considered as comparable in its environmental performance to emissions-minimised wet quenching. The second report of 12.01.2001 responded to an operator's submission of 18.12.2000 and affirmed its reservations about the comparability of emissions-minimised wet quenching with dry quenching.
72. Abbreviation for polyaromatic hydrocarbons.
73. As in the journal *Stahl und Eisen* (steel and iron).
74. The German statement from the file read: 'Um nun eine Aussage über den "wahren" Wert für den Staubemissionsfaktor treffen zu können, müssen die gemessenen Einzelwerte gemittelt werden, um so als Endergebnis einen Wert für die Netzmessung der gesamten Löschturm-Austrittsfläche zu erhalten.'
75. While the operator supplied figures and calculations which suggested that emissions-minimised wet quenching could achieve dust emissions of 10 mg per ton of coke produced, the *Land* environmental protection agency throughout the technical debates maintained a view which suggested that emissions-minimised wet quenching would lead to dust emissions ranging from 10 to 40 mg per ton of coke produced.
76. The Decision Document for the PPC licence for the integrated iron and steel works, which included the coke ovens, lists, for instance, specialist input from other EA officers on waste, noise, water quality and monitoring, in order to also scrutinise the operator's statement on air quality impacts of the site.
77. In fact two key questions were formulated by the licensing authority which guided its further collection of technical data on emissions-minimised wet quenching and dry quenching. These were:
    a) is the CSQ procedure practically suited for minimising emissions?
    b) is the CSQ procedure at least equivalent to the coke dry quenching system which is considered as BAT?

78. The *Land* environmental protection agency specified that emission values for the following pollutants had to be determined in order to come to a conclusion whether emissions-minimised wet quenching was 'at least equivalent' to dry quenching:
    - total dust
    - fine particulates (PM 10)
    - SO_2
    - hydrogensulphide
    - total sulphur
    - carbon monoxide
    - benzol and PAH (polycyclic aromatic hydrocarbons).
79. For this reason the German licensing authority also asked the state environmental protection agency to produce a technical report on what emissions were caused by emissions-minimised wet quenching and dry quenching.
80. PM 10 are fine dust particles with a diameter of 10 µg (one hundredth of a millimetre).
81. Quote from operator's lawyer's letter to German licensing authority, 25 April 2001.
82. Another example for the opening up of a technical discourse to a political discourse by invoking a language of intentions was the way in which various emission data were presented. For instance, measurement values which an external consultant had obtained for the operator, were discussed with the *Land* environmental protection agency (LUA) which provided technical expertise input for the licensing authority. A memo recording the meeting between the external consultant and the LUA stated that it was agreed not to include certain measurement values in the calculation of average emissions because a 'conservative' and 'critical' evaluation of the measurement values was required.
83. *Technischer Überwachungsverein.*
84. In German the original statement read: 'Das Messverfahren sollte einen Staubauswurf von ca $<\_$ 10 g/t Koks nachweisen können, entsprechend einer Staubkonzentration von ca. 10 mg/m^3 Schwadenvolumen. Die Volumeneinheit bei der Staub-Konzentrationsangabe ist hier das Schwadenvolumen im Betriebszustand feucht' (p. 6 of the external consultant's report in the German licensing authority file).
85. Specific reference withheld for reasons of confidentiality.
86. In the words of one of the officers involved in the licensing procedure: 'Eine Marschrichtung war schon vorgegeben.' Quote from interview no. 4 with German licensing officer.
87. There was also an issue about finding any plants as relevant cases for comparison. One coke oven plant with dry quenching was about to close. The operator thus tried to get emission figures specifically for carcinogens from coke oven plants with dry quenching in other countries, such as

Finland and Japan. No measurements were supplied from these other plants, however, because there were no measurement data for carcinogens since they were apparently very low. Moreover, the other coke dry quenching plant which was operated by the same operator applying for a new coke oven with emissions-minimised wet quenching was an old plant which was not operating at full capacity.

88. Another coke oven plant was about to close.

89. In a similar vein a language of relativity also helped the LUA to make a case that sulphur emissions from dry quenching were lower than for emissions-minimised wet quenching. The LUA's interests here included its status as an independent, technical consultant to the licensing authority and thus as an agency capable of critically questioning information supplied by the operator. The LUA based its conclusion that sulphur emissions were lower for dry quenching than for emissions-minimised wet quenching on a careful choice of comparators. It referred to sulphur emissions from dry quenching that involved an additional technical procedure which led to the removal of more sulphur from the stack emissions from the coke cooling. The operator contested this by suggesting that the LUA had chosen the wrong comparator. There were various reasons why the operator thought that the dry quenching with the extra sulphur removal technique was the wrong comparator. For technical reasons the extra sulphur removal technique could not be installed at the operator's plant. The operator also considered it only as an emerging technique that was not yet in general use. The operator also objected to it on the basis of high energy need and waste water generation.

90. A language of relativity, in terms of identifying the appropriate installation in relation to which emissions had to be assessed, was also invoked by the operator in relation to carbon monoxide emissions from coke dry quenching. The German licensing authority argued that dry quenching was associated with lower carbon monoxide emissions because the heat from the hot coke could be reused. Hence the integrated iron and steel works would need less energy supplies from outside sources of energy, such as a conventional coal-fired power station. Therefore energy reuse at the coke oven plant would help to avoid further carbon monoxide emissions. The operator's solicitor contested this view by arguing that only the emissions from the plant to which the application related, here the coke oven plant, could be taken into account, and not savings in carbon monoxide emissions from an outside power plant.

91. According to the German operator a determination of dust emissions from a coke dry quenching system also had to take into account the emissions that were caused by the wet quenching system on site. Every coke oven plant with a dry quenching system also had a wet quenching system as a standby emergency cooling system in case of a breakdown of the dry quenching system.

92. Such as polyaromatic hydrocarbons (PAHs), like benzol and benzo(a)pyren.

93. Interview no. 9 with UK permitting officer, and there were references to breaches of the 24-hour EQS PM 10 standard in the Decision Document for the site.
94. The IPPC Directive stipulates that by 2007 its obligations also have to be fully implemented in relation to existing installations, which are installations already in operation by the time the Directive came into force.
95. The environmental consultants' report stated that installation of desulphurisation equipment would bring about a 36 per cent site-wide reduction in SO_2 emissions to atmosphere from the site.
96. Environmental consultants' report, p. 16.

9 Conclusion

Introduction

This book has discussed law and EU integration relationships. What conceptualisation of law are we presupposing when we say that 'law' integrates? Is there really a distinct 'legal' dimension to EU integration? The book argues that 'the role of law in EU integration' is an empirical question. An integrating function of law should not simply be assumed on the basis of theoretical assumptions. The book therefore discusses small-scale qualitative empirical data on how determinations of 'the best available techniques' are achieved in the implementation of the EU Directive on Integrated Pollution Prevention and Control. Implementation of the Directive has been analysed at the EU, the national and the local level by reference to the licensing practices in a German and UK regulatory authority.

The book's argument proceeds in three stages. Firstly, chapters 2 and 3 discuss literature on the role of law in EU integration and examine traditional and critical perspectives. Chapter 2 argues that traditional accounts rely on notions of law which are generated internally by formal legal systems themselves. In these accounts law is portrayed as instrumental, as relatively autonomous in relation to its contexts, and as codified in formal legal texts. Chapter 3 discusses contributions – which also rely on social constructivism – that reject these assumptions, including the literature on new modes of EU governance. Chapter 4, however, argues that there is scope for further development of socio-legal analysis of EU law in action. Hence, secondly, chapters 5 to 8 discuss how political, technical and economic discourses construct BAT determinations. These chapters inductively develop small-scale propositions on the basis of the qualitative empirical data. In a third step the analysis draws on these interpretations of the data and examines what they tell us about the concept of 'EU law in action' and the intersections between a 'social' and a 'legal' sphere in particular.

This conclusion summarises the book's argument in three main sections. The first section recalls some key developments in the debates concerning law and integration and builds a case for an analysis based on 'EU law in action'. The second section outlines the main features of this concept of EU law in action and provides an analysis of how power mediates intersections between a social and a legal sphere. The third section discusses the scope and limitations of the argument. Do the empirical findings concerning the implementation of the IPPC Directive have any relevance beyond the UK and Germany? Is the account presented here significant beyond the specific focus on EU pollution control? What light, if any, do the findings shed on theories of EU integration?

Changing debates about the relationships between law and integration

Chapters 2 and 3 examined traditional and critical perspectives on law and EU integration. Chapter 2 discussed traditional accounts which draw on modernist conceptions of the social world. For instance, modernist perspectives on the state – which conceive the state as a distinct set of political institutions, exercising power on behalf of the collective interest and circumscribed within a specific territory – still feature in neo-realist accounts of EU integration. Such modernist conceptions of the state have also coloured perceptions of law in EU integration. They have privileged rather restricted images of law associated with the development of nation states and liberal constitutional orders in the eighteenth and nineteenth century in Western Europe. Here law is understood as instrumental (as capable of generating order in society), as relatively autonomous in relation to its social contexts, and hence as embodying a separation of powers as well as promoting a differentiation between a public and a private sphere. Law is also considered as a distinct set of legal rules 'in the books'. This is an image of law which still plays a role in the contemporary formal EU supranational legal order and the legal systems of the individual member states. Some contributions to the literature on EU integration, however, have begun to move away from this perspective. They broaden the conception of law by decentring the state. The state is no longer perceived to be at the heart of normative processes in EU integration. Instead the importance of networks, which bridge traditional distinctions between public and private as well as between state and civil society, is highlighted in order to explain the dynamics of EU integration. Critical accounts in the literature on EU integration have often drawn on constructivist and institutionalist perspectives. They highlight a whole range of social norms – beyond the formal 'law in the books' – as relevant to processes of integration. They also start to challenge the idea that law is relatively autonomous in relation to its social contexts. For instance, some functionalist sociologists and EU lawyers recognise the significance of economic and political contexts in the construction of law.

The concepts of law with which we work matter because they directly shape how we understand 'integration'. Conceptions of law which focus on its formal, instrumental and relatively autonomous dimensions are often associated with modernist accounts of integration. Here integration is seen as the answer to what is perceived as the key problem of how to achieve order in society:

In the barest terms, to say that a social arena is 'ordered' is to assert that that arena reflects *a substantial coordination of behaviour.*

(emphasis in the original, Tamanaha, 2001: 211)

In contrast, the 'EU law in action' analysis developed here decentres the problems of 'order' and 'convergence' as the key issues for understanding EU integration. It does so by focusing on the contribution of fluid and flexible discourses to the dynamics of EU integration. Social structures and institutions, allegedly fixed and clearly demarcated aspects of the social world, are less central to this analysis than an exploration of how perceptions of and action in the social world can shift, adjust and develop through talk and text. The book argues that integration can be multifaceted, involving not only 'co-ordination of behavior', but also disintegration (Shaw 1996, Goldstein et al., 2000) and partial integration. It highlights open BAT norms as an aspect of legal integration where the formation of norms is never finalised and remains ongoing. A modernist conception of the nation state also fades into the background when we focus on networked structures of the polity, such as the exchange of information about what constitute the 'best available techniques' under Art. 16 of the IPPC Directive, and its influence on the IPPC licensing practices of local regulatory authorities.

Hence the book seeks to contribute to existing debates concerning law and integration by developing two key methodological and theoretical issues. First, it argues that analysis of talk concerning law and integration at a micro-level can generate further insights into the dynamics of EU integration. The research has therefore focused on small-scale data about detailed implementation practices in relation to determinations of 'the best available techniques' under the EU Directive on Integrated Pollution Prevention and Control. The data has shed light on the intersections between a social and a legal sphere on a small-scale level. The book questions the differentiations between 'contexts' and 'law', which are usually invoked in EU 'law in context' studies. It argues that contexts can enter into the very construction of law and examines how this happens. By analysing how a number of discourses are mobilised in the construction of the 'best available techniques', the book sheds light on what constitutes a 'social' sphere in this scenario and how it becomes relevant to the construction of 'law'. By discussing variation in open and closed BAT norms it also examines what we should understand by 'norms' in the processes of EU integration. Do norms always possess clear boundaries that distinguish and differentiate them from their social contexts? Moreover, by applying 'law in action' analysis – usually conducted in the context of nation states – to the transnational context of the EU, the book responds to a growing recognition that the nature of law is currently being transformed through globalisation and various regional integration projects, such as the EU, Mercosur, CIS[1] and ASEAN. Hence we need conceptualisations of law which can explain legal processes across a variety of cultural and national contexts (Tamanaha, 2001: 134).

Second, the book draws on post-modernist ideas in its analysis of power and agency in 'EU law in action'. It considers language, communication and the production of knowledge as key to the construction of the social world, including EU integration processes. It thus builds on constructivist accounts of EU integration, as discussed in chapter 3. It draws on Foucault's notion of the 'microphysics of power' in order to analyse how the best available techniques are determined. Power is understood as dispersed throughout the social body and exercised through various small-scale techniques, tactics and discursive practices. This analysis questions modernist conceptions of power employed in traditional accounts of law and integration as discussed in chapter 2. In such accounts power is considered as a commodity in the hands of 'key players'. In the debates on EU integration the latter are often defined as the formal EU and member states' institutions involved in EU integration processes, together with the people who work in them, including politicians, civil servants, lawyers, citizens, as well as corporate or individual economic actors who initiate court actions. In contrast, post-modernist perspectives interpret 'agency' as an aspect of social life that is also discursively constructed in social interactions, not as a pre-given, innate characteristic of human beings. Moreover, from a modernist perspective power – and its manifestation in assertions of interests – is regarded as flowing from material social structures. It is also considered, in turn, as a structuring device (Lukes, 2005: 111). In contrast, the small-scale analysis of the operation of discourses pursued here highlights the fluid, malleable and ephemeral aspects of social life. But what light does this analysis shed on 'EU law in action'?

The 'microphysics' of power in 'EU law in action'

Understanding the nature of EU law is not just a matter of abstractly defining a *concept* of law. Empirical perspectives draw attention to legal *process*, in this case the formation of BAT technology norms. The discourse perspective focuses on how 'social actors' in the field talk about law when trying to determine what constitute the 'best available techniques'. The analysis captures an early phase in the formation of law. In this it differs from implementation studies which discuss 'law in action' at a later stage, analysing the social practices which inform how previously determined legal rules are implemented in practice. Power matters for understanding the intersections between a social and a legal sphere when legal rules are being formed. Chapter 5 suggests that actors in the field work with a complex conception of power. They draw on both post-structuralist and modernist ideas. Talk about BAT determinations during the EU BREF writing process was characterised by a tension between reference to powerful actors, such as member states, the Commission, 'regulators' and 'industry', and reference to BAT determinations as generated by opaque networks of various groups, individuals and institutions. Moreover, the empirical analysis in chapters 5 to 8 suggests that power needs to be conceptualised in broad rather than narrow terms. A political discourse which refers to interests is the most visible expression of 'power' in the construction of EU law in action here. But the 'microphysics' of power also includes how and what arguments are marshalled concerning 'the best available techniques' within a technical and economic discourse. Chapters 5, 6 and 8 trace how political points can be made with reference to technical facts and costs. This broad conception also challenges some accounts of power, discussed in chapter 4, because it does not insist on clear boundaries between power and normativity. The analysis of the empirical data suggests that political, economic and technical discourses – all central to the operation of power – feed into the construction of the 'law in action', in this case BAT technology norms. So what does this analysis further contribute to understanding normativity in the EU and the significance of social norms in EU integration processes?

Social norms and EU 'law in action'

The critical, and especially constructivist and institutionalist, perspectives discussed in chapter 3 recognise a whole range of social norms as relevant to EU integration. They discuss, for instance, how organisational rules shape the work of EU and national institutions which are involved in the development and enforcement of formal law. They also recognise social actors' values and cultural practices as significant for EU integration processes. These accounts consider social norms as different from mere social practices. Social norms are perceived as clearly bounded phenomena, differentiated from their contexts and capable of steering the behaviour of social actors.

This book seeks to broaden conceptions of law in EU integration. It recognises the significance of social norms for constructing EU law. Organisational routines and directives, such as the Environment Agency's written instructions on PPC permitting as well as specific cultural perspectives in different member states on how PPC permitting should be carried out, all played a significant role in the determination of BAT. But the book's main point is that there is a variety of norms beyond the recognition of social norms and the formal 'law in the books' in EU integration. Implementation of the IPPC Directive generates variation in *both* open and closed EU norms. Two points arise from this. First, EU integration processes do not simply involve closed norms that are clearly demarcated from their social contexts. There are also open norms, like open BAT technology norms. Clear, specific, determinate, bounded norms do not crystallise in this case. Second, this finding of a variety of norms suggests that the nature of EU law cannot be understood through developing just one specific conception of EU law (De Burca and Walker, 2005: 7, 12). Implementation of EU law 'on the ground' can generate different types of law. But how exactly does this account of EU 'law in action' go beyond traditional accounts of formal, instrumental and relatively autonomous EU law?

Formal EU law?

As discussed in chapter 2, EU law is often understood as the 'formal law in the books'. It is clear that formal law has been key to the development of EU integration, not least in the field of pollution control. Since the inception of its environmental policy in 1972 and up until 1998, the European Union has passed about 300 legal acts, mainly directives and some regulations, as well as decisions and recommendations (Guide to the Approximation of European Union Legislation, 1998: 1).[2] New forms of EU governance, however, which also involve soft law, have rendered formal state law, developed under the 'classic community method', less central to EU integration. This general trend is also reflected in EU environmental policy. Especially since the 6th Environmental Action Programme,[3] this policy relies on a whole range of measures. They include legally binding provisions, such as eco-taxes and regulation through information in labelling schemes. They also draw on non-legal measures which include voluntary regulation, such as self-regulation and legally non-binding agreements between industry sectors and the EU Commission (Lenschow, 2005).[4] Moreover, the nature of formal EU law is changing. Instead of detailed and very specific EU legislation, the Commission increasingly favours instruments like Framework Directives,[5] which leave the definition of the precise content of legal obligations to member state authorities and/or EU comitology committees, composed of member state representatives, experts, industry interests and environmental NGOs (see also Scott and Holder, 2006).

This book, however, argues that theoretical analysis of formal EU law and policy documents provides only limited insight into the nature of EU law. Whether and how EU law is changing from 'old' to 'new' forms of governance also requires empirical analysis of the kind of 'law' that is actually generated during the implementation of EU law. In fact, the book suggests that implementation practices themselves can be a further source of law. While such practices may draw on formal legal texts, they also go beyond them. The text of the IPPC Directive, national statutory provisions and secondary and tertiary rules were all relevant points of reference in debates about what constitutes the 'best available techniques'. But these formal legal provisions are also transformed by being discussed in political, economic and technical discourses. For instance, chapter 7 has traced how an economic discourse is mobilised in the determination of BAT for specific installations and industry sectors. Art. 2 (11) second indent and Annex IV first sentence of the IPPC Directive refers to the costs of techniques as a relevant factor for choosing a 'best available technique'. Chapter 7, however, argues that the actual economic discourse invoked in BAT determinations involves more than this. It also includes the costs of IPPC licensing for regulatory authorities and operators. To conclude: while 'formal EU law in the books' clearly matters in EU integration processes, it does not fully capture the role or nature of law in EU integration processes. EU integration does not just generate formal 'EU law in the books' but also EU 'law in action'. Hence analysis of the nature of EU law needs to take the idea of implementation practices into account as another source of law. So what light can EU 'law in action' analysis shed on another key element of traditional conceptions of EU law, i.e. that law can be wielded in an instrumental manner?

Instrumental EU law?

This book also questions some aspects of instrumental conceptions of law in EU integration. As discussed in chapter 2, these suggest that EU law is a key instrument for achieving convergence between member states in specific policy areas. Hence law is thought capable of realising the aims of various EU policies. The research discussed in this book, however, questions whether such an instrumental function can be attributed to the formal law, and hence whether the latter actually integrates. As far as *administrative structures of pollution control* are concerned, the IPPC Directive seems to have generated only limited integration.[6] As discussed in chapter 1, key aspects of national approaches to pollution control have been retained during the implementation of the IPPC Directive in Germany and the UK. For instance, a holistic approach towards permitting installations – taking into account how emissions to all three interconnected environmental media, air, water and land, are affected through pollution control measures – is the key policy innovation of the IPPC Directive. Elements of the UK pollution control regime put this integrated approach into practice, drawing on the system of integrated permitting which already existed in the UK before the introduction of the IPPC Directive. In the UK IPPC permitting is administratively integrated in the sense that the EA[7] brings staff with technical expertise in land, air and water pollution control all together in a single organisation. This facilitates the consideration of cross-media issues, one aspect of integrated permitting. The EA also facilitates analysis of cross-media issues through a software tool[8] which can be used by permitting officers. It allows permitting officers and licence applicants to assess data on environmental releases from an installation by quantifying environmental impacts on all media and by providing guidelines for resolving cross-media conflicts. Hence the software can help to identify pollution control options which cause the least impact on all three environmental media.[9] Moreover, UK sector guidance notes usually consider the impact of production and pollution abatement technologies on all three environmental media.

In contrast, German administrative structures – even after the implementation of the IPPC Directive – illustrate the persistence of a media-specific approach to pollution control. Each IPPC installation is licensed by one coordinating authority. But different environmental authorities – usually organised along media-specific lines – are involved in the licensing process (Kloepfer, 2004: 162–163). According to permitting officers,[10] these authorities independently contribute conditions for an IPPC licence which is issued by the coordinating regulatory authority. There seems to be limited discussion between officers dealing with media-specific issues, e.g. on waste/land, water and air when drafting IPPC licence conditions (see also Bohne and Dietze, 2004: 209). Moreover, the various technical instructions (TA),[11] which are key to the implementation of BAT in German environmental law, to a limited extent consider cross-media impacts. For instance, the TA *Luft* focuses mainly on emissions to air.[12] Part 4 of the TA *Luft*, however, recognises the impact of air pollution standards and control techniques on land contamination. It specifies that particular *Immissionswerte* (air quality standards) have to be complied with in order to avoid pollution of land, including vegetation and ecosystems. Hence Part 4 of the TA *Luft* implements the spirit of the IPPC Directive by seeking to avoid wholesale shifts of contaminants from air to land. But other technical instructions, such as the TA *Abwasser* (waste water), the TA *Abfall* (waste disposal) and TA *Siedlungsabfall* (household waste) which also implement BAT, are still very media-specific.[13]

Not just the integrated permitting approach, however, but other elements of administrative structures for the definition of BAT have also been implemented differently in Germany and the UK. For instance, the EU BAT reference documents – which are central to harmonised BAT definitions across the EU – play a different role in

German and UK IPPC licensing. In the UK, EU BREF documents feed into BAT definitions. They are taken into account when UK sector guidance notes are written. Sometimes they are directly referred to when BAT is determined for a specific plant. In Germany, however, BAT documents were only considered to a limited extent in the revision of the TA *Luft* (air) in 2002.[14] They have not yet been considered in regulations dealing with water pollution (Entec, 2006: 58). The EU BREFs' approach – which propose BAT techniques with associated emission values – is regarded as different from and potentially incompatible with the traditional German technical instructions. These are binding upon German permitting officers and hence are not just one among several factors to be taken into account. They impose emission limit values, not 'associated emission levels', for installations. Moreover, according to interviews with permitting officers,[15] EU BAT reference documents are seldom referred to directly in German IPPC licensing procedures. The different reception in the UK and Germany of a key element of the IPPC Directive, namely the EU BREF documents, thus also leads us to doubt whether 'law', in this case the IPPC Directive, has actually generated – in an instrumental fashion – greater convergence of pollution control systems.

In addition, an instrumental conception of EU law is also challenged by the discourse perspective developed in chapters 5 to 8. These empirical chapters argue that discourses are key to the construction of the 'best available techniques'. Discourses also regulate who can make what type of argument about what constitutes 'BAT'. They thereby constitute actors in BAT determinations. For instance, chapter 5 argued that a political discourse focusing on interests also constructs procedures for determining BAT in the EU Technical Working Groups. These allocate certain roles, such as 'active participant in Technical Working Groups', 'passive observer', 'expert contributor' and BREF 'author' or BREF 'writer'. They thereby construct specific forms of agency. This perspective challenges modernist accounts of EU integration in which the existence of 'social actors' is assumed rather than perceived as the outcome of complex processes of discursive construction. Modernist conceptions of social actors, however, are often central to instrumental accounts of EU law. Here 'social actors' with an innate capacity for agency wield law in an instrumental manner in order to achieve specific policy outcomes. In contrast to this, a discourse perspective suggests that agency is the outcome of complex processes of discourse mobilisation when law is implemented. Agency therefore does not exist independently as a category prior to the mobilisation of law. It therefore appears questionable whether there are prior 'social actors' who can then pick up tools of law and wield law in an instrumental manner.

To summarise: the analysis developed here questions an instrumental perspective of EU law from various angles. It questions whether the IPPC Directive (in an instrumental fashion) has in practice generated integration effects. The discourse perspective fundamentally challenges the modernist conception of agency which is central to instrumental conceptions of law. But there are also various limitations to the argument against an instrumental conception of EU law which has been developed here. First, there are limits to using evidence of divergence in pollution control practices in Germany and the UK after the implementation of the IPPC Directive as an argument for the limited instrumental capacity of the IPPC Directive to promote and achieve integration. While there may be divergence between Germany and the UK in terms of administrative structures for integrated permitting and the role of the EU BREFs, there are nevertheless harmonisation effects in relation to certain substantive BAT standards. Chapter 8 discussed one instance of this, the installation of a very similar gas cooling technique for UK and German coke ovens. It remains unclear, however, how widespread such substantive harmonisations of BAT determinations are across the EU, specifically in relation to other sectors covered by the IPPC Directive.[16]

Second, it is only possible to a limited extent to provide *general* answers to the question whether there are integration effects in EU pollution control which can be attributed in an instrumental manner to the IPPC Directive. Integration effects arise through various dynamics. There is an integration effect in the sense that all 27 EU member states are required to formally incorporate the IPPC Directive in their national law. But this does not mean that there is full harmonisation of actual permitting practices – either in terms of procedures and substantive standards – for specific IPPC plants (see also Bohne and Dietze, 2004: 202). Conversely, while there may be discrepancies in how exactly the legal obligations of the IPPC Directive are incorporated in national law, actual technology standards in a particular industry sector across the EU may be harmonised. For instance, the domination of some EU industry sectors by multinational companies can mean that in practice the same technology standards are implemented for pollution control in different member states, especially in sectors where there are only a limited number of pollution control techniques.

Thirdly, and most importantly, the analysis developed here questions only one specific aspect of the instrumental conception of EU law, namely the idea that the formal EU 'law in the books' can be wielded in an instrumental manner in order to achieve specific policy aims. But the analysis maintains that EU law in action can still function in an instrumental manner in the sense that the discourses it mobilises fulfil specific functions. As argued in chapters 5 to 8, implementation of the IPPC Directive generates a number of discourses. They fulfil the key function of coordinating interactions and debates concerning what constitute 'the best available techniques'. In fact chapter 8 argued that an EU integration effect, consisting of the installation of similar techniques of wet quenching for the German and UK coke ovens, was also due to an opening-up of a legal to economic and political discourses. Chapter 7 argued that a developed and detailed economic discourse also fulfilled the specific function of rebutting a political discourse in BAT determinations. To conclude: this book questions a specific aspect of an instrumental conception of EU law, the idea that the formal 'law in the books' can be wielded in an instrumental manner in order to achieve the pre-specified aims of EU policies. Moreover, the analysis developed here further questions an instrumental conception of law by pointing out the strong links between law and its contexts.

Relatively autonomous EU law?

Traditional accounts of EU law as discussed in chapter 2 consider law as relatively autonomous in relation to its social contexts. The analysis developed in this book questions this approach. It thereby also provides a further specific angle from which to question instrumental conceptions of EU law. Systems-theoretical approaches have been influential in debates about the limits of instrumental conceptions of law (see, for example, Teubner, 1986b). They rely on the idea of limited communication between the legal system and other social sub-systems, such as the political and economic sub-systems, in order to argue that there are limits to the instrumental use of law. The messages of law are distorted when they are translated into the self-referential processes of other social sub-systems. In contrast, the analysis developed here questions an instrumental conception of law by pointing out the strong links between law and its social contexts. But how do these links arise?

The contexts of law are mobilised through a range of discourses which are invoked during the implementation of the IPPC Directive, such as a political, economic and technical discourse. These contexts are not separate from, but are *embedded in* law. It is such intersections, rather than a differentiation between a social and a legal sphere, that characterise the 'EU law in action' here. Open BAT norms are a particularly emphatic illustration of the idea that the demarcation between a social and a legal sphere is relatively fluid. But social contexts matter in all instances of BAT determinations. There are various ways in which formal legal texts can become opened up to contexts. For instance, chapter 8 suggested that a political discourse did not displace a legal discourse in the determination of what constitute the 'best available techniques' for the cooling of coke oven gas. Instead, political considerations were addressed *within* a legal discourse. The licensing authority retained its criterion – expressed in a legal discourse – that emissions-minimised wet quenching had to be at least equal to dry quenching in its environmental performance. This was in response to the German operator's insistence – in a political discourse – on its interests to obtain an IPPC licence which authorises emissions-minimised wet quenching. This was cheaper than dry quenching which had previously been considered as BAT. Chapter 8 also argued that a technical and legal discourse was opened up to political and economic discourses through a language of relativity and purpose. Hence 'EU law in action' is not simply politicised or usurped by economics or technical expert knowledge. Instead, the account developed here suggests that there can be significant overlap and exchanges between different discourses. Participants in BAT determinations do not abandon either law, costs, politics or technical arguments. They try to mesh these arguments together.

But why does this critique of a conception of EU law as relatively autonomous matter? First, the recognition of strong links between social contexts and law further questions instrumental conceptions of EU law. From a functionalist perspective the integrating function of law is necessary for promoting coherence and order in society, once there is significant differentiation of the social system. But the empirical analysis developed in chapters 5 to 8 points to overlaps and exchanges between economic, political and technical discourses that draw on law's contexts. This questions the picture of a clear differentiation between different social sub-systems which underpins functionalist accounts of the social world. Moreover, the account developed here suggests that these overlapping contexts enter into the construction of law. It is thus questionable whether law can be wielded in an instrumental manner, in the sense that it is capable of achieving specific policy aims and thereby transforming its contexts.

Second, where it is recognised that law is not clearly demarcated from its contexts, it becomes difficult to identify a *distinct legal* dimension to EU integration. As chapter 8 suggests, this does not mean that law exercises no integrating function. But this integrating function is associated with a range of discourses which bring law's contexts into play. A resulting integration in the German and UK coke oven licensing procedure was linked to a mobilisation of economic, political and technical contexts in the construction of harmonised BAT norms. To conclude: the EU 'law in action' analysis which this book develops questions accounts of EU law as formal, instrumental and relatively autonomous in relation to its contexts. This account is developed with reference to qualitative empirical data on the implementation of the IPPC Directive at the EU level and with reference to licensing practices of a German and a UK regulatory authority. But to what extent are these findings of wider significance? Are they relevant to EU law more generally, beyond the specific focus on the IPPC Directive?

Scope and limitations of the argument

This book examines relationships between law and integration in the specific context of the implementation of the IPPC Directive. To what extent can general points about law and integration relationships be developed from this analysis? Law and integration relationships can vary according to the particular policy sector and time period of EU integration under consideration (Lange, 2007; Rosamond, 2000: 13). For instance, 'instrumental' law has been considered as particularly important for promoting an early phase of EU integration in the 1960s and 1970s. Key examples here are the ECJ's doctrines of direct effect[17] and of the supremacy of EC over national law[18] (Haltern, 2004: 179). The ECJ's creative and purposeful development of these doctrines[19] enhanced the formal law's capacity to advance integration, particularly at a time when political initiative for integration was waning in individual member states. Even if member states were not willing to fully implement EC law into their national legal systems, integration can still progress through the doctrine of direct effect. Litigants can (instrumentally) invoke EC law in their national courts in order to achieve conflict resolution in their own interests regardless of whether member states have implemented EC law.[20]

In contrast to this focus on instrumental, formal and quasi-autonomous law during the early phases of EU integration, debates in the 1990s and subsequently have located EU law more clearly in its political context through a focus on good governance and constitutional values in EU integration (Walker, 2005: 595, 598). This development has also been encouraged by the drafting of and ongoing debate about the EU constitution as well as by greater reliance on various forms of soft law and new instruments of regulation which raise issues of accountability and legitimacy in EU governance more strongly than before (Haltern, 2004: 179).

But there are no straightforward links between the particular unfolding stages of EU integration and specific types of law. Legal rules which do not easily fit in with the conception of formal, instrumental and relatively autonomous EU law were also important during early phases of EU integration. For instance, the legal procedure for enforcing EC law, under Art. 226 EC Treaty,[21] provides for diplomatic negotiation between the Commission and member state governments which have failed to implement EC law into their national legal systems. There are various steps in this procedure which encourage bargaining in the 'shadow of the law' before a formal legal action at the ECJ – considered as the last resort – commences.[22] Hence Art. 226 EC Treaty – an early cornerstone of the EU legal order[23] – envisages formal law as a trigger for informal, extensive bargaining between political actors in order to remedy non-compliance with EC law. This procedure does not seem to fit the image of formal, instrumental and quasi-autonomous law. Both Commission and member states are subject to various political pressures during negotiations. This limits the Commission's ability to achieve a specific outcome and thus to apply Art. 226 EC Treaty in an instrumental manner. Moreover, there are numerous examples which show that declaratory judgments by the ECJ – that a member state is in breach of EC law, the final step in the Art. 226 EC Treaty procedure – do not produce the specific outcome of compliance with EC law. Sometimes member states simply ignore judgments issued by the ECJ.[24] To summarise: it is difficult to identify straightforward links between specific periods of time and particular concepts of law in EU integration. Moreover, it is likely that variation in the relationship between law and EU integration has actually increased. In 'Europe à la carte' or 'multi-speed Europe' there is no single legal integration process. Instead, multiple processes of legal integration draw on various forms of law. Increasing flexibility and differentiation – itself promoted through new forms of EU governance – do not support a unified, single image of EU law as formal, instrumental and relatively autonomous in relation to its contexts (De Burca and Scott, 2006). Hence EU integration can no longer be interpreted as a search for the uniformity and harmonisation of social practices, including law. Against this background of variation in types of law employed in EU integration it remains to be assessed whether the findings concerning the implementation of the IPPC Directive merely add another single snapshot to this picture or whether they enable us to make more general points about the relationships between law and integration in the EU.

The IPPC Directive is not a unique or isolated piece of EC environmental legislation. Other EU environmental legislation, as well as legal measures in other policy fields, also share similar characteristics. It is a Framework Directive which therefore only specifies key legal obligations to a limited extent. Framework Directives are widely used. For instance, the EU Water Framework Directive also contains general legal obligations, such as the obligation of member states to achieve 'good surface and groundwater water status'.[25] More importantly, Framework Directives which impose fairly general and unspecified legal obligations upon member states are also used in other policy fields, such as consumer protection,[26] health and safety,[27] utilities regulation[28] and discrimination.[29] The EU Commission is increasingly resorting to Framework Directives in its legislative initiatives, also with reference to the principles of proportionality[30] and subsidiarity[31] and not just in the field of social policy.[32] This book argues that the implementation of the general legal obligation of the IPPC Framework Directive in practice generates both open and closed norms. Open norms may also be generated during the implementation of other Framework Directives. Moreover, the empirical analysis presented here has highlighted the significance of economic, political and technical discourses in the construction of legal obligations. While technical discourses are specific to the field of environmental law I have examined, economic and political discourses turn out to be significant for the constitution of a range of legal obligations, including policy fields beyond the environment. Hence aspects of the discursive processes discussed in chapters 6, 7 and 8 which are relevant to the construction of legal obligations under the IPPC Directive, may also be relevant to the construction of EU legal obligations in other policy fields.

Moreover, while the empirical research discussed in this book traces the implementation of the IPPC Directive on the EU level with reference to the licensing practices of a German and a UK regulatory authority, some of the empirical findings may also reflect implementation practices in other EU member states. First, the empirical analysis traces variation in open and closed BAT norms in relation to licensing practices of a UK and German regulatory authority. But open and closed BAT norms may also play a role in other EU member states, especially where EU BREFs contain open BAT norms. Variation in open and closed BAT norms may also arise here because some of the reasons for this phenomenon analysed in chapter 6 are also likely to apply. The justifications for open and closed BAT norms generated by a political and a technical discourse do not appear to be specific to Germany and the UK. Accounting for open BAT norms in a political discourse has included an emphasis on the targeting of regulatory resources through risk and new public management techniques. These are administrative policy developments which have also occurred in other EU member states. Moreover, a number of justifications for open BAT norms in a technical discourse (such as the idea that insufficient information is provided by the regulated industry, or that the dynamism of BAT as a technology standard and the complexity of some of the technical situations encountered militate against norm closure) are also likely to apply in other EU member states.

Second, various EU reports[33] suggest that further aspects of the German and UK IPPC implementation practices discussed in this book also occur elsewhere in the EU. Complex administrative arrangements for IPPC permitting, which result from federal or decentralised state structures, are not merely characteristic for Germany. For instance, the process by which a particular regulatory authority becomes involved in IPPC permitting and thus in BAT determinations also varies in Belgium, depending on whether the installation is situated in the Brussels, Wallonia or Flemish region. IPPC permitting is also decentralised in Spain where it is carried out by autonomous communities which can produce their own BAT guidance if they wish (EU Commission, First Implementation Report, 2004: 116). Moreover, not only Germany, but other member states also involve media-specific regulatory authorities in IPPC permitting. In fact, a number of member states only coordinate media-specific conditions in IPPC permits, as in Germany. This applies to Austria, Finland, Greece, Italy, the Netherlands, Portugal and Spain. There are also environmental media-specific regulatory authorities in Cyprus (Entec Report, 2006: 52). Hence more than half of the original fifteen member states have opted for a limited version of the coordination of IPPC conditions in accordance with their previous permitting system.[34] As in Germany, permits for discharges to water are also issued by a separate regulatory authority in the Netherlands. The Dutch Regional Water Boards are responsible for issuing permits for discharges to water from IPPC installations (Phare Report, 2002: 68; Gouldson, 1998, 111, 133).[35] Finally, France, as well as Germany, has instituted a bureaucratic system with *formally binding legal rules* which specify for permitters what constitutes BAT in a specific case, in contrast to the more discretionary BAT determination processs in countries like the UK, which provides only BAT national *guidance* to permitters (First Implementation Report: 113).[36]

But elements of UK IPPC implementation practices are also reflected in other member states. In the UK, for instance, the EA, a single regulatory authority, is responsible for the licensing and supervision of most IPPC installations. In Ireland too there is one single regulatory authority which deals with IPPC installations. Moreover, not just the UK, but Sweden, Ireland, Denmark as well as the Flemish and Brussels regions of Belgium have also built on their pre-existing integrated pollution control systems in the implementation of the IPPC Directive (Entec, 2006: 54).[37]

More importantly, however, the key finding of the research, the idea that formal, instrumental and relatively autonomous accounts of EU law only capture a limited dimension of EU 'law in action', is also supported by other considerations. First, the research questions an instrumental account of EU law on the basis of the disparate IPPC implementation practices in the UK and Germany. The EU reports confirm that IPPC implementation differs not only in Germany and the UK, but also in other EU member states. For instance, in an analysis of IPPC licensing procedures for thirty installations in twelve member states,[38] only fourteen, and hence less than half of the permits, included BAT conditions in accordance with the EU definition of BAT in the BREF for the relevant industrial sector (Entec, 2006: viii). In twenty out of the thirty permits examined in the Entec Report (2006), member state regulatory authorities had set certain emission limit values in IPPC permits which allowed for emissions higher than those indicated as BAT in the EU BREFs.

Moreover, the EU BREF documents, which are key for harmonising the 'best available techniques' standard across the EU, play different roles in the permitting regimes of different member states. Some member states' practices mirror UK implementation. In these cases national sector guidance notes or legislation have been produced which draw on the EU BREFs. Alternatively, BREF documents may be directly taken into account in IPPC permitting. This is the case in Ireland, the Netherlands, Sweden, Spain, Greece and the Czech Republic (Entec Report 2006: 53, 61, 75).[39] But some member states, such as Austria, the Wallonia region of Belgium, and Sweden adopt permitting practices which are much closer to the German approach to implementation. Here national BAT guidance or binding legal rules take only limited account of the BREF guidance documents. Hence there are disparate practices in relation to whether and how EU member states ensure that the specific BAT criteria in Annex IV of the IPPC Directive are taken into account in local permitting practices.[40] Member states work with different BAT definitions (European Parliament, 1999–2004: 6). The Netherlands, for instance, makes no reference to the concept of BAT but requires operators to comply with emission levels which are 'as low as reasonably achievable' (ALARA) (EU Commission, First IPPC Implementation Report, 2004:115; Drupsteen, 1999: 88). To conclude: national approaches to pollution control and interpretations of BAT have continued to be followed during the implementation of the IPPC Directive, not just in the UK and Germany but also in a range of other EU member states (EU Commission, First Implementation Report, 2004: 133; Phare Report, 2002: 72; and EP report in response to EU Commission Communication on progress in implementing the IPPC Directive, 2004: 8).[41] Given that the IPPC Directive seems in practice to have generated only limited convergence between pollution control systems in the EU, it is questionable whether it can properly be characterised as an instrument of EU environmental integration.

But further findings from the empirical research also have wider relevance. The book argues that discourses are central to the construction of the BAT standard in practice. Discourses, and hence the construction of knowledge concerning techniques through a process of communication, are also key to defining 'the best available techniques' in other EU member states.[42] For instance, a technical discourse also proves to be relevant to the interpretation of legal obligations under the IPPC Directive. In Denmark implementation of the IPPC Directive furnishes an organisational framework – the Danish 'Technical and Environment Committee' – for such technical discourses. This committee can authorise the imposition of less strict BAT standards in specific cases (Phare Report, 2002: 55). Hence in Denmark – as in the UK and Germany – emissions higher than those considered as BAT in published national guidance are sometimes considered as BAT on the basis of technical arguments. In addition, economic discourses also matter in the implementation of the IPPC Directive, not just in the UK and Germany, but in other member states as well.[43] For instance, poorer southern and some Eastern European member states are perceived as lagging behind in the implementation of the IPPC Directive (Entec Report, 2006: iii). Moreover, cost considerations in BAT are not always transparent in other member states either. The timing of BAT requirements is also a key technique in France, Italy, Spain and the Czech Republic for responding to economic pressures facing the operators of IPPC installations (Entec Report, 2006: 105; 160; 209). Deadlines for BAT compliance have also been adapted with reference to cost arguments in new and applicant EU member states. Eight out of the thirteen candidate countries[44] had already transposed the IPPC Directive into their national legislation by 2004 (European Parliament, 1999–2004: 5). But for some candidate countries, such as Poland, Slovenia, Slovakia and Latvia, there are special transition periods for up to 20 per cent of their existing IPPC installations. Installations must receive a permit by the end of October 2007, but will not be obliged to meet emission limit values based on BAT until 2008–2012 (European Economic and Social Committee, 2003).[45] Hence technical and economic discourses also matter in the construction of BAT in other member states. Thus the recognition of strong links between law and its contexts may well be applicable not only to the specific UK and German scenarios examined here, but also elsewhere in the EU. But there may be variation between EU member states in the extent to which implemented EU law is relatively autonomous in relation to its contexts. For instance, in some countries with very strong constitutional traditions of a strict separation of law and politics, a political discourse may be less significant in shaping BAT obligations than it is in countries without such constitutional traditions. The integration of economic discourses into law may also vary between different EU member states. Some[46] send experts from industry as representatives to EU Technical Working Groups for BREF drafting. Others send staff from regulatory authorities to represent their interests in EU BREF drafting.

Finally, this book has also argued that 'the formal law in the books' does not fully capture the character of EU law. The Entec report (2006) also provides further support for this approach. This report examines, in thirty case studies across a number of EU member states, not only IPPC permit conditions, but also actual emissions from IPPC installations on the basis of regulatory authorities' monitoring data. The actual emissions for several IPPC installations in various EU member states are higher than emission limits required in their IPPC licence. Hence actual operating practices represent different standards in practice from those prescribed in the formal legal site licence. The report suggests that regulatory authorities have taken enforcement action in some cases, but not in others. Hence also in these cases implementation practices 'on the ground' are also a further source for generating standards in practice. Formal legal texts, such as statutory provisions and site licences thus do not fully capture EU 'law in action'. To conclude: the findings of the empirical research discussed in this book have further ramifications. They raise questions about the nature of EU law, relevant also for other member states. But what are the further implications of this discussion about the nature of EU law for theories of EU integration?

Implications of 'law in action' analysis for theories of EU integration

How we conceptualise law also has implications for how we theorise EU integration. Concepts of law have been linked in various ways to theories of EU integration, such as supranational or intergovernmental accounts. Supranational accounts of EU integration regard EU institutions which promote common EU-wide interests, such as the EU Commission, the European Courts and the European Parliament, as key to promoting EU integration. They also emphasise the EU supranational legal order as crucial for the promotion of EU integration. In contrast, intergovernmentalist accounts still perceive EU member states as key to advancing EU integration. The member states are thought to wield significant power because their consent and support is necessary for promoting EU integration.

Hence concepts of law which focus on the formal 'law in the books' in EU integration chime with supranationalist accounts of EU integration. Formally binding EU law is a significant restraint on the sovereignty of member states. It also reflects the considerable influence of the EU Commission – a major supranational institution – as the formal initiator of EU legislative proposals. In contrast, reliance on soft law, such as voluntary agreements and open methods of coordination, has been associated with intergovernmentalist theories of EU integration. Member states retain greater influence over EU initiatives where the latter do not involve formally binding legal obligations. Moreover, they are still in the driving seat with respect to the dynamics of EU integration where this advances through an exchange of best practices and benchmarks derived from their own practices, as in some open methods of coordination.[47] Hence integration through soft law or through no law at all – an element of new forms of EU governance – further supports intergovernmentalist theories of EU integration.

But can such clear-cut relations between particular concepts of law and theories of EU integration really be established? In the first place, formal, instrumental EU 'hard law' does not simply support supranational accounts of EU integration. For it is not just the Commission, but also the Council of Ministers which exercises significant influence upon the process of passing such law. Some proposals for new EU legislation originate from member states even though the Commission formally initiates the law-making process. Hence formal EU 'hard' law can also be interpreted as an expression of intergovernmental influences in EU integration. Second, soft law and non-law approaches to integration cannot simply be associated with intergovernmentalist theories of EU integration. Soft law does not just empower member states, but in some instances also empowers the Commission, which is a key supranational actor in the EU. This is the case when the Commission promulgates soft law as a guide to the interpretation of the formal rules of hard law. This also applies where open methods of coordination are driven by Commission initiatives, such as the OMC in education. In this case, soft law actually strengthens the supranational dynamics of EU integration, rather than intergovernmental dynamics of integration. Third, an absence of formal law does not necessarily mean that there are no supranational dynamics in EU integration. Supranational dynamics such as integrated markets or EU wide political networks, including private interest groups, may still promote EU integration in the economic or political sphere, even in the absence of law. Hence non-legal approaches to EU integration cannot necessarily be associated with intergovernmentalist theories of EU integration. To conclude: it is difficult to establish specific links between particular types of law and either of the two main grand theory approaches to EU integration, namely supranationalism or intergovernmentalism. The 'EU law in action' analysis developed here recommends caution in claiming to identify links between specific concepts of law and grand theories of EU integration. Open and closed BAT norms may empower a variety of both intergovernmental and supranational actors. Open BAT norms at the EU level in

BREF documents may empower intergovernmental actors, when a member state prefers to retain influence over its definition of what constitutes BAT, for example. But open BAT norms at the EU level disempower those member states who want to see a particular definition of BAT explicitly formulated in the BREF documents. Open BAT norms at the level of site licences provide more influence for local actors, such as operators of IPPC installations themselves, thus restricting the impact of both intergovernmental actors, such as member states, and supranational actors, such as the EU Commission which organises the BREF drafting process. But 'EU law in action' analysis allows us to bring into focus a more specific aspect of the relationship between law and integration. It examines the links which are constructed between particular *characteristics of law* and the actual outcome with regard to integration. Thus the 'law in action' analysis presented in this book specifically questions the association – outlined in chapter 3 – between instrumental, relatively autonomous, 'formal law in the books' and EU integration. It thereby seeks to contribute to the development of a critical sociology of integrating law.

Notes

1. The Commonwealth of Independent States. This is an international organisation of 11 former Soviet Republics including Armenia, Azerbaijan, Belarus, Georgia, Kazakhstan, Kyrgyzstan, Moldova, Russia, Ukraine and Uzbekistan, with Turkmenistan now an associate member.
2. From 1967 to 1987 almost 200 Directives, regulations and decisions were introduced by the Commission in the field of EU environmental law (Mazey and Richardson, 2005: 109, referring to Majone).
3. Environmental Action Programmes provide an outline of EU environmental policy for a specific time period. The most recent 6th Environmental Action Programme, for instance, covers the period from 2002–2012.
4. Such as the Agreement between EU car manufacturers and the EU Commission for the reduction of CO_2 emissions from motor vehicles.
5. See, for example, the Water Framework Directive (2000/60/EC).
6. The Entec (2006) report provides evidence that even after the implementation of the IPPC Directive there are considerable differences in pollution control in the EU of 25 member states.
7. Allowing for a distinction between the Scottish Environment Agency (SEPA) and the Environment Agency for England and Wales (EA). About 85 per cent of all IPPC installations, so-called A 1 installations, are licensed by four strategic permitting groups within the EA, which also draw on consultants' input into permitting (Bell and McGillivray, 2006: 774).

8. Such as H 1. See 'Environmental Assessment and Appraisal of BAT', 2001 (last revised 20 May 2004), issued by the Environment Agency at www. environment-agency.gov.uk/business/444217/444663/298441/horizontal/ 545377/?version=1&lang=_e, site last visited 6 March 2006.

9. UK Permitting officers suggested during interviews that H1 would be used for some but not all installations in the PPC permitting process.

10. Interview no. 3 with German permitting officer.

11. In German: 'technische Anleitungen'.

12. Though it was revised in October 2000 also to implement the IPPC Directive into German law.

13. They are also authorised under statutes which are media-specific. There is a specific statute for water pollution control (the *Wasserhaushaltsgesetz* (WHG)). The *Bundesimmissionsschutzgesetz* (BimSchG) regulates mainly emissions to air, and thus air quality as well as noise. The *Bundesbodenschutzgesetz* provides a regime for the prevention and control of land contamination. There are, however, some interactions between these media-specific German environmental statutes. For instance, para. 1 BimSchG stipulates that the purpose of the BimSchG is to protect against noxious environmental impacts, including noxious impacts on land. Hence protection against land contamination can also be secured through the BimSchG. But the standards to which land has to be protected are specified in the *Bundesbodenschutzgesetz* and its regulations (Kloepfer, 2004: 1238). In the UK there are also still statutes with a focus on a specific environmental medium, such as the Water Resources Act 1991. However, the Environmental Protection Act 1990 had already introduced in the UK a system of integrated pollution control before the IPPC Directive. Moreover, UK implementation of the IPPC Directive into national law has further expanded the idea of integrating pollution controls because in the UK all landfills are now controlled through PPC permits (see the Landfill Regulations 2002 which amend the PPC regulations).

14. Part 5.1.1. of the TA *Luft* (air) further illustrates the more peripheral role of BREFs in German IPPC licensing. It suggests that for new BREFs published after the revision of the TA *Luft* the legal rules of the TA *Luft* will continue to apply and bind German permitters. A committee will then be established by the federal environment ministry (Bundesministerium für Umwelt, Naturschutz und Reaktorsicherheit) which will decide whether the new BREFs actually advance the BAT definitions which are already contained in the TA *Luft*. If the committee considers that this is the case, the committee will formally state this. Permitting officers are then no longer bound by the conflicting and older BAT definition in the TA *Luft*.

15. Interview no. 1 with German permitting officer.

16. The Entec Report (2006: 139–140; 237–241) provides data for BAT determinations in terms of emission limit values imposed in IPPC licences and actual emissions for a cement plant in the UK and a cement plant in Germany. There is limited comparability between the BAT determinations

here because emission limit values in the German IPPC licence are specified – potentially more strictly – as half-hour average, daily average and annual average for the emissions. In the UK IPPC licence emission limit values are specified simply as mg/m^3 without reference to time periods within which these emissions must be achieved, thus allowing for the levelling out of peak emissions. In the UK permit the emission limit value for dust is 85 mg/m^3. In the German permit the emission limit value is 40 mg/m^3 for the half hour average, 20 mg/m^3 for the daily average and 15 mg/m^3 for the annual average. For NOx emissions the German IPPC permit requires compliance with 1000 mg/m^3 for the half-hour average and 500 mg/m^3 for both the daily and annual average. In contrast, the UK emission limit value for NOx is 2150 mg/m^3. In the German IPPC licence the emission limit value for SO$_2$ is 570 mg/m^3 for the half-hour average, 285 mg/m^3 for the daily average and 200 mg/m^3 for the annual average. In contrast, the emission limit value for SO$_2$ in the UK IPPC permit is 375 mg/m^3. There is not much difference between the UK and German IPPC licences in the control of pollutants such as dioxins and furans which have to comply in the UK with a 0.1 ng TEQ/Nm^3 and 0.07 ng TEQ/Nm^3 in the German licence. Hence these figures show that there is variation in what is defined as BAT for cement kilns in German and UK IPPC licences. From the data presented in the Entec report (2006) it is, however, impossible to say whether these figures already indicate a greater degree of harmonisation for emissions from cement kilns than was the case before the implementation of the IPPC Directive in Germany and the UK.

17. Through the case 26/62, *NV Algemene Transporten Expeditie Onderneming van Gend en Loos v. Nederlandse Administratie der Belastingen* [1963] ECR 1.
18. In policy fields where member states have ceded sovereignty to the EC. Case 6/64, *Flaminio Costa v. ENEL* [1964] ECR 585, 593.
19. The ECJ developed these doctrines in a way that was not envisaged in the EEC Treaty 1957.
20. In the case of non-implemented EC Directives the relevant provision in the Directive has to be sufficiently clear and precise and unconditional upon any further implementing measures. In addition, the time limit for its implementation has to have expired (Craig and De Burca, 2003: 185).
21. Old Art. 169 EC Treaty.
22. Hence the fact that only a limited number of legal actions have been brought against member states is usually interpreted as an indicator of the success of Art. 226 EC Treaty.
23. Enshrined in the Treaty of Rome 1957.
24. Given significant rates of non-compliance, the Maastricht Treaty provided new powers for the Commission to apply under Art. 228 EC Treaty to the ECJ for an imposition of a penalty payment if an ECJ judgment is not implemented by a member state.
25. See the EU Water Framework Directive (2000/60/EC). For further examples of Framework Directives in the field of environmental regulation, see the Waste Framework Directive 2006/12/EC which imposes general obligations

on waste prevention, recycling and reuse. There is also the Framework Directive for the Ecodesign of Energy Using Products (2005/32/EC).

26. See the Unfair Commercial Practices Framework Directive (2005/29/EC) which imposes a general duty to trade fairly and, not unlike the IPPC Directive, provides for the setting up of expert groups composed of national officials for the exchange of information regarding national laws in relation to fair trading. Art. 10 of the Directive provides for the possibility of enforcing its provisions also through Codes of Practice. Enforcement of the Directive will also be facilitated through a European network of public enforcers of consumer protection.

27. Council Directive 89/39/EEC of 12 June 1989, the Health and Safety at Work Framework Directive.

28. Framework Directive 2002/21/EC on a common regulatory framework for electronic communications, networks and services.

29. EC Equal Treatment Framework Directive 2000/78 of 27 November 2000; [2000] O.J.L. 303/16.

30. Art. 3 b 3rd paragraph EC Treaty.

31. Art. 3 b 2nd paragraph EC Treaty.

32. The Commission has a clear preference for Framework Directives when legislating (EU Commission, 1995: 2).

33. Since the EU Commission regards the IPPC Directive as the core of EU pollution control, it has commissioned a number of studies which provide data about the implementation of and compliance with the Directive in the twenty-five EU member states. Some of these studies are based on member states' reporting requirements under Art. 16 (3) of the IPPC Directive to inform the Commission of progress in implementing the IPPC Directive. For this purpose the Commission has developed a specific questionnaire through which the original fifteen member states have reported back on implementation from 2000–2002. The detailed analysis of these questionnaire data has been published as the 'Analysis of member states' first implementation reports on the IPPC Directive (EU – 15), Final Report, 2004'. There are also the European Parliament and the European Economic and Social Committee's responses to the EU Commission's Communication on progress with the implementation of the IPPC Directive. Finally, there are also reports within the PHARE programme through which the IPPC Directive provides assistance to new and applicant member states with implementation of the IPPC Directive. The most recent draft final report dates from October 2006. This was commissioned by the Directorate-General Environment of the EU Commission. It has been compiled by the UK environmental consultants Entec UK Limited. The report provides data on progress in the implementation of the IPPC Directive in all twenty-five EU member states by reporting the number of permits which have been already issued and those which are still to be issued. Most importantly, the report provides in-depth qualitative data on the IPPC licensing and BAT for thirty installations across a range of different sectors in various EU member states.

34. Media-specific environmental regulation persists also in other ways in some member states. As in Germany, various partly media-specific environmental statutes in the Netherlands also apply for IPPC permitting, such as the Environmental Management Act and the Pollution of Surface Waters Act. These are administered by different regulatory authorities (see also Gouldson and Murphy, 1998: 111). Moreover, in some member states monitoring of environmental quality is still focused on specific media. For instance, in Denmark emissions to the aquatic environment rather than air quality monitoring near IPPC installations is a key focus of attention (Phare Report, 2002: 64). In addition, in none of the thirty permits examined in detail in the Entec report (2006: ix) was consideration of cross-media issues a relevant factor in the determination of BAT, even where trade-offs between impacts on different environmental media clearly seemed to be required.
35. Dutch provinces issue integrated licences (apart from water) for large industrial installations. Less polluting installations receive integrated licences (apart from water) from Dutch municipalities (Phare Report, 2002: 70).
36. According to the Entec Report (2006: vii) Denmark, the Flemish region of Belgium, and Sweden also use generally binding rules in permitting.
37. According to the Entec Report (2006: vi, 51) approximately half of the EU twenty-five member states had possessed integrated pollution control legislation before the implementation of the IPPC Directive.
38. These include the Czech Republic, France, Germany, Greece, Hungary, Italy, Lithuania, Poland, Portugal, Spain, Sweden and the UK.
39. The Commission's First Implementation Report (2004: 56) concludes that there are 'at least 12 member states' which 'systematically take into account BREF documents when determining BAT, either in general or in specific cases'. For a number of other EU member states, such as Denmark, Finland and Italy, the Commission's First Implementation Report states that national BAT guidance does exist, but the report does not specify whether this guidance draws on the EU BREF documents.
40. In Austria, for instance, the Waste Management Act specifies that licensing of IPPC installations must take into account the Annex IV criteria, but for IPPC installations licensed under other legal provisions BAT is defined as the installation of 'progressive techniques'. In Greece the Annex IV criteria were taken into account when national BAT guidance was developed. But in Spain and the Netherlands there is no clear and specific recognition of the Annex IV criteria for determining BAT (EU Commission, First Implementation Report, 2004: 55).
41. For the Commission and the European Parliament this is also due to a lack of clarity in some of the key provisions of the IPPC Directive (European Commission, 2003: 5,7). For instance, the threshold criteria which determine whether the IPPC Directive applies to an installation of a particular size are considered as insufficiently clear by members of the EU Technical Working Groups. So too are the definition of installation boundaries, the

very concept of 'installation', and what amounts to a 'substantial change' of an installation. Moreover, how exactly emission limit values should be derived from 'BAT' remains unclear, as is the status of the BREF documents or what is required in order to return an IPPC installation 'to a satisfactory state' after site closure.

42. How these discourses operate in detail, however, is not discussed in the various reports from EU institutions and consultants. Hence these reports shed no light on more specific findings from the empirical research, such as that an integrating function of law can also be associated with an opening up of specific discourses and exchanges between them. The EU institutions' and consultants' reports focus mainly on the formal transposition of the EU Directive into national law, rather than on detailed day-to-day implementation practices 'on the ground'.

43. These EU reports also highlight the fact that the costs of IPPC permitting itself vary between different member states. Chapter 7 has argued that the costs of permitting itself were a significant factor for the German and UK regulatory authorities because Germany and the UK have a particularly high number of IPPC installations to licence. In smaller or less industrialised member states the costs of permitting IPPC installations may not be a major issue for the regulator. The Danish Environmental Protection Agency, for instance, has suggested that it will not require any additional resources to review existing permits for compliance with the IPPC regime by October 2007 (Phare Report, 2002: 55).

44. Ten of which joined the EU in May 2004.

45. Different transition periods have been agreed for each of these countries.

46. Such as Italy.

47. For instance, in the open method of coordination for education policies in the EU.

Appendix: Methodology

The purpose of this appendix on methodology is to provide transparency in the research process and thus to facilitate critical evaluation of the research and its conclusions. It also seeks to contribute to debates about socio-legal research methods and their further development.

Reliability and validity of the data

Reliability and validity are key criteria which are often used to evaluate the quality of quantitative research in particular. Reliability assesses consistency in the data and hence whether the findings from the research can be replicated. Validity refers to whether the data really identify and measure what the research seeks to investigate (Bryman, 2001: 70, 270). These two key criteria require some adaptation for the evaluation of qualitative research. Both criteria reflect realist assumptions in so far as they expect research to reflect and replicate an objective social reality 'out there'. Qualitative research, however, and discourse analysis in particular, challenge these realist assumptions, for they explicitly recognise that social actors and researchers themselves actively construct representations of social worlds. But the question whether particular data and data collection techniques have adequately captured the social world under investigation is still an issue in some accounts of qualitative research methods (see, for example, Hawkins, 2002: 449). Especially in the context of research which involves public bodies, such as regulatory authorities, the question whether documents and interview data include 'presentational data' is debated. Given the fact that public bodies may be subject to external accountability and possibly criticism, public organisations and their staff are acknowledged to have an interest in the management of impressions and perceptions. The data collection methods employed for the present research, especially the combination of interview data with documentary data, can address, to some extent, such concerns concerning the validity of the data. Moreover, extended fieldwork periods contribute to the internal validity of the data. Internal validity captures congruence between concepts developed in the analysis and the actual observations and data (Bryman, 2002: 272). Internal validity was secured in this research through a research design which involved the researcher spending two months each with the EIPPC Bureau and the German regulatory authority. There are limits, however, to the external validity of the research because – as discussed in more detail in chapter 9 – its findings can only partly be generalised to other social settings, such as implementation of the IPPC Directive in other member states and the implementation of other EU laws.

Most importantly, however, concerns with validity and especially reliability do not capture the nature of this research project. The research was motivated by the idea that in order to understand EU 'law in action' it is necessary to understand both the *behaviour* of those involved in BAT determinations, and the specific contribution of *discourses* to BAT definitions. Examining discourses involves questioning realist positions. The interest shifts to understanding how discourses construct the social world, how they generate effects of power and how social actors' interpretative repertoires accomplish specific tasks. This requires a detailed analysis of the operation of discourses in a specific setting, rather than inquiry into a broad range of representative data. Whether discourses correspond to a 'social reality out there' becomes a secondary concern. To conclude: attention to both behaviour and discourses was considered central for grasping key aspects of 'EU law in action'. Discourses were considered as crucial in mediating the world of social actors. But attention to behaviour is considered important because discourse analysis has been criticised for its sometimes free-floating character (Wæver, 2004: 207). Discourse also needs to be anchored in a social world which involves action and specific social practices, not just knowledge production and language. One of the starting points for this research was an interest in how language plays games with actors, but also how actors can use language strategically. Moreover, attention to behaviour was also considered important in order to grasp key aspects of how social actors implement the IPPC Directive and arrive at BAT determinations.

Data sources and collection techniques

The research discussed in this book relied on various sources of data and techniques for collecting them. In order to study the implementation of the IPPC Directive at the EU level through the drafting of the BREF documents, I spent two months with the EIPPC Bureau, from 18 May to 18 July 2000. I was provided with an office in which I sat reading EIPPC background files and taking notes. I also became acquainted with EIPPC Bureau staff during informal conversations in the office, lunch and social events. I collected qualitative data during this time by writing up notes on observations and casual conversations with EIPPC Bureau staff, including BREF writers and the EIPPC Bureau management. Given the fact that my research was focused on how BAT determinations are achieved, it was clear that observation could only provide a very limited source of data since BREF writers' decision-making on BAT determinations is often pursued in private and is an internalised task, rather than being a visible or explicit work activity that could simply be observed (see also Hawkins, 2002: 448). Hence the two main qualitative data sources from this research period were documentary and interview data. First, documents included EIPPC background files, internal memos and publicly available documents about the BREF drafting process, such as the 'BREF Outline and Guide'. The EIPPC Bureau does not compile extensive or systematic background files. How much material and what specific files were compiled for the writing of each BREF document lay within the discretion of each BREF writer. The EIPPC Bureau management granted me access to the background files of BREFs in three sectors: the completed BREF on non-ferrous metals, the completed BREF for the iron and steel sector and the BREF on large combustion plants which was still being drafted at the time of the research. The files contained copies of the submissions made by trade associations and member states to the Technical Working Groups (TWGs), comments from BREF writers on those documents as well as drafts of the BREFs with comments from TWG members. In particular the inclusion of various drafts of the BREFs in the files allowed me to acquire some sense of the development of determinations of the 'best available techniques' over a period of time. Second, I conducted a semi-structured interview of one to one and a half hours with each of the BREF writers who were working during the time of my research stay in the EIPPC Bureau. This generated eleven interviews.[1] I also conducted four interviews over the two months with the EIPPC Bureau management and one interview with the desk officer for the IPPC Directive from the Directorate General (DG) Environment in the EU Commission. DG Environment also provided me with the official minutes of the meetings of the Information Exchange Forum (IEF). The official remit of the IEF is to discuss policy matters in relation to BREFs. It also formally approves BREFs before they are published by the EU Commission. The minutes of the IEF covered its meetings from the very first one on 4 December 1996 to the 7th meeting on 28–29 February 2000, as well as the IEF meetings for the years 2004, 2005 and 2006. At the time of writing the book no minutes for the 2007 meetings were yet available.

Finally, I had also asked to attend one of the meetings of the TWG for a BREF which were held during the time I spent in the EIPPC Bureau. The Bureau, however, was not happy with the idea of having a researcher present during the TWG discussions. They suggested that this might compromise the confidentiality of the group's deliberations. Instead the Bureau gave me a copy of the official audiotape which it had compiled of the 2nd meeting of the TWG for the iron and steel BREF. I transcribed the discussions of the TWG recorded on this tape. The transcript formed another source of qualitative data.

For an analysis of how 'the best available techniques' are defined at the national level I collected data both from a German and a UK environmental regulatory authority. I spent two months with a *Bezirksregierung* (German regulatory authority) involved in licensing IPPC plants, one month in 2002 and another one in spring 2004. During the second month of data collection in 2004 I shared an office with an IPPC licensing officer and read the licensing authority's background files on two licensing procedures, the licensing of the coke oven plant discussed in chapter 8 and another licensing procedure for an installation in the iron and steel sector. The German regulatory authority compiled extensive, detailed files on its IPPC licensing procedures because these files were also required for the public participation procedure according to § 10 (3) BimSchG. There were, for instance, several thick A4 lever-arch files which documented the IPPC licensing procedure for the coke oven plant. These files included reports and letters submitted to the regulatory authority by the operator, responses from various branches of the environmental administration to these letters, including the *Bezirksregierung* which was coordinating the IPPC licensing procedure, as well as the technical branch which gave expert technical advice, the *Landesumweltamt*. The files also included copies of letters from the operator's lawyer and from members of the public who had raised

objections to the licensing of the IPPC installation. The German permitting officer explained that the file to which I had been given access had
been compiled for the public participation procedure. The regulatory
authority kept another internal, confidential IPPC licensing file for the
plant which, according to the German licensing officer, included rather
more detail, such as memos recording key points of meetings between
the operator and the regulatory authority. The German fieldwork
involved contact not just with the regulatory authority who coordinated
the writing of the IPPC licences, but also with the environmental ministry in the particular *Land*, which developed policy in relation to IPPC
licensing for the *Land*. As I discussed in chapter 8, the environmental
ministry also became involved in the IPPC licensing procedure for the
coke oven. The data collected from the licensing file of the German
regulatory authority was complemented by semi-structured interviews,
ranging in duration from one to two hours with six members of staff
from various parts of the German *Land* environmental administration. These included licensing officers from the regulatory authority
(*Bezirksregierung*) which coordinated the licensing of the coke oven. They
also included IPPC licensing officers from another *Bezirksregierung* as well
as staff from the technical branch of the *Land* environmental administration, the *Landesumweltamt*, which contributed to the licensing of the
coke oven.

Fieldwork in the UK involved contact with a regional office of the
Environment Agency and the strategic permitting group based there, as
well as some local area offices which became involved in IPPC licensing.
In contrast to the German and EIPPC Bureau field work, the UK fieldwork did not involve spending time in the agency office, but involved
the conduct of interviews over a seven-month period and the analysis of
documentary data in my university office. There were two main sources
of qualitative data from the UK fieldwork. In the first place I conducted
thirteen interviews with ten IPPC licensing officers of one to two hours
duration each. Two licensing officers who were involved in the management of the unit were interviewed twice in order to clarify general
points about the organisation of IPPC licensing. The second main source
of data from the UK case study was provided by documents. The
Environment Agency does not compile files for the licensing of IPPC
plants which are as detailed and extensive as those of the German
regulatory authority. But it does produce an official record of its decision-making procedure, a so-called Decision Document for each IPPC
licence. I examined the Decision Documents and licences for 24

installations in the inorganic chemicals sector. The inorganic chemicals sector was chosen because it had been recently licensed by the EA. Thus licensing officers still possessed fresh information about the licensing of these plants when they were interviewed. Decision Documents also varied in length depending on the complexity of the installation. On average they ran to about 30 pages and thus were considerably shorter than the German file for an IPPC licence. In theory, Decision Documents represent a record of the IPPC licensing decision-making process, specifically detailing how all the legally relevant factors have been taken into account. In practice, the Decision Documents provided a formalised and condensed account of the IPPC licensing process. They provided only limited insight into the actual decision-making process and, in contrast to the files from the EIPPC Bureau and German regulatory authority, did not contain copies of reports and memos written by operators and the regulatory authority during IPPC licensing. This limitation in the documentary data was addressed through the interviews. They were conducted with the IPPC licensing officers who had written the licenses and Decision Documents. Hence the interviews provided an opportunity to develop an account of how BAT determinations were actually achieved in practice which was richer than the Decision Documents themselves.

The EA also provided me with a copy of the 'Chemicals Regulatory Package', a CD which has been prepared by the EA for the chemicals sector, including inorganic chemicals plants, in order to facilitate the licensing of installations. The 'Chemicals Regulatory Package' contains several documents, including a copy of the UK sector guidance notes for the chemical, including the inorganic, sector, general EA guidance for operators on how to produce a good IPPC application, an electronic version of the IPPC application form, a copy of the H1 software for the assessment of environmental impacts of installations, EA cross-sector guidance notes on energy efficiency and noise, copies of BREF documents for the chemicals sector as well as legal guidance by the Secretary of State, and the PPC (England and Wales) 2000 Regulations. The EA also granted me access to their internal work instructions on IPPC licensing which amounted to ten documents. These covered topics such as how to determine whether an application had been 'duly made' in accordance with Reg. 10 (2) of the PPC Regulations (England and Wales) 2000, guidance on pre-application discussions and charging, guidance on consultation upon an IPPC permit or permit variation application, guidance on how to write Decision Documents and the permit template itself. All of the data for the EU, UK and German case studies were collected on the basis of a standard confidentiality agreement according to which the identity of staff from the EIPPC Bureau as well as the German and UK regulatory authorities who participated in the study would remain anonymous. This confidentiality agreement also extended to the identity of individual industrial operators referred to in the documents to which the public authorities gave me access. All of the participants in the research who agreed to be interviewed were happy to have the interviews tape recorded. The interviews from the UK and German case studies were transcribed by professional transcribers, while I transcribed the interviews from the EU BREF writing case study. Quotes from the transcripts of the interviews with BREF writers in the EIPPC Bureau are not completely verbatim. Minor English language revisions of the quotes were undertaken after transcription at the writing stage in order to enhance the clarity and grammatical correctness of statements made by BREF writers, for most of whom English is a second language.

Access to the German regulatory authority and the Environment Agency was secured through letters to senior managers setting out the purposes and scope of the research which were followed up by phone calls. During the negotiations for access I also explained that I was undertaking an independent research project which was financed through study leave from Keele University, a grant from the German Academic Exchange Service and a small grant from the UK Socio-Legal Studies Association. The research benefited from a high level of access to information concerning determinations of 'the best available techniques'. Despite their own heavy work load licensing officers in the UK and German regulatory authority, as well as individual BREF writers, gave generously of their time in order to answer specific questions and make themselves available for interviews. The level of access granted by the German regulatory authority was particularly good and access was greatly facilitated through the researcher actually being based in the office of the regulatory authority. The fact that access proved more problematic with the Environment Agency was particularly surprising because I had worked for a number of years at UK universities in environmental law and policy and no longer possessed any German professional contacts. I had the impression that perhaps due to the extensive public participation procedure in Germany the regulatory authority was used to providing accounts of its work to 'outsiders'. Public participation clearly plays a bigger role in German IPPC licensing procedures than in the UK. Particularly in relation to large licensing procedures, such as that for the coke oven, objections to the application would usually be raised by individual members of the public or by organised environmental interest groups. In contrast to this, it was clear from the Decision Documents for the UK IPPC licences that members of the public would only rarely raise objections to IPPC licence applications. Moreover, at the time of my fieldwork with the UK regulatory authority the Environment Agency was discussing how to implement in practice the strengthened provisions for public participation which had been introduced into the IPPC Directive through its first amendment by the Public Participation Directive 2003/35/EC. The Environment Agency was, for instance, considering providing a more detailed publicly available account of how it had reached its decisions on individual IPPC licence applications in accordance with Art. 15 (5) (b) of the IPPC Directive. This was perceived as a significant change to the existing culture and working practices of the EA and was viewed by some with concern. To conclude: while there was a good level of access to research data in general, it varied somewhat as between the German and UK case study.

Finally, empirical research is sometimes portrayed as a clearly structured sequential process with the researcher first planning the project and then executing it after having obtained access. In the research discussed here the research participants were involved to some degree in the design of the research. When I first made contact with the German and UK regulatory authority, I had only limited knowledge about how IPPC licensing operated in practice and what files regulatory authorities would keep with regard to IPPC licensing. Official legal texts and publicly available documents from the environmental ministry only provided a limited picture of who actually becomes involved, and how in practice they determine BAT. Hence information and advice from the German and UK regulatory authority fed into the design of the research project: in terms of who was approached for interviews, what files I sought access to, and what range of IPPC installations would be best to study. So what are the further limitations and value of the qualitative data collected for this research?

A critical appraisal of data sources and collection techniques

The research aimed to understand the operation of discourses in the determination of the 'best available techniques'. Hence the transcript of the audiotape recording of the second TWG meeting for the iron and steel BREF as well as all the other documentary sources of data are 'original' unadulterated discourse. This discourse was constructed by the participants in BAT determinations themselves during actual BAT determinations, or after the event as the written record of a previous BAT determination. The documentary data therefore furnish high quality data for an analysis of BAT determinations from the perspective of discourse theory. They are 'natural' discourse in the sense that, in contrast to the interview data, they were not produced simply as a result of the research. But from a realist interpretative perspective the licensing files of the German and UK regulatory authority are social constructs which do not necessarily provide a complete or 'accurate' depiction of how BAT determinations are actually achieved. The documentary data, however, were examined here not as 'windows' on an external, objective social reality, but as records which show how technical, economic and political discourses are invoked and deployed in order to construct accounts of, and thereby also achieve, BAT determinations. The data from the semi-structured interviews complemented the documentary data. Written documents are always shaped by the perspectives and interests of an organisation (Hawkins, 2002: 448). Hence the interviews furnished an important additional source of data. They provided an opportunity to acquire traditional qualitative data on how IPPC licensing officers and BREF writers perceived the process of determining BAT. These data reflect a more realist perspective because they take serious account of what individual participants in BAT determinations construct as their social reality in the process of finding the 'best available techniques'. The interviews also provided an opportunity to ask about aspects of BAT determinations which were not covered in the files. To conclude: using different sources of data helped to build up a more complete picture of how BAT determinations are achieved. But the discourse perspective employed in this project does not seek to fulfil realist criteria for good research data.

The data collected for this research, however, have a specific focus. They cover a limited geographical area in so far as data were collected from one German and one UK licensing authority. The data also refer to a specific range of plants regulated by the IPPC Directive, such as installations from the inorganic chemicals and the non-ferrous metals sector, large combustion plants as well as iron and steel plants. Hence the data cover BAT determinations in three out of the six main sectors covered by the IPPC Directive.[2] These data and the focus on the discussion of coke cooling techniques in chapter 8 are quite specific. They do not cover the whole range of installations regulated under the IPPC Directive. But they cover installations which are particularly significant in terms of numbers and contribution to the EU economy. Thus 11.7 per cent of plants regulated under IPPC belong to the 'production and processing of metals' category. The chemicals sector is even more important and constitutes the third largest category of IPPC plants. Thus 13.7 per cent of all IPPC installations lie within this sector (Entec, 2006: 25). In the UK the chemicals sector is one of the largest sectors covered by the PPC Regulations (England and Wales) 2000[3] (p. 1 of the Sector Permitting Plan Chemicals). This specific focus on particular IPPC licensing procedures in the documentary data, however, was complemented through the interviews which were conducted with licensing officers who had not only licensed the plants referred to in the documents, but also a whole range of IPPC installations from other sectors. Hence licensing officers' responses to interview questions were informed by their knowledge of a wider range of IPPC installations permitted under the IPPC Directive. Moreover, the focus on documentary data from a specific range of installations helped me to acquire in-depth information. There were also pragmatic reasons in favour of the selection of data about some, but not all, types of installations covered by the IPPC Directive. First, the documents contained significant amounts of technical information. Understanding this information was facilitated by focusing on a limited number of sectors covered by the IPPC Directive. Second, the choice of sectors for the research was also a result of pragmatic decisions once the fieldwork had begun. In the German regulatory authority the coke oven licensing procedure had been a recently completed major case of such licensing. Since it involved an appeal to the EU BREF by the operator it seemed a particularly interesting case for the research. Given that the detailed analysis of an IPPC licensing procedure had been conducted in relation to a coke oven plant in Germany, I then searched for a coke oven licensing procedure in the UK. Hence the data clearly are not representative of implementation practices concerning the IPPC Directive in all sectors and all member states. Given the fact, however, that the research seeks to understand how discourses construct BAT determination processes, the research was never intended to address quantitative questions and therefore did not collect representative data.

Moreover, the German and UK data do not cover exactly the same range of installations, except for the discussion of the coke oven licensing procedures in the UK and Germany. The analysis of the coke oven licensing procedures served a specific purpose. It sought to examine the sort of law generated in a situation where there is an integration effect, in this case through the choice of very similar coke cooling techniques. It was therefore necessary to examine data about the same type of installation in Germany and the UK. But the discussion in the other chapters about how BAT determinations are achieved is not intended to be comparative, but aims to draw on a range of permitting scenarios in at least two EU member states.

Finally, the data cover a specific time period during which BAT determinations were examined. They start with data collected in 2000 on the first (iron and steel) BREF and the official minutes from the first IEF meeting in 1996. They also include data from 2003 and 2004 from the German regulatory authority and conclude with empirical data from 2006 collected from the Environment Agency. The older data from 2000 from the BREF writing process were updated through the official IEF meeting notes up until 2006. These official minutes from the later IEF meetings suggest that key issues in BREF writing identified from the earlier data collection phase were still an issue. There still seemed to be unresolved questions in some cases about what exactly constitutes the procedure for determining BAT at the EU level. Moreover, work on later BREFs also showed variation in open and closed BAT norms. Some BREFs came to more specific BAT conclusions, while in other BREFs BAT determinations remained more open also due to the existence of 'split views' in the Technical Working Groups. This chimes with Keith Hawkins's observation (2002: 458) who suggests that in institutions, where the official mandate and task for legal officials remain the same, routine and fundamental patterns in work activities of staff are likely to stay the same over a period of time, even though there may be attempts to steer or constrain their discretionary powers in decision-making. Data on the licensing practices in the German and UK regulatory authority were more recent and included official work instructions which shape BAT determination processes generally and hence are not merely valid for a specific time period involved in BAT determinations.

A critical appraisal of data analysis techniques

The data from the BREF writing case study were analysed through the Nudist software package. Nudist, the earlier version of the software, rather than NVivo was used because this cheaper version lay within the range of the budget for the project. The software was particularly good for coding the large amount of unstructured qualitative data arising from interview transcripts and notes. Through the coding key themes and topics were identified, such as 'procedure', 'actors in BAT determinations', 'characteristics of BAT determinations', 'political interests in BAT determinations' etc. The coding function helped to organise and structure the data. Memos developing ideas for the analysis of the codes were then written within Nudist. The data from the UK and German regulatory authorities were not analysed through Nudist. The German and UK case studies involved a greater amount of official documentary data from the files, which could not easily be incorporated as word files into the Nudist programme. Hence the coding for these data drew on the coding which had been developed for the data from the BREF study, and further coding was applied to the paper records themselves.

Notes

1. One of the EIPPC Bureau staff members had formerly been a BREF writer and now worked on a research project in the Bureau.
2. I collected data about coke oven IPPC licensing and the large combustion plant BREF. These installations belong to the category of 'energy industries' which are regulated by the IPPC Directive. I also acquired data about the non-ferrous metal BREF as well as the iron and steel BREF. These installations are examples of the 'production and processing of metals' activities covered by the IPPC Directive. Moreover, I examined documents in relation to the inorganics sector, covered under the 'chemical industry' category regulated by the IPPC Directive.
3. SI 2000/1973.

Bibliography

Abbott, Kenneth W. and Snidal, Duncan, 'Hard and Soft Law in International Governance' (2000) 54(3) *International Organization*, 421–456

Albertsen, Niels and Diken, Bülent, 'What is the Social?' at: http://www.comp.lancs.ac.uk/sociology/papers/albertsen-diken-what-is-the-social.pdf. Site last visited 1.11.04, manuscript on file with author

Alter, Karen, 'The European Union's Legal System and Domestic Policy: Spillover or Backlash?' (2000) 54 *International Organization* 3, 489–518

Armstrong, Kenneth A., 'Regulating the Free Movement of Goods: Institutions and Institutional Change', in: J. Shaw and G. More (eds.), *New Legal Dynamics of European Union* (Oxford: Clarendon Press, 1995), pp. 165–191

'Legal Integration: Theorizing the Legal Dimension of European Integration' (1998) 36 (2) *Journal of Common Market Studies*, 155–174

Armstrong, Kenneth and Bulmer, Simon, *The Governance of the Single European Market* (Manchester: Manchester University Press, 1998)

Armstrong, Kenneth and Shaw, Jo, 'Integrating Law: An Introduction' (1998) 36 *Journal of Common Market Studies* 2, 147–154

Backes, Chris and Betlem, Gerrit, *Integrated Pollution Prevention and Control, The EC Directive from a Comparative Legal and Economic Perspective* (London: Kluwer Law International, 1999)

Bankowski, Zenon and Nelken, David, 'Discretion as a Social Problem', in: M. Adler and S. Asquith, (eds.) *Discretion and Welfare* (London: Heinemann, 1981), pp. 247–268

Barkun, Michael, 'Introduction', in: M. Barkun (ed.), *Law and the Social System* (New York: Lieber-Atherton, 1973), pp. 1–15

Baudrillard, Jean, *In the Shadow of the Silent Majorities or the End of the Social and Other Essays* (New York: Semiotext(e), 1983)

Bauman, Zygmunt, 'Viewpoint: Sociology and Postmodernity' (1988) 36 (4) *Sociological Review*, 790–813

Bell, Stuart and McGillivray, Donald, *Environmental Law*, (Oxford: Oxford University Press, 2006)

Black, Donald, 'The Social Organization of Arrest' (1971) 23 *Stanford Law Review*, 1087–1111

Bohne, Eberhard, *The Evolution of Integrated Permitting and Inspections of Industrial Installations in the EU – First Interim Report*, (Speyer: Forschungsinstitut für Öffentliche Verwaltung bei der Deutschen Hochschule für Verwaltungswissenschaften Speyer, 1998)

The Quest for Environmental Regulatory Integration in the EU: Integrated Pollution Prevention and Control, Environmental Impact Assessment and Major Accident Prevention, (The Hague: Kluwer Law International, 2006)

Bohne, Eberhard and Dietze, Doris, 'Pollution Prevention and Control in Europe Revisited' (2004) *European Environmental Law Review*, July, 198–217

Borchardt, G. and Wellens, K., 'Soft Law in European Community Law' (1989) 14 (5) *European Law Review*, 267–321.

Bredemeier, H., 'Law as an Integrative Mechanism', in: V. Aubert (ed.), *Sociology of Law* (Harmondsworth: Penguin, 1968)

BREF Document on the Production of Iron and Steel, December 2001, at: http://eippcb.jrc.es/pages/BActivities.cfm, site last visited 10 April 2007

Brigham, John and Harrington, Christine B., 'Realism and Its Consequences: An Inquiry into Contemporary Sociological Research' (1989) 17 *International Journal of the Sociology of Law*, 41–62

Bryman, Alan, *Social Research Methods* (Oxford: Oxford University Press, 2001)

Burley, Anne-Marie and Mattli, Walter, 'Europe before the Court: A Political Theory of Legal Integration' (1993) 47 *International Organization*, 41–76

Bush, R. A. B., 'Dispute Resolution Alternatives and the Goals of Civil Justice: Jurisdictional Principles for Process Choice' (1984) *Wisconsin Law Review* 4, 894–1034

Cappelletti, Mauro, 'Foreword', in: M. Cappelletti, M. Seccombe, J. Weiler (eds.), *Integration through Law*, 1st edn (Berlin: Walter de Gruyter, 1986a), pp. v–xix

Cappelletti, Mauro, Seccombe, Monica and Weiler, Joseph, 'Integration through Law: Europe and the American Federal Experience: A General Introduction', in: M. Cappelletti, M. Seccombe and J.Weiler (eds.), *Integration through Law*, 1st edn (Berlin: Walter de Gruyter, 1986b), pp. 3–68

Chalmers, Damian, 'Environmental Law 1998-1999', (2000) 19 *Yearbook of European Law*, 493–518

Christiansen, Thomas, Knud, Erik Jorgensen, Wiener, Antje, 'The Social Construction of Europe' (1999) 6 *Journal of European Public Policy* 4, 528–544

Cotterrell, Roger, *The Sociology of Law* (London: Butterworths, 1992)

'Law and Community: A New Relationship?' (1998) 51 *Current Legal Problems*, 367–391

'Subverting Orthodoxy, Making Law Central: A View of Sociolegal Studies' (2002) 29(4) *Journal of Law and Society*, 632–644

Craig, Paul and De Burca, Grainne, *EU Law, Text, Cases and Materials* (Oxford: Oxford University Press, 2003)

Craig, Paul and Harlow, Carol, *Lawmaking in the EU* (London: Kluwer Law International, 1998)

Deards, Elspeth and Hargreaves, Silvia, *European Union Law* (Oxford: Oxford University Press, 2004)

De Burca, Grainne, 'The Language of Rights and European Integration', in: Jo
    Shaw and Gillian Moore (eds.), *New Legal Dynamics of European Union* (Oxford:
    Clarendon Press, 1995), pp. 29–54
De Burca, Grainne and Scott, Joanne (eds.), *Constitutional Change in the EU: From
    Uniformity to Flexibility?* (Oxford: Hart Publishing, 2000)
  (eds.), *Law and New Governance in the EU and the US* (Oxford: Hart Publishing,
    2006)
De Burca, Grainne and Walker, Neil, 'Conceptualizing Law and New
    Governance: Towards Reflexive Universalisability', New Modes of
    Governance Workshop; University College London, Faculty of Laws (2005)
DEFRA, 'IPPC: A Practical Guide', Third edn, February 2004
DEFRA, 'UK Article 16 (3) Report to the EU Commission', of 31 December 2002,
    DEFRA 2003
Dehousse, Renaud, 'Some Thoughts on the Juridification of the European Policy
    Process', in: F. Snyder (ed.), *The Europeanisation of Law: The Legal Effects of
    European Integration* (Oxford: Hart Publishing, 2000), pp. 15–29
  'Misfits: EU Law and the Transformation of European Governance', in:
    C. Joerges and R. Dehousse (eds.), *Good Governance in Europe's Integrated Market*
    (Oxford: Oxford University Press, 2002), pp. 207–229
Devereux, C. Jr., 'Parson's Sociological Theory', in: M. Black (ed.), *The Social
    Theories of Talcott Parsons: A Critical Examination* (Englewood Cliffs, NJ: Prentice
    Hall, 1961), pp. 1–63
Doppelhammer, Martina, 'More Difficult than Finding the Way round
    Chinatown? The IPPC Directive and its Implementation' (2000) *European
    Environmental Law Review*, August/September, 246–252
Drupsteen, Th. G., 'Integrated Pollution Prevention and Control: The Dutch
    Experience', in: C. Backes and G. Betlem (eds.), *Integrated Pollution Prevention
    and Control: The EC Directive from a Comparative Legal and Economic Perspective*
    (London: Kluwer Law International, 1999), pp. 81–90
Durkheim, Emile, *The Division of Labour in Society* (London: Macmillan, 1893)
  The Division of Labour in Society, with an introduction by Lewis Loser, translated
    by W. D. Halls (Houndmills: Macmillan Publishers, 1984)
Ehrlich, Eugen, *Fundamental Principles of the Sociology of Law*, with a new intro-
    duction by Klaus A. Ziegert (New Brunswick: Transaction Publishers, 2002)
Emmott, Neil, 'The Theory and Practice of IPPC: Case Studies from the UK and
    Hungary and the Implications for Future EU Environmental Policy' (1997) 7
    European Environment, 1–6
Emmott, Neil and Haigh, Nigel, 'Integrated Pollution Prevention and Control:
    UK and EC Approaches and Possible Next Steps' (1996) 8 (2) *Journal of
    Environmental Law*, 301–311
Emmott, Neil; Bär, Stefani and Kraemer, Andreas R., 'IPPC and the Sevilla
    Process' (2000) 10 (4) *European Environment*, 204–207
Endicott, Timothy, 'Law is Necessarily Vague' (2001) 7 *Legal Theory*, 379–385
ENDS Report, No. 309, 'IPPC Guidance Puts Squeeze on Chlor-Alkali Industry',
    October 2000, p. 52

ENDS Report, No. 319, 'Towards the Brave New World of Carbon Trading', August 2001, pp. 16–20

ENDS Report, No. 323, 'Agency Cools on Greater Role for Management Systems under IPPC', December 2001, p. 12

ENDS Report, No. 326, 'UK Convicted over IPPC Failure', March 2002, p. 58

ENDS Report, No. 336, 'Public Participation Directive to affect IPPC, EIA, Waste', January 2003, p. 52

ENDS Report, No. 358, 'UK and Netherlands Press for Nox and Sox Trading', November 2004, p. 60

ENDS Report, No. 363, 'Commission to Audit Compliance at IPPC Sites', April 2005, p. 58

ENDS Report, No. 370, 'IPPC Review Takes Shape as the "Slow Pace" of Implementation Revealed', November 2005, p. 44

ENDS Report, No. 372, 'IPPC Guidance Review Takes Shape', January 2006, p. 48

ENDS Report, No. 377, 'IPPC Review Gathers Pace', June 2006, p. 43

ENDS Report, No. 380, 'PPC-Waste Licensing Merger Moves Ahead', September 2006, pp. 38–39

Entec Report, European Commission Directorate General Environment, Draft Final Report, Assessment of the Implementation by the Member States of the IPPC Directive, Northwich, UK, 2006

Environment Agency, 'Environmental Assessment and Appraisal of BAT', issue 6, 20 May 2004

Environment Agency, 'EPOPRA Methodology, Version 3,1', April 2006

Environment Agency, UK Sector Guidance Note on Inorganic Chemicals – S.4.03, version 6.2, 12 May 2004

EU Commission, 'Better Law Making: Commission Report to the European Council on the Application of Subsidiarity and Proportionality, Principles on Simplification and Consolidation, CSE (95), 5–80 final; 21 November 1995

EU Commission, 'On the Road to Sustainable Production: Progress in Implementing Council Directive 96/61/EC concerning Integrated Pollution Prevention and Control', COM (2003) 354 final; 2003

EU Commission, 'First Report on the Implementation of the IPPC Directive, 3 November 2005, COM (2005) 540 final, at: http://ec.europa.eu/environment/ippc/ippc_report.htm, site last visited 10 April 2007

European Economic and Social Committee (ECOSOC), Opinion of the European Economic and Social Committee on the Communication from the Commission to the Council, the EP, the ECOSOC, 'On the Road to Sustainable Production', COM (2003) 354 final, Nat/199/IPPC, Brussels, 10 December 2003

European Parliament, 1999–2004, Session Document, Final A5-0034/2004, 28 January 2004, Report on Progress in Implementing Council Directive 96/61/EC IPPC, Committee on the Environment, Public Health and Consumer Policy

Falkner, Robert, 'Business Conflict and US International Environmental Policy: Ozone, Climate and Biodiversity', in: P. G. Harris (ed.), The Environment,

International Relations and US Foreign Policy (Washington: Georgetown University, 2001), 157–177

Farrel, Frank, 'How Economic Issues were Dealt with in the Non-Ferrous Metal BREF', IPTS report, manuscript with author

Farthing, Julia, Marshall, Bridget, and Kellett, Peter, *Pollution Prevention and Control – The New Regime* (Totton, UK: LexisNexis UK, 2003)

Faure, Michael and Lefevere, Jürgen, 'The Draft Directive on Integrated Pollution Prevention and Control: An Economic Perspective' (1996) *European Environmental Law Review*, April, 112–122

Feeley, Malcolm, M., 'The Concept of Laws in Social Science: A Critique and Notes on an Expanded View' (1976) 10 *Law and Society Review*, 407

Foucault, Michel, *The Archaeology of Knowledge* (London: Routledge, 1972)
  'Power/Knowledge: Selected Interviews and other Writings', in: C. Gordon (ed.), *Power/Knowledge: Selected Interviews and other Writings* (Harlow: Longman and Pearson Education, 1980)
  'Space, Knowledge, and Power' – interview with Michel Foucault conducted with Paul Rabinow, in: P. Rabinow (ed.), *The Foucault Reader* (Harmondsworth: Penguin Books, 1987), pp. 239–256

Frank, J., *Law and the Modern Mind* (New York: Coward-McCann, 1930)

Gaja, Giorgio, Hay, Peter and Rotunda, Ronald D., 'Instruments for Legal Integration in the European Community – A Review', in: M. Cappelletti, M. Seccombe and J. Weiler, *Integration through Law* (Berlin: Walter de Gruyter, 1986), pp. 113–160

Garrett, Geoffrey, The Politics of Legal Integration in the European Union (1995) 49 *International Organization* 1, 171–181

Garrett, Geoffrey, Kelemen, Daniel and Schulz, Heiner, 'The European Court of Justice, National Governments, and Legal Integration in the European Union' (1998) 52 *International Organization* 1, 149–176

Gibbs, Jack P., 'Definitions of Law and Empirical Questions', in: M. Barkun (ed.), *Law and the Social System*, (New York: Lieber-Atherton, 1973), pp. 16–37

Goffman, Erwin, 'Footing', in: M. Wetherell, S. Taylor and S. Yates (eds.), *Discourse Theory and Practice: A Reader* (Original Edition 2001, London: Sage Publications, 2002), pp. 93–110

Goldstein, Judith, Kahler, Miles, Keohane, Robert O., and Slaughter, Anne-Marie, 'Introduction: Legalization and World Politics' (2000) 54 *International Organization* 3, 385–399

Gouldson, Andrew and Murphy, Joseph, *Regulatory Realities* (London: Earthscan, 1998)

Grace, Clive and Wilkinson, Philip, *Sociological Inquiry and Legal Phenomena* (New York: Collier MacMillan Ltd., 1978)

Griffiths, Anne, 'Legal Pluralism', in: R. Banakar and M. Travers (eds.), *An Introduction to Law and Social Theory* (Oxford: Hart, 2005), pp. 289–310

Haas, Ernst, *The 'Uniting of Europe': Political, Social and Economic Forces 1950–1957*, 1st edn (Stanford: Stanford University Press, 1958)

Habermas, Jürgen, 'Between Facts and Norms: An Author's Reflections' (1999) 76 *Denver University Law Review*, 937–942

Haines, Fiona and Gurney, David, 'The Shadows of the Law: Contemporary
    Approaches to Regulation and the Problem of Regulatory Conflict' (2004) 25
    Law and Policy 4, 353–380
Haltern, Ulrich, 'Integration through Law', in: A. Wiener and T. Diez (eds.), European
    Integration Theory (Oxford: Oxford University Press, 2004), pp. 177–196
Hansmann, Klaus, Kommentar zur TA Luft (München: C. H. Beck, 2004)
Hawkins, Keith, Environment and Enforcement: Regulation and the Social Definition of
    Pollution (Oxford: Clarendon Press, 1984)
    Law as Last Resort (Oxford: Oxford University Press, 2002)
Herrnstein Smith, Barbara and Plotnitsky, Arkady, 'Introduction: Networks and
    Symmetries, Decidable and Undecidable' (1995) 94 The South Atlantic
    Quarterly 2, 380–388
Hey, Christian, 'Balancing Participation in Technical Working Groups: the Case
    of the Information Exchange of the IPPC Directive', European Conference
    on 'The Sevilla Process: A Driver for Environmental Performance in
    Industry', Stuttgart, 6–7 April, 2000
Hey, Christian and Taschner, Karola, EEB Industry Handbook (1998) at: http://
    www.eeb.org/
Hitchens, David, Farrell, Frank, Lindblom, Josefina and Triebswetter, Ursula, The
    Impact of Best Available Techniques (BAT) on the Competitiveness of European
    Industry (Brussels: European Commission, Joint Research Centre, Institute
    for Prospective Technological Studies; 2001, November)
Hunt, Alan, The Sociological Movement in Law (London: The Macmillan Press Ltd.,
    1978)
Hutter, Bridget, The Reasonable Arm of the Law: the Law Enforcement Procedures of
    Environmental Health Officers (Oxford: Clarendon Press, 1988)
    Regulation and Risk: Occupational Health and Safety on the Railways (Oxford: Oxford
    University Press, 2001)
Jarass, Hans D., Bundesimmissionsschutzgesetz (München: C.H. Beck, 2002)
Joerges, Christian, 'Taking the Law Seriously: On Political Science and the Role
    of Law in the Process of European Integration' (1996) 2 (2) European Law
    Journal, pp. 105–135
Joerges, Christian and Vos, Ellen, EU Committees: Social Regulation, Law and Politics
    (Oxford: Hart Publishing, 1999)
Johnson, Alan V., 'A Definition of the Concept of Law' (1977) 2 Mid-American
    Review of Sociology 1, 47–71
Jupille, Joseph, Caporaso, James A. and Checkel, Jeffrey, T., 'Introduction:
    Integrating Institutions, Rationalism, Constructivism and the Study of the
    EU' (2003) 36 Comparative Political Studies 1, 2, 7–40
Kloepfer, Michael, Umweltrecht (München: C.H. Beck'sche Verlagsbuchhandlung,
    1998)
    Umweltrecht, 3rd edn (München: C.H. Beck'sche Verlagsbuchhandlung, 2004)
Koslowski, Rey, 'A Constructivist Approach to Understanding the European
    Union as a Federal Polity' (1999) 6 Journal of European Public Policy 4,
    561–578

Lange, Bettina, 'Compliance Construction in the Context of Environmental
    Regulation' (1999) 8 *Social and Legal Studies* 4, 549–567
    'From Boundary Drawing to Transitions: The Creation of Normativity under
    the EU Directive on Integrated Pollution Prevention and Control' (2002) 8
    European Law Journal 2, 246–268
    'How to Conceptualize Law in EU Integration Processes? Perspectives from the
    Literature and Empirical Research', in: V. Gessner (ed.), *European Ways of Law*
    (Oxford: Hart Publishing, 2007)
Lash, Scott and Urry, John, *Economies of Signs and Space* (London: Sage
    Publications, 1994)
Latour, Bruno, 'On Actor-Network Theory – A Few Clarifications' (1996) 47 *Soziale
    Welt*, 369–381
Law, John and Mol, Annemarie, 'Notes on Materiality and Sociality' (1995) 43 *The
    Sociological Review*, 276–294
Lenschow, Andrea, 'New Regulatory Approaches in "Greening" EU Policies', in:
    A. Jordan (ed.), *Environmental Policy in the EU* (London: Earthscan, 2005),
    pp. 295–316
Lezaun, Javier, 'Creating a New Object of Government: Making Genetically
    Modified Organisms Traceable' (2006) 36 *Social Studies of Science*, 499–531
Lindberg, Leon, *The Political Dynamics of European Economic Integration* (Stanford:
    Stanford University Press, 1963)
Lindberg, L. N. and Scheingold, S. A., *Europe's Would-be Polity: Patterns of Change in
    the European Community* (Englewood Cliffs, N.J.: Prentice Hall, 1970)
Litten, Don, 'Economic Aspects in BREFs', in '*Vito Mol, International Workshop on
    Economic Aspects of BAT*, Brussels, Belgium, 10–11 February 2000
Llewellyn, Karl, 'Some Realism about Realism – Responding to Roscoe Pound'
    (1931) 44 *Harvard Law Review*, 1222–1264
    'The Normative, the Legal, and the Law-Jobs: The Problem of Juristic Method'
    (1940) 49 *Yale Law Journal*, 1355–1400
Long, Antoinette, 'Integrated Pollution Prevention and Control: The
    Implementation of Directive 96/61/EEC?' (1999) *European Environmental Law
    Review*, June, 180–184
Lukes, Stephen, *Power: A Radical View* (Oxford: Blackwell, 2005)
Macaulay, Stewart, 'Non-Contractual Relations in Business: A Preliminary
    Study' (1963) 28 *American Sociological Review* 1, 55–67
Maher, Imelda, 'Competition Law and Intellectual Property Rights: Evolving
    Formalism', in: P. Craig and G. De Burca (eds.), *The Evolution of EU Law*
    (Oxford: Oxford University Press, 1999)
Majone, Giandomenico, 'The Rise of the Regulatory State in Europe' (1994) 17
    West European Politics 3, 77–101
Mattli, Walter and Slaughter, Anne-Marie, 'Revisiting the European Court of
    Justice' (1998) 52 *International Organization* 1, 177–209
Mayhew, Leon H., 'Introduction', in: L. H. Mayhew (ed.), *Talcott Parsons: On
    Institutions and Social Evolution, Selected Writings* (Chicago: The University of
    Chicago Press, 1982)

Mazey, Sonia and Richardson, Jeremy, 'Environmental Groups and the EC: Challenges and Opportunities', in: A. Jordan (ed.), *Environmental Policy in the EU*, 2nd edn (London: Earthscan, 2005), pp. 106–121

McBarnet, Doreen and Whelan, Christopher, 'The Elusive Spirit of the Law: Formalism and the Struggle for Legal Control' (1997) 54 *Modern Law Review* 6, 848–873

McEwen, C. and Maiman, R., 'Mediation in Small Claims Court: Achieving Compliance through Consent' (1984) 18 *Law and Society Review* 1, 11–50

Mills, Sara, *Michel Foucault* (London: Routledge, 2003)

Minson, Jeff, 'Strategies for Socialists? Foucault's Conception of Power', in: M. Gane (ed.), *Towards a Critique of Foucualt* (London: Routledge, 1986), 106–148

Moravczik, Andrew, 'Liberal Intergovernmentalism and Integration: A Rejoinder' (1995) 33 *Journal of Common Market Studies* 4, 611–628

Newell, Tim and Grant, Wyn, 'Environmental NGOs and EU Environmental Law', in: Han Somsen (ed.), 2000 *Yearbook of European Environmental Law*, vol. 1, 225–252

Nisbet, Robert, *Twilight of Authority* (New York: Oxford University Press, 1975)

Pallemaerts, Marc, 'The Proposed IPPC Directive: Re-Regulation or De-Regulation?' (1996) *European Environmental Law Review*, June, 174–179

Parsons, Talcott, 'The Law and Social Control', in: W. Evan (ed.), *Law and Sociology* (New York: The Free Press of Glencoe, 1962), pp. 56–72

Parsons, T., *Sociological Theory and Modern Society* (New York: Free Press, 1967)

Pavlich, George, 'Introduction: Transforming Images: Society, Law and Critique', in: G. Wickham and G. Pavlich (eds.), *Rethinking Law, Society and Governance: Foucault's Bequest* (Oxford: Hart Publishing, 2001), pp. 1–13

Phare Report, Regional Environmental Accession Project: Development of Guidelines for Implementation and Enforcement of Issuing Integrated Permits According to Directive 96/61/EC (and EPER) for Bulgaria – Overview of IPPC Systems and Documentation in Three EU Member States, Final Report Part A (360006/04-06-RP-OO2), 21 March 2002

Picciotto, Sol and Haines, J., 'Regulating Global Financial Markets' (1999) 26 *Journal of Law and Society*, 351–368

Podgorecki, Adam, *Law and Society* (London: Routledge and Kegan Paul, 1974)

Pound, Roscoe, 'Law in Books and Law in Action' (1910) 44 *American Law Review*, 12–36

  Introduction to the Philosophy of Law (New Haven: Yale University Press, 1954)

Pinder, John, *European Community: The Building of a Union* (Oxford: Oxford University Press, 1991)

Rajotte, Alain, 'BAT and Economics: The Challenge of Integration', in *International Workshop on Economic Aspects of BAT – Proceedings*; Brussels, Belgium, 10–11 February 2000

Risse, Thomas, 'Social Constructivism and European Integration', in: A. Wiener and T. Diez (eds.), *European Integration Theory* (Oxford: Oxford University Press, 2004), 159–176

Risse-Kappen, Thomas, 'Explaining the Nature of the Beast: International Relations and Comparative Policy Analysis meet the EU' (1996) 34 *Journal of Common Market Studies* 1, 53–80

Rosamond, Ben, *Theories of European Integration* (Houndmills, Basingstoke: Palgrave, 2000)

Rose, Nikolas, 'The Death of the Social? Re-figuring the Territory of Government' (1996) 25 *Economy and Society* 3, 327–356

  Powers of Freedom: Reframing Political Thought (Cambridge: Cambridge University Press, 1999)

Ross, Laurence H., 'Housing Code Enforcement as Law in Action' (1995) 17 *Law and Policy* 2, 133–160

Sander, F. E. A. 'Alternative Dispute Resolution in the Law School Curriculum: Opportunities and Obstacles' (1984) 34 *Journal of Legal Education*, 229–236

Santos, B. de Sousa, 'Law: A Map of Misreading, toward a Postmodern Conception of Law' (1987) 14 *Journal of Law and Society* 3, 279–302

Sarat, Austin, 'Legal Effectiveness and Social Studies of Law: On the Unfortunate Persistence of a Research Tradition' (1985) *Legal Studies Forum* 9, 23–32

Schaerer, Bernd, 'Use of Cost Data in Air Pollution Control Policy in Germany', in *Vito Mol, International Workshop on Economic Aspects of BAT?*, Brussels, Belgium, 10–11 February 2000

Scheffer, Thomas, 'The Duality of Mobilisation – Following the Rise and Fall of an Alibi Story on its Way to Court' (2003) 33 *Journal for the Theory of Social Behaviour* 3, 313–346

Schepel, Harm, *The Constitution of Private Governance: Product Standards in the Regulation of Integrating Markets* (Oxford: Hart Publishing, 2005)

Schmitter, Philippe C., 'A Revised Theory of Regional Integration', in L. N. Lindberg and S. A. Scheingold (eds.), *Regional Integration: Theory and Research*, 1st edn (Cambridge, Mass.: Harvard University Press, 1971), pp. 232–264

  'Imagining the Future of the Euro-Polity with the Help of New Concepts', in: G. Marks, F. W. Scharpf, P. C. Schmitter and W. Streek (eds.), *Governance in the European Union* (London: Sage Publications, 1996a), pp. 121–150

  'Examining the Present Euro-Polity with the Help of Past Theories', in: G. Marks, F. W. Scharpf, P. C. Schmitter and W. Streek (eds.) *Governance in the European Union* (London: Sage Publications, 1996b), pp. 1–14

  'Neo-Neofunctionalism', in: A. Wiener and T. Diez (eds.), *European Integration Theory* (Oxford: Oxford University Press, 2004), pp. 45–74

Schnutenhaus, Joern, 'Integrated Pollution Prevention and Control: New German Initiatives in the European Environment Council: Update' (1995) *European Environmental Law Review*, 23–25

Scott, Colin, 'Changing Patterns of European Community Utilities Law and Policy: An Institutional Hypothesis', in: J. Shaw and G. More (eds.), *New*

Legal Dynamics of European Union (Oxford: Clarendon Press, 1995),
    pp. 193–215
'Regulation in the Age of Governance: The Rise of the Post-Regulatory State',
    National Europe Centre Paper, No. 100, 6 June 2003, Australian National
    University, at www.anu.edu.au/NEC/scott1.pdf
Scott, Joanne, 'Flexibility, "Proceduralization", and Environmental Governance
    in the EU', in: G. DeBurca and J. Scott (eds.), *Constitutional Change in the EU:
    From Uniformity to Flexibility?*, 1st edn (Oxford: Hart Publishing, 2000),
    pp. 259–280
Scott, Joanne and Holder, Jane, 'Law and New Environmental Governance
    in the European Union', in: G. De Burca and J. Scott (eds.), *Law and
    New Governance in the EU and the US* (Oxford: Hart Publishing, 2006),
    pp. 211–242
Scott, Joanne and Trubek, David, 'Mind the Gap: Law and New Approaches to
    Governance in the EU' (2002) 8 *European Law Journal* 1, 1–18
Selznick, Philip, ' "Law in Context" Revisited' (2003) 30 *Journal of Law and Society*
    2, 177–186
Shaw, Jo, 'European Union Legal Studies in Crisis? Towards a New Dynamic'
    (1996) 16 *Oxford Journal of Legal Studies*, 231–253
Smart, Barry, *Michel Foucault* (London: Routledge, 2002)
Snyder, Francis, 'Thinking about "Interests": Legislative Process in the European
    Community', in: J. Starr and J. F. Collier, *History and Power in the Study of Law:
    New Directions in Legal Anthropology* (Ithaca: Cornell University Press, 1989),
    pp. 168–198
    New Directions in European Community Law (London: Weidenfeld and Nicolson;
    1990)
    'Soft Law and Institutional Practice in the European Community', in: S. Martin
    (ed.), *The Construction of Europe* (Dordrecht: Kluwer Academic Publishers,
    1994), pp. 197–225
Stein, Eric, 'Assimilation of National Laws as a Function of European
    Integration' (1964) 58 *American Journal of International Law* 1, 1–40
    'Lawyers, Judges and the Making of a Transnational Constitution' (1981) 75
    American Journal of International Law, 1–27
Stone Sweet, Alec, 'Constitutional Dialogues in the European Community', in:
    A. Slaughter, A. Stone Sweet and J. H. H. Weiler (eds.), *The European Court and
    National Courts: Doctrine and Jurisprudence* (Oxford: Hart Publishing, 1998),
    pp. 305–330
    The Judicial Construction of Europe (Oxford: Oxford University Press, 2004)
Tamanaha, Brian, *A General Jurisprudence of Law and Society* (New York: Oxford
    University Press, 2001)
Teubner, Günther, 'Substantive and Reflexive Elements in Modern Law' (1983)
    17 *Law and Society Review*, 2, 239–285
    'The Transformation of Law in the Welfare State' in: G. Teubner (ed.), *Dilemmas
    of Law in the Welfare State* (Berlin: Walter de Gruyter, 1986a), pp. 3–10

'After Legal Instrumentalism? – Strategic Models of Post-Regulatory Law', in
   G. Teubner (ed.), *Dilemmas of Law in the Welfare State* (Berlin: Walter de
   Gruyter, 1986b), pp. 299–325
'Autopoiesis and Steering: How Politics Profit from the Normative Surplus of
   Capital', in: R. in't Veld et al. (eds.), *Autopoiesis and Configuration Theory: New
   Approaches to Societal Steering* (London: Kluwer, 1991), pp. 127–141
Timasheff, Nicholas, *An Introduction to the Sociology of Law* (Cambridge, Mass.:
   Greenfield, 1939)
Trubek, David, Cottrell, Patrick and Nance, Mark, Jean Monnet Working Paper
   02/05, ' "Soft Law", "Hard Law" and EU Integration: Toward a Theory of
   Hybridity' (New York: New York University School of Law, 2005), 10012 at
   http://law.wisc.edu/facstaff/trubek/HybridityPaperApril2005.pdf, site last
   visited 4 April 2007
Tushnet, Mark, 'Post-realist Legal Scholarship' (1980) 15 *Journal of the Society of
   Public Teachers of Law*, 20–32
Twining, William, 'Two Works of Karl Llewellyn – II' (1968) 31 *Modern Law
   Review*, 165–182
   Globalisation and Legal Theory (Oxford: Butterworths, 2000)
Unger, Roberto M., 'The Critical Legal Studies Movement' (1983) 96 *Harvard Law
   Review* 3, 561–675
Valverde, Mariana, *Law's Dream of a Common Knowledge* (Princeton: Princeton
   University Press, 2003)
Vercaemst, Peter and Dijkmans, R., 'Integrating Economic Aspects when
   Determining BAT – A Framework', *Vito Mol, International workshop on economic
   aspects of BAT*, Belgium, Brussels, 10th to 11th of February 2000
Walker, Neil, 'Legal Theory and the European Union: A 25th Anniversary Essay'
   (2005) 25 *Oxford Journal of Legal Studies* 4, 581–601
Wallace, William, 'Introduction: The Dynamics of European Integration', in:
   D. Wallace (ed.), *The Dynamics of European Integration* (London: Pinter/RIIA,
   1990), pp. 1–24
Wæver, Ole, 'Discursive Approaches', in: A. Wiener and T. Diez (eds.),
   European Integration Theory (Oxford: Oxford University Press, 2004),
   pp. 197–215
Weber, Max, *Law in Economy and Society*, translated by Max Rheinstein
   (Cambridge, Mass.: Harvard University Press, 1954)
Weiler, Joseph, 'The Community System: The Dual Character of
   Supranationalism' (1981) *Yearbook of European Law* 1, 268–306
Wickham, Gary, 'Power and Power Analysis: Beyond Foucault?', in:
   M. Gane (ed.), *Towards a Critique of Foucault* (London: Routledge, 1986),
   149–179
Wiener, Antje and Diez, Thomas, 'Introducing the Mosaic of Integration
   Theory', in: A. Wiener and T. Diez (eds.), *European Integration Theory* (Oxford:
   Oxford University Press, 2004), pp. 1–21

Wincott, Daniel, 'The Role of the Law or the Rule of the Court of Justice? An "Institutional" Account of Judicial Politics in the European Community' (1995) 2 *Journal of European Public Policy* 4, 583–602

'A Community of Law? European Law and Judicial Politics: The Court of Justice and Beyond' (2002) 35 *Government and Opposition* 3, 3–26

Winter, Gerd, 'The IPPC Directive: A German Point of View', in: C. Backes and G. Betlem (eds.), *Integrated Pollution Prevention and Control: The EC Directive from a Comparative Legal and Economic Perspective* (The Hague: Kluwer Law International, 1999), pp. 65–79

Zocttl, J., 'Towards Integrated Protection of the Environment in Germany?' (2000) 12 *Journal of Environmental Law* 3, 281–291

Index